AUG   2009

ALSO BY LEORA TANENBAUM

Slut! Growing Up Female with a Bad Reputation

Catfight: Rivalries Among Women—from Diets to Dating,
from the Boardroom to the Delivery Room

TAKING
BACK GOD

TAKING
BACK GOD

American Women Rising Up

for Religious Equality

LEORA TANENBAUM

Farrar, Straus and Giroux   New York

3811800092744 8

Farrar, Straus and Giroux
18 West 18th Street, New York, 10011

Except when otherwise noted, translation of the Hebrew Bible is from *Tanakh: The Holy Scriptures: The New JPS Translation According to the Traditional Hebrew Text*, copyright © 1985 by the Jewish Publication Society. Used with permission.

Translation of the New Testament and Deuterocanonical Books is from the *Holy Bible: New Revised Standard Version*, copyright © 1989 by the Division of Christian Education of the National Council of the Churches of Christ in the United States of America. Used with permission.

Translation of the Qur'an is from *The Sublime Quran*, trans. Laleh Bakhtiar, copyright © 2007 by Laleh Bakhtiar. Used with permission.

Library of Congress Cataloging-in-Publication Data
Tanenbaum, Leora, 1969–
    Taking back God : American women rising up for religious equality /
Leora Tanenbaum.— 1st ed.
        p.   cm.
    Includes index.
    ISBN-13: 978-0-374-27235-7 (hardcover : alk. paper)
    ISBN-10: 0-374-27235-2 (hardcover : alk. paper)
    1. Women and religion—United States.   I. Title.
BL458 .T35 2009
200.82'0973—dc22

                                                    2008031413

www.fsgbooks.com

1   3   5   7   9   10   8   6   4   2

The stories recounted in this book are based on the author's interviews with individuals across the United States. All names are real, except when a first name appears alone without a surname. In those cases, the name is a pseudonym used at the request of the interviewee.

In memory of
Barbara Rosner Seaman
and
Sassi Lonner

CONTENTS

PREFACE

Because the topic of religious reform is volatile, it's important that I reveal who I am religiously. Often, when women in a religious community demand gender equality, they are accused of just trying to stir up trouble: they have disavowed their femininity, they are not "really" religious, and/or they are feminist Jezebels. Therefore, you should know that religion is central in my life, as is motherhood. I have chosen to represent the new class of devout women—those seeking to expand women's rights within their faith—because, well, I share many of their beliefs.

I am an observant Jew. I freely choose this lifestyle. I respect Jewish law and adhere to it to the best of my abilities. Jewish law guides many, if not most, of the small and large actions I take every single day. I observe Shabbat (Jewish Sabbath) and Jewish holidays, observe *kashrut* (Jewish dietary restrictions), believe that the Jewish sacred texts are holy, and raise my two children and maintain my household in a way that is connected to centuries-old Jewish laws, customs, and culture. Yet I also am committed to equal rights for women, and I thoroughly enjoy contemporary, twenty-first-century American culture.

As you can imagine, my life is filled with contradictions. I experience tensions between preserving Jewish tradition and living a modern life. In this regard, I probably represent the typical observant Jew of today. But I don't wring my hands over reconciling my Jewish identity with my modern inclinations. For one thing, I'm too busy (the kids, the career, the Shabbat cooking . . .) to overanalyze. Besides, despite the inconsistencies, things just kind of hang together. Somehow I make sure that it all works.

Some background: My parents made sure that I got a high-level Jewish education. From kindergarten through twelfth grade I attended modern Orthodox Jewish day schools. These were private religious schools that included classes in Hebrew language and Judaic subjects (such as Torah and Talmud) as well as math, world history, science, and English literature. I always loved the unique academic challenges, especially the Hebrew and Judaic subjects.

In hindsight, I know that my early Jewish education, though coed, did not teach religious equality for boys and girls. At the time, I was aware that only the boys learned how to lead prayer services and that only the boys learned key Jewish skills (such as chanting from the Torah), but I was not disturbed. I accepted that as the way things were supposed to be. I did not think about gender equality in any milieu, religious or otherwise. I learned about feminism only in college, at which point caring about and fighting for equality for women became a defining element of my identity.

Being Jewish has always been very important to me. Being Jewish is much more than following Jewish religious laws. It's also about being part of an ethnic group—the Jewish people—who have a long, fascinating history and a rich literary, culinary, and linguistic culture. Being Jewish is also about feeling connected to Israel as the homeland of the Jewish people. I cherish all of these connections. I want my children to establish these connections as well so that they can pass them on to their children.

I'm an enormously fortunate person. I married a man I love; I have the economic safety net of my husband's salary; I enjoy reproductive freedom, and therefore my two children were planned and wanted; I enjoy my work, and I am respected for it. I have so much freedom and so many choices that today I can follow paths my grandmothers could only have dreamed about.

Yet at the same time, there is a strict and narrow path that I don't want to abandon: the Jewish way. Following the Jewish path keeps me sane in the face of endless—often confusing—choices.

I am lucky to be part of a religion that takes women seriously as fully capable. It is good to be a Jewish woman, particularly in the United States. Here we have a strong Jewish feminist presence, which has pushed for egalitarianism in the liberal (Reform, Conservative, and Reconstructionist) movements. Women in the most stringent (Orthodox) movement also enjoy the freedom and privilege to participate in Jewish life in meaningful ways.

Nevertheless, the issue of women's status in Judaism remains a sore spot for me and for many other women. There is more work to be done in the struggle for women's equality, especially within the Orthodox movement, which segregates the sexes and assigns them different roles.

Jewish sacred texts such as the Bible and the Talmud reflect a male-centered point of view. Aside from a few exceptions, the women in these texts are subordinate to men and far less powerful. But it is my belief that these texts are a product of their times. Judaism is not inherently or necessarily biased against women. *Halakhah* (Jewish law) has a certain measure of fluidity, and great rabbis throughout the ages have decreed changes in the law. Thus, one can argue that it would actually be very "Jewish" to make reforms to improve conditions for women.

Unfortunately, despite centuries of Jewish reform, many Orthodox religious authorities today believe that the realities of contemporary life should not dictate change in Jewish law or custom. They ground their viewpoint in their belief in God: it is against Jewish custom (which is divinely inspired) and, more important, against God's law, for women to become rabbis or to read from a Torah scroll or even to participate in group prayer only with other women—they say. But the great rabbis of yesterday felt free to debate God's intentions, and they were guided by the customs of the people when interpreting Jewish law. The leading Orthodox rabbis of today could do the same—if they wanted.

Tellingly, Jews tend to refer to Judaism not as a faith, but as a religion, because faith, while important, is not the end-all and be-all. Actions are far more important. Assembled at the foot of Mount Sinai en route to the Promised Land, the people of Israel were given God's commandments. After hearing what was expected of them, the Israelites declared: "All that God has spoken, we will do and we will listen" (Exodus 24:7).* Note that the people vowed to *do* the commandments first and to absorb and understand them later. On the one hand, the Israelites trusted God: they had faith in the commandments. On the other hand, the Israelites accepted the obligation to perform the commandments no matter what—even if they never arrived at a complete understanding or faith.

I am loyal to Jewish law and I take Jewish law seriously. I trust in the importance of the law, and I respect its wisdom. I will do and I will listen. Thus, I observe not only laws for which rational explanations exist, called *mishpatim*, such as the commandments not to murder and not to bear false witness, but also the laws whose purposes cannot be understood by humans, called *hukkim*, such as the dietary laws and the commandment not to wear clothes made of a blend of wool and linen. I recognize that some Jewish obligations do not make rational sense, yet they serve a purpose. Although none of us can understand the specific purposes of each of the hukkim, I recognize that these laws bind the Jewish people together in today's fragmented world; they have been practiced for centuries and therefore connect the generations that have lived and those that are yet to be born; they force us to limit our behaviors, which can lead to a heightened awareness of boundaries and the carving of space and time; and they instruct us not to take the world's resources for granted.

But while I accept the laws, I also leave open the opportunity to struggle with them. And this includes struggling over my place as a woman in Judaism.

My biggest source of frustration is connected with prayer in synagogue. I prefer an Orthodox service and Orthodox prayer book, but traditional Orthodox synagogues exclude me. I am deeply disturbed that in my synagogue women must sit in an upstairs gallery, far from the action, where our presence counts for nothing. (Women do not sit upstairs in all Orthodox synagogues, but they are always segregated from the men in a separate section.) I am insulted that women are categorically denied the honor of leading any part of the liturgical service. How do I resolve my conflict? I sit in that upstairs balcony on most Shabbat mornings because despite my frustrations, I gain spiri-

*Translation from the Hebrew is mine.

tual strength from many aspects of the service. But I also attend a different monthly service in which women are given the maximum leadership possible within the constraints of Jewish law. In this service, I have taken on different leadership roles, including reading from the Torah. I have also led the weekday morning service at a Conservative synagogue. At both venues I bring my young sons so they can see that yes, women can be religious leaders too.

My own struggle, as you see, is mild. Many other American women face greater obstacles to spiritual fulfillment, obstacles that prevent them from realizing themselves fully. And of course, we can't forget that millions of women living around the world are not free to determine their relationship with their faith: religion, interpreted narrowly and often brutally, is forced upon them. But American women are free to choose whether or not to be loyal to their faith. Many decide—after soul-searching, reading and rereading their sacred texts, speaking with their religious leaders, participating in classes at their religious institutions, and speaking with friends or even strangers on the Internet—not to abandon their religion. Instead they make the commitment to stay and to challenge their faith to become more inclusive of women and thereby become stronger itself.

TAKING
BACK GOD

ONE

Women on the Verge of an Uprising

Go to your local church, mosque, or synagogue, and take a look around during worship. Who is leading the service? Who is preaching? Are women mentioned positively, negatively, or at all? Is God described exclusively as Father, as Father and Mother, or in gender-neutral terms? How are the women dressed—are they covered up, even on a scorching-hot day? Wait—where are the women, anyway? Oh, there they are—all the way in back. Or upstairs. Or in another room.

If you've witnessed the preferential treatment of men in America's houses of worship, you will not be surprised to learn that there is an explosion of millions of women in this country rising up and demanding religious equality. More and more, religious women—Christian, Muslim, and Jewish—are declaring that they expect to be treated as equal to men in the religious sphere. They want the same meaningful spiritual connections enjoyed by their brothers, fathers, husbands, and sons. They are critical of their faith's male-oriented theology and liturgy. They reject the interpretations of their religious tradition that give women a different, and to their minds lesser, status.

These women agree with their priests, pastors, imams, and rabbis that the word of God is revealed in their faith's sacred writings. And they embrace the word of God. Yet they believe that God always intended for women to be treated as equals to men. The problem is not God's intention, but rather a distortion of God's plan.

I am one of these women: I too live with deep conflict. I am com-

3

mitted to my religion, but increasingly I am frustrated with the place my tradition assigns me as a woman. In writing this book, I have connected with many of these women, and share their experiences here to raise awareness that conflict and contradiction sometimes can be good things because they can impel positive change. For when there is tension between the desire to be religious and the desire to be treated as equal, religious women inevitably question the status quo, leading them to study the foundations of their faith. This process strengthens religion for everyone involved. Blind faith, on the other hand, weakens religion for everyone involved.

We are living at a pivotal moment. Catholics have been active in the movement for women's ordination as priests since 1975, and the first woman was ordained as a rabbi three years earlier in the Reform Jewish denomination. In 2006 we saw the installation of the first female presiding bishop of the Episcopal Church in the United States. But today the movement has deepened. It still pushes for ordination in those faiths where it remains forbidden, but it has widened its focus beyond that one issue. And it encompasses Muslim women, who are also speaking up against women's discrimination. It has germinated a new class of religious women who are infusing their faith communities with palpable energy. That energy is alive: it is growing and spreading.

These women are not abandoning religion. Nor do they seek to overturn it. On the contrary: *they want to stay within their religious heritage but make it better by allowing women full rights.* They want to transform religion while maintaining tradition. Many of these women seek out like-minded folks, both men and women, in order to practice their faith together in a way that is spiritually fulfilling rather than spiritually disabling. Others work from within to reform their church, mosque, or synagogue to become more inclusive of women. All of these devout women recognize that religion, when practiced together with a commitment to gender equality, can empower women rather than limit them. At the same time, by creating opportunities for women, they are making their religion stronger and more durable.

Historically, men have monopolized God. Today, women are taking back God for themselves. Says forty-six-year-old Catherine Shannon, a practicing, churchgoing Catholic and stay-at-home mother of four in suburban Connecticut, "I don't feel equal at all, and I struggle with it.

I watched the installation of Pope Benedict XVI on TV, and I found it repulsive. It was all these men—no women. Women are allowed to become 'Eucharistic ministers,' but they're not allowed to consecrate the Eucharist. Only a male priest is allowed to do that. I would feel better if women could do it."

Syeda Reshma Yunus, a forty-seven-year-old traditional Muslim woman who was born in India and lives in California, feels similarly. She is offended that many mosques forbid women from entering and exiting through the main door (a separate door for women is sometimes found on the side or rear of the building) and that nearly all mosques in the United States require the women to worship behind the men. "You know how you're supposed to come back from the mosque feeling good and spiritually recharged? I never feel that way. When I come back from the mosque, I just want to throw something at those people!"

For her part, Ariele Mortkowitz, a twenty-seven-year-old Orthodox Jewish woman living in Washington, D.C., shares this sense that as a woman, she's getting the short end of the religious stick. She disagrees with her tradition's rule that women, but not men, must dress modestly. "You need to cover your hair [as a married woman] and you need to cover your body because women are considered sexual beings. A male friend [not from my community] once said to me, 'Doesn't that make you feel good, though, knowing that you are looked at as a sexual being?' But no, it doesn't! I don't want to hide who I am, but I'm supposed to because I'm a source of negative influence for my male counterparts in society."

Many religious people consider these sentiments heretical. When excommunication wasn't considered punishment enough, the medieval Catholic Church burned heretics at the stake. When women in our country during the colonial period challenged their congregations, their punishment was swift and fierce. In 1638 in the Massachusetts Bay Colony, Anne Hutchinson was excommunicated and banished from the colony because she had held meetings in her home to discuss the Sunday sermon and to provide a forum for her own theological ideas. In 1660, a supporter of Hutchinson who preached her own sermons, Mary Dyer, was hanged on the Boston Common. Other women who expressed provocative views about Christianity and the church hierarchy were also hanged, pilloried, or whipped.[1] Some were lucky merely to be publicly insulted. In 1848 the suffragist Elizabeth Cady Stanton—an evangelical Protestant who claimed that opponents of women's rights were misreading the Bible—was stung when she was denounced as an "infidel" by her hometown preacher.[2]

Today's equality-seeking religious women are sometimes considered heretics and branded as pagan, a term used to describe one who believes in more than one god. After an international conference of mainstream Protestant women, held in Minneapolis in 1993, participants were labeled pagan because they "reimagined" God as possessing both feminine and masculine characteristics. Even today, any religious woman who tries to broach the topic of alternate ways of representing God is at high risk of being silenced as a pagan— which also means one who stands outside the faith community. These women are told that nothing can change, because the way things are now is the way God decreed they should be, as revealed in the sacred texts.

Despite the insults flung at them, the women in this book remain deeply religious, faithful people. They are in awe of God as their creator, redeemer, and sustainer, and they wish to live lives that serve their God. By and large, they are mainstream, conventional people— schoolteachers, social workers, office managers, nonprofit directors, lawyers, physicians, church administrators, soccer moms, retired grandmothers. And they appear mainstream: they dress modestly—nothing too attention-grabbing, nothing outrageous. They tend to be particularly well educated (since higher education leads to critical thinking), yet they are also average Americans. For the most part, they just want to be left alone to worship Jesus Christ or Allah or Hashem—quietly, without causing a ruckus, without being in-your-face about it. But also with dignity and not as second-class citizens within their faith.

They are activists by necessity. To get to the point where they can worship the way they want to, they know that action is required. And action they are taking. Catholic women are supporting female ordination ceremonies, risking excommunication by the Vatican because the Catholic Church not only forbids female priests but also forbids support and even *discussion* of the subject. Evangelical Christian women are engaging in serious, high-level Bible study in which they challenge scriptural interpretations that place husbands as heads over wives, who are instructed to be subservient. Muslim women are participating in prayer services in which a woman recites the *khutba* (sermon) and women pray adjacent to men, not behind them. Observant Jewish women are attending prayer services in which the curtain dividing the women from the men is pushed aside so that a woman can *layn* (chant the words of) the Torah.

I want you to get to know this new breed of devout women—who they are, why they are dissatisfied with their faith, and what they are doing about it. Millions of religious women, together with like-minded men, are having an enormous impact on churches, mosques, and synagogues across the United States: they are reshaping organized religion to become more inclusive of women not only as worshippers but as leaders. There are no hard numbers, but everyone involved in the professional world of women and worship agrees that more and more women are standing up for their religious rights. In no small part, these women are gaining momentum through the Internet, which enables otherwise disparate individuals to come together.

"Women in these traditions are taking a very hard look at the conflict they have been living, between trying to be faithful and coming against certain elements of their tradition that are baldly unequal to women," observes Cyra Choudhury, the executive director of the Foundation for the Advancement of Women in Religion. "We are seeing a groundswell. There are regular women, women not engaged in the academy, asking more questions. They don't necessarily want to become priests or rabbis or imams, but they want their questions answered and they don't want to just accept the answer, 'Well, this is the sacred law; this is just what it is.'"

I have chosen to explore five communities of American women struggling for women's religious advancement: Catholics, evangelical Protestants, "mainline" (nonevangelical) Protestants, Muslims, and Orthodox Jews. Obviously, there are many other communities in which women are similarly rising up. A website called Feminist Mormon Housewives offers a space for Mormon women to vent frustrations with their narrow role. There are disgruntled women in the Eastern Orthodox, Mennonite, and Pentecostalist churches and in the Jewish Conservative movement too, not to mention members of

Eastern religions. Rather than attempt to tackle all denominations and movements, I limit this inquiry in order to paint a vivid landscape.

In 2006 I traveled to Chicago to attend an international gathering of United Methodist clergywomen to celebrate the fiftieth anniversary of their full clergy rights. Fifteen hundred women, most of them ordained, converged at the Hyatt Regency convention center at McCormick Place, their numbers limited only by lack of space. This was the last place I expected to find disgruntled voices—the event was, after all, billed as a celebration, a landmark anniversary, a weeklong gala party. Besides, aren't mainline Protestants very open to women's new roles?

When I showed up to claim my name tag, I encountered two cheerful volunteers overseeing the registration materials. At first they couldn't find my name on their list; they leaned over the table and scanned the names, finally locating me under "Media."

"Media? Are you a reporter?"

I explained that I was writing a book about women who are devoted to their faith but ticked off about their status within it.

"Well," said one of the volunteers, a friendly woman with short white hair and vivid blue eyes. She straightened her shoulders and flashed me a wide, welcoming grin. "You've come to the right place."

More and more, *any* place where religious women gather is the right place to find women demanding equality.

What motivates them? To find out, I engaged in intense interviews with women seriously devoted to their faith, living across this country from far-flung rural Oregon to densely packed New York City. To seek them out, I attended five conferences of religious people in support of women's advancement—in Charlotte, North Carolina, for a conference of the Evangelical and Ecumenical Women's Caucus; in Chicago for the United Methodists' fifty-year anniversary of clergywomen's rights; in Milwaukee for the Catholic reform group Call to Action's annual conference; in Manhattan's Times Square for the historic Women's Islamic Initiative in Spirituality and Equity; and in Manhattan's Upper West Side for the tenth-anniversary celebration and conference of the Jewish Orthodox Feminist Alliance.

Many other women reached out to me after seeing the advertisements I placed in the politically left-of-center Christian magazine *So-*

journers, the feminist Jewish magazine *Lilith*, the progressive Muslim website *MuslimWakeUp!*, and the secular liberal journal *The Nation*. (Many women who read conservative publications also want equality. I chose liberal publications, guessing that in those venues I would have a good chance of finding women willing to speak with me.)

Overall, I spoke with ninety-five women—Catholics, Protestants, Muslims, and Jews. Their ages range from nineteen to ninety-five, and they live in twenty-four different states across the country. Some refer to themselves as feminist; others avoid the term as strongly as they wish Eve had spurned the serpent's fruit. (In this book I describe people and organizations as "feminist" only if they already define themselves in this way.) Except for several interviewees who had left their religious community because they couldn't reconcile their beliefs with their tradition, all are seriously committed to their religious tradition yet simultaneously believe that women are not treated as they should be. They base their beliefs on their understanding of the sacred texts of their faith.

These women collectively voiced four goals:

1. *They want to see women in leadership roles within their church, mosque, or synagogue*—even if they personally do not desire to hold such a position themselves. By extension, they believe that women should be permitted to participate in the same rituals available to men. Because conservative religious women do not plunge forward and claim for themselves a responsibility or ritual without authorization from a respected religious authority, they are educating themselves about existing interpretations that favor increased participation by women.

2. *They want women represented in the language of their liturgy.* In some cases this means wanting God to be described with feminine as well as masculine images (Mother as well as Father, Queen as well as King); in other cases it means simply wanting the liturgy to refer to human women (foremothers) as well as human men (forefathers).

3. *They want religious recognition that their physical bodies are normal and not aberrant.* Despite the millions of women who are proud of their bodies and enjoy wearing revealing

clothes, many other millions—who grew up in religious households—have been taught that the female body, which menstruates, nurtures a growing fetus, gives birth, and lactates, is inherently offensive. Sadly, many women come to believe this is true.

4. *They want to be recognized as people created fully in the image of God.* The idea that human beings are created "in the image of God" and therefore share some aspects of the divine is very powerful and important in Judaism and Christianity. In Islam, it is believed that humans have the potential to share some characteristics of God but can never fully achieve a mirroring of God.

Genesis 1:27 reads, "And God created the human in His image, in the image of God He created him; *male and female He created them.*"[3] In mirroring God to some extent, humans are elevated. If God is compassionate and just (as all three religions maintain), and if we have the capacity to act as God acts, then we have the power and responsibility to behave in compassionate and just ways. Moreover, if all humans are like God, then all humans must be treated with respect. But what happens if only men are believed to be "in the image of God"? Christian leaders throughout the centuries have argued that only men reflect the divine image, while women *require men* to complete them to achieve the same status. As a result, many Christians believe that women are not as valuable as men in the eyes of God—and therefore, by themselves, cannot be "saved."

To achieve these goals, much more is required than to "add women and stir." Theology itself—the ideas that undergird the religious practices—must reflect the lives of women too. Since the 1970s, academics in the area of religion and women have reexamined and reinterpreted Christian and Jewish theology. More recently, Muslim academics have also turned to women's issues in theology. They have called attention to Judaism, Christianity, and Islam as religions created by men. Whether or not one believes in a supernatural God, there is no arguing against the fact that the architects of each religious tradition were people—men.

Historically, women have been shut out of the power structures of each faith. As a result, a male point of view has molded each faith's core ideas about God and about who has access to the privilege of serving God.

More fundamentally, the three religious traditions have tended to regard women as inferior and subordinate to men. "It is not possible for woman to achieve equality with man," is how the theologian Elisabeth Schüssler Fiorenza sums up the prevailing belief, "because this is against divine law and biblical revelation."[4] There are, to be sure, exceptions and ambiguities that also are part of the theology of these religions, but speaking generally, it has been understood that there is a hierarchical relationship between man and woman, that man is the one with the power, and that this is the divine truth.

Woman's supposed inferiority, it has been explained, is innate or circumstantial, caused by (pick your favorites):

Sin (eating from the forbidden Tree of Knowledge in the Garden of Eden)

Child-rearing responsibilities

The capacity to sexually arouse men, who might then participate in forbidden sexual relations

Having a woman's body, which does not reflect the image of God

Having a woman's body, which is closer to nature than man's body, and therefore removed from transcendent reason, which is godlike

Having been created second instead of first

The fact that Jesus was a man and not a woman

The fact that God is most often described as male and not female

When you take a step back and examine each explanation, you can't help but see the flaws:

Adam ate the forbidden fruit too.

Child-rearing responsibilities do not last a lifetime, and besides, doesn't the capacity to give birth make women more godlike than men?

Men can learn sexual restraint, and if men are natural leaders, why are they so weak?

The Bible says explicitly that both women and men are created in the image of God.

A person can give birth and also possess the ability to reason.

If being first is better than being second, why are animals not superior to humans?

Jesus was not only a man but also Jewish, yet Christians don't consider themselves inferior to Jews.

The Hebrew Bible (also accepted as sacred by Christians and Muslims), as well as the Qur'an, refers to God in feminine as well as masculine terms and images, and Jesus refers to himself in female imagery.

The whole enterprise of explaining man's supposed superiority to woman is specious and suspicious.

The feminist theologian Mary Daly was one of the first modern thinkers—along with Valerie Saiving, Rosemary Ruether, Letty Russell, Judith Plaskow, and a few other trailblazers—to analyze the woven bond of sexism and religion. She wrote in 1971,

The Judaic-Christian tradition has served to legitimate sexually imbalanced patriarchal society. Thus, for example, the image of the Father God, spawned in the human imagination and sustained as plausible by patriarchy, has in turn rendered service to this type of society by making its mechanisms for the oppression of women appear right and fitting. If God in "his" heaven is a father ruling "his" people, then it is in the "nature" of things and according to divine plan and the order of the universe that society be male dominated . . . Within this context, a mystification of roles takes place: the husband dominating his wife represents God himself. What is happening, of course, is the familiar mechanism by which the images and values of a given society are projected into a realm of beliefs, which in turn justify the social infrastructure. The belief system becomes hardened and objectified, seeming to have an unchangeable independent existence and validity of its own. It resists social change which would rob it of its plausibility. Nevertheless, despite the vicious circle, change does occur in society, and ideologies die, though they die hard.[5]

These are stinging words. Daly was arguing that Christian theology reinforces sexism in society. To put it another way, there is something wrong with Christianity because it is sexist. But she also hinted at the possibility for reform: social change *could* happen; it just wouldn't be easy or pretty. At the time she wrote this passage, Daly was personally committed to feminist reform of the Catholic Church. But since 1971 she has changed direction. Today she believes that the Christian tradition is *inherently* oppressive to women because its core symbols, such as a male Christ, are essentially sexist. She now argues that Christianity cannot be reconciled with the drive for women's equality—and therefore it must be abandoned.

I disagree. Reform is not impossible. To my mind, Judaism, Christianity, and Islam are strong enough that they can withstand a little reform without compromising their core values. The issue is not a matter of "if," but "when." We can reread our sacred texts and interpret them through the lens of women's equality. There are many truths to our sacred texts, not just one, and we can expose multiple meanings that enrich, not strip away, the validity of our faith.

Even if one is adamant that the divine voice is unalterable, it still cannot be denied that the divine voice always has been, and always will be, filtered and interpreted by humans. It is our job to figure out the most authentic way of understanding this voice, and to do so, we must use human knowledge. Today, we know that women are full human beings with the same intelligence, leadership skills, and spiritual capabilities as men. It is incumbent upon us to use this knowledge in our understanding of sacred texts.

Christian women seeking equality emphasize that Jesus treated women as fully equal to men, that men and women together were equal disciples in the earliest Christian mission, and that Jesus lived his life and suffered his death to be in solidarity with all who had faith, including the marginalized—women, poor, outcasts, sinners. And yet how many Christians today are even aware that their religion valued what we call inclusiveness? Christians must look back at the early history of the church and recapture the gender equality that was part of its foundation.

Muslim women seeking equality similarly point out that the prophet Muhammad treated women very positively, but that through the centuries this has been forgotten or ignored. The Qur'an—the Muslim holy text believed to be the literal word of God as it was revealed to Muhammad—gave women legal rights of inheritance and divorce, which was revolutionary in seventh-century Arabia. One revelation addressed women directly (something not done at all in the Hebrew Bible or the New Testament) and stated that women and men are morally and spiritually equal. The prophet's first wife, Khadijah, was a successful merchant and an older woman, and it's clear that Muhammad held women in general in high esteem. "Islam gave women rights," the author and translator Laleh Bakhtiar tells me, "and the men took them away." Muslim women seeking equality want to return to the attitudes toward women expressed in the Qur'an and through Muhammad's example.

Observant Jewish women seeking reform remain committed to halakhah, the code of Jewish law, which is built upon a foundation of gender inequality. Nevertheless, these women say that even within halakhah their roles can and should be expanded greatly. They point out that halakhah has always been fluid and flexible and has changed throughout the centuries when rabbis have deemed change necessary. These rabbis have found interpretations in Jewish law to support their changes. If the leading rabbis of today wanted to give women rights, they could and they would.

"The problem with much theology," writes the theologian Judith Plaskow, "is not that it speaks from male experience—it must speak from some experience—but that it claims universality for its particular perspective . . . Theology cannot deal with 'universal human experience' not simply because human reason is finite, but also because experience itself is so varied." Plaskow, unlike Daly, does not throw up her hands and walk away. Instead, she calls on groups that have not been represented to speak up so that their insights can be included in "a multifaceted theological exploration of the human situation."[6] The challenge is to avoid repeating the error of our forefathers, who presented their own male experiences as universally human ones.

If we accept this challenge, we can achieve our goals. Women *can* take on leadership roles in their churches, mosques, or synagogues. Women *can* be represented in the language of their liturgies. Women *can* be taught that their bodies are normal. Women *can* be recognized as having been created in the image of God. We can achieve these things. We do not have to abandon our faith communities. We can stay and make them stronger. And for this to happen, we cannot be polite. The religion reporter and papal biographer David Gibson observes that with the Catholic priest shortage, laypeople, women and men, are effectively running the parishes. "If all these people went on strike for one week, the Church would come to a grinding halt."[7]

And for those who would prefer that Catholics go a week without confession before they would allow a female priest, remember that without women, there is no religion. Says the religious studies professor Christel Manning,

> Women are still the heart of most families. When parents divorce, mothers usually get primary custody. When Christian families homeschool their children, it is almost always the mother who does the educating. It is the mother who determines how closely a Jewish family will observe the kosher laws. And it is women who, by joining the labor force, are challenging traditional religious gender roles. Women therefore have a powerful influence both on what it means to be [religious] today and what it will mean for the next generation.[8]

In other words, even if religious leaders don't care about justice for women, they should give it to them anyway—for the sake of the continuity of their tradition. It is shortsighted not to.

The ancient sage Hillel asked, "If I am not for myself, who will be for me?" Meaning: If I don't look out for my own interests, who will? He continued, "If I am only for myself, what am I?" Although I must look out for my own interests, I can't look out *only* on my behalf. I must also help others in need. Otherwise, what kind of person would I be? Hillel's questions point to the conflict between the interests of the individual and the interests of the community to which she or he belongs. So which one takes precedence?

The answer is embedded in the great rabbi's final question: "If not now, when?" Meaning: There will always be conflict between the individual and the community, and this conflict might never be resolved. But that need not stop me—and you—from doing what needs to be done now.

Devout American women of different faiths are arriving at the same conclusion: religion must become more inclusive of women, and action must be taken *now*. These women are living with an enormous conflict—between their needs and the long-held interpretations of their religious tradition. But they are moving beyond the impasse of conflict to take matters into their own hands.

Even if you feel no personal stake in religion, it has an enormous influence over your life. More and more, religious values influence the political direction of our country. In fact, religion affects everyone in the United States, whether they are Episcopalian, Quaker, Buddhist, Reform Jewish, Wiccan, or atheist. A whopping 90 percent of Americans believe in God.[9] Only 10 to 14 percent of Americans have no ties to a congregation, denomination, or faith group.[10] Of those with religious ties, the overwhelming majority are Christian. A quarter of adult Americans are Catholic (51 million) and 52 percent are Protestant (105 million), making three-quarters of all adults in this country self-described Christians. Less than 2 percent are Jewish (2.8 million), and less than 2 percent are Muslim (2.35 million).[11] The Jewish and Muslim figures are slippery; if a Jew is defined as anyone with Jewish parentage, the number could be as high as 5 million, and many Muslim organizations claim that there are between 5 to 7 million Muslims in the United States. Moreover, for those who are spiritually hungry but turned off by the more popular U.S. religions, there is a smorgasbord of alternate options ranging from Hinduism to Scientology to the mystical religion Madonna strangely calls Kabbalah (it bears only a passing resemblance to the Kabbalah of Jewish tradition).

No matter how you crunch the numbers, it is indisputable that America is a country filled with religious people, the overwhelming majority of them Christian, and that most take their religion seriously. The 2008 presidential campaign was strewn with Bibles. Recognizing that Americans take politicians' religion into account on election day, each candidate jostled for the position of Most Pious and Authentic Christian. Even Rudy Giuliani, not a religious man, described himself in spiritual terms.

A full third of Americans describe themselves as born-again or evangelical[12]—the word "evangel" means "good news," and evangelicals believe they are obligated to spread the good news that Jesus can save sinners. Millions of evangelicals believe in the inerrancy of the Bible—that it is without error and that there is only one "true" meaning of the words of the Bible, which was written by God. Among those who hold this belief are some—commonly called fundamentalists—who believe that interpretations other than their own are false and not worthy of attention, perhaps even blasphemous. If a Christian strays from the accepted understanding of key biblical passages, she may not have "faith" (appropriate belief in Jesus Christ as savior) and therefore may not be "saved" (brought to heaven instead of hell after death) by Jesus. When Christine, a white thirty-eight-year-old stay-at-home mother living in rural North Carolina, was growing up, she would occasionally tell her evangelical parents that she disagreed with some verse in the Bible. "My parents would tell me, 'Well, you really need to work on your faith.'"

Many evangelicals are politically right-wing. Some don't support the separation between church and state, religion and politics. Instead, they make a concerted and often successful effort to align the political and social landscape with fundamentalist Christian ideas. Known as the religious right, they are members of well-organized, politically conservative Christian groups such as the Christian Coalition, Moral Majority, and Focus on the Family, and along with groups like the Catholic Council, they have massive grassroots support. These groups include enormously influential people with the power to determine and enforce national and state laws, people who want to impose their own vision of what America should look like onto everyone else.

Faith-based politics have led to classrooms in which attempts are made to replace the science of evolution with either "intelligent design" or creationism.[13] Religion in politics has tied the hands of medical researchers who want to use fetal stem cells to save existing lives

17

and has led to massive support of a constitutional amendment to ban same-sex marriages. Meanwhile, "Faith Nights" at football and baseball games around the country (not only in the Bible Belt) offer Christian music, giveaways of Christian toys, and testimonials from the players themselves. Some Christian faculty members at the U.S. Air Force Academy in Colorado have proselytized the cadets, who include Jews and other religious minorities. When George W. Bush tapped Harriet Miers to sit on the Supreme Court in 2005, he indicated to Americans that they could trust her because she is a born-again Christian like himself.[14]

To say that the religious right does not support equality of the sexes would be like saying that Noah's ark got wet during the flood. Many on the right don't even support adequate *education* for females. Because of the political muscle of the religious right, millions of girls do not receive complete information abut sexuality and contraception, as they are subjected to "abstinence-only sex education," which has been shown to be both ineffective and dangerous. Boys don't receive decent sex ed either, which is also tragic, but it's the girls who get pregnant. Some of these pregnant girls or adult women seek help in health-care institutions that receive federal funds but do not inform women about their full options, which include abortion.

Not all evangelicals are fundamentalist or politically right-wing. According to Anne Eggebroten, a research scholar with the Center for the Study of Women at UCLA, herself an evangelical Christian and one of the founding members of the Evangelical Women's Caucus in 1974, the religious right "is a cultural movement that gives people a black-and-white world where abortion is wrong and homosexuality is wrong. Their belief is that if you just stay within certain boundaries, you will be safe and happy and have a strong spirituality. And that approach has worked for a lot of evangelical churches." Eggebroten is a white fifty-nine-year-old woman living in Santa Monica, California. When I meet her, she looks relaxed in khaki pants and Birkenstocks, her chin-length gray-blond hair tucked casually behind her ears. But she is anything but laid-back when it comes to her commitment to women's and gay rights. She is a tireless critic of fundamentalist Christian politics in her columns for *Women's eNews* and in her groundbreaking book, *Abortion: My Choice, God's Grace*, in which evangelical

Christian and Catholic women discuss their decisions to have abortions. She asks me,

> Why are abortion and gay rights the big issues right now? People didn't care all that much in the 1950s. The common denominator pushing all of these conservative groups is fear. You have women controlling their own bodies and the empowerment of gays and lesbians. There is a lot going on in society that is still relatively new and scary. So I think there's a huge appeal to a time that never was when things were safe and nice and women and gays were in their place. There's a tremendous attraction to that, and I think that it fuels the popularity of forms of faith that give people a clear sense of rights and wrongs and going back to a mythic time when things were easier and answers were clearer. People also want a scapegoat. If they have a scapegoat, they don't have to look at their own behavior. A lot of fundamentalist preaching is about how bad gays are and how they're going to take over the world, how bad feminists are and abortions are. If you look at the men who have been active in fighting abortion, the way they got into it is the mentality of, "Wow, these people are so bad, but I can save the world!"

Given the political-religious environment today, the inclusive vision of today's equality-seeking religious women creates not only an alternate way of worshipping God but an alternate way of being a citizen in this country. We believe that those who are politically conservative should not have a monopoly on religion. In the 2008 presidential campaign, Democratic senators Barack Obama and Hillary Clinton appealed to the spiritual side of voters, weaving religious themes into their campaign rhetoric. Although I usually become concerned when politicians invoke religion, because this can lead to the blurring of church-state separation, at the same time I found it refreshing that Democrats were the ones referring to God. Every year at its annual convention, Planned Parenthood Federation of America holds an optional interfaith prayer breakfast. To me, this is encouraging. No, I don't think being religious is a prerequisite for being pro-choice—or, for that matter, for being *anything*. Being religious has no bearing on whether someone is a moral, kind, empathetic person or whether she is cruel and hurtful. Religion is used to justify any and all behavior. But I want people to be aware that many women who support the full range of reproductive health care, including the legal right to an abortion, are religious too.

There is a history of devout women in the United States agitating for social reform. Today's ticked-off religious women have illustrious predecessors: Lucretia Mott and Elizabeth Cady Stanton, leaders of the first wave of the women's rights movement, were raised in religious households—Mott as a Quaker, Stanton as a Presbyterian. They were vehemently antislavery and called for immediate abolition based on their understanding of God's law. These women organized the Seneca Falls, New York, convention of 1848, in which they unveiled a Declaration of Sentiments, modeled on the Declaration of Independence, that called for women's suffrage and reform of marital and property laws. Historians date this convention as the beginning of the organized women's movement in the United States. The two founders were motivated by their understanding of the Bible, which they believed taught the message of equality of all human beings.

Vivian Gornick, the essayist and biographer of Elizabeth Cady Stanton, reminds us that when the great women's rights leader was coming of age, religion was as inescapable as the air she breathed:

> In the Cady household, as in innumerable American homes at the time when she was growing up, there prevailed an unreconstructed Presbyterianism that posited original sin as one given, and the ever-present threat of an eternity spent in hell as another . . . It is hard to overstate the religious cast of this culture. In 1800 the rhetoric of Christianity informed the dailiness of American life, all popular notions of virtue were visibly bound up with a Christian definition of moral obligation, thousands of young men routinely contemplated a life in the church, and in colleges and universities religious thought and practice were thoroughly intermingled with every kind of intellectual inquiry.[15]

Against this religious backdrop, women's rights activists formulated their revolutionary ideas. They peppered their speeches and pamphlets with references to being "anointed," "sanctified," and "baptized" by their savior to fight for this cause, which was "sacred" and divinely ordained.[16] Angelina Grimké, active in the antislavery and women's rights movements, wrote a letter to Stanton in 1841, urging her not to move to Boston (where Stanton's husband wanted to live) from upstate New York. She wrote:

> I greatly fear this contact for thee, because thou has not given thy heart to God, and therefore this preserving power cannot uphold thee. He has blessed thee with talents which if devoted to his service will be a blessing to thy self, to thy husband and family, and to the world . . . In Boston there will be little to make thee so, much to draw your heart away from God. I long to see you sitting at the feet of Jesus, hearing his words and doing his will. This is all you need to place you among the choicest instruments for doing good.[17]

This appeal to God was typical among the earliest American feminists. At the 1848 Seneca Falls Convention, held in a church, Lucretia Mott urged everyone present to "be as the Jesus of the present age."[18] The activist Elizabeth Oakes Smith, speaking at the Syracuse National Women's Rights Convention in 1852, similarly said that "we who struggle to restore the divine order to the world should feel as if under the very eye of the Eternal Searcher of all hearts, who will reject any sacrifice other than a pure offering."[19]

These women believed that it was *God's* plan—not their own—that women should be allowed to vote, own property, and initiate lawsuits. Stanton argued that all you have to do is take a look inside your Bible to see that, just as "representative women have in all ages and nations walked outside the prescribed limits and done what they had the capacity to accomplish . . . the women of the Bible form no exception. They preached, prayed, prophecied, expounded principles of government to kings and rulers, led armies, saved nations and cities by their wisdom and diplomacy, conquered their enemies by intrigue as well as courage."[20]

In the late nineteenth and early twentieth centuries, some evangelical Protestant women also took on the temperance cause—the fight to get people to moderate their consumption of alcohol, if not abstain from it completely; to close down saloons, where men congregated and often came home drunk and violent; and to eliminate prostitution. Frances Willard, the president of the National Woman's Christian Temperance Union in the last quarter of the nineteenth century and a devout Methodist, used preacher language in her lectures around the country. Together with many suffragists, temperance movement activists allayed the fears of those who opposed the reformers for being antifamily. These reformers bent over backward to prove how loyal they were to their roles as wives, mothers, and home caretakers. They declared that the home, with mother at the helm, was an essential pillar of moral society because women were morally superior to men. In so doing, they elevated female domesticity at the same time that they pushed for women's equality in the larger world.

This position, contradictory and complicated, has bedeviled supporters of women's rights for generations: we have had to work double time to show that men are also moral role models, within and outside of the home, and that women must not be limited to the domestic sphere. But at the time, the reformers' position allowed Christian women to demand civil rights without compromising their status as wholesome and pious. It also gave them license to meet together publicly and to speak in open forums, which were taboo for women throughout the nineteenth century. (In 1838, Quaker abolitionist women met in Philadelphia to talk about slavery, and a mob of ten thousand men circled the building, shouted at the women, threw stones through the windows, broke the doors and windows, and set fire to the building after the women, unable to continue their work, walked out.[21]) These women's strategies were resoundingly successful, leading ultimately to the passage of the Eighteenth Amendment to the Constitution (putting Prohibition into law) and the Nineteenth (giving women the right to vote). Along the way, reformers like Willard also promoted the cause of increased participation and leadership for women within the church.

Meanwhile, Elizabeth Cady Stanton became increasingly disillusioned with Christian theology. Instead of calling Christians to task for misreading the Bible and distorting its message, she began to challenge the Bible itself. She came to believe that the message of the Bible, not the messengers, were at fault. As Gornick puts it, Stanton came to see that "it wasn't that the Bible *served* patriarchy, the Bible *was* patriarchy,"[22] and she came to disavow Christianity altogether. In trying to spread her message, she worked on a book, *The Woman's Bible*, a collection of biblical references to women together with feminist commentaries. Published in two parts, in 1895 and in 1898, the book came under fierce attack, and Stanton, the guiding force of the women's movement, lost all credibility among her activist sisters. Even the National Woman Suffrage Association publicly declared the book "harmful to its cause."[23]

White Protestant women were not the only ones who spoke up for reform. Catholic women and Jewish women, outsiders to Protestant culture, along with black Christian women, addressed other areas of reform. They were not invited to join the suffrage and temperance movements, and they weren't interested anyway in the banner of moral purity; many of them had to earn a living and therefore did not agree that women had a special responsibility to make the home a moral haven. They were too busy making ends meet to worry about protecting the home.[24] As the twentieth century rolled forward, these groups became involved in other areas of social reform—labor issues such as worker safety and workers' rights, pacifism, socialism, outreach to the poor, civil rights, and reproductive rights. Like white Protestants, they too were strongly influenced by their religious conviction of the need to help those less fortunate.

What I find striking about the suffragists and temperance activists is that religion so strongly informed their work, yet they bypassed their pastors. They took on the mantle of authority for themselves. They had the confidence of their religious knowledge, the assurance of their mastery of Scripture. They listened to their own religious beliefs and their own opinions about God and justice; they did not merely say amen to whatever their pastor said. They did not ask anyone's permission to speak up: they just did. In their day, religious leaders were elevated to sky-heights and had real power over community life. Yet these women fearlessly decided not to defer to them. And because of these women—and their male supporters—we have abolished slavery, given women the right to vote, empowered women within the legal system, and obtained a model of feminist religious scholarship.

Today's devout women seeking change share their predecessors' impatience with religious leaders. Catholic women are justifiably disgruntled over being ignored during the selection of Pope Benedict XVI and outraged over widespread sexual abuse by trusted priests and the ensuing cover-up by bishops. Meanwhile, many Protestant, Muslim, and Jewish women are respectful, often reverent, toward their pastors, imams, and rabbis; but they also believe that these leaders by themselves will not facilitate change to women's advantage.

"Change comes from grassroots pressure," says Susan Aranoff, a leading activist on behalf of married Jewish women who can't get religiously divorced from their husbands. (Jewish law unilaterally favors men in divorce, and some men exploit this advantage, sometimes to extort money.) "Change comes from the bottom," she continues, "and *then* it is acknowledged and solidified by the leaders." In other words, *the "leaders" are followers.* The true leaders are ordinary people who use their collective power to press for change from the inside.

It was grassroots pressure that led to the March 1973 conference of the emerging Jewish women's movement, which successfully pushed for the inclusion of rituals honoring girls and women among Jews of all denominations. Grassroots pressure led Episcopal bishops in 1974 to ordain eleven women as priests, without church approval, which prodded the Episcopal Church hierarchy to sanction women's ordination to priesthood two years later, leading ultimately to the 2006 installation of the first female presiding bishop. The lesson is clear. "We need to make facts on the ground," contends Renée Septimus, an observant Jewish woman. "That is the only way things are going to change. Well-educated laypeople will make changes, not the rabbis, because the rabbis don't lead. The laypeople will lead and the rabbis will follow. That is the only way change is made."

Septimus is concerned that many Orthodox Jews, while ferociously well versed in the minutiae of Jewish history and law, have lost sight of the big picture, which includes human responsibility. "To me, Judaism is an evolution of a partnership between the divine and the human.

Because if you look at Judaism through history, you see that so much of Jewish law has changed! But today the rabbis don't want to change anything. They have a vested interest in their power. And people are afraid of their rabbis and don't want to do anything that their rabbis would disapprove of."

Muslim women face a similar challenge because their religion, like Orthodox Judaism, is built upon a legal foundation. "Women are going to change the religion because we have nothing to lose," says Mona Eltahawy, an international journalist who writes about Muslim issues and whose work appears in all the major Arab and U.S. media, including Egypt's *Al-Dastour* newspaper, *The Daily Star* of Lebanon, BBC World, and the *International Herald Tribune*. Eltahawy is usually busy jetting around the world to various Muslim hot spots, but on this afternoon she is home in New York City. We meet at a walk-in-closet–size Afghan restaurant. Her striking looks are framed by shiny, thick hair and black rectangular glasses, and she wears a choker, rings, and bracelets inscribed with Arabic writing.

"*Sharia* [Islamic law] is applied and interpreted differently in every country and it's not divine revelation," Eltahawy tells me in her precise accent, an Anglo–Middle Eastern hybrid. "It was codified several hundred years after the Prophet's death. Those of us who say that we can't continue to live as if it were the year 900 want to maintain the spirit of the religion when it was revealed to the Prophet, but to apply it to today. Changes must be based on the scholarship. There are progressive scholars doing interesting interpretations. They are mostly men and a few women. The changes should be based on what they are doing."

Born in Egypt in 1967, Eltahawy has lived in Britain, Saudi Arabia, and Israel and has seen up close the ways in which sharia is interpreted and applied strictly and rigidly. "We need a whole multitude of voices to represent Muslims. We need voices to say things like, 'Women should not be in the back' and 'It's wrong to mutilate girls' genitals' and 'It's wrong to force a girl or young woman into an arranged marriage she doesn't want to be in.' I think American Muslims are the best hope for Islam. We have freedoms here that Muslims don't have in other countries. Muslim American women are leading the way. This is a very exciting time to be a Muslim woman in America." Eltahawy looks at me intently from across the table. "If we ask for permission to make changes, we won't get it. We just have to do it."

"I believe very firmly that we have to take actions to back the new interpretations," says the Muslim activist Asra Nomani, confirming the current thinking. Nomani is the author of *Standing Alone: An American Woman's Struggle for the Soul of Islam* and a major force behind the drive for women's equality in U.S. mosques. Nomani is whispering to me on her cell phone while she sits on a pew at a local church, where her teenage niece is taking a driving course. "The new interpretations are out there—there is scholarship that shows that women can be witnesses, women can be imams, women can drive cars, and women are not allowed to be beaten. So now we have to walk the talk. We have to actualize the new interpretations. We have to put them out in the world." Nomani is breathlessly impatient to get things moving. "I differ with some other people who think we should wait and get more consensus," she says, carefully modulating her voice so that her words don't bounce off the church walls. "That will never happen. We're up against this entire empire that has a consensus *against* us, so we will never turn the tide if we wait for our rights to be given to us."

Christian women also are taking matters into their own hands. In a number of Protestant denominations, women have the advantage of the right to become pastors and thereby usher in reforms from a position of leadership. But being a leader doesn't give one a free pass. Rev. Amy DeLong, an ordained United Methodist minister in Wisconsin, has twice been appointed to lead conservative churches, and she has found over and over that congregants want to hear a different perspective on God. "The idea of universal salvation—that everyone is saved—is considered heretical because that is not the doctrine we are taught. And yet it resonates with almost every average person sitting in the pew. People say, 'I like the idea that God loves everybody, whether we do right or wrong.' They don't want to think of God as mean. But we've been taught a mean image of God." Despite congregants' desire for alternative interpretations of Scripture, she was challenged for exposing them to new ways of thinking about their theology.

DeLong, who is forty but could pass for a college student, has bleached cropped hair, blue eyes, and a friendly face. Her example is a good illustration of what can happen when someone questions long-held traditional beliefs. She is the director and founder of a progressive Christian organization composed primarily of United Methodists from Wisconsin. It is called Kairos CoMotion—the Greek *kairos* signifies God's time when something special occurs, while the word "co-Motion" refers to movement, spirit, and energy—and it supports gay rights, women's rights, and alternate ways of understanding the meanings of Jesus' life, death, and resurrection. In 2005 DeLong organized a Kairos conference called, tongue very much in cheek, the Extreme Makeover Conference. The theologian Rita Nakashima Brock, a prominent scholar and author, was the keynote speaker. Her topic was the doctrine of atonement (Jesus dying for human sin) and the related concept of redemptive suffering—the belief that a person can be saved by Jesus Christ through her suffering, which is reminiscent of the cross Jesus bore. This concept has been challenged by feminist theologians because historically, a married woman has been expected to submit her own will to that of her husband and children. Women have been told that if submission causes them to suffer, that is a *good* thing, leading to salvation for themselves and their families. In many cases, this idea of suffering being good has been used to justify domestic violence and abuse.

DeLong had specifically invited Brock, a known critic of the doctrine of atonement and its sanctification of suffering, because she wanted to shake things up and get people to think outside the box. Among the registration materials was a flyer that contained what DeLong called an Atonement Quiz. The quiz asked, "Was Christ's death payment for our sins? Does God require suffering? Did God send Jesus to be a blood sacrifice for salvation? Is violence necessary for redemption?" It went on: "If you answered 'Yes' to any of these questions, then your Atonement Theology may be in need of an Extreme Makeover! Join the CoMotion and let God get under your skin."

DeLong intended the Atonement Quiz to be provocative—and, well, it was. A month before the conference she received a letter from the Wisconsin executive committee of a conservative movement within the United Methodist denomination—called the Confessing Movement. It was signed by ten people. It had been sent to all the board members of Kairos, and to local bishops and lay leaders, intended to threaten and intimidate them. The letter asked DeLong to defend her biblical grounds for an alternate understanding of the theory of atonement. It suggested that she check the United Methodist qualifications for ordination and the responsibilities of a pastor, and it went on to say, "We fear that rejecting the United Methodist understanding of the atonement (held in common with nearly all Christians for 2,000 years) may jeopardize your own salvation and relationship with God through Jesus Christ, as well as potentially damage the church's witness to the Gospel and weaken the faith of others."

DeLong was livid. She scoffed at the attempt to scare her, but she worried about others less secure in their place within the United Methodist community. Church members may want to question doctrine—not necessarily reject it—but how can they feel free to question, let alone challenge, religious ideas when they are made to feel like heretics? "This intimidation hurts ordinary, churchgoing people," DeLong fumes, "because they come alive with these new ideas. They eat it up! They get to hear a message they didn't even know existed. They are sitting in the pews dying, spiritually, for messages like this." Despite the letter, did she hold the conference anyway? "Of course!"

The call to speak up is perhaps best expressed by Sister Joan Chittister, a Benedictine nun and tireless activist for reform in the Catholic Church. Chittister, a Julia Child look-alike with enormous charisma, had a question for the three thousand Catholics assembled in Milwaukee in November 2006 to celebrate the thirtieth anniversary of the reform organization Call to Action: "Why should Catholics speak up for reform?" Her thunderous answer: "What happens in the world and in church does not depend on God. It depends on *us*. It is not God's fault if things we have done already do not change. It is *our* fault! We are the ones deciding who is sacred enough to touch the chalice at the Eucharist, so we can *undecide* it!"

Chittister went on to relate the story in II Kings (6:24–7:10) of the four Jewish lepers in ancient Israel. Everyone in the packed conference hall knew the tale—a classic scriptural story, beloved by Jews as well as Christians and repeated often. Nevertheless, with her booming voice and flair for dramatic pauses, Chittister had her audience sitting on the edge of their seats. She spoke of the lepers, poverty-stricken and left to die of hunger. Because their disease was contagious, they were put outside the walls of the city of Samaria to fend for themselves: those within the city had washed their hands of them. Meanwhile, the enemy, the Aramaean army, had surrounded the city walls, and since there was no food allowed into the city, the people inside were also starving, so desperate that they had turned to cannibalism.

The lepers turned to each other and decided to go over to the enemy's camp. They were going to die anyway, so what did they have to lose? Maybe they could find some food scraps. Worst case, the soldiers would kill them—but they would die anyway if they just sat there. So the lepers went to the Aramaean camp, and behold, the soldiers had fled. And they had left behind abundant food, drink, and wealth! The lepers had their fill and helped themselves to gold and silver, and then they did something remarkable. They went back to the very people who had cast them out, to share with them the good news: The siege was over. Samaria was free! The lepers recognized their responsibility, and they acted on it—even though it was tempting to do nothing and thereby exact their revenge.

Chittister continued: "The lessons are clear, aren't they? First, the work of renewal is ours. We cannot blame God for what we do not do to save ourselves. Second, as the lepers know, unless there are those who care enough for the community to risk for it, renewal is out of the question and the entire tradition is in danger. Unless there are those willing to think *newly*, to begin again, the people cannot be saved. Unless someone rises up, whatever the thinking of those around them—who are equally sincere, yes, but seriously paralyzed by old-world views—a new world will never—*can* never—come . . . Rise up and take responsibility . . . Rise up and use the gifts you've been given. Rise up, rise up, and go!" Her audience of reform-minded Catholics roared with applause. They, along with reformers among Protestants, Jews, and Muslims, realize that if no one rises up—as the prophets did, as the lepers did—no one will be saved.[25]

Sojourner Truth, the nineteenth-century black slave and devout Christian who broke free of her bondage to become a legendary abolitionist and women's rights activist, was confident that the world could be made a better place if women would unite and rise up together. "If the first woman God ever made was strong enough to turn the world upside down all alone," she declared, "these women

29

together ought to be able to turn it back and get it right-side up again!"[26]

Many women cannot rise up. If they did, they would risk losing their friends, their community, even their jobs. One fifty-eight-year-old Catholic woman who spoke to me on the condition of anonymity is afraid to voice her criticisms of the Catholic Church. As a Latina from Venezuela, now living in Texas, she is adamantly opposed to the church's positions against abortion, divorce, and women's ordination. But, she says, "I can't tell people my opinions and lose my friendships and lose my relationships just because I want to say what I think. I have to work very hard, be invisible, and not make waves"—she speaks in a halting voice—"in my job and also in my religion. To survive, I can't voice my opinions, because I depend on people, especially my friends from church. I'm Catholic but I do have my own beliefs that are not always the beliefs of the church. But I do believe in God and I do need my faith to survive. I have a hard, hard time in this country, but my faith keeps me going. If I leave the church, I will crumble."

Others feel too intimidated to speak up, simply because of the social pressure to conform to religious teachings. "When a woman speaks up or stirs things up," explains thirty-two-year-old Kimberly Harper, a black doctoral student who converted to Islam and lives in North Carolina, "they say that she's a 'bad sister,' but if she does what she's supposed to, she's a 'good sister.'" Harper herself is outspoken about women's status within Islamic tradition, but she recognizes that not everyone has her courage or the luxury to be critical. A more typical approach is that of Kristin Wurgler, a white twenty-five-year-old evangelical Christian living in Orange County, California. "I've been in situations in the church so often where I completely disagree with a lot of what people say, but when you speak up, they completely shun you. They think that you're not one of them anymore." In certain situations, she remembers, she used to "keep [her] mouth shut and not make a big deal out of it," although now she is more likely to stand up for what she believes in.

No matter what her circumstances, the woman who speaks up to confront her religious tradition, especially if she chooses to remain committed to the tradition and therefore maintain bonds with her community, takes risks. If her community is not ready to listen to her, she may be branded a heretic or a pagan and treated as an outcast (as a leper?)—along with her family. But without public criticism, nothing will change. And the way things stand now, there *must* be change. The consequences for those who conform uncritically to their tradition's expectations of women can be devastating.

When your faith instructs you that you are inferior and subordinate, this is how you come to view yourself—and not only in the religious sphere. If a religious woman's church or synagogue or mosque—the central institution of authority in her life—tells her that women categorically cannot be leaders, perhaps that women categorically should not be visible to men during worship, she internalizes the belief that she is not capable of leadership and that she is not worthy of being a full participant in essential activities that are labeled "For Men Only." This is a disempowering message. Think about what it means. She will not even try to develop a number of skills and talents that will forever be cut off. She will not pursue professional or intellectual ambitions. She will feel awkward and probably discouraged if she decides to assert herself and, as a result, may very well decide not to bother.

Obviously, there *are* assertive women who refuse to take no for an answer. God bless them. But for so many others, the message of religious inferiority is smothering.

Meanwhile, boys grow up with a sense of entitlement that they don like a comfortable robe: they are entitled to serve on the Catholic altar, even to become priests if that is their ambition, and to enjoy the company of other men alone (no complaints of breast-feeding or hot flashes!). They are entitled (even required) to be the "head" in their relationship with their wives and leaders within their communities without any competition from the ladies. They are entitled to celebrate Ramadan evenings, when eating is finally permitted, with elaborate and delicious dishes cooked by women who are not allowed to attend the celebration. They are entitled to all the synagogue honors, which they have to share only with other men. Are you seeing a pattern here? Do you see the implications? Religious males stand in the center of their world; females are told to move to the periphery. Is it any wonder that God is described as male? God is the center of the universe, so how could God be thought of in female terms? And if God is male, then men become accustomed to thinking of themselves as godlike. As Mary Daly famously quipped, "If God is male, then the male is God."[27]

It's true that in many aspects of American society, women have come a long way. Over the last forty years we have made tremendous progress. Nevertheless, many religious women set a bar for themselves in the world at large (not only the religious world) that is lower than the one set by their male peers. They don't expect to be listened to, so they don't speak up. They let men fill most of the slots in politics and religious-community affairs. They don't expect to command much respect, so they pursue low-prestige, unchallenging jobs and leave the well-paying positions for the guys to pursue. They can't imagine opportunities outside of marriage and motherhood, so they get married and have babies (and more babies) before they are ready, and they take on a far greater share of the domestic responsibilities than they can handle without being worn down.

Could their religious background have something to do with this?

TWO

A Love-Hate Relationship
with Tradition

In the religious sphere, change is a dicey subject. The whole point of organized religion—its main appeal for most people—is precisely the fact that it is steeped in long-held tradition. If you fiddle with the tradition, the tradition ceases to exist. That is the fear of those who oppose making such changes as referring to God in feminine as well as masculine terms, or allowing women to preach in fundamentalist churches, or calling up women to read from the Torah, or allowing families to sit together for *jum'a* (Friday noon Islamic prayer service). Opponents of change believe that the word of God has one meaning and is inviolable; tampering with tradition would mean creating a new religion. If you crave change, they ask, why not just leave and go find yourself a pagan ritual group or a Reconstructionist synagogue or a Unitarian Universalist church?

But changing tradition is not an oxymoron. Judaism, Christianity, and Islam have changed throughout time and continue to change. Religious leaders want adherents to think that tradition is bedrock, but that is plainly not true, as anyone with a passing acquaintance with history can see:

- Christianity was fundamentally and enormously altered when Martin Luther, a sixteenth-century German monk, questioned Catholic tradition and became the architect of the Protestant Reformation. The Reformed tradition encompasses Lutheran,

Calvinist, Presbyterian, Baptist, Anglican, and many other denominations and movements.

- From 1962 to 1965 the Roman Catholic Church convened the Second Vatican Ecumenical Council, known as Vatican II. Out of this council came sweeping changes affecting the lives of Catholics around the world, including increased participation by the laity (non-ordained Catholics) and a reconsideration of the position of the church in the modern world. It is now acceptable to recite the Communion prayer in English or Spanish instead of Latin, and the wafers representing the body of Jesus increasingly can be gluten free, among other changes.

- Clothing restrictions on Muslim women have changed since the time of Muhammad, depending on the interpretations of different Islamic ruling factions and governments over the last fourteen hundred years. The Qur'an instructs men to talk to Muhammad's wives from behind a curtain or screen (Qur'an 33:53), and it instructs Muslim women to draw their cloaks or veils close to them when they go out in public so as not to be harassed (Qur'an 33:59–60). The point is that Muslim women should dress modestly. Over the centuries, many different forms of clothing have been understood to satisfy this requirement, ranging from a hair covering or face veil to a full-body garment or regular Western-style street clothes that are loose in cut. Some Islamic cultures have also required women to be completely secluded from men.

- In the twentieth century, Orthodox Jews accepted the creation of the bat mitzvah (religious coming-of-age ceremony for girls that originated within the Reconstructionist movement), baby-naming ceremonies for girls, and the insertion of special hymns praising God on the anniversary of the creation of the modern State of Israel, among other modern innovations. It is believed that Jews must not turn to God for answers, but must discuss and debate their questions among themselves and reach their own conclusions. According to the Talmud (Baba Metzia 59b, based on Deuteronomy 30:12), even if God called out an answer, the Jews are to ignore the divine voice and defer to rabbinic—human—

opinion. Thus, every generation may revise the Jewish legal code to reflect its current situation.

Custodians of religious tradition do not oppose change per se. And sometimes females even benefit from religious change. But when it comes to women taking charge at the highest leadership echelon, forget about it: male religious authorities say that their hands are tied because having women in power violates religious tradition. Why is the battle cry of "Tradition can't be changed!" voiced most loudly when it comes to giving power to women? For the same reason that nonreligious institutions fear secular feminism: Upholders of the-way-things-supposedly-have-always-been-done worry about the blurring of gender roles. They say that women will forget they are women: they will cease to take care of children, and nuclear families will forever be ruined. "Who will look after the children?" they ask with dread and horror. (Oh, no. The answer couldn't be . . . men!) Will women even *want* to get married if they have the same rights as men? If not, there won't be any children at all, which means the religious tradition will die.

Relax, defenders of the-way-things-supposedly-have-always-been-done. When it comes to devout women, most are emphatic that they do not want to be the same as men. They want *equal* opportunities and *equal* treatment, which is not the same as wanting to be *identical* to men.

The overwhelming majority of women I spoke with are mothers, and each mother holds her parenting role as a very high or the highest priority in her life. Nearly all believe that during the years in which they are taking care of children, they should be given some leeway so that they are not expected to fulfill exactly the same responsibilities as men. Yet they also believe that they should be permitted to fulfill responsibilities outside the home if they choose to, and that their partners must take on an active fatherhood role too. Some want women and men to be treated equally, yet believe they should have separate responsibilities. This is the belief of Kimberly Harper, a convert to Islam. "The man should be the breadwinner," she says, "and the woman should have the option to work if she chooses. They have different roles in dealing with the children. Women have certain qualities, like being able to express their emotions, and the differences are there to create a balance."

Others, however, have moved beyond this distinct-but-equal attitude. These women see no need for strict separation between gender roles. Syeda Reshma Yunus observes that "it's easier for human beings to have separate roles, because then they don't have to do a lot of thinking. But the Qur'an says that men and women are garments unto each other, and that goes beyond roles—that message is about mutual respect. The prophet Muhammad actually had a crossover role himself. He did housework and was very affectionate with his children, activities that we usually think of as the woman's role. His wives also crossed over in their roles. His first wife, Khadijah, was a businesswoman, and his youngest wife, Aisha, led a war." Yunus sums up her approach: "You can't straitjacket people into different roles. There needs to be flexibility. The more difficult task, but the better task, is negotiation between the husband and wife over the roles."

Writer and scholar Anne Eggebroten, speaking with the perspective of an evangelical Christian, couldn't agree more. I ask her point-blank: Does she think that in the church there should be separate roles for men and women? "No," she replies, and proceeds to broaden my question. "You can make an argument that within a marriage there are different gender roles because only women give birth, and many women do nurse their children. So for at least a short period of time, there are differences in the roles for men and women. It's then up to the individual couple to decide how to share roles with child raising within their family. If they don't have children, there is less of a reason to have a gendered division of labor.

"But within society as a whole," she continues, "and within the church as a whole, this is a very tenuous argument. To argue that women should have different roles than men, you would have to argue that women and men are different intellectually and emotionally. Those arguments were popular in ancient Greek and Roman culture, with Saint Augustine, Thomas Aquinas, and other fathers of the church. Most women nowadays have concluded that there is no reason to have a separate division of labor, that women can be presidents of colleges, doctors, and dentists, that they can write books and teach classes. And they can also lead their churches. The idea that you need to have a penis to preach or to have a spiritual connection to God is no longer held by many people."

Eggebroten arrives at her most persuasive point. "Religious women are looking to their Scriptures for guidance. And many of these women are realizing, 'Wow, we have been misled on how to read our Scriptures! We have been mistaught! There just isn't much scriptural basis for the gendered division of labor! These lessons did not come from the Bible!'"

Devorah Zlochower, head of the *beit midrash* (house of learning) of the Drisha Institute in Manhattan, a progressive institution of Jewish study for women, arrives at more or less the same conclusion as her evangelical counterpart. "I'm not super-attached to traditional gender roles," she says. "I'm attached to *choices*. It's about presenting an array of models to girls and boys and to show that there is not only one way to do things. I'm not concerned about the price of giving up the traditional roles, because the traditional roles work for some people but not for everybody. That was always the case and will always be the case. I don't want to ditch the traditional roles, but I also don't want to privilege them. It's up to those who wish to privilege them to do so, and that is their right."

Zlochower is one of a growing number of brilliant Orthodox Jewish women who have achieved the same high level of Judaic education that men have always been allowed to achieve. If she were male, she would be a rabbi, and not just any rabbi—an esteemed, no doubt powerful one. It is worth noting that Zlochower, whom I met in her office at Drisha, is clearly a woman who wants to look like a woman and not like a man. It was a sticky day, and she wore a long blue denim skirt, a pink short-sleeved polo shirt, a blue denim cap that covered most of her curly hair, and very clean athletic sneakers—typical busy Orthodox mom attire. (In addition to her prestigious position, Zlochower has two children.) Remember, equal does not mean identical. Zlochower expects to be treated like a full human being in her religion—not as a man clone.

Yet how can a woman be treated as an equal within a tradition that does not recognize women as equals? Isn't this impossible by its very nature, especially if women are not considered identical to men? Zlochower addresses this conflict head-on and uses herself as a living example.

"When I first wanted to start learning Gemara [a compilation of rabbinic discussions that is part of the Talmud, one of the critical holy texts in Jewish tradition], I was twenty-five. I came to Drisha as a student. This was my first opportunity to learn Gemara, something I had wanted to do my whole life but couldn't, because girls did not learn Gemara in my [ultra-Orthodox] community growing up. So I had to insert myself into the system. But my experience was that as a woman, I was not able to do that. The texts I was studying were not talking to me. Sometimes they were talking *about* me, often saying derogatory things, but never *to* me. I was never the assumed audience of the text. So I started doing this dance, which is a dance of both loving and revering the tradition but critiquing it at the same time, and being very aware that the tradition doesn't fully embrace me. I can't fully embrace it unquestioningly, since I don't get embraced back. While on the one hand I don't want to mess with the tradition, I also want the tradition to expand to include people like me—yet *it can't without changing.* It just can't. [The exclusion of women] is fundamentally built into the system. So the tradition has to change if it's going to encompass people like me. I'm not willing to say, 'Keep the tradition the same, and I will sacrifice.'"

Why do women like Zlochower even bother with this "dance" of loving the tradition and critiquing it at the same time? Why don't they just leave? In the United States, Protestants and Jews in particular can seemingly have their cake and eat it too, since they can stay within their religion yet switch denominations—something their Catholic and Muslim sisters are less able to do, since Catholics and Muslims practice within take-it-or-leave-it faiths. Yet ask any devout woman, including a Protestant or Jew, "Why don't you leave?" and more often than not you'll be met with a look of confusion to rival the builders' expressions at the top of the Tower of Babel.

"You don't just leave your family!" was the aghast response I heard countless times. "No one has the right to tell me that I don't belong," a twenty-eight-year-old Presbyterian college chaplain told me defiantly. "I come from generations and generations of Presbyterians. This is a part of my identity." Says an undergrad at a Jesuit (Catholic) campus in Milwaukee, "I'm not going to jump ship. Someone has to stay to look out for gays and women and other minorities and people who are suffering. We have to stick with it to make sure someone is protecting them." A religious studies scholar in North Carolina responds, "As a person of faith, I don't want to leave the church, because it's as much my church as it is theirs [the people who oppose reform]." An Orthodox Jewish woman in New York City tells me, "You can't make change except from within. And if I leave, who will push for change?" A Presbyterian studying at Harvard for her master's of divinity degree (a requirement for ordination) sighs, saying, "I wouldn't be doing this if I weren't called to do it. I really have wrestled with it. The experience [of being mistreated because I'm a woman] has taught me about compassion and instilled in me a desire for justice that I think is important in ministry." Says a Muslim grad student in California, "You have to hang in there and be stronger than the oppression that faces you."

I love these answers, all of them. But I have particular fondness for the justification of the essayist Nancy Mairs, who was raised in the Congregationalist tradition but converted to Catholicism as an adult. In her book *Ordinary Time*, she relates that her son-in-law, confused as to why she sticks with Catholicism despite all her complaints, asks her why she doesn't just start a new church of her own. Mairs goes on to say that she adores her son-in-law,

> But how do I explain to this thoroughly secular young doctoral student in biochemistry that one doesn't start churches the way one starts experiments on immune responses to immortal cells introduced into nude mice or turtle bladders, that the search for God differs axiomatically from the search for cancer? The tug—the aesthetic, mystical, moral, eschatological—of Catholic tradition would mean as little to him as the results of his painstaking assays would mean to me.
>
> "I don't want another church," I say to him simply. "I just want to get this one right."[1]

For some women, especially those within the evangelical world, leaving just isn't an option, period. This is their universe—their family, their community, their support system. "A break with this community," writes the religious studies professor Julie Ingersoll in her book *Evangelical Christian Women: War Stories in the Gender Battles*, "means much more than just attending a different church on Sunday morning. It means breaking from one's family of origin; it may mean breaking childhood connections for women who attended Christian schools;

it may well mean breaking college ties as well, since many of these women went to Christian colleges." It may even mean "the dissolution of one's marriage." Ingersoll, who teaches at the University of North Florida, admits that for those of us outside the evangelical tradition, it can be hard to understand the problem: If a woman feels alienated from her church, why can't she just switch denominations? The answer is that to a conservative, evangelical Protestant, the liberal or mainline denominations are not considered authentically Christian. To her, switching to another denomination would be akin to leaving Christianity entirely, and that is very seldom the desired end result.[2]

Religion promises to fill the holes in people's lives with meaning. And for many people around the world, religion does deliver. The rituals—with their scents, tastes, beauty, singing, instant community, and the sense that God is watching and caring about us on planet Earth—can make people feel good about themselves and their purpose in the world.

Many who have suffered abuse, illness, addiction, or the death of loved ones turn to God. They see God around them, and this cheers and comforts them. Helen Markey, a devout Catholic born in 1939 who lives in Ramsey, New Jersey, relates that she first turned to God as a child because her father suffered from rheumatoid arthritis and was in a lot of pain over the course of many years. "I heard my father crying in pain at night, and I was frightened. There was nothing I could do about it but pray." Today Markey loves to see evidence of God's presence around her. "God is what centers me, God is what grounds me," she says, her face shining with excitement. "There are highs and lows in my life, and God is there not only in the heights but also in the depths. This morning there was a gorgeous sunrise and the light was hitting the trees, and they looked pink! I said, 'God, thank you!'"

"Jews, Christians, and Muslims have developed remarkably similar ideas of God, which also resemble other conceptions of the Absolute," writes Karen Armstrong, a historian of religion. "When people try to find an ultimate meaning and value in human life, their minds seem to go in a certain direction. They have not been coerced to do this: it is something that seems natural to humanity."[3]

It's clear that for many people, religion is not something you just walk away from—even when you are treated like a second-class citizen.

A devout woman may be disgruntled with her religious role, but that doesn't mean she wants to jettison every aspect of her religious life. A critical determinant of whether she will stay or ultimately leave is her point of view of her faith's sexism: Is it a coating that has stuck to the tradition and can be scrubbed off? Or is it inherent in the tradition and therefore can never be eliminated? The theologians Carol Christ and Judith Plaskow write that the ticked-off women who stay within Christianity and Judaism recognize their religions as patriarchal,

> but they deny that patriarchy is what these religions are about. They find in tradition a valuable core that has proved liberating to them personally and that, they believe, can liberate tradition itself from its patriarchal bias. Some women discover this core in themes dealing explicitly with liberation—the exodus from Egypt, the prophetic plea for justice, or Jesus' concern for the poor and oppressed . . . Wherever this core is located, it is taken as the "true" tradition, as a more fundamental statement of the nature of Judaism or Christianity than sexist images of institutional structures.[4]

But of course, there are always people who wrestle with their faith—and ultimately do decide to walk away. These are women like Mary Daly, who famously said goodbye to Catholicism because she found its symbols of God the Father and the male Christ "oppressive." To these women, explain Christ and Plaskow,

> the essential core of the traditions is so irreformably sexist that it is pointless to tinker with them in the hope of change. Emphasizing the symbolic portrayal of God as male within Christianity and Judaism and pointing to the ways in which institutional religion has supported sexism, they argue that the best way for women to free themselves from sexist traditions is to reject any loyalty to them.[5]

Cynthia, forty-nine, the mother of three children, who lives near Washington, D.C., fits this description. She left the Catholic Church a year ago. She had loved her Catholic childhood, her Irish Catholic identity, her Catholic education, and the experience of going to Mass.

Leaving the church was not easy. But she felt she had no choice. "I was a faithful Catholic who kept searching for answers within my faith," she told me. "I finally and sadly concluded that I couldn't find them there. The pedophilia scandal was a major factor in my disgust with church leaders, and that led me to question the entire hierarchy and its abuses of power. I believe that if women had a say in dioceses, the pedophilia would not have gone so far. I stopped going to Mass, because by going to church, I was showing approval. This is my protest."

A doctoral student at the University of North Carolina at Greensboro, Ann May, similarly left the Episcopal Church. At the age of fifty-three, she decided she had had enough. May, who has three adult children, had been involved in Bible-study groups, where "I was part of a community where everybody believed the same thing. But I was presented with a hierarchical structure that says there is a designated place for women, and I would think, This is my place as a woman, as a wife and a mother. It was a nice, neat little package. Whenever I had a question, instead of just living with the question, there was an answer there waiting for me." May was given answers before she even had formulated the questions. After ten years in this cozy world, she began to have anxiety attacks.

What triggered May's decision to leave was a realization that came out of psychiatric therapy. She came to understand that she was looking at God the same way she had looked at her own father. "He was someone I could never please, and that was the same way I looked at God." May reevaluated her need for a godlike father figure, which led her to question the hierarchy of the church. "It's so male centered. The structures, the rituals, the symbols, and the liturgy reinforce the myth of male superiority. There are female priests, but in its foundation God is always viewed as male, and it's like the imagination is shut down when it comes to women." She sighs. "I still have spiritual yearnings, but I feel hemmed in by the church. I do miss the sense of community I used to have. I wish there were a space for people to ask tough questions instead of just being given easy answers."

The religious studies professors Miriam Therese Winter, Adair Lummis, and Allison Stokes have coined the expression "defecting in place" to describe the phenomenon of women who rebel and protest but have not actually jumped ship. "Alienated women are remaining active in congregations with the hope of changing the church," they write.[6]

For these women there are no answers, only more and more questions. Let us meet three—Catholic, observant Jewish, and Muslim—who are alternately dancing and wrestling with their traditions. How do they negotiate the conflict between desire for equality and love of tradition?

Karen Napolitano is a forty-three-year-old mother of three living in Gaithersburg, Maryland. She is a social worker and the director of volunteer services at a nonprofit interfaith social justice agency that serves people in crisis. In March 2006 she saw a classified ad I had placed in the liberal political journal *The Nation*, in which I stated that I was an author seeking to speak with women who were devoted to their religion but dissatisfied with their status within it. She sent me this letter:

Hi, I am a woman whose religious convictions are defined by an oxymoron: I am a liberal practicing Catholic. I regularly attend Mass and receive the sacraments. I have chosen Catholic education for my children. The mystical elements of our faith tradition give me joy and bring me to a heightened understanding of the world around me, and yet, my politics and social beliefs are frequently out of step with the policies of the Catholic Church.

I ask: Why does the Catholic Church maintain such a hard line against the ordination of women? This policy comes from church law and tradition, not from [sound] theology. Where is the place for women who feel a true calling to the priesthood and who would give freely and fully to God and to their congregations? As the church faces diminishing numbers of priests, it only seems prudent to invite women into the "full experience" of the Catholic Church. In my church, women are always "lesser" members, defined by the limited symbols presented to us: Mary the virgin, Mary the Mother of Jesus, pious women saints who sacrificed all to the service of the church, or Mary Magdalene the whore who begs forgiveness from Jesus. Of the seven sacraments available to us in the church, women can only partake of six. No woman can be ordained [the

*seventh sacrament], therefore, the full experience of the church is
closed to all women.*

*In the 1970s, I was raised in a Catholic church that was pro-
gressive, inclusive, propelled by the momentum of egalitarianism,
and fueled by a genuine vision of an idealized world in the wake
of Vatican Council II. This is the Catholic Church that I embraced as an adult, but I now find myself a minority member in a
vanishing church. The Catholic Church I experience today seeks to
weed out dissenting voices, to curtail discussions of any kind that
flow against the mainstream edicts from Rome, to limit the possibility of inclusion, and to focus its support of public policy in the
narrowest terms. The same priests who will not speak out against
the invasion of Iraq will then condemn from the pulpit Terri Schi-
avo's husband for "murder." The same priests who tell tearful
women that God will give them the strength to handle their eighth
pregnancy rage from the pulpit about a husband and wife's in-
ability to control the lustful impulse. The Catholic Church's organized, political "pro-life" agenda is diminished to nothing more
than an effort to ban abortion. I do not hear official Catholic
voices speaking out against poverty, promoting responsible elder
care, pursuing economic parity, or advocating against the death
penalty. Where is the Catholic Church's public voice and advocacy
role for life after conception?*

Feel free to contact me with any questions or comments.
Sincerely,
    Karen Napolitano

I raced through this letter, then read it again more slowly. It was so
well expressed and powerful. Napolitano had personalized the conflict
experienced by women who love their religion but are fed up with inequality. She had included her home phone number, and as soon as I
read her letter, my fingers were itching to dial it. We spoke for a few
moments and arranged to speak at length a few days later.

On the phone, Napolitano was congenial and relaxed, bending
over backward to show me that the church infuses her daily life in
very positive ways. Intriguingly, she didn't sound terribly critical. She
shared happy memories of her "cradle Catholic" upbringing and chat-

ted about having felt "safe and protected" as a child because of her family's faith. She told me how Catholicism had led her to her profession as a social worker because "a fundamental teaching of Catholicism is to be other-centered, to live as Jesus did, to live in a way that compels you to focus on the world around you and not on yourself. It's not about *your* salvation; it's about helping those around you."

All well and good, I thought. Then I steered the conversation to the topic of women's place within the church. Napolitano told me that she was pro-choice and that she uses contraception, positions "incongruent with the traditions of the church," but that she could "live with the discrepancy. I'm okay feeling like I can participate in sacramental life and the community even though some of my beliefs are incongruent with the church's teachings. I think that many of the teachings are flawed. They have grown out of tradition and history, and they are not infallible teachings. But rather than leave the church and try to seek something else, for me it feels more right to stay and be a voice, a presence, and work for change."

I was surprised that Napolitano expressed her conflict so mildly, and I told her so. I reminded her that just a few days ago, she had sent me an e-mail that to my mind sounded angry or at least indignant. Napolitano was taken aback. "It's interesting that you see my e-mail as angry, because I didn't feel that way when I wrote it," she responded. "I was articulating some of the things I carry around with me, but I don't feel a sense of anger." After we hung up, I went back to the e-mail and read it again. I hadn't imagined it: the letter truly expresses outrage. I shrugged off Napolitano's denial with the understanding that living with conflict, by its nature, causes people to veer one way one day, and the next day the other way. I reckoned that the day of our talk was a "Catholicism is terrific" day, and I thought nothing more about it.

But a few days later she sent me a follow-up e-mail.

Dear Leora,

Thank you again for the opportunity to share my experiences of Catholicism with you. Many times over the past week, I have reflected on your comment that my original e-mail was "angry." I believe that I was not wholly honest with you when I responded

*somewhat defensively to this characterization. You're right. I do
feel anger when I reflect on the limited role of women in the
Catholic Church, yet my impulse is to deny that anger and to temper it with positive comments. If I am truly honest with myself, I
must admit that Catholicism has "trained" me to respond in this
way. The church stresses obedience to its teachings and "oneness" as
a community. Catholics are routinely chided from the pulpit or in
private for actions that "divide" the spirit of community. We are
taught that dissent is "sinful" and damaging to us personally and
communally. Obviously, this method is effective because the Catholic
Church has successfully maintained its centralized control over the
hearts and minds of billions of people for millennia!*

 Peace,
  Karen Napolitano

Once again, Napolitano had expressed the dilemma of countless
women in a personal and powerful way. Although she genuinely feels
anger, her impulse is to deny her anger, "to temper it with positive
comments" because Catholicism has "trained" her to "respond in this
way." Yes, that is precisely true, and not only for Catholics. Religious
women (and men) are conditioned to keep their negative comments
to themselves. Through this conditioning, the status quo is maintained because those who voice dissent are dismissed as wacky people
on the fringe and not representative of the mainstream. Therefore,
their opinions don't have to be taken seriously.

For Napolitano, writing to me was her act of rebellion. For now, it
appears that this is as far as her rebellion goes. She is still working
through her dual allegiance to the church and to the cause of women's
equality. She is deepening her thinking about her place within the
church. It's clear that she takes the church seriously and that her criticisms are serious and well considered.

For some women, quiet disagreement isn't enough. Renée Septimus of Manhattan is an observant Jew who speaks up to make change
from within, and along the way, she herself is changed. I meet with her
early on a Friday afternoon, the busiest time of the week for observant
Jewish women, but Septimus is relaxed. A social worker, like Napolitano, and fifty-five years old, Septimus is an attractive, slim woman

with medium-length auburn hair. She is wearing cropped pants, a trim T-shirt, and sneakers. She has four children, ages twenty through thirty-one. Her Shabbat cooking is well under way, and she has a chunk of time she can devote to speaking with me. (Since cooking is not permitted after sundown on Friday, it must be completed in advance.) We sit in her eat-in kitchen; a gracious host, she serves fresh fruit, cookies, and coffee. My own Shabbat cooking will wait until I return home, and I'm impressed both with her culinary organization and her Zen-like ability to sit still for an hour and a half without even once getting up to tend to burners or grills.

Septimus grew up in what is called a modern Orthodox background, meaning that her family was religiously observant but also participated fully in American culture. "At that time," she explains, pushing the plate of cookies to my side of the table, "modern Orthodoxy was very clear about its goals. When I grew up, I could live a completely observant life but also go to museums, movies, and be a part of the larger culture. Back then, we wore pants, we wore short sleeves. It's not like the way it is today," when observant women wear only skirts and many wear only long-sleeved shirts and therefore do not appear fully assimilated into American life. "We held hands when we were dating, we had mixed dancing [boys and girls together], we had pool parties."

To Septimus, modern Orthodoxy has been increasingly dominated by a strain of Orthodoxy that is not terribly interested in being modern. She attributes this trend in large part to the *ba'al teshuvah* movement—the movement of people not previously religiously observant who come to embrace observance as adults. "The *ba'alei teshuvah* are way more *frum* [observant] than people like me who grew up modern Orthodox. They tend not to see shades of gray [in theological and ritual matters]. They tend to see things as all black or all white. And they influence the whole community, which has turned to the right. Many of the men in my generation are as well-educated religiously as our rabbis are, and in fact studied with them in the yeshivas [Judaic schools], which gives my generation the confidence to question things. But many observant Jews today don't question things, and they have turned against the secular world. The women stopped wearing pants, and they started covering their hair."

"There's also not as much intellectual honesty as there used to be," Septimus continues. "There's no more room to ask questions and debate the halakhah [Jewish law]. It used to be that nothing was taboo. But today if you ask the same questions [that we used to ask a generation ago], people say you're an *apikores* [heretic], and once you accuse someone of that, the conversation stops."

Septimus married at age twenty-one to a man who at the time was more observant than she was, but he never pressured her to take on religious obligations that she didn't feel comfortable with. When they first married, he asked her to cover her hair, "so I tried it for a few weeks, but I didn't like it, so I stopped, and he was okay." Nevertheless, she is a seriously observant Jew, someone who always follows the halakhah and never presumes to go around the law. So how does she handle her conflict? Septimus sighs, tries once again to get me to eat a cookie (I gamely put one on my plate so she'll stop checking), and says, "I have been on a religious journey, and it has been lonely. I have struggled to learn to be a woman within Orthodox Judaism and feel comfortable in the synagogue, in the community, and, most importantly, in my relationship with God. The basic tenet of my whole belief system is that I have a personal God that is watching me and to whom, so to speak, I can talk. My frustration comes from the way Orthodoxy looks at women, the way it looks at me. And if you are at all honest, you see that we are second-class citizens. You have to be deaf, dumb, and blind not to see it. If you look at the [sacred writings] and you read some of the things that the rabbis have said about us, it makes you feel just horrible about yourself. There's a lot of misogyny, a lot of anxiety about women's sexuality. You have to keep these feelings to yourself because most people don't want to hear about them.

"When I was in my early thirties, we lived in Queens, across the street from the *shul* [synagogue]. And when they rebuilt the shul, we kept the Torahs in our house on the dining-room table. After they had been there for several weeks, I said to my husband, 'You know, I have never seen the inside of a Torah.' My husband opened up one of the Torahs for me. That was such an intense moment.

"When I was in my forties, we lived in Manhattan, and I started going to Darkhei Noam [a traditional yet controversial synagogue in which women can participate more fully than usually permitted], and the first time I was there, I literally started to cry. It was the first time I'd seen and heard women getting *aliyot* [being called up to the Torah] with women and men together. It was just an intense experience.

"Eight years ago, my husband was awarded a Wexner [prestigious Judaic] fellowship and we were invited to a program held near Salt Lake City with people from all the denominations. On *Shabbos* [Sabbath] morning, I went to the Orthodox service, found it uninspiring, finished my *davening* [praying] alone outside the room where the service was being held, then went to the Reform service to see what it was about. The singer Debbie Friedman was there with her guitar, and everyone was dancing. And I, who never dance and had never gone anywhere near a guitar on Shabbos [because observant Jews believe that playing musical instruments is forbidden on Shabbat], was incredibly moved. I went and danced with the women. I had tears in my eyes, it was so incredible. And for the rest of the program, every day I woke up early and returned to that Reform service with my own Orthodox *siddur* [prayer book]. Me, an observant woman! What does that say to you? It says that this service touched me in a way that my own belief system had never been able to do.

"When my son, who's now twenty, was bar mitzvah, I knew that I wanted my name included in his *aliyah*. [In Orthodox synagogues, only the father's name is included as part of the son's name, as in "Isaac, the son of Abraham" rather than "Isaac, the son of Abraham and Sarah." In the other denominations, the mother's name is included.] I got an opinion from a respected [Orthodox] rabbi saying it was permitted to include the mother's name. I gave my rabbi the written responsum, and he was terrible to me. He said, 'Well, my wife and my mother don't feel that they need to be included, so why should you?' This was the rabbi of a modern Orthodox synagogue in Queens. After the ceremony I gave a speech in front of all of our guests, 225 people. I told them that during my son's bar mitzvah, I had been excluded. I wasn't included in the aliyah, I couldn't kiss my son when he was finished reading Torah [because I was in the women's section], and I couldn't even see his face during the service! And then I read a personal prayer I had written from me, his mother, to my son. And our guests were so moved. People were wiping away the tears. I still remember a friend of ours, a big man, probably six feet two, and he was sobbing with everyone else!

"In the middle of the dinner, I realized that the rabbi had left without saying goodbye to me, and that he must have been insulted by my speech. So on Saturday night I called him, and the next day my husband and I went over to speak with him to try to engage with him, because I had not meant to insult him. And he told me that from then on, I was not allowed to teach classes anymore at the shul.

"I decided I would sponsor a lecture series for the community, and I would invite all the speakers saying interesting things about Orthodoxy, all the big names. I deliberately chose speakers and topics I knew the rabbi did not allow in his own lecture series sponsored by the shul. The issues were controversial and cutting-edge. For three years, over the course of the winter months, I ran this lecture series at the Y in Queens. It was a huge success. So many people came—although one woman told me, 'I can't go, because the rabbi wouldn't like it if he knew.' *The Jewish Week* did a two-page spread with pictures.

"This was one of the high points of my life. I took something that was very negative—the way I had been treated as a woman by my rabbi and by Orthodoxy—and I made it positive and constructive for the community. I stood up for something I believed in.

"The one negative thing is that this has been a lonely journey. I did the whole lecture series by myself. I knew that if I didn't do it, no one else would. The experience emphasized for me that in many ways, I am alone within Orthodox Judaism.

"My observance level remains the same. I keep kosher. I keep *mikvah* [immersion in ritually pure water once a month after menstruation, after which marital relations are permitted]. I keep Shabbos. I continue to observe these things because that is what God wants, and because Judaism won't continue without observance. But my beliefs have changed. I don't believe that gays deserve capital punishment. I don't believe that God would give half the human race fewer talents and abilities than the other half, and I certainly don't believe that once God gave us our talents and abilities, God wanted us not to use them. To me, it's a sin *not* to use my abilities and talents as a woman."

Septimus reminds me of a modern-day Elizabeth Cady Stanton: a woman with the confidence of her knowledge of her religion's sacred teachings, who defers to *her* understanding of God's law, not to interpretations she sees as unjust. This self-assurance is a critical ingredient in rising up. Unfortunately, too many women lack this ingredient. Therefore, religious women must become learned in their sacred texts. If they don't, they will forever be dependent on others who have their own interpretations.

Napolitano and Septimus are from different religious backgrounds, but they share something critical: they feel some sense of permission to criticize aspects of their religious traditions—possibly because they are white and assimilated into white American culture. When a Muslim woman voices gender dissatisfaction, however, whether she is white or a woman of color, she is in a tenuous position: very many Americans believe Islam to be a backward religion, in large part because of the way Islam is perceived to regard its women. Many Muslims are of course assimilated into mainstream American culture, but the dominant perception is that they are not. Therefore, criticizing Islam for its treatment of women can make a Muslim woman feel like a traitor, or at best as if she is airing dirty laundry.

It is against this backdrop that Hana, a twenty-six-year-old grad student in California, talks with me. We speak on the phone on a summer afternoon. She can't see me, but she knows I'm white and Jewish, and she tells me that the very act of expressing her dissatisfactions makes her nervous. She doesn't know what my assumptions are about her religion and culture, and she doesn't know if she can trust me. Fair enough. I too am protective about my religious culture, and I can relate to her concerns, even while I recognize my privileges.

Hana, who is studying toward a Ph.D. in feminist Muslim thought, was born in the United States to Pakistani parents who were wed in an arranged marriage. Trained as a microbiologist in Pakistan, her father changed professions and became a businessman while her mother worked in retail, and Hana was raised in a suburb of a southeastern city. Growing up, she attended public schools and learned to recite the Qur'an phonetically from a woman in the community who was hired to teach her about Islam. "It's considered a great feat as a child if you can complete the recitation of the entire Qur'an in Arabic," she explains. "It's a huge rite of passage, and they give you a big party. I was sort of the teacher's pet. She always held me up as one of her best students, if not her best student. I responded to Islam very enthusiastically. I was very diligent. I did all my memorizations. Word got around the community that I was a pious child, and even though the five prayers a day were not incumbent upon me, because I was so young, I was already praying diligently five times a day starting at age ten. I never missed a single prayer. My friends would be outside playing, but I would be inside praying. I had this almost ascetic discipline.

"Looking back, that level of religious fervor came out of a fear of God. I thought I had to be a good Muslim, otherwise God would punish me, and I was horrified at the thought of doing anything wrong. If I messed up one word, I would redo an entire prayer. I would repeat my ablutions two or three times if I thought I had missed one drop of water on one tiny part of my wrist. And I was rewarded for this: I was praised in the community. This made my parents extremely proud."

When she was sixteen, Hana started to ask questions about her religious tradition. She started to become aware, from the white students around her at school, that Islam is perceived to be oppressive to women. She internalized this perception and began to see herself as backward and oppressed too. At eighteen she went off to college, where the feminists and the Muslims held opposing viewpoints, with never the twain to meet. Hana felt caught in the middle.

"In my sophomore year I took my first women's studies class, and there was this misinformed, outsider view that you can't be a Muslim and also be a liberated woman. I also came into contact with the Muslim Student Association and ended up running for office and taking on a leadership position. Then I ran for president and won that also. It was like I was living in two separate worlds. I co-majored in English and women's studies. But the women's studies undergrads had no racial awareness. I had a lot of trouble with the perspective of many of the students. I was always calling 'racism' in class. I was just working it out, trying to figure out what my perspective was. I finally arrived at the conclusion that perhaps the Western feminist perception of women in Islam is wrong, and that perhaps it was misinformation about Islam that had made me believe Islam was oppressive to women."

But, I pointed out, she herself is critical of women's status within Islam, so isn't she contradicting herself?

"I'm still figuring things out. It's not entirely clear yet that we can be fully human and equal participants in the religion. But I have overwhelming confidence that I can figure it out, that the egalitarian impulse and the gender justice are there within Islam. I have to uncover them through theological study. It's possible that Islam has never been egalitarian. There have been periods in history that were better than others. But because of the male domination of theological studies, we have so many layers to peel back before we can figure out how Islam can be just to women."

It is because of men's domination of Islamic customs that women are discriminated against, Hana says, and not necessarily because of the core of the religion itself. Still, given the nearly total way that men have interpreted the "right" way to be Muslim, it's hard to be a Muslim woman. Hana speaks carefully, slowly, hesitantly: she is a scholar first and foremost, but she also wants to share her emotional point of view. She wants me to know that her personal feelings and her scholarly inquiry are two separate things; in fact, she yearns for the possibility that her scholarship will yield an Islam that allows for a very different emotional response.

"Going to the mosque makes me feel humiliated and isolated. It's gotten to the point where I can't even stand to hear the sound of the sheikh's voice on the loudspeaker. I become so angry that I can't concentrate on my prayers. Going to the mosque makes me feel disconnected from God rather than more connected. I think, This can't be Islam. Putting us women away in a small room with screaming children, giving us a loudspeaker that sometimes works and sometimes doesn't, it just can't be Islam."

Again we see the ambivalence of a woman caught in a love-hate relationship with her religious tradition. At one moment Hana is proud of her tradition; at the next moment she agonizes over it. And because of widespread anti-Islamic sentiment, she is constantly self-conscious about how to criticize her tradition with respect.

I have highlighted these three women because they demonstrate the complicated status of the devout-but-critical woman. Each is engaged in a challenging process. Napolitano attempts private reconciliation with her Catholic faith. Septimus confronts members of her community to think about Jewish law in a fresh perspective. Hana is seeking to disentangle the way Islamic customs have been understood from the core of her heritage. These women could have walked away from their heritage, yet all have chosen to stay. They represent millions of others like themselves.

To my mind, they are worthy of respect because they have chosen to live with something profoundly difficult: ambiguity. They have an appreciation for nuance and complexity and a respect for different viewpoints. These are essential ingredients when contemplating the mystery of the divine. Absolute certainty, when it comes to theological matters, is a danger sign, an indicator of narrowness of thought.

THREE

Catholic Women vs. the Vatican

The thing you should know about Catholic reformers is that they are far from humorless. Actually, they're quite funny. This could be because, up against an authoritarian pope and an unyielding church hierarchy, their struggle for the inclusion of diverse voices in church decision making necessitates a gallows humor. Otherwise, how would they find the strength to go on? The theologian Mary Hunt refers to herself and fellow reformers as "the best and the brightest of the bad girls," and audiences laugh with the realization that as earnest as she is, she does not take herself too seriously. Patricia Fresen, a Dominican nun for forty-five years now training and ordaining women as priests against the wishes of the church, jokes that "Jesus had a new vision, and we really haven't caught up with him yet!"[1] Call to Action, the Catholic reform organization, sells T-shirts with the slogan QUESTION AUTHORITY. JESUS DID.

These reformers are also creative. The Women's Ordination Conference (WOC), an organization that promotes the ordination of women to a renewed priestly ministry, uses grassroots efforts to challenge church policies with their Ministry of Irritation. (The goal is to irritate the church hierarchy just as a grain of sand irritates an oyster, creating a pearl.) To bring public attention to the issue of women excluded from church leadership, this "ministry" set off pink smoke bombs at the Shrine of the Immaculate Conception in Washington, D.C., (the largest Catholic church in the United States), as well as at churches around the country, during the papal conclave in April 2005, when 115 cardinals in Rome secretly chose the new pope. The pink smoke contrasted with the black and white smoke emitted in Rome (black signaling that no one had been chosen yet, and white proclaiming the decision completed). The point was that women were not included in the conclave—it was, as usual, all men. In April 2008, when Pope Benedict XVI visited Washington, D.C., WOC created a large mobile billboard that stated, POPE BENEDICT, HOW LONG MUST WOMEN WAIT FOR EQUALITY? ORDAIN CATHOLIC WOMEN. It was posted on a truck and followed the route of the popemobile.

Those who say that there is no valid reason for excluding women from the priesthood are absolutely serious about the importance of their message. And they know that the way things stand now, their ordination ceremonies may appear futile, since the Vatican does not and will not recognize them as anything other than an invitation for excommunication. And yet the feeling is, why not? The important thing is that these ceremonies have symbolic value. Their ministry announces that women can and should be included in the church, that women can and should represent God just as men do. These women prod ordinary Catholics to think in new ways about the priesthood and the role of women in the church. As more ceremonies take place, their symbolic value grows, along with the discontent of countless Catholics. A 2006 *National Catholic Reporter* survey of U.S. Catholics found that 62 percent of respondents support ordaining women as priests and 81 percent support ordaining women as deacons. An Associated Press/Ipsos poll conducted in April 2005 found that 64 percent of U.S. Catholics support women's ordination.[2] Moreover, these ordinations are not futile. Although women priests are not recognized by the hierarchical church, they do minister as priests to people on the margins.

Women's ordination among Catholics is not only about achieving justice but also about confrontation. Extending this sacrament to women could very well force real change within a church that desperately needs change to maintain any sense of moral legitimacy in the wake of its horrifying sexual scandals. These priests motivate Catholics to look at religious leadership in a new way, and isn't that precisely what Jesus did? Even I, a non-Christian, have been deeply moved to witness a Roman Catholic woman priest presenting the bread and wine that she had consecrated for the Eucharist at a Call to Action Mass. There is something powerful about a woman acting as mediator between people and God. It strengthens our understanding of women, of humanity, and of the divine.

To be sure, Catholic women have many other issues to complain about aside from the exclusion of women from the priesthood: the church's systematic cover-up of the sexual abuse that took place over decades, mandatory clerical celibacy, prohibition of birth control and abortion, denigration of gays and lesbians, exclusion of those who divorce, lack of gender-neutral language, and a theology that defines women by their sexuality as virgins, mothers, or sinners. In fact, ordinary U.S. Catholics do not agree with many church teachings. But the movement for women's ordination is "the most provocative thing going on right now in the Catholic reform movement," says Angela Bonavoglia, the author of *Good Catholic Girls: How Women Are Leading the Fight to Change the Church*, a riveting account of Catholic women's reform. "If you want to challenge the church, this is definitely a way to do it."[3] According to Deborah Halter, a religious studies lecturer at Loyola University in New Orleans, women's ordination is not just a publicity stunt. She writes in her book *The Papal "No": A Comprehensive Guide to the Vatican's Rejection of Women's Ordination*, "I believe that women's ordination should and will take place within the sacramental life of the church."[4] Says Aisha Taylor, WOC's executive director, "These women hear the call from God to the priesthood. They are taking ownership of their power and saying, 'The hierarchy can't tell me what to do anymore. I am going to live out my call to service. God created women and men as equals and this is God's plan for the church.'"

Joan Houk looks like the devoted grandmother she is. Age sixty-six, she wears her gray-white hair just past her ears, and she has small wire-rimmed glasses. Her clothes are neat and matronly: modestly cut black pants, comfortable sneaker-shoes, white blouse buttoned up to the neck, a coral knit cardigan. But Joan Houk is not only a gentle mother and grandmother. She is also on the front line of the battle for women's ordination. Houk was blessed by female bishops, themselves ordained in apostolic succession (part of the line of bishops said to go back to the apostles). The bishops "laid hands" on Houk and anointed her with oil during a ceremony that took place on a boat in Pittsburgh on July 31, 2006.

Houk has been a loyal Catholic her entire life. Her grandfather ushered in the faithful at the 6:00 a.m. Mass and stoked the church furnace. She was educated in Catholic schools, got married, raised six children (three of them adopted), and then spent the next two decades working for her church as a parish volunteer, then employee. In 1992 she was "called." She felt with certainty that God wanted her to become a priest. "It was an intuitive thing. I figured that I would be ordained—in the normal way," she says calmly. On the surface it sounds as if Houk had lost her mind—*of course* she couldn't become a priest. All Catholics know that only men can become priests! What on earth was she thinking?

Houk simply assumed that at some point down the road the pope would change his mind. To her it was transparent that the church needed women and therefore the church would ultimately open the doors to the priestly ministry and let women in. She had been working for the church, taking on more and more responsibility, until finally she had done the most a layperson was allowed. She took theology classes at the University of Notre Dame, and a few years later she had earned a master of divinity degree on full scholarship. The M. Div., as it's called, is the usual academic requirement for becoming a priest or minister within the Catholic and Protestant traditions. "It didn't make sense that I would be accepted into the program, even have it all paid for, and the Holy Spirit was calling me, and then I couldn't be ordained? So I truly believed that I *would* be ordained. It didn't even occur to me that I *wouldn't* be ordained." Houk had never been an activist. "No, I have not been out there with posters or prayer vigils or stuff like that. I just went to school and continued working for the church, and the whole time, I thought that the bishop would ordain me with the pope's blessing."

After all, there is a serious priest shortage around the world. In the United States, 16 percent of parishes have no priest and are run by a layperson, usually a woman. Female "lay ministers" actually outnumber the priests. Eighty percent of the church employees who work as parish administrators, youth ministers, and directors of religious education are women, and women perform pastoral duties in hospitals, prisons, and colleges.[5] Priestless parishes are growing: there are more priests in the United States over the age of ninety than under thirty,[6] and with church funds going to pay the claims of victims of priest pedophilia, there are no financial resources to build up parishes in need of funding.

Someone with Houk's credentials is therefore in demand because she is capable of running a parish, even though as a woman she is not permitted to consecrate the bread and wine for the Eucharist. Thus, after earning her degree, for three years Houk served as pastoral director for a parish in Jackson, Kentucky, that did not have a priest. "The bishop installed me, and I took care of the people in that parish on a day-to-day basis. There was a priest who came in on Saturday nights to preside over the Eucharistic liturgy, but other than that, I did everything." Houk presided over baptisms and funerals and tended to the sick and needy—everything a priest does, aside from the Eucharistic consecration. For the next two and a half years she served as pastoral director for another church in Kentucky that also did not have a priest.

Houk returned to her hometown of Pittsburgh in 2002 because her mother was ill and dying. Busy and absorbed with events at home, she didn't follow the news and had no idea that a controversial women's ordination ceremony had occurred that summer. It had taken place on a boat on the Danube River between Austria and Germany, out of any bishop's jurisdiction. Seven women were ordained by a renegade bishop, Rómulo Braschi of Argentina, who had broken with the church in 1998 to form a schismatic church in Brazil. Cardinal Joseph Ratzinger, then head of the Congregation for the Doctrine of the Faith and today the pope, immediately excommunicated all seven women. "Even after I heard about it, I was not in favor of it," Houk says to me. "And then I put it out of my mind." She was still assuming that one day she would become ordained in the same Vatican-approved ritual through which men become clergy. So why should she support some crazy women on a boat in the middle of nowhere?

In 2005 she and her husband attended a morning lecture by the theologian Patricia Fresen at a nearby conference, and Houk's perspective on illicit ordinations completely reversed course. I have heard Fresen myself and I can tell you that she is electrifying. A white woman who grew up in South Africa, she speaks with a proper Anglo accent and dresses smartly, with a scarf tied neatly around her neck—in short, she is another activist who appears more at home running the church gift shop than taunting the pope. But looks can be deceiving.

In her speeches Fresen compares the status of blacks in racist society with that of women in the Catholic Church, and she uses her own experiences in South Africa to buttress her argument. "It's not only wrong but *sinful* to deny women ordination," she declared to a standing ovation at a speech I attended in 2006. Like me, Houk found her persuasive. "We sat there and listened to her talk about growing up in South Africa and having to break the apartheid laws and actually go to prison, and then seeing apartheid done away with," remembers Houk. "She compared apartheid with canon law that keeps women from being ordained. She said it was an unjust law and that she had learned from apartheid that when you can't change an unjust law, you must break it. And she had chosen to break the canon law."

Fresen, who holds a doctorate in theology, had been ordained a priest in Barcelona in 2003 by Bishops Christine Mayr-Lumetzberger and Gisela Forster, both of whom had been ordained bishops by anonymous male bishops claimed to be in good standing with the Vatican. (Obviously, if they revealed their identities, they would lose their good standing.) Under pressure from Rome, Fresen's order of Dominican nuns did not officially support her ordination, and she was given the choice of repenting, repudiating her ordination and staying in the order, or leaving. She chose to leave. She moved to Germany, where she currently lives and coordinates women's ordinations with a group called Roman Catholic Womenpriests, an international organization. In 2005, together with two other women priests, Fresen was ordained a bishop by several Roman Catholic male bishops who have also kept their identities secret but are said to be in good standing with the Vatican.

After Fresen's lecture in 2005, Houk and her husband bought sandwiches and sat down at a table to eat lunch. They didn't say anything to each other for a few moments. "And then both of us discovered that we had experienced the same realization at the same time:

that I must do this. I am called to the priesthood. I am prepared for the priesthood. The church is not changing anything, and this would be a way to force change and to achieve justice."

The ceremony in which Houk was ordained, in July 2006, was the fourth group ordination of women priests and the first such event within the United States. On this day, eight women were ordained as priests and another four as deacons by Fresen together with two other women bishops, Gisela Forster and Ida Raming. The ceremony took place on a chartered boat because no priest or bishop would volunteer his church for this purpose. The symbolism of water was also too good to resist: water gives life and ebbs and flows, and Jesus often preached from a boat. Water is also necessary for a valid sacramental baptism.

Since the 2002 Danube ceremony, there has been a ceremony on the St. Lawrence Seaway between Canada and the United States in July 2005, in which five were ordained as deacons and four as priests, and another on Lake Constance, between Germany, Austria, and Switzerland, in June 2006, in which one was ordained as deacon and three as priests. There has also been one group ordination of women deacons, again on the Danube in 2004. In 2008 alone, a Roman Catholic Womenpriests ordination ceremony took place in Vancouver, and an additional seven ceremonies were held in the United States (in Pismo Beach, California; Portland, Oregon; St. Louis; Boston; Lexington, Kentucky; Santa Barbara; and Chicago). Though not associated with Roman Catholic Womenpriests, since 2001 there have also been several individual ordinations of Catholic (though not Roman Catholic) women priests conducted by Bishop Peter Hickman of the schismatic Old Catholic Church.

In all, there are now more than sixty-one Roman Catholic women deacons or priests in the United States, with an additional thirty worldwide. There are approximately ten additional women priests ordained in independent Catholic (not Roman Catholic) churches. Many are married, and one identifies as lesbian; none of the ordaining bishops has required celibacy.

As all rite of ordination ceremonies do, the Pittsburgh ritual in which Houk was ordained included prayer, Scripture readings, a homily, calling forth the candidates, examination of the candidates, and prostration before the altar and cross while the Litany of the Saints was chanted. (Typically during prostration a candidate lies down, forehead touching the floor, with the bishops in front of him, but in women's ceremonies the candidates lie prostrate to the altar and cross, in order to symbolize their obedience to Jesus and not to the bishops.) Then came the "laying on of hands"—in which the bishops placed their hands on the heads of the candidates in silence—followed by the prayer of consecration and vesting in stole for the deacons and stole and chasuble for the priests. Then the priests' palms were anointed with oil.

I spoke to Houk a few days later and asked her what went through her mind while she lay on the floor (actually the boat's dance floor) for those long minutes. She chuckled at my question but gave a serious answer. "When we were lying there, the Litany of the Saints was recited as a chant. I listened to the names of the men and women. It gave me a lot of strength, and I knew that what I was doing was the right thing at the right time. There are a lot of people who have gone before me who have done the right thing at their right time, and some of them lost their lives for it." She continued, "People say to me, 'You're so brave! I admire you.' But I'm not brave! I felt no courage in doing this. I'm just doing what I need to do from day to day. There *have* been brave people—people who have knowingly faced death and still have done what they needed to do. And do you know who else was brave? The people who came on the boat to support us. Some of those people work for the church, and if their identities become known, they can lose their jobs. They knew that, and they came anyway. So those are the people *I* admire."

Before the ceremony, Houk wrote to Bishop Wuerl of the Pittsburgh Diocese—an open letter intended to "be shared with the faithful"—in which she explained her decision. Citing Canon Law 1024, which states that "a baptized male alone receives sacred ordination validly," Houk wrote:

> *Competent Catholic scriptural scholars and theologians find no scriptural or divine law against a woman being ordained. As a matter of fact, history and archaeology reveal examples of ordained women in the early Church . . . As it stands now Canon 1024 is an unjust law. Just as many unjust laws had to be broken*

in order for the laws to be changed (such as during the civil rights movement), I believe Canon 1024 must be broken . . . It is a sin for the church to discriminate against women and blame God for it. The Church's discrimination is part of the systemic discrimination that results in the physical violence, rape, mutilation, bondage, harassment, poverty and abandonment of women. I admonish the church to turn away from this sin of discriminating against women. In obedience to the Gospel of Jesus, I will disobey this unjust law . . .

    Your sister in Christ,
    Joan Clark Houk[7]

The Pittsburgh Diocese, as expected, was not supportive. Through a spokesperson, the diocese issued a statement saying that the ordination undermined the unity of the church. Although the term "excommunication" was not used, the diocese in effect banished the ordinands by withholding the sacraments from them. How does that make her feel? "I'm sad I can't take Communion. I made my first Communion when I was seven years old, and I have gone every week, sometimes every day. This Sunday will be hard because it will be the first time I will have to sit in the pew. But there are a lot of people who can't take Communion, and I will be in solidarity with them."

For all my enthusiastic support of Houk and the other women ordained, I have to admit that at times I did feel as if we were speaking in a parallel universe. Houk, Fresen, and the WOC activists use the words "ordained," "deacon," "priest," and "bishop" as if they were imbued with the value conferred by the Vatican—and yet without the pope's blessing, weren't these words meaningless? "If a male were to go to the bishop with the same story of being ordained on a river by a bishop whose name he couldn't reveal, the bishop would go 'Hmmm,'" observes Roberta Ward, a spokesperson for the Pittsburgh diocese. "In the eyes of the official church, they are not priests or deacons. Priests get ordained for service to a diocese or a religious order. These people don't belong to any particular diocese. They are out of the loop."[8]

But the only way to challenge the canon law forbidding women to become priests is to assert that women *can* become priests. And therefore the term "priest" is used deliberately and meaningfully. Using another term would not challenge the canon law, because priesthood would continue to be the province of men alone. "By staying outside of official church structures," says Patricia Fresen, "we will achieve nothing. We are already excluded, and this would mean accepting our exclusion."[9] This was the same logic of the legendary "Philadelphia 11"—the women who were illicitly ordained as Episcopal priests in 1974 by three retired bishops. They refused to accept their exclusion, and their action resulted in the denomination's approval of women's ordination two years later. "We changed a church that would not change itself," said one of the women ordained in 1974, Betty Bone Schiess.[10] That is precisely what Catholic women are trying to do too.

"No one save mad feminists will give [this ceremony] any credence," said Catholic League president Bill Donahue. "Indeed, this happens every day in the asylum: some actually think they're the pope."[11] But he's wrong. If I woke up one morning and declared myself queen, I wouldn't have any subjects—but these women deacons and priests actually *do* have Catholics taking them seriously. It's true they have no brick-and-mortar churches; nevertheless, they are busy presiding over baptisms, marriages, funerals, and Eucharistic services for the increasing number of faithful who believe that women can represent God just as men can. For now, they tend to serve as priests in small, liberal "house churches" that meet in someone's home for prayer and Communion.

In any event, these women believe that it is *God* who is calling them to this job, and that *God* is the one who wants them installed as priests. Who can quibble over semantics when God is calling?

"Even though I'm sad that I can't join people in the line [going up to receive the consecrated wafer and wine]," says Houk, "it's okay because I can feel Jesus surrounding me and holding me. And nobody can take that away—no priest, no bishop, no pope. And therefore I can do what I am doing. This is what God wants me to do. And God is not going to leave me."

Houk and the other women who have been ordained are role models for younger Catholics, many of whom report that their discovery, as girls, that women can't become priests has had a defining impact on their Catholic identities. Emily Waldron, a student at the University of Puget Sound in Tacoma, Washington, told me that in high school catechism class in the small Colorado farming community where she grew up, she learned that women couldn't be priests—"and what bothered me was that there was no good reason. It didn't seem well justified. The reason I was taught was that it was tradition." Laura Eppinger, a student at Marquette University, a Catholic university in Milwaukee, also remembers being told by a nun in her Catholic high school that women could not become priests. "I couldn't understand it, and I still don't understand it," she tells me. "I know that I have the same spiritual and intellectual capacity as any man. So I don't understand why it's not an option for me. I see the rule as invalid and wrong." Nicole Sotelo, the media coordinator for Call to Action, also attended Catholic school. She reports that when she was in third grade, she wanted to become an altar server. "The priest came into our classroom, but he only wanted boys. I realized at that moment that something was not quite right."

In the Catholic tradition, a priest is one who receives the Holy Spirit through the sacrament of "holy orders," in which a bishop (in essence a "high priest," said to be one link in the long chain of bishops dating back to the time of Jesus and the apostles) lays his hands on the candidate. The newly ordained (or "ordered") priest is then entrusted to serve the church with divine grace.

Here's the problem: Jesus never mentioned anything about a priesthood. Neither did Paul. All evidence shows that in fact, the leaders of the early church never intended to have a formal priesthood; they wanted to break from the Jewish tradition, which did have priests. *All* people who believed in Jesus Christ were said to be priests because they were part of a "priesthood of believers." *All* faithful followers of Jesus, not just clergy, were understood to be equal under God. *All* were considered "ordained" or "ordered" at baptism. Instead of designating a special caste of priests, the early church from the time of the apostles had deacons, who did the day-to-day church work. Women could and did serve as deacons.

The equal footing of all believers lasted a few hundred years. Then a formalized hierarchy was created, and Christianity was forever altered. An ordained priesthood was established in the year 313, when Constantine, the emperor of the Roman Empire, legalized Christianity. The role of deacons diminished; they became low-level clergy, while the power of priests grew and the bishops, the "overseers," became responsible for most church decisions and teachings. Thus the clergy became an elite group that assumed more and more power, while the laity (everyone else) was stripped of power and became more passive within the church. No mention was made of excluding women until the twelfth century, when ordained priests were granted the power to absolve sin and to transform the bread and wine into the body and blood of Christ. In 1517, reacting to the power of the clergy and their tendency to abuse it, Augustinian monk Martin Luther protested the church and propelled the Protestant Reformation. This led to the Council of Trent (1545–63), which further strengthened the boundary between clergy and laity. The council issued an official list of seven sacraments for males and six for females: ordained priesthood was the one sacrament denied females. The council further stated that ordained priests were on a higher level than the priesthood of believers. This boundary became even more pronounced in 1954, when Pope Pius XII said that ordained priests represent Christ and laypeople are witnesses. Women, therefore, could never transcend the role of witness.

These ideas about the special power and privilege of the clergy came under debate just a few years later. After being selected pope in 1958, John XXIII did something shocking, brave, and monumental: he called for a worldwide gathering of bishops to discuss the role of the church within the modern world. Dubbed Vatican II, the Second Vatican Council proceedings took place from 1962 through 1965. (The First Vatican Council, held in 1869–70, dealt with doctrine and papal infallibility and was never completed owing to the outbreak of the Franco-Prussian War.) One of the outcomes of Vatican II was the "Dogmatic Constitution on the Church" in 1964 (*Lumen Gentium*), which elevated the laity from mere spectators to active participants as people of God. This dogma referred to the faithful as a "royal priesthood" who "exercise that priesthood by receiving the sacraments, by prayer and thanksgiving, by witness of a holy life, and by self-denial and active charity." The church was on record emphasizing that non-clergy are also priests and even declaring that church teachings cannot be considered valid un-less the faithful actively "receive" or accept them. In that spirit, the laity—composed of women and men—was encouraged to become more active in church life and not to simply cede all activity to the clergy.[12]

To be sure, Pope John XXIII was no feminist. In Deborah Halter's indispensable book on the church's rulings about women and the priesthood, *The Papal "No,"* she relates that only men were invited to observe Vatican II proceedings and only men were invited to serve as spokespeople for women's organizations. One week before the third session opened, in 1964, Pope Paul VI (who succeeded after John XXIII died, in 1963) discovered that there was public criticism of the council's exclusion of women, and only then did he allow "some de-vout ladies" to attend as auditors for several ceremonies. During the final session in 1965, twenty-two women were allowed to serve as auditors among the three thousand men.[13]

On the other hand, the council issued a historic statement over-turning the concept developed by Aristotle, Augustine, and Aquinas that men were the heads of women because they were created first. The "Pastoral Constitution on the Church in the Modern World" of 1965 (*Gaudium et Spes*) says,

> All women and men are endowed with a rational soul and are created in God's image; they have the same nature and origin and, being redeemed by Christ, they enjoy the same divine call-ing and destiny; there is here a basic equality between all and it must be accorded ever greater recognition.[14]

For the first time, the church had officially recognized women and men as equals before God.

After Vatican II, Catholics were energized. Finally they had a stake in the decision-making process. For the first time, large numbers of ordinary Catholics began to study the Bible on their own, to educate themselves about what Scripture *really* said. Immediately, Catholic women started asking questions. If they were equal to men, why couldn't they become ordained? After all, the Bible doesn't say any-thing about ordination for anyone, female or male. Meanwhile, women in other sacramental Christian denominations—such as the Episcopal Church in the United States and the Anglican Church in Canada—*were* being ordained, so what was the holdup in the Roman Catholic Church? Reform was in the air, and in 1975 the first Women's Ordination Conference was convened. Twelve hundred women came to Detroit for this event, and five hundred more wanted to come but were turned away for lack of space. The organized movement to protest the exclusion of women from the priesthood was born. It had the backing of theologians and biblical scholars. It was poised for progress.

I would love to tell you that the rest was history. But new leadership in Rome, threatened that their power might be chipped away, virtually erased the achievements of Vatican II. In fact, the progressive spirit of Vatican II on the part of the Vatican was extinguished almost as soon as it was lit. Pope Paul VI's attitude about women can be summed up with two words: "Humanae Vitae." That is the name of the infamous encyclical of 1968, in which he acted against the recommendation of the special Papal Birth Control Commission and condemned all forms of contraception aside from the rhythm method (abstinence during a woman's fertile time of month), which is notoriously unreliable. "Humanae Vitae" told women that they were not allowed to take control over their bodies; in effect, they could not take control over their lives.

Paul VI's successor, John Paul II, installed just a few years later, in 1978 (after the thirty-three-day papacy of John Paul I), represented a giant step backward: he was unrelentingly conservative, particularly with regard to women's autonomy. He led the church for twenty-seven long years, during which time his authoritarian nature and anti-Vatican II stance became increasingly evident. John Paul II, writes Angela Bonavoglia, "set in veritable stone the church's opposition to birth control, sterilization, infertility treatments, condoms even to prevent the spread of AIDS, the morning-after pill even in cases of rape, stem cell research, and pregnancy termination in virtually all circumstances." He also "condemned homosexual behavior in the harshest terms, as well as divorce and remarriage" and "refused to accept even the most unimposing inclusive language, replacing the proposed 'for us and for our salvation' in the Apostles' Creed with 'for us men and for our salvation.'"[15] The essayist Nancy Mairs tells me, "John Paul II was a disaster from an ecclesiastical point of view. He wasn't evil incarnate, but he was too interested in his own power."

Meanwhile, Catholics protested the unbending doctrine at cathedrals around the country, and they were not crazy radicals. They were faithful Catholics with legitimate, thoughtful concerns. From the beginning, nuns—the most credible of the faithful—were at the forefront of the reform movement. Yes, *nuns.* Despite their reputation for blind obedience to the hierarchical church, nuns became radicalized during the 1960s and '70s and began to challenge the Vatican. The Vatican had sent twenty thousand nuns to work as missionaries in Latin America, where they were exposed to liberation theology (the idea that Christian teachings could be used to help the poor and oppressed, which often leads to a mixing of Catholicism with left-of-center politics) and developed their own ideas about being agents of change. Nuns supported the Equal Rights Amendment and opposed legal restrictions on abortion (and two of them were forced out of their religious order as a result). More and more, they studied in divinity programs and earned their master of divinity degrees. And many nuns were present in Detroit at the first Women's Ordination Conference and subsequent WOC events.

Sister Joan Chittister was one of those radicalized nuns.[16] In 1952, at the age of sixteen, she entered the Mount Saint Benedict Monastery in Erie, Pennsylvania. The teachings that came out of Vatican II turned her into a reformer. She earned her doctorate in communication theory, and today she is a bestselling author and globe-trotting public speaker on Catholic reform. She eloquently and knowledgeably challenges the church to embrace gender-neutral language and the ordination of women. In 2000 in Rome, she spoke to a thousand nuns about feminism. "The notion that God would create women with brains in order to forbid them to use them paints God as some kind of sadist," she said. "The notion that the God of Mary and Eve . . . trusts more to men than to women in the divine plan for salvation ignores the very place of women in the Christian tradition."[17]

The Vatican decided to teach this nun a lesson—and not with a slap on the arm with a ruler. It instructed U.S. dioceses to boycott a 2001 National Catholic Education Association conference in Milwaukee because Chittister was the keynote speaker. As a result, many Catholic teachers were not given the funds to attend. Chittister, surrounded by bodyguards, delivered her address before a packed audience that gave her a standing ovation before she had even ascended the podium. Refusing to be silenced, even by the pope, she declared, "Today's heresy is tomorrow's social dogma." What a dramatic moment! A nun was speaking out against the Vatican, even declaring outright that heresy can sometimes be a good thing. This scene alone offers a vivid picture of the defiance of the faithful in the face of an out-of-touch leadership.

Ever in demand, Chittister was invited to speak a few months later at the first conference of a new organization, Women's Ordination Worldwide, in Dublin. The Vatican found out and told her she was forbidden to attend, saying that if she did, there would be "grave penalties." The prioress of the Erie Benedictines, Sister Christine Vladimiroff, was warned that if she did not officially forbid Chittister from going to Dublin, she faced the risk of excommunication or even the disbanding of the order. Chittister begged Vladimiroff to forbid her so that she alone would incur the church's wrath, but Vladimiroff, with the support of 127 out of 128 active sisters, told the Vatican that she would not stop Chittister. Chittister did go to Dublin, where she addressed an audience of thirteen hundred supporters from around the world, and the Vatican did not follow through on its threats to the Erie Benedictines. Vladimiroff issued a statement in which she said that faithful Catholics are "scandalized when honest attempts to discuss questions of import to the church are forbidden." Chittister told the press, "I did not do this in defiance of the church. I did this because the best history of the church is in discussion. To suppress discussion is a sin against the Holy Spirit."[18]

The Erie Benedictines are not the only sisters who openly question church hierarchy. In 1979, when the newly installed Pope John Paul II came to the United States and held a prayer service at the Shrine of the Immaculate Conception in Washington, D.C., five thousand nuns were invited to attend. Theresa Kane, a Sister of Mercy and president of the Leadership Conference of Women Religious, was selected to issue a greeting to the pope. After the requisite niceties about the importance of his work on behalf of the world's poor, Kane went on to discuss the significant but unrecognized contributions made by women in the

Catholic Church. "Our contemplation [as women] leads us to state that the church, in its struggles to be faithful to its call for reverence and dignity for all persons, must respond by providing the possibility of women as persons being included in all ministries [including priesthood] of our church."[19]

The nuns responded with enthusiastic applause, but the pope did not address Kane's remarks. This was to be expected, given John Paul II's consistent disrespect of devout women attempting to serve the church. A decade later, in 1989, when the Communist regime in Czechoslovakia fell, it was discovered that there had been an underground church. Catholics in Czechoslovakia, who totaled 66 percent of the population, had been persecuted for practicing their religion since the 1948 Communist takeover. To keep the church alive, Bishop Felix Davidek was consecrated with Vatican approval to secretly ordain priests and to organize an underground seminary. (When his church activities were discovered some years later, he was sentenced to prison for fourteen years.) Many of the priests were married men, and there were five or six women who had been needed to serve Catholic women imprisoned by the Communist government.

When all this information finally came to light, the Vatican determined that the unmarried men could continue as priests. The married men could no longer serve as priests, but their priestly actions in the underground church were recognized as valid. But the priestly actions of the women who had served the church were declared "invalid," which meant that all the sacraments they had performed would not be recognized by the church hierarchy.

In 1996 Ludmila Javorová,—the first of these women priests to have been ordained by Davidek—was notified by her local bishop that she was "formally prohibited" from performing priestly duties and that she was to keep this prohibition secret. Javorová had served as vicar general of the underground diocese for twenty years under threat of torture and death. This was how the Catholic Church repaid her.[20]

From the moment the Catholic women's ordination movement formed, the Vatican has countered it with periodic statements purporting to explain why women cannot become priests. However, "most of the documents addressing the issue are decidedly inaccessible to most Catholics," comments Deborah Halter. "The texts are written in densely technical language; they present a maze of arguments drawn from biblical metaphors sometimes taken out of context; they depend upon unevenly applied biological differences and obsolete cultural stereotypes; they are often delivered late to the world's bishops, who are then unable to study the documents in advance of their release to Catholics and the media; and, their general tone is patriarchal and often patronizing."[21] Halter implies that this obfuscation is deliberate. Vatican II had emphasized that doctrine was not valid unless the faithful assented to it—but if they can't *understand* it, they can't disagree with it, and thus the Vatican can unilaterally assert its will.

In the early 1970s a Pontifical Biblical Commission was given the task of settling the issue of women's ordination "once and for all." But guess what? The commission concluded that there was no valid scriptural reason not to ordain women, because the concept of the priest who consecrates the Eucharist was developed after the time of Jesus and the New Testament.[22] The Congregation for the Doctrine of the Faith, a powerful Vatican agency, overturned the commission's conclusions, and in 1976, one year after the first WOC conference, the CDF issued its own statement, the "Declaration on the Admission of Women to the Ministerial Priesthood" ("Inter Insigniores").[23] The prefect of the Congregation at that time, Cardinal Joseph Ratzinger, now goes by the name Pope Benedict XVI.

According to this document, the primary reason that women cannot be ordained is that they are unable to act *in persona Christi*—they cannot represent Christ—because they do not resemble Christ in his maleness. Critics pointed out that Jesus never said anything about maleness—or about a priesthood. The claim that priests must be male is certainly not based on the Bible, and it contradicts the Christian idea that all who are baptized are in the image of God (*imago dei*). Halter points out that "Inter Insigniores" ignored the fact that salvation is said to come from the humanity of Jesus, not from his maleness. His sex had never been privileged before. After all, in Galatians 3:26–28 Paul declares, "In Jesus Christ you are all children of God through faith. As many of you were baptized into Christ have clothed yourselves with Christ. There is no longer Jew or Greek, there is no longer slave or free, there is no longer male and female; for all of you are one in Christ Jesus." Moreover, Ratzinger's logic opened the door to issues of race, ethnicity, or nationality: Could it also be said that blacks could not be ordained because Christ was not black?

After the Episcopal Church in the United States began to ordain women, in 1976, the Vatican became particularly defensive because the Episcopal Church, like the Catholic Church, has an apostolic priesthood supposedly dating back to Jesus telling Peter, "On this rock I will build my church" (Matthew 16:18). In 1984 John Paul II wrote a letter to the archbishop of Canterbury, Robert Runcie, in which he stated that the ordination of women in the Anglican churches created an obstacle in friendly relations between the two institutions. After consulting with Anglican leaders around the world, Runcie outlined the Anglican position: there is no basis in Scripture or tradition for objecting to the ordination of women; the exclusion of women from priestly ministry is not rooted in divine law; and the Catholic emphasis on maleness as part of in persona Christi is in fact *detrimental* because it weakens the priesthood by failing to include all Christians.[24] In 1992 the church of England followed its American counterpart and approved women's ordination as well.

In 1988 John Paul II wrote "On the Dignity and Vocation of Women" ("Mulieris Dignitatem"), in which he said that since Jesus chose men as apostles, it follows that women are unsuitable for the priesthood.[25] However, the term "apostle" is a contested one. Distinguished from a disciple, meaning a follower of Jesus Christ, apostle often refers to the twelve men selected by Jesus to be special missionaries. Yet confusingly, the term can include people beyond those twelve. For instance, Paul described himself as an apostle and Luke is considered an apostle, even though they were not handpicked by Jesus. Since both Paul and Luke considered themselves apostles, they had to expand the definition of apostle beyond the twelve originally chosen by Jesus. According to Paul, an apostle was someone who witnessed Jesus Christ when he was resurrected and was told to proclaim the gospel (1 Corinthians 9:1–2). According to Luke, an apostle was someone who met the qualifications to replace Judas (who had betrayed Jesus): one who had accompanied Jesus during his ministry and also witnessed his resurrection (Acts 1:21-22). Women fit both Paul's and Luke's criteria according to all four Gospels; therefore women were apostles, even though they were not among the twelve chosen to sit on heavenly thrones to rule the twelve restored tribes of Israel. Mary Magdalene is considered an apostle, as is Junia, an early church leader. Women were Jesus' closest companions, walking with him from Galilee to Jerusalem and witnessing his death as well as his resurrection.

Meanwhile, there was internal dissent among U.S. bishops. In 1983 the U.S. Catholic bishops' conference voted unanimously to develop a pastoral letter regarding women's concerns about the church. A committee of six bishops, together with seven female consultants, coordinated discussions with seventy-five thousand Catholic women across the country. The committee created a document in which it quoted women in their own words expressing their opinions on myriad societal and religious issues, including teachings on sexuality and ordination. Unacceptable to the Vatican, the document was rewritten and rewritten. The final version deleted all of the women's quotations. The bishops refused to approve the document, and it was not released.[26] Since that failure, U.S. bishops have not written major pastoral letters for fear of being in conflict with the Vatican.

In 1994 John Paul II realized that he needed to do something to quell the rising internal dissent. Thus, he formally permitted females to serve as religious educators and as Eucharistic ministers, in which they lead Mass and offer but do not consecrate the bread and wine. (Women were already serving in these roles anyway.) However, two months later he issued another document on women's ordination, "On Reserving Priestly Ordination to Men Alone" ("Ordinatio Sacerdotalis"), a major apostolic letter reemphasizing that women cannot be priests.[27] Cynics—and their numbers were increasing—theorized that the pope's chain of events was deliberate and strategic: by throwing a bone to the ladies, John Paul II figured that they would be less inclined to complain about the apostolic letter. In this document, John Paul II praised "the dignity of women and their vocation." Women, he continued, were "the holy martyrs, virgins, and the mothers [who] bravely bore witness to their faith and passed on the Church's faith and tradition by bringing up their children in the spirit of the Gospel." The pope further declared that the prohibition of women from serving as priests was to be held "definitively"—meaning that no future pope or ecumenical council would be allowed to reverse the judgment. In response, the Belgian bishops' Commission on Woman and the Church released a document that said that Jesus' maleness was being "exaggerated beyond reason." In 1995 the pope continued his emphasis on women's special roles as virgin or mother. In his "Letter to Women" on the occasion of the United Nations Fourth World Conference on Women, in Beijing, he wrote that women had a "special genius" (an essential nature) that men did not have.[28] This "special genius" precluded them from the priesthood.

The criticisms did not abate, leading the Vatican to drastic measures. Several months later, in late 1995, Cardinal Ratzinger published a responsum in which he claimed that the Vatican's prohibition of women from the priesthood was "infallible"—free from error and irreversible. Only 150 words long, the responsum declares that this prohibition is founded on the word of God and that the subject is no longer open for discussion. Women's ordination may not be discussed in public. Those who defy this ban may be excommunicated.

(As a non-Catholic, I can't be excommunicated, but I can be ignored. I never received a response to my request for an interview with a Vatican representative on the subject of women's ordination.)

Many Catholics were dismayed with the Vatican's hardball. "There are literally millions of Catholics in the U.S. alone who see no reason why women can't be ordained, and they're not going to decide they're not Catholic," said the Reverend Richard P. McBrien, a theology professor at the University of Notre Dame, in response to Ratzinger's statement. "It is the pope and the Vatican who will be seen as out of step."[29]

In 2004 Ratzinger penned a "Letter to Bishops of the Catholic Church on the Collaboration of Men and Women in the church and in the World," a confusing document. It condemns the "lethal effects" of feminism, although it also embraces the rights of women in the workplace and respect for women choosing to work inside the home. The implication is that feminism is not about women's equality, but about something entirely different—a destructive desire for power, it seems. As usual, there are no quotations or voices of actual women, and it appears that Ratzinger—the pope—has no idea what women's lives are really like.[30] Most recently, in May 2008, the Vatican decreed again that all ordained women and the bishops who ordained them are immediately and automatically excommunicated.

Joan Houk's husband never expected to part ways with Rome, but in reaction to the Vatican's rationalizations for exclusion, he feels he has no choice. "Our church has been flying apart since the election of John Paul II, and we thought that the new pope would be someone chosen to bring us together. Instead they elected someone commonly referred to as the 'junkyard dog of theology.'" A retired civil engineer who has been a committed Catholic his entire life, he speaks slowly and carefully. Like his wife, he is an accidental activist who never dreamed he would ever violate anything the church dictated. "Now there is no opportunity for dialogue. There is no opportunity to showcase women's abilities. The church is using the only tool left to them when they have failed to convince—which is to exclude [through excommunication]. This is the only tool they have left because they have not convinced people. What is left to us? What is left to us is confrontation."

He continues, "This is really a bigger issue than women's ordination. This is about thinking less of people because they are different. We have to fight against that. The tragedy is that the church says this is God's will. The church is putting God behind its bigotry. It is using God to support its bigotry. We need to stand up and say, 'God does not do this.'"

If you read the New Testament, you can only conclude that the church's denigration of women has no biblical foundation whatsoever. This is an important point because Catholic tradition values biblical foundation and because the Vatican purports to ground its prohibition on the Bible. Yet in black-and-white there is abundant evidence that women were the backbone of the Jesus movement and of the early church. However, for generations and generations the church has de-emphasized the importance of these women (if not banishing them entirely from church history), so that even though they've been there all along, most Catholics have not known these women existed. Many Catholics today continue to remain ignorant of this part of their religious history.

During the early Christian ministry, the idea that women were capable of mediating with God was well established; women had been serving as priests for a thousand years in ancient Mediterranean polytheistic cults. In *Portrait of a Priestess: Women and Ritual in Ancient Greece*, Joan Breton Connelly dispels the long-held belief that the women in the pre-Christian era were powerless and kept inside the home. In fact, there was a caste of powerful priestesses who enjoyed prestige, honor, and influence.[31] Thus, in Jesus' day and in the several centuries that followed, no one would have raised an eyebrow at the sight of women serving as religious authority figures.

Over and over the New Testament shows that women believed in Jesus and he repaid them by treating them as equals. When a woman who had been suffering from uterine bleeding for twelve years (from fibroids, perhaps) touched the hem of his cloak, he healed her rather than shunned her, despite her status as ritually impure (Luke 8:40–48).

When he was asked to judge an adulterous woman, he saved her from being stoned by stating, "Let anyone among you who is without sin be the first to throw a stone at her," causing the would-be stoners to slink away (John 7:53–8:11). (According to biblical scholars, this story was not originally included in the New Testament, but was added later by scribes. Nevertheless, many believing Christians consider it part of their sacred text. For our purposes here, the issue of authorship is less important than the point conveyed in the story, which is that Jesus was regarded as someone who wanted to help women and expose hypocrisy.)

It was a woman, Mary Magdalene, who was the most loyal to Jesus, and for this reason she has been traditionally called the "apostle to the apostles." Mary Magdalene was a devoted disciple and steadfast friend. With other women, she remained with him during his crucifixion and was the first to discover his empty tomb, the first to witness his resurrection, and the first to spread the "good news" about his resurrection (Matthew 28:1–10; Mark 16:1–8; Luke 23:55–24:10; John 20:1–2). In the narrative of the life, death, and resurrection of Jesus, there couldn't be anyone more central. As it says in the Gospel of John 20:11–18:

> Mary stood weeping outside the tomb. As she wept, she bent over to look into the tomb [where she expected to find the dead body of Jesus, whom she had seen crucified, and was shocked to discover that his body was not there]; and she saw two angels in white, sitting where the body of Jesus had been lying, one at the

head and the other at the feet. They said to her, "Woman, why are you weeping?" She said to them, "They have taken away my Lord, and I do not know where they have laid him." When she had said this, she turned around and saw Jesus standing there, but she did not know that it was Jesus. Jesus said to her, "Woman, why are you weeping? Whom are you looking for?" Supposing him to be the gardener, she said to him, "Sir, if you have carried him away, tell me where you have laid him, and I will take him away." Jesus said to her, "Mary!" She turned and said to him in Hebrew, "Rabboni! [my master, my teacher]." Jesus said to her, "Do not hold on to me, because I have not yet ascended to the Father. But go to my brothers and say to them, 'I am ascending to my Father and your Father, to my God and your God.'" Mary Magdalene went and announced to the disciples, "I have seen the Lord"; and she told them that he had said these things to her.

Other women also accompanied Jesus on his travels, some of them providing for him and his disciples financially and devoting their lives to him (Mark 15:40–41; Luke 8:1–3). Women traveled with Jesus during his final trip to Jerusalem and remained with him during the crucifixion until the end, while all the male disciples fled (Matthew 27:55). In Romans 16:7, Paul refers to Junia, "prominent among the apostles" who was "in Christ before I was." There are also numerous references to female deacons and other female leaders throughout the New Testament—Phoebe, Lydia, Prisca (also known as Priscilla), Joanna, and others.

The biblical scholar Elisabeth Schüssler Fiorenza revealed the vital role played by women in the life of Jesus in her 1983 book *In Memory of Her*, whose title refers to the unnamed woman at Bethany who anointed him. In Mark 14:9 a woman carries "an alabaster jar of very costly ointment," which she pours on his head. The disciples become enraged, saying that the ointment should have been sold, with the money going to the poor. But Jesus defends her, saying, "She has done what she could; she has anointed my body beforehand for its burial. Truly I tell you, wherever the good news is proclaimed in the whole world, what she has done will be told in remembrance of her."

According to Schüssler Fiorenza, the woman's act was a prophetic recognition that Jesus was the Messiah. Alone among the disciples, she recognized that Jesus was Christ. The irony, of course, is that Jesus instructed his disciples to keep her memory alive, yet much about her has been forgotten. The name of the betrayer, Judas, is remembered, Schüssler Fiorenza drily points out, "but the name of the faithful disciple is forgotten because she was a woman."[32]

Don't feel bad if you are unfamiliar with these women: it's no wonder. The church over time has erased or devalued them. Church scribes changed the name of Junia, the important female apostle, to Junias, a made-up masculine name without precedent, rendering the female apostle invisible. After the respected New Testament scholar Bernadette Brooten of Brandeis University uncovered this fraud, Junias was changed back to Junia in 1989 in the New Revised Standard Version of the New Testament.[33] The indispensable role of female deacons in the early church—who preached, baptized, performed marriages, and buried the dead—has been downplayed at best, ignored at worst.

And don't feel guilty if you thought that Mary Magdalene was a woman of ill repute. No, she was not a prostitute—that was a fiction that began with Pope Gregory I in the sixth century. He identified Mary Magdalene as Mary of Bethany, who in turn has been identified as the unnamed "sinner" who anointed the feet of Jesus in Luke 7:36–50. Scholars believe that these in fact were three different women who have become conflated into one—Mary of Magdala. Pope Gregory I did not call Mary Magdalene a prostitute, but he planted the idea that she was a sinner, and the idea that her sin was of a sexual nature became widespread. The adulterous woman Jesus rescued from being stoned also became associated with Mary Magdalene, despite no evidence.

To maintain the lie that the disciples and apostles were all men and that the early church was led exclusively by men, the church hierarchy has performed extensive cover-up work. The official lectionary, which designates New Testament readings for Mass in Catholic churches throughout the year, includes passages about women only for weekday church services, when relatively few of the faithful are present. Sister Christine Schenk, the executive director of FutureChurch, an organization promoting the full participation of all baptized Catholics in the life of the church, laments the fact that the women in Jesus' life are absent from Sunday Scripture readings. The account of the woman of Bethany who anointed Jesus and whose memory Jesus specifically said should be kept alive, for example, is recited only on Easter Monday, not Easter Sunday, when the pews are filled to capacity. For that holy day, other readings are chosen instead. Likewise, Romans 16:1–19, in which Paul cites by name the women who led the early church, is never recited, and the reference to Junia is included in a reading recited once every three years, on Saturday. Furthermore, on each Sunday during the Easter season, Catholics hear about the male disciples, but the female disciples are relegated again to weekday readings. The encounter between Mary Magdalene and the resurrected Jesus is also relegated to a weekday (Easter Tuesday). "Adding insult to injury," says Angela Bonavoglia, "Jesus' appearance to Thomas—who had doubted him—is read on the second Sunday after Easter every single year."[34]

This erasure of women from church history is the result of a negative Christian view of women that developed as Christian theology became influenced by Greek and Roman culture. Augustine, the fourth-century bishop, was strongly influenced by Aristotle's belief that men are inherently superior to women. Augustine argued that woman by herself is not created in God's image, and that she could only image God in a relationship with a man. Thus, a woman is inherently secondary and subordinate to a man.

As a result of this thinking, Thomas Aquinas declared in the thirteenth century that women could not be priests. Meanwhile, deacons grew weaker and weaker in power while priests grew more powerful. The priesthood became less concerned with helping the needy and more focused on the liturgy of the Eucharist. In 1139, at the Second Lateran Council, it was determined that priests must remain unmarried and celibate in order to protect church property, which otherwise was lost to priests' wives and their families. Underlying this concern about property was the belief that women were subordinate to men and that therefore, celibate life, free of women, was holier than married life.

A few European women resisted their systematic patriarchal exclusion from the church hierarchy. They recognized that the only way they would ever be allowed a professionalized religious life was through the claim that they had a direct, mystical relationship with God. Hildegard of Bingen (1098–1179) claimed that she spoke to God and was heard by God—and people believed her. Because she was regarded as an authentic mystic, explains the historian Gerda Lerner, she was able to break through multiple barriers for women of her time: she wrote extensively, traveled, and became very influential. Likewise, Julian of Norwich (1342–ca. 1416) and Margery Kempe (ca. 1373–ca. 1438) also became public figures through their claims of an ecstatic, visionary way of knowing God. However, nearly all women who attempted to carve out this unique role paid a steep price. Kempe, accused of heresy, was imprisoned. Women known as the Beguines, who basically functioned as nuns and administered to the needy, were accused of heresy and witchcraft during the early 1300s. One Beguine, Marguerite Porète, was burned at the stake for heresy.[35] By the time of the Council of Trent, women were shut out from leadership roles entirely, and the privileging of masculinity was as firmly rooted as a carob tree in the Holy Land.

Female Christian leaders must be given the same level of respect as male leaders not to "make women feel good," an accusation often leveled against feminists when they attempt to uncover historical facts and set the record straight, but because otherwise, Christianity— founded on the ministry of Jesus and the leadership of the disciples, apostles, and deacons who built the early church—is falsified. Believing Christians deserve to know the truth about their history. They cannot be expected to devote their lives to a faith that obfuscates the truth. As long as these lies are perpetuated, the contemporary church leadership will believe it has permission and legitimacy to subordinate women.

Even those women who do not support women priests admit that their opposition lies not in a belief that women are incapable of doing the job well, but in their simple fear of change. I had a delightful lunch with four devoted Catholic women, mothers and grandmothers in their sixties and seventies, in Ramsey, New Jersey. The host, Helen Markey, went out of her way to prepare a vegetarian quiche out of respect for my observance of kashrut, the Jewish dietary restrictions. For two hours we spoke about a wide range of issues pertaining to women and religion, but the topic of women's ordination sparked the most heated and surprising discussion. At first, when I asked if they supported women's ordination, only one, who years before had served as a pastoral associate, would admit it. But as our conversation deepened, the three opponents of ordination admitted that it's something they could get used to once they overcame their fear of doing something different.

One of the women, seventy-five years old, shared with us her belief that women should be allowed to be deacons. So why not priests? "I don't know why exactly"—long pause—"except"—long pause—"it's tradition. I'm not saying I would reject it, don't get me wrong. But I would have a hard time with it." If one morning her parish had a woman priest, she would grumble about it at first, but over time she would accept the change.

Another woman at the table, also seventy-five, mused, "There are a lot of very spiritual, holy women out there who might make better priests than the priests we have. Things will change, and I'm not saying I'm against that. I do visualize men as priests, but I'm not against having a woman as a priest. I do feel that women, as nurturers, would do a much better job at keeping the church together. I think that men, especially if they're not married, have no idea what goes on in family life—the trials and tribulations you have in raising children. They are just oblivious. So I feel it would be very beneficial to have women come into the church."

The third holdout also came around. She admitted that it would be difficult for her to accept "the first wave of women priests," because she would always consider them "radical extremists and very vocal," but she could probably make peace with women priests once they were to become established.

I suspect that even those Catholics who claim that women cannot be priests, because women do not image Christ, could be persuaded simply because of the urgent priest shortage. Wouldn't a woman priest be better than no priest? Listen to Robin Imbrigiotta, a hospice chaplain in Akron, Ohio: "There've been situations where someone has died and the priest didn't get there in time," she told Angela Bonavoglia. "The family is standing around the bed, and I'm comforting these people, and we're talking about the patient. The priest walks in, takes off his hat, looks at everyone, and says, 'Oh, I'm so sorry.' And they'll say, 'Father, say a prayer.' And Father will say a prayer [and] then walk out. They're like, 'Oh, thank God Father was here.'"[36] It's ludicrous that people believe they cannot receive the same solace from a woman, and it's sad for those who hold this belief when they are in pain and there is simply no male priest around.

Are illicit ordination ceremonies really the best strategy for confronting the exclusionary priesthood? Among those who desperately want a renewed priesthood, there is sharp difference of opinion.

Frances Kissling, the former president of Catholics for a Free Choice (an organization representing Catholics who support women's right to reproductive choices), advocates for change in the priesthood but is not convinced that these ceremonies are the most practical method of achieving it. "Most Catholic women don't even know about these ceremonies," she pointed out to me, "and if they did know, they probably wouldn't approve of them. Going on a boat with a secret bishop ordaining you? Some of them are anonymous and some of them aren't? Messing around with the liturgy? This is beyond the scope of what most people will accept." She added, "Most of the women who have participated in these ceremonies do not have parishes; they do not have congregations. There is no structure for them. So they don't have a way to expose ordinary women to what they are doing."

The theologian Mary Hunt, codirector of the Women's Alliance for Theology, Ethics and Ritual in Silver Spring, Maryland, is skeptical of women's ordination ceremonies because in her mind, they are not radical *enough*. Nevertheless, she does support the efforts of Roman Catholic Womenpriests and the women who dare to become ordained. Hunt uses the term "kyriarchy" to describe the church structure. Coined by the theologian Elisabeth Schüssler Fiorenza, kyriarchy is from the Greek word "*kyrios,*" which means "lord." It refers to the rule of a master over his subordinates, in contrast with patriarchy, which refers more narrowly to the male domination of women. Kyriarchy encompasses other forms of oppression, through top-down power structures, in addition to male domination. "The Catholic Church is the quintessential form of kyriarchy," she told me, "because a very few people on the top, the ordained, make all the decisions for all the people at the bottom, the laity. So simply getting women into the ordained structure will not change the structure and probably will even shore up that structure. I think a moratorium on the ordinations, until a little more thinking is done, would not be a bad idea."

To Hunt, Schüssler Fiorenza, and other radical reformers such as Rosemary Ruether, ordaining women maintains the kyriarchy and does not dismantle it. Therefore, ordaining women in and of itself keeps alive an oppressive power structure. Their ultimate objective is to declericalize the church—to eliminate the privileges of the clergy—and to create a "discipleship of equals" in which there is no power differential among the faithful; everyone who is baptized would be considered "ordered."

"I worry that in the current climate, even our best efforts to confront kyriarchal powers result in reinscribing the importance of ordination and, however inadvertently, elevating those who are ordained," Hunt declared at a Women's Ordination Worldwide conference in Ottawa, Ontario in 2005. "Co-optation is still, in my view, the most serious danger. One day, may it be soon, when the house of cards comes tumbling down, even the present pope will see the wisdom in recognizing women's ministry on kyriarchal terms and in ordaining women [and recognizing the ordinations that have already taken place illicitly] in order to preserve the kyriarchal system of power."[37]

Don't let Hunt's radical ideas and jargon fool you. She is congenial, sarcastic without being off-putting, and razor-sharp smart. "It's funny," I told her, "because from where I sit, these ceremonies seem very radical."

"They're radical because they happen," she shot back. "What's not radical is that they are the same ceremony that the men use" within the same structure that forces so many Catholics to be passive and subservient.

"But won't the kyriarchy be overturned if women could be priests?" I pressed.

"That's the question," she replied. "But did Hewlett-Packard become a cooperative just because it has had women CEOs?"

"But the women priests are themselves radical and want to make changes."

"Yeah, but how much can a few individuals really do to change the system? The question for me is: Will kyriarchy be overturned before these women are co-opted? And I think the answer to that is no."

Nancy Mairs shared with me the same line of thinking. A convert to Catholicism, she grew fed up with the prevailing hierarchy and has turned to an alternative method of worship. Mairs, who lives in Arizona, is involved in a "house church" called the Community of Christ in the Desert, in which some thirty-five people meet in one another's homes and say the Eucharistic prayer together without a priest in sight. Increasingly popular among breakaway Catholics, there are between three hundred and four hundred small "house churches" across the United States. "It's our way of having our cake and eating it too," she explained. "I've let go of the idea of women's ordination. It's a false promise, because what we need is something *really* new: we need a priesthood of the people. Ordination is bad for men because it's a bad kind of power." So why would it be good for women?

I certainly see the attraction of a "discipleship of equals" or a "priesthood of the people," but would such a religious movement be, well, *Catholic*? Or would it be something else entirely? What is the essence of Catholicism, anyway? These questions form the fault line between those who oppose and those who support women's ordination. In fact, a radical organization that spun off from the Women's Ordination Conference, Women-Church Convergence, refers to itself not as Catholic, but as "Catholic-rooted."

Supporters of women's ordination very much see themselves as part of the Catholic tradition. They do not want to jettison the rituals that they love and that comfort them—and those rituals presume clergy. In an effort to maintain legitimacy with those Catholics willing to at least entertain the idea that these irregular ceremonies have value, the bishops presiding over them have been careful to keep the traditional chain of apostolic succession. "We are not selling out," Patricia Fresen insists. "We are building a new model of priesthood. Later, we can move on to another model."[38]

"We need a broader model of priesthood," agrees Nicole Sotelo of Call to Action. "We are all ordained at baptism; that is part of our theology as Catholics. So we need to work toward that broader model, to get to the day when we can all affirm our baptismal ordination and enter into service in whatever ministry we've been called to by Christ. But in the meantime, we shouldn't discredit the ordinations, because they help Catholics, both here in the U.S. and abroad, question the discrimination that is happening within our church. They are a good starting point we can use to get to that broader vision of greater equality. They have sparked the movement and made people across the world aware of the oppression in our church."

This "ordination today, discipleship of equals tomorrow" strategy is keeping the movement humming. "A discipleship of equals is a wonderful vision," Angela Bonavoglia tells me over a cup of decaf at a Manhattan coffee shop. "But I don't personally think you can get from an institution like the Catholic Church, which is so hierarchical and rigid, to a discipleship of equals without opening up the priesthood to everybody—men, women, gay, married, parents. Once you open it up, the power structure would change. Then I could see that vision of a discipleship of equals down the road. But you can't go straight to that final vision."

Bonavoglia supports the public challenge to the church, but she is partial to what she calls "organic" ordination—when a community clamors for a specific woman to be ordained because they want her, with her individual talents, to be their leader. The perfect example is Rev. Mary Ramerman, the pastoral administrator of the Spiritus Christi Church in downtown Rochester, New York. Spiritus Christi began its life as Corpus Christi, a tiny, poor, struggling parish, led by Father James Callan and Father Enrique Cadena, that was committed to serving the poor. Ramerman began working there in 1983. One day, Father Enrique asked Ramerman to hold the chalice with the sacred wine while he held the bread during Mass. Although this angered some parishioners, others were thrilled to see a woman in that role for the first time in their lives. Soon after, the liturgy committee asked Ramerman to wear priestly garb—a long white linen tunic and a stole—and before long she began to celebrate the Eucharist when the priests were out of town.

In 1998 the Vatican ordered the bishop of Rochester to remove Father Jim from the parish. (Meanwhile Father Enrique had married and joined the Episcopal Church.) When Mary Ramerman stepped in and celebrated Mass, she in turn was fired. So many parishioners were angry that in 1999 they formed their own parish, which they named Spiritus Christi. Father Jim, who joined this new parish with Ramerman, was expelled from the priesthood by the Vatican. The parish, which had grown from a tiny, struggling church to a thriving, successful one, wanted to ordain Ramerman. She was reluctant: ordination had not been her ambition. But in 2001 she relented, and three thousand people attended her ordination ceremony at the Eastman Theatre in Rochester.

"And that ordination was one of the most moving things I've seen in my entire life," gushes Bonavoglia. "It was a public challenge. And the singing was spectacular. The bishop who did the ordaining is from the Old Catholic Church, which has the same apostolic succession as the Roman Catholic Church through the 1870s, at which point it broke away over the issue of infallibility. Three thousand people that day saw a woman ordained a priest, and that does not leave your soul very quickly."

Having attended a Spiritus Christi Eucharist, I can report that Ramerman has a strong presence. She has a humble way about her and comes across as pious but not rigid. In her white robe and rainbow-hued stole, with her sandy, shoulder-length hair feathered back from her face, Ramerman smiles, jokes pleasantly, speaks gently but forcefully, and is clearly comfortable in her role. She creates an atmosphere in which everyone feels included in the service and connected with one another. And isn't that the point of public worship?

By itself, women's ordination will not fix the top-down power structure in the Catholic Church. But it forces people to reexamine the current structure and to reflect on the need for inclusiveness. "When the church discriminates against women, it tells society that it is morally acceptable to discriminate against women," says Joan Houk. "When it says that women cannot be ordained, because they cannot represent Christ in persona Christi, then society degrades women, leading to violence, abuse, exploitation, and even death. The academics say not to ordain, because we will get co-opted. I say we must ordain, or women will never be accepted as fully human, deserving of respect and protection under the law. By its silence, my church is responsible for the ongoing violent treatment of women in the church, in the family, in the neighborhood, and in the world. Silence equals approval."

For now, women's ordination fulfills both practical and spiritual needs. Men and women both are renewed spiritually when they communicate with their God through diverse humanity.

FOUR

Evangelical Women Spread the
Good News About Women and the Bible

I was en route to Charlotte, North Carolina, and if I had any confusion about it, traveling on a highway named the Billy Graham Parkway clarified that I was in the Bible Belt. It was July 2006, and I was on my way to a four-day gathering of seventy evangelical Christian feminists. I arrived with a suitcase and two expectations: one, that there wouldn't be any kosher food in the vicinity (hence cans of tuna fish and protein bars jostled with shampoo and toothpaste in my luggage); and two, that Bible-thumping women would regard my Jewishness as a challenge and would try to convert me. Well, I was right about the food. But the members of the Evangelical and Ecumenical Women's Caucus (EEWC), an organization that supports empowerment of women in church, society, and at home, went out of their way to show respect for my religious background. They helped me find a safe place to light my Shabbat candles. They came up to me to make sure I was okay with their references to Jesus Christ. A few even greeted me with "Shalom." All enveloped me with a hospitality that made me feel completely welcomed.

My assumptions about Bible thumping were also turned on their head. These women, along with a few men, who refer to themselves as "biblical feminists," clearly love the Bible. They quote the Bible, they sing songs and hymns that cite the Bible, they are comforted by the Bible, they study the Bible, and they enjoy the occasional, ecstatic yell of "Hallelujah" or "Amen" in approval of the Bible. Yet they find meanings in the Bible that are quite different from those extracted by the more conservative evangelicals and fundamentalists around them. They do this through "hermeneutics," or principles of biblical interpretation.

One of the sessions at this gathering, for instance, was a Bible study led by Reta Halteman Finger, a New Testament scholar at Messiah College in Grantham, Pennsylvania. This study session cut deeply against the grain of much of what is widely taught in conservative evangelical schools and churches. Finger, with a professor's talent for being back-straight yet approachable, examined Paul's letter to the Ephesians—people living in the city of Ephesus, an early Christian center within the Roman republic (in today's Turkey). This letter contains an oft-quoted passage commonly used to justify male dominance in the husband-wife relationship:

> Be subject to one another out of reverence for Christ.
>
> Wives, be subject to your husbands as you are to the Lord. For the husband is the head of the wife just as Christ is the head of the church, the body of which he is the Savior. Just as the church is subject to Christ, so also wives ought to be, in everything, to their husbands.
>
> Husbands, love your wives, just as Christ loved the church and gave himself up to her, in order to make her holy by cleaning her with the washing of water by the word, so as to present the church to himself in splendor, without a spot or wrinkle or anything of the kind—yes, so that she may be holy and without blemish. In the same way, husbands should love their wives as they do their own bodies. He who loves his wife loves himself. For no one ever hates his own body, but he nourishes and tenderly cares for it, just as Christ does for the church, because we are members of his body. For this reason a man will leave his father and mother and be joined to his wife, and the two will become one flesh. This is a great mystery, and I am applying it to Christ and the church. Each of you, however, should love his wife as himself, and a wife should respect her husband. (Ephesians 5:21–33)

This passage has caused enormous grief to untold numbers of women because the lines "Wives, be subject to your husbands" and "the husband is the head of the wife" have been overemphasized while the verses before and after have been overlooked. Ever wondered what is the basis of the bridal wedding vow to "love, honor, and obey"? This is it.

But Finger demonstrated that the message is in fact positive, even beautiful—a vision of equalizing love, not unbalanced power. "This is a document of resistance," she said, explaining that the description of households was actually intended to be subversive when compared with the prevailing family structure under Roman rule. She also noted that most respected biblical scholars today strongly doubt this letter was written by Paul; the historical evidence points to a later author who wrote in Paul's name. Since its date is later, its message of feminine subordination needs more contextual analysis.

Finger called on participants to read the letter aloud, and along the way a lively discussion sprang up. These women and men had previously pored over Ephesians many, many times. A number of them knew much of it by heart. And yet they came to the text with openness and curiosity and a desire to seek out fresh meaning. They excitedly raised their hands, tested out possible interpretations, asked questions about the historical circumstances, and listened to one another—in short, they held up a biblical passage that many others would simply dismiss as sexist or troublesome or irrelevant, and they treated it with respect and renewed understanding. I was disappointed when the time ran out. And I had learned something far more profound than what Paul did or did not say to the people living in Ephesus in the first century of the Common Era: that engaging in hermeneutics can be a radical act.

"People might be surprised that the very instrument that has been used for oppression—interpretation of the Bible—can also be the source of liberation," says Alena Amato Ruggerio, a professor of communication at Southern Oregon University. Hermeneutically speaking, Bible study can be approached in myriad ways, just as any book or poem or play or song can be experienced in multiple ways by various people and even by one person. Bible study per se is not radical; it's how you go about doing it. "*Everyone* who reads a text always automatically engages in the process of interpretation," continues Ruggerio. "But we [biblical feminists] choose to emphasize historical context. We choose to bring to the forefront voices in the Bible that had been silenced. We choose to read individual passages within the frame of the whole. *That's* what is radical."

In contrast with Catholicism, in which the hierarchical power structure determines who has access to religious rituals and objects and who does not, evangelical Christianity has the potential to infuse spiritual power within each individual. There is no concept of priesthood in evangelical Christianity but instead an emphasis on the individual's relationship with Jesus Christ. Nevertheless, many evangelicals choose not to exercise their own personal power. They doubt their own ability to make sense of their religion, and they prefer reassurance from an authority figure: their pastor. Many churchgoers are afraid to think for themselves lest they be denied the treasure dangled before them as a reward for their devotion: a place in heaven. This reliance on religious leaders is most evident when it comes to interpretation of the Bible.

"When I was five or six, my parents gave me a gerbil for Easter," remembers Martha of her fundamentalist upbringing in St. Louis, Missouri. Martha is forty-one with five children, but with her fresh complexion, she could pass for thirty. She has shoulder-length dark hair and brown eyes, and she offers me a wry, friendly smile. "A friend of mine from down the street came over and I bragged about my gerbil. I said something like, 'I have a gerbil, and it's mine.' My mother pulled me aside and told me that bragging was a sin and that it was wrong. She got out a children's Bible-story book and read to me 'Nobody Likes a Braggart.'" Martha's parents took biblical warnings about pride to mean that God did not want young, enthusiastic children to show off their new pet gerbils to their excited friends. "It really affected me," says Martha. "To this day, I have a hard time saying that I did something well. The idea that I'm a good parent and a good wife comes really hard to me."

The Bible was used as a weapon to stifle Martha, but it was the hierarchy within her family that really suffocated her. There was never any doubt about who was in charge—her father, the head of the household and the disciplinarian. "My mother was never allowed to be outspoken," she recalls. "When my mother did speak up, my father belittled her. So she just kept her mouth shut. She never had any say in anything that went on. I was also not allowed to speak up, although my younger brother was allowed to. When I was a teenager, around fourteen, I started to question things. I became very mouthy because I began to resent the teachings and I wasn't being listened to. I was never given permission to ask any questions. So I would say things like, 'Well, why does it have to be this way?' My father was very violent. He was physically abusive. He followed James Dobson [a very influential fundamentalist preacher and media personality], who supports breaking the will of the child through physical punishment and says it is biblically based."

This hierarchy of power with the father at the top is widely believed to be God's desire. In many evangelical and fundamentalist Christian families, it is a given that men and women marry and have children, and that once married, the man is the "head" of the household, with final authority, while the woman and children must "submit" to him. But evangelical women seeking equality challenge this belief—and they are using Scripture to support their views. In addition to EEWC, another organization, Christians for Biblical Equality (CBE), promotes a more egalitarian understanding of key New Testament passages demonstrating that neither Jesus nor Paul intended for men to rule over women. Most evangelicals have never heard of EEWC or CBE; nevertheless, the organizations have succeeded in spreading their message of women's equality to the wider evangelical community.

Kristin Wurgler, twenty-five years old and married last year, is a perfect example of the new evangelical woman. She questions the theological belief in male headship and how it is used to limit both women's and men's abilities. Because Wurgler is evangelical ("not as harsh as Jerry Falwell but a similar mentality" is how her younger sister Emily described their upbringing to me), before the wedding she was required by her church in southern California to take several different personality tests and to attend a premarital counseling class. The class met for four hours on four consecutive Saturdays, and it was taught by a family counselor at the church, which is nondenominational. Many evangelical churches are not affiliated with any particular Protestant denomination, because evangelicals tend to value institutional independence.

"Since this was a Christian class," Wurgler explains, "they told us that girls need to remember that not only does the man need to feel like a man by being in control and being a leader, but that this is what

God wants, so we have to give up the leadership and defer leadership to the husband. It's important for the girl to be in a relationship where it's easy for her to give the leadership away. If you're with a guy who you don't want to give the leadership to, then it's an unhealthy situation."

There were fifteen other couples in the class, and it would have been easy for Wurgler to just sit there politely and deferentially, nodding her head and pretending to take notes. Unfortunately, she stuck out from the pack: her personality tests had tagged her as someone with a "leader personality," she was told, and her fiancé was characterized by these same tests as someone who lacked this personality trait—a circumstance that the family counselor highlighted as a serious potential problem. Wurgler describes her husband as "laid-back, go with the flow. He's not necessarily a follower, but he doesn't like to take control." They were the only couple in the class in which the woman had the so-called leader personality and the man did not (although in one couple, both were identified as leaders). While everyone in the class had to listen to the same lectures about male headship and female submission, Wurgler and her fiancé were singled out as needing to pay extra special attention lest they turn their backs against their God-given roles.

"If God is real and God created me, then God created me with this personality in order for me to take a leadership role," she protests. "I'm called to be a leader in certain situations, and if it's my personality to step into that role, then I should do it rather than sit back and submit. I think God created me this way for a reason, and it's not an accident that I'm this way, and it's not something cultural that happened to me to make me this way and that therefore I shouldn't be this way. So I've come to the conclusion that a lot of people, including myself, just don't understand what the Bible is saying."

"Do *you* think men and women should have separate roles?" I ask her. "No," this devout evangelical Christian tells me. "I think roles should be defined by the strength of the person. We will probably end up assigning things to each other, like the person who's good at finances will be in charge of the finances, that kind of thing. I don't think it has to do with gender."

Wurgler is disturbed by these church teachings but not outraged. Her sister Emily, however, an undergrad at the University of California in San Diego, isn't sure if she wants to consider herself a Christian any longer. She's searching for answers and is indignant about the whole "wives must submit to their husbands" belief. In high school, her pastor's wife explained that the husband gets the final say in household matters and that this is necessary because "you can't have two coaches on a football team," Emily recalls, and "you just have to trust God that this is the right way."

"But why should a woman have to change her personality to fit into this little box of what a wife and husband should be?" she asks. "Leadership should correspond with ability. Lots of women want to get married and have a Christian family, so they fit themselves into this role of submitting because they believe that this is what you need to do to have a good Christian family, that this is the way God wants it."

The terms "evangelical" and "fundamentalist" are often used loosely and interchangeably, but they have specific histories and meanings. An evangelical is a Protestant who is "born again" to a life marked by a sense of personal connection with Jesus, who believes that Scripture is the word of God, and who tries to convert others by spreading the "good news" that Jesus can save those who have faith in him. Politically, an evangelical may be right wing, centrist, or left wing. A fundamentalist Christian is an evangelical who believes that modernity is corrupt and that every word in the Bible is literally true; he or she is generally right of center in the political realm.

According to a Gallup poll in 2002, a whopping *46 percent* of Americans describe themselves as born-again or evangelical.[1] (Today almost no one describes herself as a fundamentalist, because of its associations with Islamic terrorism.) Evangelical teachings obviously influence the thinking and behavior of an overwhelming number of Americans.

Evangelical Protestantism has gone through phases over the course of its development, but it has long been the dominant religious force in this country. Its roots lie in Puritan New England, but it was energized by the religious revivals known collectively as the Great Awakening (1730s–60s) and the Second Great Awakening (1820s–30s), which emphasized the experience of being "reborn" as a Christian through an ecstatic encounter with Jesus. Participants in revivals experienced a frenzied emotionalism and a commitment to preaching the gospel to those not yet converted. Religious expression became very personal, not distanced and mediated through dry ritual. The leaders of most Protestant denominations were strongly influenced by the revivals and, as evangelicals, became the ruling voice throughout American culture. The great political and social activists throughout the nineteenth century and the early twentieth century, including suffragists, were evangelicals.

In the 1920s evangelicalism became divided. This was a time when enormous changes in the world at large and in the United States specifically altered the way Americans looked at themselves, God, and the role of religion. In the wake of a devastating world war, urbanization, increasing immigration and exposure to diverse cultures, scientific advances, and new ideas about literary and biblical criticism, many evangelicals came to embrace a modern worldview. This strand became what is known as mainline Protestantism: Christianity that is theologically liberal, interested in science as much as Scripture in explaining the world, devoted to social reform, and open to diversity and pluralism. Meanwhile, others clung ever more fiercely to conservative doctrine. These conservatives were named fundamentalists because they upheld the ideas promoted in a series of twelve booklets known as *The Fundamentals*, published between 1910 and 1915. In opposition to mainline Protestants, they adhered to "inerrancy," a literal understanding of the Bible, which they believed to be free of factual error even in areas of science and history. A third strand, Pentecostalism, also emerged from the evangelical split; this tradition emphasizes an ecstatic religious experience and supernatural signs of baptism, such as "speaking in tongues." Because this ability or "charism" is considered a spiritual power that is a gift from God, Pentecostals are sometimes called charismatics, and some Catholics are also considered charismatic.

The mainline-fundamentalist split became hardened with the 1925 Scopes Monkey Trial in small-town Dayton, Tennessee. John Scopes was a science teacher (hired by the American Civil Liberties Union) who taught the theory of evolution in public school even though state law forbade the teaching of any theory that denied the biblical story of creation. Scopes was charged with violating the law, and the ensuing trial showcased two larger-than-life personalities—defense attorney Clarence Darrow representing Scopes and William Jennings Bryan, public statesman and orator, representing the fundamentalists. (Bryan, a populist and a fundamentalist himself, associated Darwinism with eugenics.) Scopes was found guilty of violating the law, but on appeal the court set aside the conviction.

The trial, publicized widely, did not help the fundamentalist cause: most Americans decided they preferred scientific over religious explanations of how the world began. Mainline Protestantism became the new dominant religious voice in the United States. Fundamentalists realized that they were in the minority and chose to embrace this identity with pride. They saw themselves as pious holdouts against an increasingly secular and immoral culture. Thus they distanced themselves from certain aspects of modern culture: natural history and science, biblical and literary criticism, new family arrangements. In his book *Fundamentalism and Gender*, John Stratton Hawley notes that fundamentalists regard themselves as embattled victims fighting against the onslaught of an immoral world, and they are nostalgic not for early Christian society during the time of Jesus or the early church, but for "an idealized version of home and community life in the small towns of rural, nineteenth-century America" in which, they believe, there was "no tension between secular and religious loyalties, and in which the authority of Scripture defined a community where truth was undiluted by the relativity of knowledge."[2]

If the evangelicals of the nineteenth century essentially disappeared, then who are the evangelicals of today? They trace their history back to another split, this one between fundamentalist factions in 1942. Billy Graham, Charles Fuller, Harold Lindsell, and other emerging leaders met in St. Louis and proposed to renew the evangelical ideal through engagement in the modern world. "If fundamentalism had abandoned the culture and liberal Protestantism had abandoned historic Christianity, the new evangelicals would do neither," writes the sociologist Sally K. Gallagher.[3] These "neo-evangelicals" launched an incredibly successful movement of conservative, doctrinal Christians who were ready to interact in politics, science, education, and the arts. They subscribed to conservative theology and the need to be born-again, yet they also evangelized in increasingly sophisticated ways. Billy Graham began speaking to huge audiences at international evangelical "crusades," hosted radio and television programs, ran evangelism-training conferences, and published a monthly magazine, in addition to organizing relief work. Charles Fuller and Harold Ockenga founded the Fuller Theological Seminary, the flagship evangelical school and intellectual center. *Christianity Today* was launched, among other mainstream evangelical magazines. By 1976, a born-again president, Jimmy Carter, was elected—evidence that evangelical Protestants were once again the leading religious force within the wider society.

But Carter's born-again status alone wasn't enough to satisfy many of his evangelical constituents, who felt that his left-wing politics made him un-Christian. Right-wing politics and evangelical religious beliefs were becoming entwined. Republican evangelicals strengthened and consolidated their power through a coalition that became known as the religious right—composed of various right-wing Christian organizations, including fundamentalists and Pentecostals. In 1979 the fundamentalist preacher Jerry Falwell created the hugely influential Moral Majority, which supported "family values" and opposed abortion, gay rights, pornography, and the Equal Rights Amendment to the U.S. Constitution (which, if ratified by the necessary thirty-eight states, would provide equal rights to all citizens regardless of sex). This group was buoyed by the election of Ronald Reagan in 1980 and was joined by Focus on the Family, the Christian Coalition, Concerned Women for America, and the Eagle Forum. These organizations have reached hundreds of millions of voters.

Right-wing pastors are politically influential, especially when their pulpits stand in megachurches (which can attract up to fifty thousand worshippers on Sundays). "There is an expectation that if you're Christian, you are Republican," says thirty-eight-year-old Christine, a born-again mother of two in small-town North Carolina, the heart of the Bible Belt. "When the first Bush ran against Clinton in 1992, I walked out of several churches because the pastors were telling people to vote for Bush. During the 2004 election we put up a John Kerry sign on our lawn. I had never done anything like that before—I never put bumper stickers on my car—but I wanted to get people to think for themselves. I wanted Christians to know that they don't have to be

Republican. Anyway, the pastor of one of the biggest churches in town, who lives across the street from us, drove up and just stopped and stared at our sign. He never really talked with us again after that. He probably thinks, Oh, I guess they're not Christian."

Evangelical pastors consistently use their pulpits to proselytize politically. Caitlyn, twenty-nine, grew up Southern Baptist and is now Episcopalian. When she was in high school in Atlanta, she says, "we had a pastor who talked about the 'demon-crats' and who criticized President Clinton and even said cruel things about Chelsea Clinton. My parents are very strong Democrats even though they are very devout Southern Baptists, so I grew up hearing that as a good Christian, I should take care of the poor and take care of the environment. What I heard from the pulpit was a real disconnect." In 2008 a right-wing evangelical organization called the Alliance Defense Fund recruited fifty pastors to deliver sermons that endorse political candidates, even though doing so violates tax exemption rules.

There are diverse points of view, to be sure. Evangelicals today tend to skew younger, more financially comfortable, and better educated than twenty-five years ago. In addition to the EEWC, there are other organizations founded on the premise that evangelicalism and social justice are inherently linked. The Evangelical Environmental Network claims that environmental problems are ultimately spiritual problems, and that Christians must solve environmental threats. Call to Renewal, together with *Sojourners* magazine, works to overcome poverty. "Evangelicals come in a continuum that runs the political gamut from extreme left to extreme right," points out Virginia Ramey Mollenkott, an author on feminism, gender, and evangelicalism and a leading figure in the EEWC. "What Christian evangelicals have in common is the conviction that meaningful living requires a direct personal relationship with God, and that the Bible should be taken seriously. But what that means can differ widely, and our social attitudes differ tremendously."[4]

Concerned that the word "evangelical" has become synonymous with a politically right-wing agenda, a group of prominent evangelicals circulated an "Evangelical Manifesto" in May 2008. Its purpose, said the document's drafters, was a "call to reform—an urgent challenge to reaffirm Evangelical identity, to reform Evangelical behavior, to reposition Evangelicals in public life, and so rededicate ourselves to the high calling of being Evangelical followers of Jesus Christ."[5] The manifesto was signed by a broad spectrum of evangelical leaders, including those on the political left (such as the author and editor Jim Wallis) and the political right (such as James Tonkowich, president of the Institute on Religion and Democracy). But its predominant message was that evangelicals have become too involved in conservative politics. It distinguished between fundamentalists (code for the religious right) and evangelicals. The document states,

> Fundamentalism has become an overlay on the Christian faith and developed into an essential modern reaction to the modern world. As a reaction to the modern world, it tends to romanticize the past, some now-lost moment in time, and to radicalize the present, with styles of reaction that are personally and publicly militant to the point where they are sub-Christian . . .
>
> Fundamentalism . . . all too easily parts company with the Evangelical principles, as can Evangelicals themselves, when they fail to follow the great commandment that we love our neighbors as ourselves, let alone the radical demand of Jesus that his followers forgive without limit and love even their enemies.[6]

More than anything else, the manifesto is evidence that evangelicals are divided between the old-school political conservatives and the younger adherents who are also interested in politics but in a broader and more sophisticated way.

Still, evangelicals are largely Republican. In 2004 they accounted for 40 percent of the votes cast for George W. Bush. In 2008 60 percent of young white evangelical registered voters identified themselves as Republican or leaning Republican.[7] The Republican-evangelical connection remains tight. Tellingly, Richard Land, head of the public policy arm of the Southern Baptist Convention, the largest Protestant denomination in the United States and very closely aligned with George W. Bush, did not sign the Evangelical Manifesto.

From the point of view of women's religious equality, the history of evangelicalism and fundamentalism looks like a gender tug-of-war. Women in these communities actually *have* held significant leadership roles; therefore the men who subsequently seized power have had to be especially aggressive in keeping the ladies in line. The fact is that for many years women *were* the face of evangelical Protestantism. During the revivalist periods, women claimed that the Holy Spirit had infused them and called them to spread the gospel; although the men placed limitations on women, they didn't stop them. In 1754 Methodist leader John Wesley allowed women to preach, but only if they were "under the extraordinary impulse of the Spirit"; they were also not permitted to speak in uninterrupted, lengthy sermons.[8] The Second Great Awakening coincided with industrialization and the carving of the social world into the male public sphere and the female private sphere, but Christian women claimed they were gripped with evangelical fervor. Thus they shrewdly managed to break free of domestic confinement (although they continued to bear responsibility for safeguarding the home) and entered the public realm. In the mid- and late 1800s, women rose to prominence as missionaries, pastors, preachers, Bible teachers, and social activists. Again, they had to be mindful always to conform to ladylike conduct, but they did penetrate the stained-glass ceiling of their time. In fact, most Bible institutes admitted female students into their ministerial programs and taught them how to prepare and deliver sermons.

By the twentieth century, however, the men of the newly emergent fundamentalist movement became determined to put the brakes on women's leadership. Threatened by women's power within the churches, they decided to reshape their religion as unquestionably masculine. In the 1920s, when American women gained the right to vote and enjoyed postwar economic prosperity, fundamentalist men invoked Scripture to claim that women needed to obey men. Theological schools instituted restrictive quotas for female students; those who managed to be accepted were steered toward "feminine" work, such as teaching children.[9]

Meanwhile, fundamentalists developed an emphasis on "inerrancy." Protestants believed in the centrality of the Bible, but by the 1920s there was a new belief: that the Bible was completely without error and infallible, not only regarding religious issues such as faith and salvation but also regarding science and history. The Bible was to be understood as literally true. The sociologist Nancy Ammerman explains inerrancy in her book *Baptist Battles* as the belief that "the Red Sea really became dry land, and Jonah really spent three days in the belly of a great fish." She quotes the prominent Southern Baptist preacher Jerry Vines:

> I'll tell you what I believe. If these fellows with their television cameras had been on the mountain that day they would have seen Jesus leave from a literal mountain, on a literal cloud, through a literal sky, in a literal body, going back to a literal heaven, to sit down on a literal throne. And in a literal body he's coming again. Literally. I really believe it.[10]

Belief in inerrancy is common among both fundamentalists and evangelicals today and tends to dovetail with belief in male headship.[11] Millions upon millions of Americans believe that husbands are the leaders of their families and that wives must play a supporting role. Day to day, the specifics of leadership include getting the family to church on time, leading prayers at mealtimes, and modeling behaviors such as reading the Bible. But in the general sense, leadership equals being "in charge." The husband has the responsibility of making major family decisions—which can be arrived at after discussion with his wife—and then following through with those decisions. As a forty-one-year-old mother told Sally Gallagher,

> He has the main vote. We sit down and we discuss it and I give him my opinion; but whatever we decide, it is ultimately his decision. Sometimes we disagree, but we decided from day one that we would sit down and we would discuss things and he would tell me his ideas and I would give him my ideas and then we would come up with a reasonable solution. But ultimately it would be his decision because he is the head of the house.[12]

To run smoothly, every two-parent household is built on a division of labor: one parent is largely responsible for certain tasks and the other parent takes over for the other tasks. Because of gendered expectations (such as women being better at holding babies and men being better at turning off the fuse box) coupled with financial reality (fathers usually earning more than mothers), most American mothers in nuclear families take on a disproportionate share of nurturing and routine household maintenance, whether or not they work in the labor force; most fathers take on mechanical and outdoor tasks, such as anything involving a toolbox or lawn mower. If you ask most parents to justify their division of labor, they will probably answer that each is doing what he or she does best, or that the arrangement works best for them and their children, or that they don't have a choice, because of their economics. Perhaps in the future things might be different, but this is the way it is now.

But those who believe in headship assert something else: that God wants households run in a certain way. Once God enters the equation, there is no arguing and there is no possibility for change. It doesn't matter what you think about headship—if you don't like it, if you don't agree with it, if it doesn't work in your particular family. To the conservative devout, the only thing that matters is following the wishes of God. Conservative evangelical leaders repeatedly make the point that it makes no difference if Christians *agree* with God's plan; they have to follow it anyway. And these leaders claim to know precisely what God wants. James Dobson, the conservative radio-show host, psychologist, and chairman of the right-wing organization Focus on the Family, who reaches more than two hundred million listeners a day, says that "whether women's activists like it or not, a Christian man is obligated to lead his family to the best of his ability . . . God apparently expects a *man* to be the ultimate decision maker in his family."[13]

Focus on the Family is a powerful media empire with a $100 million a year budget. Its website offers lots of advice on how to put headship into practice. In "How a Husband Should Handle His Wife's Submission," Stormie Omartian tells her male readers that if their wives are having trouble submitting to them, they should remind their wives that submission is really "a matter of trusting in *God* more than trusting in man" and that "a wife will more easily make the choice to submit to her husband if she knows that he has made the choice to submit to the Lord. It will be a sign to her that it is safe to submit to him. And the goal here is to help her, not force her, into proper alignment."[14]

According to Focus on the Family, men and women are inherently different creatures with essentially different and nonoverlapping roles.

In a ten-part series, Masculinity 101, the author Nancy Kennedy claims that "Guys are primarily task and goal oriented," "Guys are competitive," "Guys are cave dwellers when problems strike," and so on.[15] Dobson, for his part, shares with his readers that his wife, Shirley, likes to keep the heat in their home on high, while he prefers it cold. This is crucial information because it demonstrates that "women typically operate at a lower rate of metabolism than men. It is only one of the countless physiological and emotional differences between the sexes." He continues:

> It is important to understand some of the other ways men and women are unique if we hope to live together in harmony. Genesis tells us that the Creator made two sexes, not one, and that He designed each gender for a specific purpose. Take a good look at male and female anatomy and it becomes obvious that we are crafted to "fit" together. This is not only true in a sexual context but psychologically as well. Eve, being suited to his particular needs, was given to Adam as "help-meet." How unfortunate has been the recent effort to deny this uniqueness and homogenate the human family! It simply won't square with the facts.[16]

Actually, Dobson is the one who doesn't "square with the facts." He omits the key information that Genesis offers *two* creation stories. In the first chapter of Genesis, man and woman are created at the same time. It's only in the second creation story, recounted in the second chapter, that Eve is created to be a companion to Adam. So Shirley's preference for a well-heated home must go back to the second creation story, since the first is a pesky nuisance in the explanation of male difference and superiority.

Even in households in which both the husband and wife work outside the home, the expectation among "headship" believers is that the wife does all the laundering, housecleaning, meal planning, cooking, grocery shopping, diaper changing, child raising—and in many cases, clothes sewing and homeschooling. At Southwestern Baptist Theological Seminary, a homemaking major is open only to women. Some of the classes are taught by Dorothy Patterson, the wife of the seminary's president. One student, Emily Felts, reports that her relatives want her to become a lawyer, and that in fact she could be a good lawyer—but she prefers to master homemaking. "My created purpose as a woman is to be a helper," she told the *Los Angeles Times*. "This is a college education that I can use." Whether or not she wants to become a lawyer is beside the point. "It really doesn't matter what I think. It matters what the Bible says."[17]

If you believe the Bible is the word of God, but you also believe that male headship is wrong, what do you do? You sit down, crack open your beloved copy of the good book, and reread it carefully to see if God, through the church's early leaders, really did call for headship. You examine the evidence from the text, you reflect on the overarching messages contained within, you take into account the historical circumstances of the era in which it was written, and then you draw conclusions. "A lot of us originally came from fundamentalist roots," remembers Nancy Hardesty, a founding mother of the biblical feminist movement, "so for many of us the Bible is the authoritative source for our issues and the Bible is the way we approach things."

Two women, Hardesty and Letha Dawson Scanzoni, were the first to offer alternative biblical interpretations to mainstream evangelicals. In 1966 the centrist evangelical magazine *Eternity* ran a provocative article by Scanzoni—then a freelance writer, author of three books, and wife of an Indiana University sociologist—on "Women's Place: Silence or Service?" She questioned why evangelical churches allowed women to proselytize but not to teach classes with male students. Two years later the magazine published a second piece by Scanzoni in which she argued for partnership, not headship, in marriage, and she offered biblical support for her argument. This time, *Eternity* ran not only the article but also a photo of Scanzoni with her husband and children. "This was something the magazine never did," recalls Hardesty, who was an assistant editor there. "We seldom even published pictures of authors. But in this case the managing editor apparently felt we needed photographic proof that Letha was a 'normal' wife and mother!" Hardesty had been the one to arrange for the photo, and through their communication they became fast friends. Like Scanzoni, Hardesty was unconvinced that the Bible advocated women's subordination to men.

At the time, Scanzoni was busy writing an outline for a book, grounded in evangelical beliefs, demonstrating that the Bible supports the full equality of women and men at home and within the church. She turned to her new friend and asked if she would coauthor it. "It was a turning point in my life," says Hardesty. "She was living in Indiana, and I had just left Philadelphia, where *Eternity* was located, to teach in Illinois. I went to her home in Indiana and we basically divided up the chapters. We knew we would be compatible." They worked on their book at the same time that Billy Graham told the *Ladies' Home Journal* that "wife, mother, homemaker—this is the appointed destiny of real womanhood."[18]

I met Scanzoni and Hardesty in Charlotte in 2006 and was struck by their similarity in appearance. Both women, now scholars in their sixties who have published multiple influential books that have changed countless lives, have short hair and glasses; they have warm eyes and friendly smiles; and they wear the loose, comfortable knits that are imperative for those who are always dashing off to worship, deliver a lecture, or pull down a book from a library shelf. These two women, who seamlessly coresearched and cowrote their book *All We're Meant to Be: A Biblical Approach to Women's Liberation* from 1969 to 1972, are evidently in sync with one another.

As they searched for a publisher, left-of-center evangelicals were forming a social justice movement. Ron Sider and Jim Wallis, then emerging leaders, wanted to bring an evangelical perspective to the work of equalizing people across races, ethnicities, and social classes and to counter the growing strength of right-wing evangelicals. (The religious right at that time was in gestation.) But women's rights were an afterthought, as they were with the secular New Left of the late 1960s. In 1973, fifty evangelicals met at a run-down YMCA in Chicago over Thanksgiving weekend to discuss social issues and to form a new organization, later named Evangelicals for Social Action (ESA).

Nancy Hardesty, then a doctoral student in the history of Christianity at the University of Chicago Divinity School, was one of only five or six women invited.[19] "The convening committee—all male—had prepared a draft of a statement for the group's consideration. It included lengthy paragraphs on racism, poverty, economic justice, and militarism, but no mention of women at all," she recalls. "Eventually I raised my hand and pointed this out." A member of another all-male committee given the responsibility of redrafting the statement leaned over to Hardesty and whispered, "Give me something to add to the statement and I'll try to get it in." Quickly she scribbled on a scrap of paper: "We acknowledge that we have encouraged men to prideful domination and women to passive irresponsibility. So we call both men and women to mutual submission and active discipleship." With one minor change ("passive irresponsibility" morphed into "irresponsible passivity"), her sentences were adopted and became part of the statement, known as the Chicago Declaration. Sider later asked Billy Graham to sign the statement, but he refused because of those two sentences.

Hardesty remembers with a sly chuckle that she shrewdly volunteered to be the secretary of the planning committee that organized the second conference. "As we say in the South, my momma didn't raise no fool!" Given the task of inviting people who qualified in some way as being "evangelical leaders," she made sure that thirty women, including Letha Dawson Scanzoni, attended the second conference, in 1974. Hardesty chaired a women's group, the "evangelical women's caucus," which called for nonsexist language in Christian educational materials, equal pay for equal work in Christian institutions, and endorsement of the Equal Rights Amendment. The women decided that their caucus needed a conference of its own, which was planned for the following year.

The timing was so perfect that it seemed God must have arranged it: just a few months before the 1974 ESA gathering where the Evangelical Women's Caucus was formed, *All We're Meant to Be* was published by Word Books. Publicity for the book led Anne Eggebroten and others to read it, contact Scanzoni, and attend the conference. In their book, Scanzoni and Hardesty demonstrated, clearly and patiently, that Christianity supports full equality for women. They introduced readers to what is now called a "hermeneutics of suspicion"—the method of examining the Bible from an alternate point of view that is not the dominant one through a questioning of underlying presuppositions. (The phrase "hermeneutics of suspicion" was coined by the

French philosopher Paul Ricoeur in 1970 in reference to Marx, Nietzsche, and Freud, but it became widely used among biblical feminist scholars after the theologian Elisabeth Schüssler Fiorenza adopted it in 1984.)

Scripture has been misunderstood, Scanzoni and Hardesty claimed, leading to teachings that are incorrect. Instead of jettisoning the Bible because of the antiwoman messages extracted from it, they have chosen to take it seriously as the word of God.

> We believe that all who would call themselves Christians must grapple with the Bible. We must take seriously the Scriptures as we find them, primarily because they represent the central locus of authority in the Christian tradition. To depart too far afield from Scripture and church tradition is to create one's own religion. Thus while we understand some feminists' attempts to resurrect goddess worship, we choose to stay within the Judeo-Christian tradition.[20]

Passages that have been interpreted as limiting women have been wrongly understood as normative and universal commands, they argued, rather than provisional regulations for specific populations within a specific situation. For example, many Christians agree that some practices accepted in the Bible no longer apply today, such as the right to own slaves. Some teachings are also culture based, noted Scanzoni and Hardesty. For example, Paul declared in 1 Timothy that women may not braid their hair or wear gold or pearls, yet nearly all Christians today find it perfectly acceptable to wear braids, gold, and pearls. Christians, like Muslims and Jews, determine which passages in their sacred texts they consider prescriptive and timeless and which ones they understand as descriptive and limited to the era in which they were written. The Bible contains countless admonitions and guidelines, so by necessity anyone looking to glean meaning must isolate the overarching values and place *those* as timeless, the two women argued. Jesus preached equality of all people and never even hinted that women were subordinate to men, so Christians today should follow his example.

Scanzoni and Hardesty also looked closely at biblical language, turning words around to discover hidden meanings. When Paul declared that a man is the "head" of a woman, for example, he used the Greek word *"kephale."* Scanzoni and Hardesty argued that *kephale* does not mean "authority over," but rather "source" (in reference to Eve having been created out of Adam's rib). They supported their argument with other statements made by Paul, such as Galatians 3:28, that "there is no longer male and female; for all of you are one in Christ Jesus." (In later editions of their book, they argued that *kephale* does mean "head," in the simple sense of being in conjunction with "body," as a metaphor for unity in the human race, in marriage, in one's spiritual relationship with Christ, and in the church. Without that union, a person dies, a marriage is dead, one is spiritually lifeless, and the church is no longer alive.)

"Jesus himself reinterpreted the Hebrew Scriptures from a theological perspective that sometimes conflicted with the theological leaders of his day, the Pharisees and the Sadducees," they reminded their readers. "Never was Jesus satisfied merely to repeat traditional interpretations of Scripture; he constantly sought to uncover fresh meanings and new insights that had escaped others. He revealed the heart of God's message to his hearers."[21]

Immediately *All We're Meant to Be* was recognized as brilliant and paradigm altering. It received the book-of-the-year award in 1975 from *Eternity* magazine. Christian stores couldn't stock it fast enough, so the publisher had to keep printing more copies. *All We're Meant to Be* was so influential that twenty-two years later, the flagship evangelical magazine *Christianity Today* honored it as one of the "top 50 books that have shaped evangelicals" (ranked Number 23). "We didn't really know how big it would be," Hardesty tells me. "We knew that some liberal Catholic women and Protestant women were starting to agitate and write on these issues, but this was the first book within the evangelical world that dealt with feminism."

Social movements have a habit of bubbling over practically overnight, and this one was no exception. Biblical feminism was boiling in different corners of the evangelical world. Lucille Sider Dayton launched and edited a biblical feminist journal, *Daughters of Sarah*, that grew out of her Bible-study group. She and her study partners collected thirty dollars to pay postage and copying, and they mailed two hundred copies of their first issue to friends and acquaintances as well as to names collected by Hardesty in her role as secretary of the ESA planning committee. The response was so overwhelmingly positive that they continued publishing articles on controversial topics— divorce, incest, abortion, prostitution—always from an evangelical point of view. (The journal was later edited by Reta Halteman Finger, and it folded in 1996.) Meanwhile, the prominent theologian Paul Jewett wrote *Man as Male and Female*, which argued that Paul had been mistaken when he called for women's subordination to men. The author Patricia Gundry wrote *Woman Be Free*, also about Christian women as second-class citizens, and the renowned John Milton scholar Virginia Ramey Mollenkott wrote *Women, Men, and the Bible*, which suggested that New Testament comments about women must be understood within their historical context and not be considered eternally binding. A movement of women and men who were serious about Scripture and equally serious about inclusiveness was under way.

The Evangelical Women's Caucus held its first independent gathering on Thanksgiving weekend of 1975 in Washington, D.C. (Only years later did the organization change its name to the Evangelical *and Ecumenical* Women's Caucus.) Three hundred and sixty women came to attend lectures and workshops on the topic of women's liberation in the church. Mollenkott delivered the keynote speech, in which she claimed that the Bible is a product of a patriarchal culture and that its patriarchal elements are not authoritative in the present day.

Many evangelicals were outraged by the idea that the Bible promotes gender equality rather than male domination. They accused biblical feminists of denying God's authorship of the Bible, a claim that Gundry called "an all-purpose silencer."[22] Conservative opponents also made the accusation that biblical feminists were more influenced by the secular world—and feminism in particular—than they were by the authority of Scripture. But Scanzoni insists, "We did not become feminists and then try to fit our Christianity into feminist ideology. We became feminist because we were Christians."[23] Many women who secretly supported the EWC were afraid to join up, for fear that their conservative husbands, pastors, friends, or employers would be dismissive or punitive.

They were not wrong in thinking so. When Scanzoni's initial article, "Woman's Place: Silence or Service?" was published, in 1966, one *Eternity* reader wrote in to question why Scanzoni couldn't understand Paul's "simple rules" against "overambitious" women studying the Bible; another letter writer suggested that the article should have been titled "Woman's Place: Silence *in* Service." A third opined that "most women seem to be incapable of consistent logic when their emotions are involved."[24] A decade later, Paul Jewett was censured at Fuller Theological Seminary for his controversial book; Gundry's husband, who taught at the conservative Moody Bible Institute in Chicago, was asked to resign.

"We faced a lot of challenges," Hardesty sighs. Hecklers would interrupt her when she gave public lectures or would interrogate and contradict her during the question-and-answer period. "At first we were very defensive, whether or not we appeared so. I never felt I was wrong, and spiritually I always felt sure of what I was saying, and right that women were equal and should be treated as equal. But it was also hard because as women we're taught that we should be nice and people should like us—and it was clear that a lot of people didn't like us, and still don't!"

The organization's second conference was held in 1978 and cosponsored by Fuller Theological Seminary in Pasadena, California, where members of the faculty led many of the seminars. One thousand people attended. The organization put forth a statement of faith:

> We believe that God, the Creator and Ruler of all, has been self-revealed as the Trinity. We believe that God created humankind, female and male, in the divine image, for fellowship with God and one another. We further believe that because of human sinful disobedience, the right relationship with God was shattered, with a consequent disruption of all other relationships. We believe that God in love has made possible a new beginning through the Incarnation, in the life, death and resurrection of Jesus Christ, who was, and is, truly divine and truly human. We affirm a personal relationship with Jesus Christ as Savior and Lord. We believe that under Christ's headship and through the work of the Holy Spirit we are freed to exercise our gifts responsibly in our churches, home and society. We believe that the

Bible which bears witness of Christ is the Word of God, inspired by the Holy Spirit, and is the infallible guide and final authority for Christian faith and life. We believe the church is the community of women and men who have been divinely called to fellowship with God and one another to seek and do God's will, looking forward to God's coming glorious kingdom.[25]

This was a heady time for biblical feminists. Women and men who felt a close relationship with Jesus Christ but were dissatisfied with the rhetoric of male domination now had a community of their own.

Internal disagreement about homosexuality, however, divided the Evangelical Women's Caucus in 1986. In solidarity with the lesbian members of the organization, Anne Eggebroten proposed a motion urging civil rights for gay men and lesbians. The motion passed, but some members believed that homosexuality was forbidden according to Scripture. They wanted their biblical feminism to focus exclusively on issues of male headship, full stop. These members also wanted to maintain legitimacy within the conservative evangelical world; they worried that association with an organization promoting gay rights would tarnish them. Therefore, they disassociated from the caucus. Led by Catherine Clark Kroeger, an expert on classical Greek language and literature, in 1987 these former caucus members created a new organization, Christians for Biblical Equality (CBE). In 1990 CBE published a statement in *Christianity Today*, "Men, Women, and Biblical Equality," which laid out the biblical rationale for gender equality. The organization has since eclipsed EEWC in popularity. (CBE claims two thousand members and an additional two thousand individuals connected to the organization in some way; EEWC in its heyday boasted the same number of members, but today the roster is down to well less than a thousand.)

CBE embraces gender equality within a traditionalist perspective. Aside from its rejection of gay men and lesbians, the organization also eschews the term "feminist." It has ties with influential evangelical organizations such as the National Association of Evangelicals and the Lausanne Committee for World Evangelization. The CBE Statement of Faith declares commitment to the belief "in the equality and essential dignity of men and women of all ethnicities, ages, and classes" and states that "all persons are made in the image of God and are to reflect that image in the community of believers, in the home, and in society." It also declares that "as mandated by the Bible, men and women are to oppose injustice." But in all other respects, the Statement of Faith is theologically conservative—in its beliefs about the Bible, the Trinity, human sin, and salvation. It also pointedly reads, "We believe in the family, celibate singleness, and faithful heterosexual marriage as God's design."[26]

Most evangelicals have not heard of EEWC or CBE, but they have been influenced by them. The wider evangelical world has stealthily accommodated a good number of the core beliefs of these organizations. For instance, today many evangelical wives work in the labor force, even when their children are young. Since its censure of Jewett, Fuller Theological Seminary has changed course and endorsed biblical feminism by allowing lecturers to bring this perspective into the classroom and requiring students to use gender-inclusive language. There is certainly more critical awareness of gender roles. Conservative Christian women who reject male headship feel freer to formulate their own ideas about how their households should be run. "Sometimes the result is a creative blending of traditionalism and feminism," writes Julie Ingersoll, the religious studies professor and author, "often backed by Christians who feel no need to choose between the two."[27]

Supposedly the ideology of male domination has been softened into a belief in what the sociologist Sally Gallagher terms "complementary interdependence"—that women and men are essentially different but are partners who complement each other. Gallagher calls this "pragmatic egalitarianism." According to her research on 429 self-identified evangelicals, more than 90 percent claimed in a written survey to believe that the "husband should be the head of the family," with half saying that headship means "final authority."[28] But at the same time, 87 percent claimed that marriage should be an equal partnership. This contradiction, Gallagher explains, demonstrates that evangelicals are merely paying lip service to male headship and that they don't truly live it out in their private lives. Moreover, she believes that feminist ideas about egalitarian marriages have led evangelical fathers to take on a more active parenting role than in previous generations and to be more affectionate and attentive with their children.

But the concept of complementary interdependence can serve as a ruse, a way to keep male headship intact but undercover—which may be more insidious than being out in the open. And isn't it possible that the opposite of Gallagher's hypothesis is true—that evangelicals are merely paying lip service to egalitarianism, not to male headship? Gallagher admits that after interviewing her research subjects in person, she discovered that only 5 to 10 percent truly held egalitarian views on marriage.[29] Looking at the organizations devoted to advancing complementary interdependence, I'm not surprised: many appear to use the phrase simply to get women off their backs. They appear to have no intention of participating in equal partnership with women.

Promise Keepers, a hugely influential evangelical organization in the 1990s, was a response to biblical feminists that has advocated a "muscular" yet "tender" masculinity. Founded by Bill McCartney, the University of Colorado football coach, and supported financially by James Dobson's Focus on the Family as well as other right-wing evangelical organizations, Promise Keepers was known for its men-only events at football stadiums; they resembled revivals, with chants, hymns, and "We love Jesus, yes we do!" cheers. (Because of mismanagement and financial difficulties, the organization exists today purely through local chapters and does not have a national presence.) Its purpose was to reclaim masculinity by emulating the warrior aspects of God while remaining sensitive and caring so that Christian men could become better husbands and fathers.

And how are men supposed to reclaim their manly nature? By following the advice of Tony Evans, who offers a detailed script:

> Sit down with your wife and say something like this: "Honey, I've made a terrible mistake. I've given you my role. I gave up leading this family, and I forced you to take my place. Now I must reclaim that role."
>
> Don't misunderstand what I am saying here. I'm not suggesting that you *ask* for your role back, I'm urging you to *take it back*. If you simply ask for it, your wife's likely to say, "Look, for the last ten years, I've had to raise these kids, look after the house, and pay the bills. I've had to get a job and still keep up my duties in the home. I've had to do my job *and* yours. You think I'm just going to turn everything back over to you?"
>
> Your wife's concerns may be justified. Unfortunately, there can be no compromise here. If you're going to lead you must lead. Be sensitive. Listen. Treat the lady gently and lovingly. But *lead*![30]

It's no wonder that women were forbidden from entering the football arenas in which Promise Keeper events were held. No doubt they would have stormed the fields in disgust.

Another organization, the Council on Biblical Manhood and Womanhood (CBMW), was founded to counter biblical feminism. John Piper, the senior pastor of Bethlehem Baptist Church in Minneapolis, and Wayne Grudem, a theology professor at Trinity Evangelical Divinity School in Deerfield, Illinois, teamed up in 1987 with several other evangelical leaders in Danvers, Massachusetts. They created a "Danvers Statement," summarizing their need for the CBMW, which several years later was expanded into the book *Recovering Biblical Manhood and Womanhood: A Response to Evangelical Feminism*, a densely packed tome of 566 pages. The book refutes the claims to women's equality advanced by Scanzoni, Hardesty, Gundry, and their CBE peers, and it uses Scripture to demonstrate that men and women have different but complementary roles. Men lead, and women submit, but because Piper and Grudem use the term "complementary," they imply that women have nothing to complain about. After all, isn't "complementary" better than "dominating"?

On paper it does look better. But put into practice, complementary roles is just another phrase for unreconstructed male headship. This is made perfectly clear by the contributor Raymond C. Ortlund, Jr., an ordained minister and Bible professor at Trinity Evangelical Divinity School, who says that both "male-female equality and male headship, properly defined, were instituted by God at creation and remain permanent, beneficent aspects of human existence." His definition of male-female equality: "Man and woman are equal in the sense that they bear God's image equally." So far, so good. But here is his definition of male headship: "In the partnership of two spiritually equal human beings, man and woman, the man bears the primary responsibility to lead the partnership in a God-glorifying direction."[31] How is the marriage a "partnership" if one is the leader and the other is de facto the follower?

Editor John Piper adds a psychological dimension in his description of "mature" men and women:

At the heart of mature masculinity is a sense of benevolent responsibility to lead, provide for and protect women in ways appropriate to a man's differing relationships. At the heart of mature femininity is a freeing disposition to affirm, receive and nurture strength and leadership from worthy men in ways appropriate to a woman's differing relationships.[32]

Male leadership extends, of course, to sexual relations. Piper warns women not to initiate sex with their husbands, although they may signal interest. It is up to the man to "lead in a way as only a man can, so that she can respond to him." He is particularly repulsed sexually by physically strong women:

Consider what is lost when women attempt to assume a more masculine role by appearing physically muscular and aggressive. It is true that there is something sexually stimulating about a muscular, scantily clad young woman pumping iron in a health club. But no woman should be encouraged by this fact. For it probably means the sexual encounter that such an image would lead to is something very hasty and volatile, and in the long run unsatisfying. The image of a masculine musculature may beget arousal in a man, but it does not beget several hours of moonlight walking with significant, caring conversation. The more women can arouse men by doing typically masculine things, the less they can count on receiving from men a sensitivity to typically feminine needs.[33]

Piper acknowledges that there are times when it just can't be avoided: a man is going to have to be led by a woman—though I pray for his sake that when this happens, she does not have "masculine musculature." He provides the example of "a housewife in her backyard" who is asked by a man how to get to the freeway. It is her responsibility, he intones, "to direct the man [so] that neither of them feels their mature femininity or masculinity compromised."[34] In general, however, women are not to hold positions of authority in any institution, religious or otherwise, because men should not be placed in a role in which they expect to be subordinate to a woman. *Christianity Today* chose this as its book of the year in 1993.

On the one hand, the very existence of CBMW signals a victory of sorts for biblical feminists. The folks at CBMW are on the defensive, always reacting against the feminists in their midst. In fact, Wayne Grudem's recent book, published in 2004, is titled *Evangelical Feminism and Biblical Truth*—another reactionary work. On the other hand, male headship is still intact. It's all around us. One newlywed husband told Ingersoll that he decided to practice headship by taking complete responsibility for the family's finances. He did not allow his wife to have access to their checking account. Every time she needed money, she had to come to him and explain what she needed it for; if he agreed the expenditure was legitimate, he would give her the amount he thought she needed.[35]

She may be an extreme example, but Andrea Yates shows us that male headship can wreck and literally end lives.[36] In 2001 Yates drowned her five children in their bathtub. She was the murderer, it's true, not her husband—but he shoulders much of the responsibility. Rusty Yates controlled his wife's life absolutely. Before they married, Andrea Kennedy (who was raised Catholic) had been valedictorian of her high school class, worked as a nurse, and had a social life. When she dated Rusty, they studied Bible together and became involved in a fundamentalist community that insisted that women were good for only one thing: having and raising children. The two married and did not use birth control; they wanted to bear as many children as God would give them. In eight years of marriage, Andrea Yates had five children and one miscarriage, and she suffered from postpartum depression. After their first child, she gave up her job. A few years later she began homeschooling her kids.

Rusty Yates, who insisted that as the head of the household he make all the decisions, moved the family out of their four-bedroom house and into a motor home that had been converted from a bus. That's right: Andrea Yates homeschooled her children inside a bus. She was also busy baking cakes and chicken potpie, sewing costumes, and doing all the other ceaseless, thankless work of full-time motherhood—with no babysitter to ease some of the burden. She lost touch with her friends and relatives and became convinced that she was a terrible mother: a traveling evangelist had persuaded her that as a descendant of the sinful Eve, she was inherently bad. After she attempted suicide—twice—her husband finally agreed that they could move back into a house.

But it was too late. When the police found her after she had murdered her children, she told one of the officers that she had planned the act ever since she had "realized I have not been a good mother to them," and quoted Matthew 18:6, which instructs anyone who causes children to sin to put "a great millstone" around her neck and be "drowned in the depth of the sea." Anne Eggebroten, in an essay on the tragedy, observes that in the eyes of Andrea Yates, killing her children was actually a merciful and selfless act because it would send them to heaven, where they would be saved, for if they lived to the age of accountability and were influenced by her "bad" mothering, they would end up in hell. Andrea Yates knew that in the state of Texas she would be executed, which is exactly what she wanted. She believed that she did not deserve to live. She told the doctors that she wanted her hair cut and cropped in the shape of a crown to emulate the "crown of life" Jesus promised those who were faithful (2 Timothy 4:8, Revelation 2:10).

Andrea Yates was mentally ill, to be sure. When she committed the murders, she was taking antidepressants and antipsychotic drugs. Nevertheless, millions of perfectly sane women are also oppressed by male headship. Her story sheds light on what can result from a marriage with an all-controlling husband. No one who espouses male headship believes that a husband should *completely* control his wife, but the distinction between being in charge and being abusive can be subtle. And when a husband abuses his power, who is there to stop him? Moreover, women may internalize their submissiveness, policing themselves and becoming reluctant to stand up to abuse, fearful of God as well as their husband. Many women end up doing what they think God would want, ignoring what they themselves want or what is rational or sane.

"There are a lot of stay-at-home moms here in North Carolina, and that's their job," says Christine, who was raised in a conservative evangelical family and is unsure whether she wants to continue using the label "evangelical" to describe herself today, a mother of two at age thirty-eight. "A lot of the men don't do anything. They come home and then go out to poker night. They could help out at home, but they don't. And I connect this with their religious beliefs." She goes on: "All of us are supposed to be servants of God, but women interpret this differently than men do. Women tend to sacrifice themselves. It creates unhealthy boundaries, and it hurts us more. Women are supposed to submit to their husbands. We learn to be people pleasers, but this is detrimental. We think we have to take care of everybody and we have to put ourselves last. We become submissive, and we think that this is what God wants."

Biblical feminism has raised awareness about the dangers of male headship, but without question there is much more work to be done. Emily Wurgler relates to me that when she spoke recently with a pastor about gender roles, he told her, "In Ephesians, God delegated the role of head of household to husbands, and though it may not always correspond to ability, I have to trust his reasoning." When women interpret the Bible for themselves, they develop hermeneutical skills and come to trust their *own* understanding of God's reasoning.

Those who want women to "submit" to men don't limit their vision to matrimony alone. They want female submission institutionalized in schools, churches, and all religious organizations. And in some denominations they are getting what they want. The Southern Baptist Convention (SBC), the single largest Protestant denomination in the United States, with more than sixteen million members, officially calls for women to be treated as second-class citizens in every aspect of their lives. The SBC has enormous political clout and well over $10 billion in assets.[37]

"In my Southern Baptist church growing up, which was fundamentalist," remembers Sheri Shepherd, thirty, "women could not be pastor or deacon. They could teach kids in Sunday school, but they couldn't teach adults unless they were team teaching with their husband. My mom filled in a few times for the music director, but there were other churches we went to that didn't want her to fill that position, so instead they would have a man be music director even if he couldn't read music."

Today's Baptists have their roots in the seventeenth century, when they opposed the church of England. A group of Baptists left England for the British colonies to avoid religious persecution, and in 1639 Roger Williams founded the first colonial Baptist church in Providence, Rhode Island. Baptists were heavily involved in the Great Awakenings in the United States, and in the nineteenth century they became the predominant religious force in the South. They are evan-gelicals: they emphasize the importance of experiencing Jesus in a per-sonal, emotional way. They believe that only those who profess faith in Jesus Christ as their savior will go to heaven, and they take their bap-tism seriously, fully immersing the new Christian in water—but only a child or an adult; no one is baptized as an infant, before being old enough to choose Jesus. Baptists also believe in the absolute authority of Scripture, but they are wary of adopting creeds. Each Baptist church is autonomous, and many Baptists eschew affiliation with any denomination; nevertheless, national organizations such as the South-ern Baptist Convention, founded in 1845, provide a coalition for those churches that do want some unity through a larger structure.

Theologically, Baptists are not necessarily opposed to women's or-dination; they value an individual's relationship with the divine and a personal sense of spiritual calling. In 1964 the first Southern Baptist woman was ordained to the ministry (in North Carolina), and in the following years, many women enrolled in Southern Baptist divinity schools in preparation for ordination. Although their numbers were small, women were poised to become a presence in Southern Baptist ministry.

But in the blink of an eye, everything changed. In 1979 a con-servative faction of the SBC initiated a well-organized effort to elimi-nate moderates from the denomination. At the flagship SBC school, Southern Baptist Theological Seminary in Louisville, Kentucky, mod-erate faculty were asked to leave or resigned throughout the 1980s and 1990s. Faculty members who remained were required to affirm conservative views, not only on the need to accept Jesus in order to achieve salvation but also on three social issues, all related to gender: homosexuality, abortion, and women's ordination. The measuring stick to determine who was orthodox and who was moderate—who was on the conservatives' side and who wasn't—shifted from biblical inerrancy to conservative views on women, according to Julie Inger-soll. Inerrancy was still unquestionably important, but it was no longer part of the litmus test.

At its 1984 convention the SBC passed a resolution opposing the ordination of women with the rationale that the Bible excludes women from pastoral leadership positions and besides, such a ruling would "preserve a submission that God requires because man was first in Creation, and women was first in the Edenic fall."[38] In 1998, the SBC passed an amendment that read, in part:

> The husband and wife are of equal worth before God. Both bear God's image but in differing ways. The marriage relation- ship models the way God relates to his people. A husband is to love his wife as Christ loved the church. He has the God-given responsibility to provide for, to protect, and to lead the family. A wife is to submit graciously to the servant leadership of her husband even as the church willingly submits to the headship of Christ. She, being "in the image of God" as is her husband and thus equal to him, has the God-given responsibility to respect her husband and serve as his "helper" in managing their house- hold and nurturing the next generation.[39]

Although the word "complementary" is not used here, the concept frames this amendment: women are equal to men in the sense that they are created in God's image; nevertheless, they are different. They are assistants and followers, never leaders. It appears that the SBC in- serted language about women's equality purely for show.

And if a woman's husband is wrong about a decision, should his wife graciously submit to his leadership? Why, yes, she should. "As a woman standing under the authority of Scripture, [I do so] even . . . when I know he's wrong," said Dorothy Patterson, the homemaking instructor. She is also a theology professor who served on the commit- tee that wrote the amendment—and, not coincidentally, a member of the board of the Council on Biblical Manhood and Womanhood, and wife of the president of Southwestern Baptist Theological Seminary. "I just have to do it and then he stands accountable at the judgment."[40]

The SBC made its strongest statement against women's leadership at its 2000 convention: it prohibited women from serving as pastors. "While both men and women are gifted for service in the church, the office of pastor is limited to men as qualified by Scripture," the new statement read. The result has been the exclusion of women from SBC seminaries, agencies, and churches except in connection with teaching children or, sometimes, playing music (as long as they aren't "leading"). Baptists not affiliated with the SBC have also been influenced by the new extreme views on women. When Ingersoll interviewed women attending Baptist schools as undergraduates, she found again and again that they were pressured to choose lives as homemakers and to avoid career paths. Those who actually made it to graduate school were doubted, contested, and scorned. "That which would be called sexism in a secular context," she observes, "is often seen as being endorsed by God" in Christian higher education. Not that things get better after grad school: one woman was hired by a church as assistant pastor, only to arrive on her first day to discover that the church bulletin had introduced her as "the new staff person in the office."[41]

Here is the scriptural support for female submission in church:

Women should be silent in the churches. For they are not permitted to speak, but should be subordinate, as the law also says. If there is anything they desire to know, let them ask their husbands at home. For it is shameful for a woman to speak in church. (1 Corinthians 14:34–35)

Let a woman learn in silence with full submission. I permit no woman to teach or to have authority over a man; she is to keep silent. For Adam was formed first, then Eve; and Adam was not deceived, but the woman was deceived and became a transgressor. (1 Timothy 2:11–14)

On the face of it, these passages appear cut-and-dried. But before you denounce female theologians, teachers, and pastors as heretics and Jezebels, you have to know a few facts about the larger biblical context.

These passages, both supposedly written by Paul, have been questioned by nearly all respected biblical scholars. It is very widely believed that Paul supported women's participation in church, as Jesus did, but that later writers or scribes wanted to turn the clock back on women's rights and shrewdly inserted these verses to give them the weight of biblical authority.

Bart Ehrman, an expert on the early church and author of *Misquoting Jesus*, points out what many scholars have known for years: the modern New Testament is riddled with errors not present in the original manuscripts. There are no surviving Greek manuscripts of the New Testament. There aren't any copies at all of manuscripts from the first few centuries of Christianity—they do not exist. As a result, the texts we have today are filled with mistakes, some simple errors made during manual copying, others created deliberately for theological purposes. Paul's letters in particular—and especially the verses pertaining to women within those letters—have undergone serious reassessment. For example, the letter of 1 Timothy is understood to be written not by Paul, but by one of his followers in the second century, using Paul's name.

As for 1 Corinthians, no one doubts that Paul wrote most of the letter, but verses 14:34–35 raise a red flag to scholars because they are placed in different parts of the letter in different manuscripts. It is very possible that the verses were inserted in the wake of the faux 1 Timothy letter. It is also clear that within 1 Corinthians, the verses about women come out of nowhere and break up a section about the role of prophets that otherwise flows seamlessly.[42]

It also appears highly unlikely that Paul intended to prohibit women's leadership; that would contradict so many other passages which no one doubts he wrote. In 1 Corinthians 11:5, Paul *does* permit women to preach in the churches—and why would he contradict himself, especially within the same epistle? In the eleventh chapter Paul is very specific and provides guidelines, saying that women should always wear a head covering while leading public prayer or prophesying. (Ironically, that which Paul permitted—women preachers—is being forbidden today, while that which he forbade—to pray or preach with an uncovered head—is widely permitted.) And remember, Paul also said in Galatians 3:28 that "there is no longer male and female; for all of you are one in Christ Jesus." Moreover, we know that Paul often mentions women serving as church leaders with his approval. According to Ehrman, 1 Corinthians 14:34–35 "was no doubt made by a scribe who was concerned to emphasize that women should have no public role in the church, that they should be silent and subservient to their husbands. This view then came to be incorporated into the text itself, by means of a textual alteration."[43]

Given what scholars today know about the New Testament, it is a stretch for someone to rest his case for female submission on these specific passages, which contradict not only other scriptural passages but indeed the overarching message that Jesus spread of erasing social distinctions. Citing these passages as authentic and true reflects a desire to keep power limited to men, something Jesus would not have approved of.

Rev. Nancy Hastings Sehested grew up in the Southern Baptist Church. "My grandfather was a Southern Baptist minister. My dad was a Southern Baptist minister. This was our tradition going back for a hundred years," she tells me. "No one told me when I was growing up that women couldn't be pastors. I had the calling to tell the 'good news'"—to become a pastor. Her news was not good to the SBC, however, which disfellowshipped her church in 1987 because she, a woman, was the minister. "The greatest hatred I have known comes from people who claim the same redeemer I claim," she comments.

I met Sehested when I attended the Evangelical and Ecumenical Women's Caucus conference in North Carolina. She led a workshop for twenty people, "Doing Justice and Loving Mercy," in which she talked about her current position as chaplain in a maximum-security prison for men. It's hard to imagine Sehested working with murderers and sex offenders. She is petite and delicate-looking, with short, curly honey-colored hair and rimless glasses. The day of the workshop she wore a bright pink cotton skirt, a lavender polo shirt, and thong sandals, adding a backdrop of cheerful colors to the serious, contemplative conversation of the workshop. As we sat in a circle in a small conference room, Sehested discussed the "mark of Cain" in Genesis 4:15—the mark God put on Cain after he had murdered his brother Abel. God placed this mark after giving Cain a curse, in response to Cain's complaint that anyone who found him would kill him. To Sehested, "the mark of Cain is mercy. God marked Cain so that no one would kill him. Mercy should be for everyone, not only those people you think deserve it."

One woman spoke up, an African American Pentecostal pastor. Sehested's comments had particular significance for her. She said that as a child, she was taught that all blacks had been cursed with dark skin color—that they had their own "mark of Cain," their skin color—but it was a curse, not an act of mercy. Everyone silently digested this information, that religious teachings can lead to self-hatred, but alternative religious teachings can lead to love and mercy. I knew at that moment that Sehested had a gift for spreading wisdom.

Sehested is a pivotal figure in the history of women in the Southern Baptist Church.[44] She grew up in Texas and moved to New York City for her education—the City College of New York for her undergraduate degree and Union Theological Seminary for her divinity degree. It was at Union where she saw women in pastoral roles for the first time, and it was there that she felt "called" to serve God in the ministry. She returned to the South, first to Georgia, then to Tennessee. In 1987 a tiny Memphis congregation, Prescott Memorial Baptist Church, the first Baptist church in the city to accept blacks as members and the first to ordain women as deacons, chose her from a field of eighty candidates to be their new pastor. She was thirty-six years old. Her gender might have gone unnoticed, at least for a while, but the president of the SBC at the time, Adrian Rogers, was from Memphis and led a megachurch of seventeen thousand members. "I had moved into Mr. Rogers's neighborhood," Sehested says wryly, "but he did not like me just the way I am."

The executive board of the Memphis-area Baptist association, which represented 120 local churches, investigated Prescott's "doctrinal soundness," and its credentials committee met with Prescott representatives. Prescott had prepared a thirteen-page paper demonstrating with scriptural evidence that women had an important leadership role in church history. "They were really surprised that we had a scriptural basis for calling a woman pastor," said Tom Walsh, who was vice chair of Prescott's board of deacons. "What it shows is that when someone disagrees, they assume that we're not spiritual or that we're not Christian."

One month later the association met behind closed doors. While the motion was being debated, Sehested approached the microphone to speak. The association was following *Robert's Rules of Order*—a widely used parliamentary procedure—and when someone saw her about to speak, he called a motion to close debate. According to Robert's Rules, she was not allowed to speak once this motion had been made. "Too late, too late, you can't speak," the men shouted at her. "As Baptists, we are told that everybody has a voice, and we believe in the priesthood of believers—that we are all equal under God, and that there is not a hierarchy over us," Sehested tells me, recalling that fateful meeting. "The authority is Christ. So I was stunned that they wouldn't at least hear my voice. To me, *that was an incredible violation of the word of God.*"

But Adrian Rogers allowed her to take the microphone, explaining that "out of Christian courtesy" they should "allow the lady to speak." Sehested walked up the aisle to the pulpit, holding her Bible. "At that moment, we were operating outside of *Robert's Rules of Order*, so I didn't have to limit myself to two minutes. And something in me took over. It was an electrifying moment. I knew that for them, my opponents, I was not a human being; I was an issue. I was symbolic of what they did not want and what they wanted to eradicate." She had to make herself real and human to them if she had any chance of persuading them that she could serve as a religious leader.

She spoke extemporaneously for ten minutes. "I am Nancy Hastings Sehested, messenger from Prescott Memorial Baptist Church, pastor of Prescott Memorial Baptist Church, and servant of our Lord Jesus Christ," she told those assembled. She continued:

By what authority do I preach? That question you ask of me. It is not a new question. It is a question that was asked of our Lord Jesus Christ on a number of occasions. He had not the authority of the religious establishment, nor the authority of the state, [but] the authority of none other than the Holy Spirit that moved in his midst.

And by what authority do I preach and bear witness to my faith? By the authority of the Southern Baptist Convention? By the authority of the Shelby County Baptist Association? By the authority of Prescott Memorial Baptist Church?

No. No, my brothers and sisters. By the authority of the Lordship of Jesus Christ, who did not count equality with God a thing to be grasped, but emptied himself, becoming a servant.

And following in his footsteps, as a servant of Jesus Christ, who took the towel and the basin of water and exemplified the kind of servanthood that each one of us is called to live under, I found a towel with my name on it. And each one of us has a towel with our name on it.

And who was it that taught me this wonderful freedom of

the Spirit? My Sunday school teachers. My pastor. My Southern Baptist Church, who nurtured me and said, "God calls each one of us, so listen!" And so I listened.

They never said, "God calls each of you and with God everything is possible, remember, except to be able to stand behind a pulpit. Women can't do that." They never said that. They said, "With all things—God is able to do all things."

The winds of the Spirit blow where they will. And we do not know whither they come and whither they go . . .[45]

Sehested sat down, and the moderator took a vote. She watched while 80 percent of those present voted against her church for choosing a woman, not a man, to serve as their pastor.

Sehested recounted for me this unbelievable moment nineteen years after it had occurred. Listening to her, I had to catch my breath. It seemed so . . . impossible. This had taken place in 1987, after all, years and years after women had gained so many rights within the larger American culture and legal system.

"So let me get this straight," I said to her. "They opposed you not because of your theology, but only because you were female?"

For the first time in our conversation, her soft voice rose. "They didn't know *anything* about my theology! I was just doing pastoral work for this little congregation. And then I became this symbol. It had *nothing* to do with my theology. *Nothing.* It was *purely* because I was a woman. And I had entered the ministry because I felt called by God, *not* to make a statement about women."

She continued. "I got so much hate mail. People called me Jezebel; they called me whore of Babylon. They said that I was the cause of the breakdown of the family. And things have not gotten better for Southern Baptist women since 1987. The issue boils down to power." Her voice became soft again, and she spoke deliberately, choosing each word with enormous care. "I was surprised by how much hatred was spewed out by people claiming allegiance to the same God I do, and in the name of the same God they do harmful and hateful acts. It is tragic that these things happen in the name of God."

Lest you think that what happened to Nancy Hastings Sehested could not or would not happen today, consider that in January 2006, a theology professor in a tenure-track position at Southwestern Baptist Theological Seminary, Sheri Klouda, was told to leave because women are supposedly biblically forbidden to teach men. The president of the board of trustees told the Associated Press that the seminary had been mistaken to hire a woman in the first place. "There was a momentary lax of the parameters," he said, but now the seminary had "returned to its traditional, confessional, and biblical position."[46] Also in 2006 the First Baptist Church in Watertown, New York, voted unanimously to fire the church's eighty-one-year-old Sunday school teacher, who had taught there for fifty-four years, because her students included men.[47]

There is no message of female inferiority or subordination in the New Testament as it was originally written. Passages that seem to lead to subordination may have been created later and then ascribed to Scripture in order to give them the weight of uncontestable authority. Or, as feminist evangelicals argue, the meaning of these passages in their original context may not have been as restrictive as their interpretation today—or not even intended by God as a message for all times and cultures.

"We all want so badly to truly access the divine, to draw near to God," points out Alena Amato Ruggerio, the communication professor. "We're taught in church that the Bible is one of the best means of achieving that goal." For millions upon millions, the Bible *is* the best way to achieve communication with God. But it is impossible to communicate effectively when someone else does all the interpreting.[48]

FIVE

Are Mainline Churches Making Men Less Manly and Women Too Prominent?

Women and men around the world had been waiting for generations for this historic moment. For the first time, a woman was officially recognized as a major religious leader. But those who had hoped that a woman could unite different religious factions will have to keep waiting.

On November 4, 2006, Bishop Katharine Jefferts Schori formally took office as head of the Episcopal Church, the United States arm of the Anglican Communion, which is the third largest Christian body in the world (after the Roman Catholic and Orthodox churches). Wearing vestments reminiscent of Joseph's many-colored coat, with violet, royal blue, green, and a splash of crimson, and carrying the primatial staff (a ceremonial long stick with a stylized cross), she presided over the Holy Eucharist for thousands of Episcopalians gathered at Washington's National Cathedral. On that day, Bishop Schori became the highest-ranking woman in the communion of churches associated with the church of England and led by the archbishop of Canterbury, with eighty million members worldwide. With its dramatic history—created by King Henry VIII when he broke with the pope to annul his marriage with Catherine of Aragon and marry Anne Boleyn—the Anglican Communion is a significant force in world religious affairs. Having a woman in such a visible role is a loud announcement that women, like men, can access the divine.

Bishop Schori was ordained at age forty in 1994 and quickly rose to become bishop of Nevada in 2001 before being elected presiding bishop (the Episcopal term for archbishop) of the entire 2.4-million-member denomination. But her whirlwind rise up through the religious ranks is not the only thing that makes her unique. Before her ordination she was an oceanographer, specializing in squid and octopuses, and she is a licensed pilot who flies small planes. (When she served as the bishop of Nevada, Schori flew her plane from parish to parish, since they were so spread out across the state.) She can literally see the world from different perspectives—that of a sea creature swimming along the current and also of a bird soaring above the clouds.

Unfortunately, not all members of the Episcopal Church wish to look at things from different viewpoints. Her election may very well fracture the already divided church: conservative Episcopalians actively oppose her. This is because Bishop Schori has upheld the rights of gay Episcopalians. In 2003 she supported the consecration of an openly gay bishop, Rev. V. Gene Robinson of New Hampshire, and the blessing of same-sex unions.

Around the world, Anglican leaders are displeased, some outraged. More than a third have curtailed their involvement with the American church. At an international meeting in Tanzania in February 2007, eight archbishops refused to take Communion with Bishop Schori. They issued her an ultimatum: bar gay men and lesbians from becoming bishops and halt the blessing of same-sex unions, or leave the Anglican Communion. One-quarter of the world's bishops boycotted the 2008 Lambeth Conference, which takes place only once every ten years in Canterbury, England, and which Bishop Schori attended. Here in the United States, one-tenth of congregations nationwide have cut their ties with the Episcopal Church, affiliating with conservative Anglican provinces overseas. There is, in effect, a schism.

Bishop Schori's opponents zero in on her support of gay men and lesbians. But the fact that she is female also girds their criticism. "The strength of the reaction by conservatives around homosexuality is partly because of a sense of offense around the ordination of women," says the Anglican expert John L. Kater.[1] In the United States, several Episcopal dioceses do not ordain women. Overseas, many Anglican provinces do not ordain women as priests or deacons, and only three ordain women as bishops. And, as many women in Christian leadership do, Bishop Schori is willing to describe Jesus in language that opens the mind to new metaphors for God. After being elected to presiding bishop, she preached a homily in which she evoked "Our mother Jesus" who "gives birth to a new creation—and you and I are His children."

So far, Bishop Schori has been unflappable. After all, she's been in this water before. "The first time I was chief scientist on a cruise," she explains, "the captain wouldn't speak to me because I was a woman."[2] But as a scientist, Jefferts Schori could prove that she is as intelligent as any man. In the religious realm, intelligence is often beside the point. Heterosexual manliness, it is widely believed, is close to godliness.

Relatively speaking, women in mainline Protestant denominations have it pretty good. Unlike women in the Roman Catholic Church, Eastern Orthodox churches, the Southern Baptist Convention, and smaller fundamentalist groups, women in most of these mainline denominations may be ordained. As they rise through the leadership ranks, they gain a stake in decision making. These denominations— the United Methodist Church, the Evangelical Lutheran Church in America, the Presbyterian Church (U.S.A.), the Episcopal Church, the United Church of Christ, the Christian Church (Disciples of Christ), and the American Baptist Churches USA, among others— emphasize inclusiveness, and therefore they tend to avoid language, rituals, and theology that exclude women.

The United Methodist Church, the largest Protestant denomination in the United States, for instance, in 1992 adopted a resolution, "The Status of Women," that today reads,

> Christianity was born in a world of male preference and dominance. Practices, traditions, and attitudes in almost all societies viewed women as inferior to men, as having few talents and contributions to make to the general well-being of society aside from their biological roles . . . But the life of Jesus, the Redeemer of human life, stood as a witness against such cultural patterns and prejudices. Consistently, he related to women as persons of intelligence and capabilities. He charged women as well as men to use their talents significantly in the cause of God's kingdom. His acts of healing and ministry were extended

without distinction to women and men . . . To regard another as an inferior is to break the covenant of love; denying equality demeans, perpetuates injustice, and falls short of the example of Jesus and the early church.[3]

This resolution is as feminist as you can get. Its message is that Jesus regarded women as equal; therefore Christians should regard women as equals too. Likewise, the Presbyterian Church (U.S.A.) urges its churches to use inclusive language to describe those who worship God (since words like "brotherhood" and "mankind" exclude women and imply that women are not created in the image of God) and to describe God (since masculine terms are simply metaphors, not actual descriptors, and therefore feminine terms could be used too). The church's brochure, "Well-Chosen Words," states that

Inclusive language is needed because words, and the images they invoke, have the power to shape our beliefs and attitudes; male-dominated language creates and reinforces a hierarchical order in which women are regarded as subordinate; [and] words indicate our basic belief and assumptions about ourselves, about others and about God.[4]

For anyone who cares about women's religious equality, these denominations seem to offer a comfortable fit.

In fact, according to conservative critics, many of whom identify as evangelical, women have it *too good* and are included *too much*—leading to a "feminization of Christianity" that repels heterosexual men, driving them away from church services and making them feel "emasculated" and "impotent," while it breeds "radical feminists" who deny a transcendent God and instead worship themselves. The mainlines must become more manly, conservative critics charge, to survive. (A parallel phenomenon of feminization is also said to be occurring in the liberal Jewish denominations.)[5]

Women have long attended church in greater numbers than men, in Europe as well as in our country. In the late 1600s, the Puritan minister Cotton Mather wondered about it.[6] In the mid-1800s, two-thirds of New England churchgoers were women.[7] Since then, the lopsided ratio has not budged: it's still primarily women who get up early on Sunday mornings, wedge their children's feet into shiny dress shoes, smooth down their unruly cowlicks, and hustle them out the door and to church and Sunday school while their husbands may or may not choose to join them. In 1959 Norman Rockwell lampooned lazy dads in his *Saturday Evening Post* cover *Sunday Morning*: it depicted Mother and three children filing out of the house in their Sunday best, Bibles tucked close to their hearts, while Father slumps in a high-backed chair, hiding out in his pajamas, slippers, and bathrobe while reading the newspaper and smoking a cigarette. "Next time you're in church," writes the essayist and author Frederica Mathewes-Green, "count the number of adult heads and divide by the number of pairs of panty hose. If the panty hose contingent makes up more than half the total, there's a word for your church: typical."[8]

The gender gap is accompanied by a steep decline in mainline church attendance in general. In 1968 mainline denominations had more than twenty-six million members comprising more than 13 percent of the U.S. population. By 2003 the mainlines represented 6.8 percent of the population.[9] In the New York City area alone, membership in the mainlines has fallen by 45 percent since 1960. There are a thousand churches in the region for only three hundred thousand members. A third of the United Methodist churches in the region did not add a single new member in 2001, while more than a third of Evangelical Lutheran churches have seventy-five or fewer members. For comparison's sake, in one New York county, five Episcopal parishes served a thousand people in 2000, while five Catholic parishes served fifty-three thousand people.[10]

One reason mainline numbers have been declining is that members tend to have low birthrates, especially compared with Catholics, Eastern Orthodox, and evangelicals. But there are other reasons too. Most mainline Christians are very involved in secular culture and don't feel as strong an urge as their grandparents and great-grandparents felt to attend church and become involved in religious matters. Protestants who are strongly committed to Christian doctrine—the hard-core religious—tend to join evangelical and Pentecostal churches. Indeed, over the last four decades, membership in conservative, evangelical Protestant denominations has risen dramatically. In 1960 there were almost two million more Methodists than Southern Baptists, writes the foreign policy expert Walter Russell Mead, but "by 2003 there were more Southern Baptists than United Methodists, Presbyterians, Episcopalians, and members of United Church of Christ combined."[11] Critics say that mainline churches have lost their religious fervor, replacing the trinity of Father, Son, and Holy Spirit with a new trinity of "peace, justice, and inclusiveness."

This liberal bent, it is argued, appeals to women and effeminate men, not "masculine" heterosexual men. Conservative critics claim that church services are too feminine. They are filled with music, singing, and flowers. They emphasize community and relationships; helping the needy; and a sense of nurturing and inclusiveness of people of different affectional orientations, races, and ethnicities. Doctrine is often considered less important than soup kitchens. If Jesus is depicted at all, he has a slight build, with long, flowing hair and soulful eyes—looking more like a hippie folksinger than a brawny fellow who will build a kingdom of God. In his book *The Church Impotent: The Feminization of Christianity*, Leon Podles complains that "the Methodist Church is a women's club at prayer." He advises churches: "first of all, do not make matters worse. Feminism and homosexual propaganda dominate the liberal churches, and both drive men even further away."[12]

According to the Institute on Religion and Democracy (IRD), an evangelical watchdog organization that monitors and criticizes U.S. mainline churches and seeks to reform them, the churches are definitely in trouble. Alan Wisdom, the vice president for research and programs, writes to me in an e-mail,

> Does the absence of men sap a church of its vitality? Or does a dysfunctional church drive away the men sooner than it does the women? I suspect it's more the latter than the former. I would theorize (without evidence, I'll admit) that men are more impatient than women with institutions (such as churches) that seem to have lost their sense of purpose. When a church isn't clear about what it believes, doesn't articulate any goals for its work, and doesn't seem to be making much of an impact in the lives of its members or in the community, men may be quicker to say, "I don't need to waste my time in this place. I'm out of here." Women may be more inclined to stay for the sake of

cherished personal relationships, even though privately they know that the church is stagnating. But this is just my personal theory.

He suggests that renewing the churches to make them healthier will draw more people, men and women. That would mean putting a greater emphasis on Jesus, prayer, the sacraments, Bible study, pastoral care, and "a greater sense of the presence and power of the Holy Spirit as the motivation for worship and service." Likewise, Podles suggests that churches emphasize the holiness of God—because holiness, which is distinguished by being separate from the non-holy, is a "masculine category," as "men develop their masculine identity by a pattern of separation, both biological and cultural . . . The more transcendent God is, the holier he is and the more masculine he is."[13]

The mainline churches are all about "the meltdown of liberal Christianity," echoes the Beliefnet editor Charlotte Allen. She believes that declining membership is a direct result of liberal thinking. "When your religion says 'whatever' on doctrinal matters, regards Jesus as just another wise teacher, refuses on principle to evangelize and lets you do pretty much what you want, it's a short step to deciding that one of the things you don't want to do is get up on Sunday morning and go to church," she writes. Meanwhile, for the sake of comparison, Allen upholds evangelical and Pentecostal churches that "generally eschew women's ordination" and are "growing robustly."[14]

The historian Ann Douglas, in her book *The Feminization of American Culture*, traces the collapse of "muscular" Protestant religion in this country and the rise of sentimental, "feminine" religiosity, arguing that this phenomenon occurred in tandem with the disestablishment of American religion. Since the United States was created with a separation between church and state, religious affiliation became voluntary. Clergymen therefore felt insecure about their status and future and appealed to another group similarly plagued with feelings of powerlessness: women. By the mid-1800s, the theologian Henry James, Sr., complained that "religion in the old virile sense has disappeared, and been replaced by a feeble Unitarian sentimentality."[15]

Historically, heterosexual Christian men from time to time have asserted their manliness—through "red-meat theology"—to take back their religion from those darned sentimental ladies and emasculated clergymen. From the 1880s through 1920 the "muscular Christianity" movement told men that being a good Christian meant being physically strong and healthy. As we saw with modern evangelical Christians, Promise Keepers and the Council on Biblical Manhood and Womanhood have been engaged in a similar modern crusade. "One day I was sitting in church, and all of a sudden it dawned on me that the target audience of almost everything about church culture was a fifty- to fifty-five-year-old woman," says David Murrow, author of *Why Men Hate Going to Church*. Murrow's mission is to figure out how to get men into the pews. "We don't have to have hand-to-hand combat during the worship service," he reassures. "We just have to start speaking [their language], use the metaphors they understand and create an environment that feels masculine to them," and stop singing what he calls "love songs to Jesus."[16]

A United Methodist men's organization tries to attract manly men. "Men like adventures. Men like challenges. We like in-your-face sermons. We need to be pursuing God on our own, and not expecting the preacher to change our spiritual diaper each Sunday," says Rev. Mark Winter of Fort Worth, Texas. "All week long, we're given projects, goals and challenges by our bosses. We like to sink our teeth into projects. If a pastor can theologize that this is what Jesus did, it stirs men's hearts. We want to be impacting our world for Christ." At the Wesley Memorial United Methodist Church in Columbia, South Carolina, the men's group repairs homes of elderly members and participates in Men Cook with Fire monthly meetings at which the men grill meat and eat it together as they listen to an inspirational speaker.[17]

In mainline seminaries, women now outnumber the men studying for divinity degrees. This stirs fear among conservative critics because it means that clergywomen could become even more visible and powerful in the near future. Rolling back women's gains and "defeminizing" the churches, they argue, will strengthen mainline Protestantism because it will bring back muscular conservatism to the congregations and therefore draw more men to the pews. (The Institute on Religion and Democracy does not oppose women's ordination, as long as the women ordained are theologically conservative.)

Allow me to point out the flaws in this argument. First, there is nothing inherently feminine about such liberal values as inclusiveness, justice, and community. Indeed, these are values that Jesus himself preached. In denigrating these values, are not critics denigrating Jesus himself? Besides, mainline churches embraced liberal values decades before they ordained women. In recent times they became intensely involved in social justice activism during the civil rights movement under the leadership of Rev. Martin Luther King, Jr., but now that female pastors are highly visible, liberal values are attributed to the ladies.

Likewise, there is nothing inherently masculine about the things that "muscular Christians" like to emphasize: religious doctrine, physical activity, grilled meats. I can tell you authoritatively that many women, myself included, find that all three are life enriching. The definition of what is masculine, as with the term "feminine," often varies from culture to culture. In fact, in traditional Jewish and Islamic cultures, men are expected to engage in religious practices that may be considered feminine according to the values of many Christian Americans. Traditional Jewish men are praised and valued for spending time indoors studying Jewish texts—limiting physical activity—and for chanting and singing the words of the Torah. Islamic worship, meanwhile, involves extensive bending and prostrating in submission as well as standing with shoulders touching those of worshippers on either side. And in some circumstances, both traditional Jewish and Muslim men don cloaks that could pass for women's attire. Yet these men are held up as unimpeachably masculine.

There is no reason to believe that stripping women of their vestments and offering barbeque along with the Holy Supper will usher in more men. The mainline churches would still have too much competition from secular and evangelical cultures. Besides, as we have seen, the gender gap in the pews goes back centuries; it is not a new phenomenon and has nothing to do with increased women's rights.

The most troubling aspect of the argument is that anything devalued is named feminine while anything elevated is termed masculine. When conservative critics lament the feminization of churches, they are simply deriding inclusive values that they oppose, often for political reasons. Shrewdly, they label these values feminine because they know that most Americans, including women, want to distance themselves from anything considered "feminine." Just as female-dominated professions (elementary school teaching, nursing) are devalued because women run the show, religion that is said to be female-dominated is likewise debased. Femininity and liberal values are bundled together, allowing them to be belittled simultaneously.

Devaluing of femininity goes hand in hand with denigration of gays and lesbians. (Different Christians interpret the scriptural passages on homosexuality differently, with many unconvinced that gay sexuality is in fact a sin. Regardless, nearly everyone agrees in principle that one should love the sinner even while scorning the sin, just as Jesus did; yet many people do not put this theory into practice.) Gay men, it is believed, are similar to women, while lesbians are defective women (so they don't benefit from the cultural advantages of masculinity). Misogyny and homophobia are thus inextricably linked. Whenever churches seek to curtail the rights of gays and lesbians, they are also seeking to curb the rights of women—and vice versa.

Cotton Mather, who noticed that women attended his Puritan church in higher numbers than men, went on to initiate the Salem witch trials, which led to the execution of fourteen innocent women and six innocent men. Today the word "witch" is discredited, but accusing someone of being a heretic, a pagan, or a goddess worshipper is very much in vogue. The Institute on Religion and Democracy (IRD) has been leading the way in manufacturing panic among conservative evangelical Christians who believe that mainline churches are bewitched by "radical feminist" women.

Created and funded by right-wing secular foundations, the IRD targets progressive Christian policies and structures within the United Methodist, Presbyterian (U.S.A.) and Episcopal churches. Among the financiers of the IRD are the foundations named for Richard Mellon Scaife, Howard Ahmanson, Lynde and Harry Bradley, Adolph Coors, Smith Richardson, Randolph Richardson, and John Olin. The goal of the IRD is to take control of the mainline churches by getting right-wing evangelicals (who oppose women's rights and gay rights) into the top leadership positions within the churches. To achieve this goal, the IRD provides support to right-wing groups within each church, which in turn distort and publicize any and all inclusive measures within the churches. Specifically, the IRD opposes feminism, gay rights, abortion, environmentalism, affirmative action, hate-crime legislation, social welfare, and antiwar measures.

"You're familiar with the right-wing takeover of the Southern Baptist Church?" asks the religious studies professor Rev. Dr. Rebecca Todd Peters of Elon University in North Carolina. "A parallel process has been afoot in the Presbyterian Church for over twenty years. There's a right-wing movement within our church that has different organizations of its own. There is an attempt to discredit women's ministry within the church and also feminist theology in general."

In the United Methodist Church, organizations called Good News, Renew Women's Network, and the Confessing Movement, among others, actively work to reshape the denomination to make it predominantly evangelical and politically right wing. Good News is known for its magazine, which is mailed to thousands of United Methodists whether they want it or not. (Good News encourages individual members to send in their church's directories of members' names and addresses, invading the privacy of regular churchgoers. The organization thereby creates a direct-mailing list of United Methodists in the United States.) Renew is devoted to attacking the Women's Division of the United Methodist Church. The Confessing Movement—its name angers many Christians because "Confessing Church" was also the name selected by German Christians who opposed Hitler—has a statement of faith that claims, "We repudiate teachings and practices that misuse principles of inclusiveness and tolerance to distort the doctrine and disciple of the church . . . We deny the claim that the individual is free to decide what is true and what is false, what is good and what is evil."[18]

"The need for sound doctrine is not in dispute," responds Rev. Scott Campbell, a United Methodist leader in Cambridge, Massachusetts. "The question is not whether a church ought to articulate its theological beliefs, but, rather, *how* such formulations ought to be used to *guide* the faithful." Unlike the Roman Catholic Church, Eastern Orthodox churches, and other churches that are defined by conformity to particular creeds, Methodism has some flexibility built into it by founder John Wesley in the mid-1700s. "We do not use doctrine as a club to coerce compliance, but as an indispensable aid in deepening our discipleship," says Campbell, noting that Wesley "was a ruthless abridger and amender of the so-called classical doctrines. He took the thirty-nine Articles of Religion of the church of England, chopped off fifteen and revised others to suit his own purposes."[19]

In the Presbyterian Church, meanwhile, the IRD-funded Lay Committee publishes a newspaper, *The Presbyterian Layman*, that routinely attacks anyone who doesn't adhere to its narrow idea of what it means to be a Christian: right-wing politically and fundamentalist theologically. As *Good News* is mailed to United Methodists, *The Layman* is sent to five hundred thousand Presbyterians unsolicited, their personal addresses provided to the IRD without their permission, six times a year. It is staggeringly well funded, receiving millions of dollars from the Howard Pew Freedom Trust and other conservative foundations.

The Lay Committee was founded in 1965, but it didn't get real momentum until 1993, the year of an international ecumenical colloquium called the Re-Imagining Conference, which was funded by a number of sources including the Presbyterian Church (U.S.A.), the United Methodist Church, and the Evangelical Lutheran Church in America. Two thousand people, mostly women, converged in Minneapolis in November 1993 to "re-imagine" or reexamine Christian theology and worship from a feminist perspective. They came from forty-nine states and twenty-seven countries—theologians, clergy, and laypeople. Approximately four hundred were Presbyterians, and the Presbyterian Church (U.S.A.) contributed $66,000 to the cost, as well as travel expenses for church staff who wished to attend. The event was part of the Ecumenical Decade of Churches in Solidarity with Women, an initiative of the World Council of Churches, an international and ecumenical organization. Its purpose was to encourage churches to commit to the full participation of women.

Feminist theology had been explored for twenty years at this point, and in fact none of the presentations at the conference introduced ideas that were new. Yet to most American Christians, who had been exposed only to the dominant liturgy and rituals of their home churches, the feminist ideas at Re-Imagining were radical.

Instead of God or Christ or Lord, many of the lecturers used the word "Sophia"—the Greek term for wisdom or God that is found in the New Testament (similar to the feminized personification of Wisdom in the Hebrew Bible)—in order to expand metaphors for divinity and to emphasize that God is not a man. (For discussion of the history of the term "Sophia" and its use in Scripture and worship, see Chapter 9.) A United Church of Christ pastor presented a ritual substituting milk and honey for bread and wine that was accompanied with the words,

> Our mother Sophia, we are women in your image:
> With the hot blood of our wombs we give form to new life.
> With the courage of our convictions we pour out our life
>   blood for justice.
> Sophia-God, Creator-God,
> let your milk and honey pour out,
> showering us with your nourishment . . .
> Our sweet Sophia, we are women in your image:
> With nectar between our thighs we invite a lover, we birth a
>   child;
> With our warm body fluids we remind the world of its plea-
>   sures and sensations . . .[20]

Delores Williams, a theology professor at Union Theological Seminary, declared, "I don't think we need a theory of atonement at all . . . I don't think we need folks hanging on crosses and blood dripping and weird stuff. We do not need atonement; we just need to listen to the god within."[21] One of the workshops was titled Prophetic Voices of Lesbians in the Church, and at least ten of the speakers identified themselves as lesbians.

The Lay Committee had been poised for action, and it pounced. With support from the IRD, it had sent to the conference reporters who hovered over tables and flashed their camera bulbs. As conference goers left Minneapolis, *The Layman* delivered the news to mainline Protestants around the country, complete with photojournalistic evidence: wacko feminists en masse had ridiculed Christian doctrine. They had made a mockery of the holy trinity of Father, Son, and Holy Spirit. They had participated in a heretical gathering of goddess worship. They were pagans who had disavowed Jesus. And this had been sanctioned and paid for by institutional churches.

Articles in *The Layman* were picked up by multiple Christian news outlets, leading to mainstream news coverage. The reaction from conservative church members was sheer horror. For millions of average American Christians, this sensational portrait of self-indulgent blasphemy was their first exposure to feminist theology. They worried that Sophia was coming soon to a church near them.

No question about it, speakers at the Re-Imagining conference did deviate from established church doctrine. They stretched the boundaries of accepted theologies. They questioned the legitimacy of long-standing rituals and practices. Yes, the conference was radical. But that was precisely the point; there was a reason the title *Re-Imagining* had been selected. The conference was intended as a safe place to tinker with tradition, to play with religious practice. It was an opportunity for Christian women disaffected by traditional ideas and worship to figure out ways to relate their Christianity to their lives in meaningful ways. *The Layman* highlighted the most extreme examples of what it considered anti-Christian practices, but the fact is that participants did firmly identify as Christian. "I did not perceive at any time that we were worshipping a goddess or making God into a different image," says one participant. "I was comfortable with new words and enjoying new insights."[22]

"It was the first international women's theological conference on a really large scale," remembers Rev. Dr. Barbara Dua, a Presbyterian minister and former associate director of the office of women's ministries for the Presbyterian Church (U.S.A.). "I believe *The Layman* was waiting for an opportunity to slam what women were doing in theological and biblical studies. Otherwise, I don't think *The Layman* would have attended the conference. I think they had been waiting for the opportunity to discredit women, to say, 'These women are heretics.' They portrayed a very unbalanced view."

As part of its well-organized response to Re-Imagining, the IRD created a Christian Women's Declaration. It was originally drafted by the IRD's late president, Diane Kippers, together with Janice Crouse, now a think-tank fellow at Concerned Women for America, a conservative fundamentalist organization. (The declaration has been revised since, most recently in November 2004.) Seven pages long, it condemns "radical feminists" for, among other things, developing an agenda that "leads to women being demeaned, their lives destroyed and their spirits enslaved."

The use of "radical feminist" was deliberate. Alan Wisdom explains to me that the IRD does not reject feminism, but it does reject radical feminism. What's the difference? "If by 'feminism' one meant 'equal rights for women,' then [Kippers and Crouse] were all for it. But if one were referring to a whole host of other theological and political positions that have become associated with contemporary feminism, then they would be more uneasy." Viola Larson, a board member of Voices of Orthodox Women, an evangelical Presbyterian women's organization affiliated with the IRD, informs me that she used to consider herself a "Christian feminist." "But having encountered too many feminists in the mainline churches who call themselves Christian feminists but who are in reality radical feminists, I no longer identify myself that way." In her mind all feminists are radicals.

What troubled Kippers and Crouse the most was the "movement to 're-imagine' two thousand years of Christian faith. We repudiate the assumption that Christian faith and teachings were first 'imagined' by men and now should be 're-imagined' by women."[23] Kippers and Crouse argued that the belief that Christianity has been formed and shaped by human beings goes hand in hand with the negation of God's revelation and sovereignty. Those who "re-imagine" Christianity are making it into something it's not, and therefore they reject Christianity.

However, it is my own conclusion that the IRD, not the conference participants, were the ones with wild imaginations. I've spoken with several women who attended the conference, and I've read multiple firsthand accounts of the event. Each one disagrees that the intent of the speakers was to disavow Christianity. The Reverend Jeanne Audrey Powers, a consultant to the conference and an interreligious affairs officer for the United Methodist Church who was interviewed by *The New York Times*, "did not dispute the accuracy of the quotations but said that they were unusually hyperbolic or dramatic expressions that were taken out of context and give a misleading impression of the conference as a whole." Indeed, the *Times* reporter listened to the tapes of the conference and concluded that "the sessions sounded like serious theological discussions taking place in a high-spirited atmosphere, with much bantering about traditional beliefs."[24]

"Some have said that the problem with the use of Sophia was that it did not conform to the reformed Trinitarian formulation for God.

Neither does 'Rock of my Salvation,' but we use that language all the time and people don't start screaming about rock worship," said Rev. Jeanette Stokes, a Presbyterian minister from North Carolina who attended the conference. "The use of Sophia was an attempt to try something new but something biblical. It always surprises me that so many people get so upset when we replace male language for God with female language. It reminds me that they must believe that God is male."[25]

"I remember being there and hearing women say that this was the first time they ever felt comfortable in worship, because they were included," Rebecca Todd Peters tells me. "There was an assumption at this event that women were equal to men in creation, that women were equal to men in the church. This assumption was not something they were getting from their local churches. So it was a very empowering experience for them." To the critics who claimed that participants were not practicing Christianity, Peters replies,

> It's a different way of defining what it means to be Christian. But that doesn't mean that it's not Christian. As part of the Reformed tradition, that's what we are all about. One of the mantras of our tradition is that we are "reformed and always reforming." It's not that the Reformation happened in the sixteenth century and stopped. It's a process in which we continually seek to understand the divine and learn new things about the divine.

The Catholic theologian Mary Hunt, one of the speakers, recalls that no one expected any controversy. "It was my view that nothing said at the conference was new," she tells me. "There was nothing that hadn't already been said in the seminaries or been published. But the IRD instrumentalized the conference very deliberately." What threatened conservative evangelical critics, Hunt believes, is not the progressiveness of the ideas per se, but the fact that ordinary Christians were embracing it. "The women loved it. They were not lunatics. They were serious mainstream people." If average, mainstream Christian women were not spiritually satisfied with traditional doctrine and ritual, the mainlines were in even more serious trouble than anyone had thought. After all, as we have seen, like it or not, ordinary women are the backbone of these churches.

Re-Imagining was a symbolic turning point for mainline women willing to embrace new ideas about religion. As a direct immediate result of the fury, the director of the Presbyterian Church's Women's Ministry Unit, Mary Ann Lundy—one of the coordinators of the conference—was forced to resign. The church lost millions of dollars in withheld contributions. But the larger repercussions have been more significant: a clampdown on any alternative way of thinking about Christianity.

For example, in the late 1990s an eighty-three-year-old United Methodist woman from Sacramento, Elaine Jacobson, created a small group for the United Methodist women in her area. Jacobson and a friend had been attending a monthly one-hour meeting of United Methodist women at the University of California, Davis, campus that discussed recent books and articles. The two women enjoyed it so much they decided to form something similar in Sacramento. They named it the Sophia Circle. "Since 'Sophia' is the word for wisdom in the Bible, we decided to use it," she explains. "Additionally, most of us are older and considered that we were wise." The group, which had eleven members, was chartered by the district United Methodist Women president. The women decided to draw from a publication called the *Re-Imagining Newsletter* as a conversation starter. Because of its name and its decision to even look at something with the word "re-imagining" in its title, the group was targeted by the Renew Women's Network, which has demanded that it change its name and ways or disassociate from United Methodist Women.

"What are they so afraid of?" asks Jacobson. "Many of us are leaders in our local churches . . . We have no formal connection with the Re-Imagining community." She continues: "I find it hard to understand the fuss. I am stimulated by new ideas, some of which I discard and some of which I incorporate into my life and thinking. That is how we grow, spiritually, mentally, and personally."[26]

College-age women are especially apt to explore new ideas. In the early 1990s a campus ministry organization, the National Network of

Presbyterian College Women (NNPCW), formed. It soon spread to eighty-five campuses nationwide with a mission to spiritually engage young Christian women through worship, Bible study, and discussion. Rev. Kate Holbrook, today an assistant chaplain at Colorado College in Colorado Springs, was very active in NNPCW when she was an undergrad at Bates College in Maine. She loved the organization so much that she became a member of the steering committee. Clean-cut, fit, and athletic, with wavy brown hair and hazel-brown eyes, Holbrook is the picture of vibrant health. She remembers, "In my first year of college, I couldn't find any religious community on campus, so it was a hard year. I didn't really have a religious community, and the only community there was too conservative for me. But then I discovered the Network. It was designed to help connect women on campuses interested in faith and feminism. In my sophomore year, 1997–98, I did an independent study on why women stay within their faith. It was a very empowering year for me. I even went to a conference in New York City at Union Theological Seminary that had the best women theologians out there. It was great. I reclaimed my faith for myself and brought together my love of the Bible and Christianity along with my interest in social justice work and feminism. I met all these amazing young women, and it was just incredible. It was so empowering." The NNPCW "was the kind of thing that I wished had existed when I had been in college," says Rebecca Todd Peters, cofounder of the organization.

In June 1998 the NNPCW made a routine request for continued funding at the denomination's General Assembly—the meeting of the governing body of the church, known as the GA—which was held that year in Charlotte, North Carolina. At the time, it received $50,000 a year from the church. No one at NNPCW had a clue about what was to follow.[27]

During the GA, the executive editor of *The Layman*, Parker Williamson, made a surprise attack on the NNPCW. He called the GA's attention to a pamphlet written by NNPCW students—*Young Women Speak*. Williamson said that the pamphlet contained blasphemy and was inconsistent with Scripture, especially with regard to discussion about sexual matters such as premarital heterosexual sexuality and gay sexuality. For instance, one woman had written, "God is letting me know that it doesn't matter whether I have a relationship with a man or a woman, just as long as I remember that God is the center of the love." Another had written, "I view the message of the Bible to be very helpful to my society. However, I also understand that there are issues of both long ago and today that are uniquely distinct to the particular period of time."[28]

"It was a resource publication with different articles by young women that had been published in the early 1990s, soon after the NNPCW had been started," Holbrook tells me. "One of the articles was about sexuality and spirituality. One was about racism. There was a section about gay and lesbian issues. It was a neat resource for young people asking questions."

Peters adds, "The core material was generated from the young women." In fact, she tells me, one of the pieces was a letter she herself had written to her father when she was in college, about inclusive language being important to her. "One of the lines in that letter said that the lack of female images of God in the Christian tradition had caused me to look at other religious traditions that did have female images. And somehow, this line got translated [by the conservative critics of the NNPCW] as our promoting goddess worship! This was one line in one piece. They didn't just take it out of context; they changed the meaning in a way that was inflammatory."

It was recommended that the GA vote not to continue funding for the organization. "Here we were, a group of young women excited about our faith, which is pretty amazing when you think about it, since so many people complain that young people are not involved enough in the church," points out Holbrook. "But the representatives of the church considered us a problem that had to be solved." After a demonstration led by NNPCW students, the vice moderator of the GA arrived at a compromise solution: the church would continue to fund the NNPCW for one more year, during which time a special review committee would examine the organization's activities and bring recommendations to the next GA the following year.[29] The review committee, it was announced, would be composed of three men, all ordained and known Presbyterian leaders, as well as four women, none of whom was recognized as a leader in the church.

The GA ended, but *The Layman*'s accusations were not over yet.

In a renewed effort to get the church to quash the NNPCW, Parker Williamson wrote to the GA chair two weeks later with the allegation that anyone who visited the official Presbyterian Church (U.S.A.) website and clicked on the link to the NNPCW Web page could follow hyperlinks to other sites, including online pornography and dating services for lesbians and gay men. He published his letter in *The Layman* and on the newspaper's website. "The NNPCW pages have been serving as an Internet gateway to hard core homosexual pornography," he claimed, in an overt attempt to strike fear in the hearts of Christian parents.

> Following links initially recommended as resources by NNPCW I found my way to a lesbian dating service (only three key strokes from the official church page). Continuing through interlocking links that started with an NNPCW recommendation I reached animated pictures depicting aberrant forms of sexual behavior including, but not limited to, oral and anal sex, sadism and masochism, and an entrance to "live chat rooms" in which potential partners may discuss their fantasies . . . Like a doorway leading from a Presbyterian sanctuary, it all starts on the official church web page . . . [T]his network *has been leading college women into pornography.*[30]

Everyone associated with the NNPCW at the time is fervently adamant that the links were unintentional and unwanted. Holbrook reminds me that at the time, not everyone was as familiar with the Internet as they are today. A student had informally created the website. "No one on our end was able to figure out how there was any link to pornography, although we did have a link to PFLAG," a support organization for parents, families, and friends of lesbians and gay men.

"The thing about their accusation is that we were always working *against* pornography and sexual violence!" protests Rev. Dr. Barbara Dua, who had just begun serving as the associate director of the women's ministries for the church. Dua, like any good church leader, wears a conservative suit with a printed scarf for a controlled dash of color. Her dark, wavy hair falls below her ears. Her voice is as youthful as that of a college student. "That they would turn that around and point to the women themselves as promoting pornography was so un-believable! The moderator of the GA, Rev. Douglas Oldenburg, the former president of Columbia Theological Seminary in Atlanta, came to talk with me privately and asked if there was any truth to the claim that we had intentionally offered pornography on the Internet. I was blown away that someone of his caliber seriously considered that what *The Layman* was saying was true."

In January 1999 the review committee met in the boardroom of the church's national headquarters in Louisville, Kentucky, to assess the NNPCW. "The review committee didn't call it a trial, but to us it was a trial," recalls Holbrook. "We were attacked, and we had to de-fend ourselves and our right to exist." There were approximately a hundred people in the room—the review committee, members of the NNPCW steering committee, Presbyterian staff people, and support-ers. Also present were representatives of *The Layman*, which presented a slide show that began with an artist's depiction of Eve and attempted to demonstrate that women in the church have a long history of anti-Christian activity.

"I remember there was one guy on the review committee who kept asking—he must have asked at least three different times—'How could you not know there was a link to a link to a link to pornogra-phy?'" recalls Holbrook. "We said, 'We didn't know.' 'How could you not know?' They didn't believe us and wouldn't listen to us." Echoes Gusti Newquist, who worked under Dua in the Louisville national of-fice and was also present at the hearing, "I couldn't believe that any-one took the pornography charge seriously. It was so ridiculous. The committee asked us about it, and I told them, 'None of us had ever followed these links before.'"

The review committee determined that the Network was allowed to exist and would continue to receive funding, but it was no longer permitted to print *Young Women Speak*. If the organization wanted to publish a new pamphlet in the future, it would not be permitted to do so without a biblical scholar and theologian, both chosen by the church leadership, overseeing the project.

From where I sit, it seems that *The Layman* or any other organiza-tion is absolutely entitled to question church-funded groups that pro-mote beliefs violating church doctrine. However, *The Layman* and its supporters have engaged in ugly tactics that, to my mind, override their right to offer critique. First, *The Layman* got personal. The college women themselves were attacked as blasphemous. Remember, to a devout person of faith, being called blasphemous or heretical is extremely painful and shameful. "These young women were pawns," says Dua. "I knew these women, and they were our best and brightest. They were the Phi Beta Kappas. They were the most spiritually mature. They were more spiritually mature than most of people in that General Assembly. And they were getting dragged through the sewer. I just sat there thinking, These are our daughters and our granddaughters, and we are treating them like dirt. It was just unbelievable to me."

Dua herself was also personally targeted. Just as her predecessor, Mary Ann Lundy, had been mocked and attacked as a fringe feminist goddess lover and summarily fired, so too was Dua singled out as anti-Christian. "In many ways *The Layman* tried its best to ruin my reputation as a woman in the church," she says. "They ran all these articles about me that said I was leading the church on a 'detour into darkness.' People still find these articles online. I tried not to take a lot of this personally, because I realized I was a symbol for other things. Still, it was hurtful." Dua no longer works for the Presbyterian Church. She is executive director of an ecumenical organization, the New Mexico Conference of Churches.

Moreover, the accusations were without merit. It appears that *The Layman* and its supporters leveled the accusations merely to create a campaign of intimidation against feminists within the church and to demonstrate that the church would be better served without feminists, who are heretics and can't be trusted. After all, the NNPCW never made any statement indicating that church doctrine supported premarital and gay sexuality; the group merely raised these as legitimate issues for discussion. All young people discuss sexuality. It's foolish to tell Christian women that if they want to discuss sexuality, they should do it in a non-Christian setting; after all, isn't the whole point of campus ministry to keep young people *connected* to the faith? As for the porn charges, the review committee ultimately concluded that the Web links were never intentional.

Today, "the Network still exists, but the freedom of the group has been taken away because it's under scrutiny," laments Dua. "You begin to be afraid of what you might say. And if you've spent any time at all with college kids, you know that it's just deadening to think that someone will file a report on what you want to say." Newquist disagrees somewhat. "As the years went on, in my view the group became more publicly feminist," she says. "The group reclaimed the term 'feminist' and made up T-shirts that said, 'Jesus Loves Feminists' in 2003."

On the other hand, "I definitely felt constrained about discussing sexuality. That was the place where we were coming against church policy, which in my opinion is problematic. The church policy in my view does not take into account the real-life situation of young women. Our church's statements on sexuality are inadequate. I always had to be clear about what the church said about sexuality—that it is against premarital and gay sexuality—but I never said that I personally believed that what the church said was right." Newquist points out that "the formal accusations against the group were all about sexuality. They were not about the group identifying as feminist or about using alternative God language. It was sexuality."

It's no accident that attacks on the college women centered on sexuality. This issue can whip people into a frenzy of panic and horror in a way that perhaps no other issue can. Conservative critics homed in on sexuality as a rallying cry because this enabled them to "unleash people who had a smoldering resentment of women taking on roles in the church," theorizes Dua.

We see that when pressured by conservatives, mainstream denominations do not welcome feminists or stand up for women. "It's very hard for liberals to be effective in organizing against *The Layman*" and the other conservative evangelical critics, says Peters, since the latter "truly believe that they are right. They truly believe that the only way to be saved is through Jesus Christ, that abortion is wrong, that gays and lesbians are wrong. That's why it's so hard for liberals to be effective in organizing around them. Because liberals come out of a worldview and a mind-set that believe in openness and dialogue, and that it's okay if the conservatives want to have those beliefs. But the conservatives want to push their ideas onto other people; that's part of their ideology."

Newquist sums up the whole saga succinctly. "We were a good money-raising tool for *The Layman*."

For all the complaints that the churches are too feminized or that they are in danger of being overrun by radical feminists, women do not match heterosexual men in clerical power, not by a long shot. The stained-glass ceiling is as impenetrable as ever.

In 2006, at the fiftieth anniversary celebration of clergy rights for United Methodist women, which was held in a Chicago conference center, I was dazzled when I entered the room. It had been given over to vendors, and in addition to books and jewelry, they were selling stoles and clergy robes in gorgeous, vibrant colors—royal purples, grassy greens, blood reds, oceanic blues. I laughed to myself: maybe women wanted to be ordained so they could wear these clothes? But then I found the small conference room where a documentary, *And Your Daughters Shall Prophesy*, was being screened. It consisted of interviews with working United Methodist pastors. One typical interviewee, a middle-aged black woman, attractive and professional in appearance, related that parishioners have said to her, "We do not want a female pastor, because we do not want to go to hell. Because God does not want female pastors." She looked into the camera and said, "And that is really painful."

In 1853 Antoinette Brown, a Congregationalist (today's United Church of Christ), became the first ordained woman in the United States. Women from other Protestant traditions, however, had to preach without full clergy rights (if they were allowed to preach at all) for another century. Methodist and Presbyterian women could become ministers only in 1956, Lutheran women in 1970, and Episcopalian women in 1976. (Non-Orthodox Jewish women were also becoming rabbis—in 1972 in the Reform movement, 1974 in the Reconstructionist movement, and 1985 in the Conservative movement.)

The pioneers who became ordained at mid-century were not feminist activists. Not trying to prove a point about the capabilities of all women, they explain that they simply followed "God's call" to the ministry. Rev. Marion Kline of Des Moines, Washington, age ninety-five, worked for the Methodist Church beginning in the 1940s but only received full clergy rights in 1956. "I didn't ever intend to be a minister," she insists to me on the phone, her mind focused and unspooling with vivid memories. "But I heard the call to Christian service. People ask me if I was discriminated against, and the answer is, Yes! In the 1940s, during wartime, I was assigned to a little church in the country in Wisconsin. They didn't really want a woman, but they got used to it. I remember hearing someone say to a new family that was moving in that the church didn't have a minister. As if I didn't exist. Then, another minister was brought in to replace me, and nobody told me. When the vote went through to allow women to get clergy rights, it was a whole change in clout."

Rev. Grace Huck, born in 1916 and today living in Spearfish, South Dakota, recalls shuttling from one tiny rural Methodist congregation to another—churches that considered themselves lucky to have anyone preaching, even a woman. If you met Huck, you would never guess that she has been alive for nearly a century. She stands ramrod straight, wearing a big gold cross over her perfectly starched, ruffled white blouse. In her autobiography, *God's Amazing Grace,* Huck recalls a typical incident that took place in North Dakota when she was twenty-nine. When it was announced that she was appointed pastor of one of the parishes, a congregant pounded on the back of the pew and shouted, "There will be no skirts in this pulpit while I am alive!"[31] You get the idea of what these trailblazing women were up against sixty-odd years ago.

So here we are, fast-forwarded to the twenty-first century. Women form the majority of students studying in mainline Protestant seminaries for master of divinity degrees, yet women constitute less than 18 percent of ordained clergy. More than half of the local churches in mainline denominations have only one or zero lay (not ordained) women preaching; and of churches with a male-only clerical staff, more than three-quarters never invite a single woman to guest preach.[32]

Ordained women report that they have a much harder time than their male peers do in getting good pulpit jobs. Congregations still prefer men. Church search committees, even in liberal congregations, want young men with children, married to stay-at-home wives who do church volunteer work. The congregations willing to offer jobs to women tend to be small, with fewer resources, clout, and influence than large ones. After having been ordained for a decade or more, 70 percent of men have clergy positions at medium- and large-sized congregations, compared with 37 percent of the women, who are stuck in small and struggling churches.[33] Additionally, even the small congregations prefer to have a man in the senior pastoral position and offer only the assistant position to a woman.

Female clergy are also consistently paid less than their male peers. Even when women are hired for the exact same types of jobs as the men, within the same denomination in the same size church, they are still paid less—91 cents to the dollar—after adjusting for differences in age, experience, and education.[34] Put another way, the sole reason why female clergy are paid less than male clergy is that they are female rather than male.

In the past, the prejudice was unabashedly out in the open. Rev. Dr. Barbara Dua relates that in 1977, when she entered Princeton Theological Seminary as an M.Div. student, she walked into her first-semester preaching class and was shooed away by the esteemed homiletics professor, Rev. Dr. Donald MacLeod. "You are too short to preach and your voice is not deep enough!" he declared to her—even though she is five feet eight inches tall and he had never heard her speak in public or preach.

Today few employers of mainline clergy would say outright that women are less capable than men—but many of them continue to think it, consciously or not. Rev. Elaine Puckett had long dreamed of leading a large United Methodist congregation in her hometown, Atlanta. But eighteen years after being ordained, the men she was ordained with have become leaders of big churches while she has worked in subordinate positions in a string of jobs—associate pastor at one church, leader of another church that doesn't have the resources to survive, then back again in an associate pastor position somewhere else. "You begin to question your competence," she told *The New York Times*. "When you look at the endless cycle of one appointment after another after another like these, your endurance runs low." Rev. Dottie Escobedo-Frank, pastor of CrossRoads United Methodist Church in Phoenix, relates that in a former associate pastor position, a colleague told her that he was too distracted by the fact that she is a woman to focus on what she was saying from the pulpit.[35]

One pastor tells me that she used to intern in a rural midwestern town at a church with tight financial resources, working with a pastor in her sixties. "I remember one Sunday there was a church member helping me get ready for Communion. We were setting up the grape juice in the little cups, and I said, 'It seems like things are going really well here with Pastor Joanna.' And she said, 'Oh yes, we really appreciate her because we could never afford a man.' The church felt that the only way they could afford a full-time pastor was to have a woman. Her benefits package was horrible."

Once hired, female clergy have to face another tough layer of prejudice—from their congregations. People in the pews—women as well as men—continue to find it difficult to see women as figures of religious authority. One man in Escobedo-Frank's former congregation covered his eyes whenever she preached. Rev. Kate Holbrook guest preaches at various parishes, and she tells me that when she greets people after a service, she gets more comments about the way she looks than about the content of her sermon. "That's a nice dress you have on today," congregants say to her.

Clergywomen with young children face an additional hurdle. Clerical work is more than full-time—congregations expect to be able to reach their spiritual leaders any day, anytime. Since child-care responsibilities are seldom evenly shared, falling disproportionately on mothers, clergywomen with young children scramble to meet their children's needs while they serve their congregations. Indeed, Barbara Brown Zikmund, Adair Lummis, and Patricia Chang found that three times as many clergywomen as clergymen (30 percent to 9 percent) report that it is "very difficult" to combine ministry with parenthood. This is hardly a surprise, since 43 percent of the women in full-time ministry had the primary responsibility for caring for their children, compared with only 3 percent of the men in equivalent jobs.[36]

Rev. Emily Goldthwaite Fries is an associate pastor in a large and growing United Church of Christ congregation in Urbandale, Iowa. She is striking-looking, with large brown eyes, straight hair pulled back from her face, and a slender build. She's also young, in her late twenties, so she hasn't yet faced the motherhood-career balancing act, but she has seen enough discrimination already. "Pastor Emily," as she is known, lays it all out for me. "Is there sexism? Absolutely. Being young and female, there are a lot of times when I enter a room and people don't take me seriously until they listen to me speaking. There are people who see me as the senior pastor's assistant, which I'm not. But for many people, it's natural to them that I'm an assistant and that the senior pastor is the one in charge." Nevertheless, Goldthwaite Fries feels blessed. "In most churches," she says, "it's normal for the female associate pastor to be very subordinate to the male senior pastor. I'm lucky because in this congregation I'm given the opportunities I should be."

Even today, many women report that they are the first woman ever hired as a pastor in the church they are currently serving. Being a token raises the stakes for job performance because of congregants' expectations. Goldthwaite Fries says, "For a lot of the churches I interviewed with, if I had taken the job, I would have been their first woman pastor. And my denomination has been ordaining women for a very long time. Antoinette Brown was ordained over a hundred and fifty years ago. A lot of people think that they need a male minister, or that it's a step down if their male minister left and they have to hire a woman; they're disappointed with that. But if their experience with a female pastor is a positive one, it transforms everybody in a positive way. But it's a huge burden on the female pastor's shoulders. When I was searching for a job, I can't tell you how many times people said to me, 'If the experience with you is good, then from then on this church will be accepting of a woman minister. If you don't do an excellent job, it will give people an excuse to reject all future women ministers and they would never want another one.' I would have had to set a standard for all women ministers."

Being a token, and therefore being isolated, can also lead to far more serious consequences. Female clergy face the threat of sexual harassment, stalking, physical threats, actual physical attacks, and even rape. One female pastor tells me that this problem is widespread, but nobody wants to go public with it because it compromises a woman's already tenuous ability to get a job or keep the one she has. And as Goldthwaite Fries says, when you are a token, you hold an unbearable weight on your shoulders of representing all female clergy. No one wants to speak up about sexual harassment or violence if it means that all female clergy will be regarded as walking targets or, worse, that women in positions of religious authority are getting what they asked for.

Despite the risks, isolation, name-calling, covered eyes, and inequitable salaries, women are storming the seminaries. They want to serve God and they want to assist people in the pews to connect with God. God is calling them to do this important work, they say. And if being a woman in this work is out of the norm, then so be it. A call is a call.

"Everywhere I go, I surprise people because I'm a woman," says Goldthwaite Fries. "At least once a week I have an interaction where I have to explain that yes, women are allowed to do this." But that can be a good thing. The unexpected wakes people up. "I speak differently than a man does," says Escobedo-Frank. "To hear the fullness of God's voice, you need to hear both men and women. People's ears are opened more because of the surprise, and they are delighted by surprise."[37]

"I've had ninety-year-old women come up to me and say, 'I've never heard a woman preach before,'" Goldthwaite Fries adds. "They're not sure how they feel about it. Then they sit there and they listen to me, and they come up to me after I've preached and they say, 'It's really powerful to hear a woman preaching.' For many people, it can be profound and powerful that I'm doing this at all."

SIX

The Alarm Has Rung and
Muslim Women Are Wide-Awake

Muslim prayer, *salat*, is harmonious communication with God. One of the five "pillars" or foundational requirements of Islam, it is methodical, lyrical, and physical. The *muezzin* (announcer) chants over a loudspeaker in Arabic that it's time for prayer. Before entering the sanctuary, worshippers remove their shoes and engage in a cleansing ritual, *wudu*, in which they clean their faces, arms, head, and feet in order to be ritually pure before God. They wear loose-fitting clothing, with men sometimes choosing to cover their heads with a *kufi* (cap) and women most always covering their hair with a scarf, *hijab*. Upon entering the sanctuary, they join in straight, organized lines, standing barefoot atop rugs that are often beautifully decorated in the Persian style, facing in the direction of Mecca, the birthplace of the prophet Muhammad and the holiest city in Islam. They stand so close to one another that their shoulders touch: everyone is on the same level, the same rank, in the presence of God.

Worshippers take their cues from the *imam*, prayer leader, who melodically chants "*Allahu Akbar*" (God is greater)—a phrase that reminds Muslims that God is supreme and transcendent—and proceeds to recite verses of the Qur'an (the sacred text of Islam, said to contain the words of God as they were revealed to the prophet Muhammad) in the original Arabic. Worshippers bow, prostrate themselves, and stand up in unison during each recitation. Their physical movements demonstrate their surrender or submission (*islam*) to God. They

158

thank God, praise God, and emphasize their devotion to God. For many, the sight of these choreographed body movements and the sound of the ancient language are soothing, even therapeutic.

That is, unless you are shoved as an afterthought into a tiny space and told during the sermon that you don't have the same rights as your husband, brother, and son.

Muslim women in the United States, like their Christian and Jewish sisters, and like many of their Arab sisters, are becoming less and less willing to put up with the religious status quo. (Muslim women in the United States are not the first Muslims to insist on gender parity. For many years, women from Damascus to Cairo have been demanding ample prayer space.) They are contesting theology that has been interpreted exclusively by men, which situates women as subordinate to men. With regard to their treatment in the mosques, they are sick of being told that they must enter from a back door instead of the main entrance, as is the practice in some but not all U.S. mosques. (It is not mandatory for Muslims to pray in a mosque, but many attend regularly because they enjoy the community experience or because it is their custom.) No longer are these women tolerating being squeezed in the back behind a wall or herded into an upstairs gallery, which is often dirty and almost always means not being able to see the imam. They are refusing to listen to khutbas (sermons) delivered by male imams telling husbands that they are permitted to beat their wives or have sex with them without consent. U.S. Muslim women—American-born, immigrants, and converts—are rising up and demanding to be treated with equal dignity, which is precisely what the Qur'an instructs.

"The women are upstairs, and they bring their children and it's cramped, and the children get very restless," is how Kimberly Harper describes the scene. Harper, an African American woman who converted to Islam, lives in North Carolina and is a board member of the first Islamic sorority, Gamma Gamma Chi. "And the brothers say, 'Sisters, please control the kids!' And we can't see the imam at all. Personally, this is my largest frustration. I feel like Islam is all about family, so they should encourage families to come. But the way it is now, it's difficult to come with your children. They should make the *masjid* [mosque] more welcoming for the sisters. I don't mind a man leading the service; I just want access. It's an all-boys network, and the message is: women are not welcomed. The men don't even say '*As-salaam aleikum*' (Peace be upon you) to us, even though you're allowed to give salaams to members of the opposite sex."

Nasreen Aboobaker from Fremont, California, remembers attending communal prayers on the holiday of Eid ul-Fitr, which marks the end of Ramadan, the month of fasting. Her mosque had rented out space at a local Hilton to accommodate the huge number of worshippers. The men were assigned the ballroom, the women, a small conference room where they were to listen to the prayers over the sound system. The women waited an hour for the imam to begin. Suddenly the door opened and their husbands were fetching them to take them home. Little did the women know, but the sound system had failed. "We did not even know the prayer had ended," she told *The New York Times*. "We were locked up like sheep and cows."[1]

Mosques in the United States did not used to restrict women's space. This is a new movement, begun in the last two decades. Muslim women who grew up in the United States are galled in part because when they were girls, mosques were friendlier to them. They experience the situation today as an anomaly that should not be.

Women's unequal treatment extends beyond the mosque, but in the United States this issue has become emblematic for a new vanguard that calls itself a "progressive" Muslim movement. These Muslims, women and men, are scholars and activists working in synchrony. They respect their intellectual heritage, based on the Qur'an, *hadith* (the collection of traditions of Muhammad), and sharia (the code of law). Yet they also insist on exploring new ways of interpreting the tradition and law. And they do this within the framework of being American and holding American values.

In 2003, UCLA students Ahmed Nassef and Jawad Ali created a cutting-edge website, *Muslim WakeUp!* (muslimwakeup.com), with Nassef serving as editor in chief and Patricia Dunn, Nassef's then-wife, serving as managing editor. *Muslim WakeUp!* is not just another collection of articles floating in cyberspace. It is an international water cooler for forward-thinking Muslims who are fed up with the status quo. It provides space for uncensored points of view on all things Islamic. Its mission is to bring together Muslims and non-Muslims in America and around the globe in efforts that celebrate cultural and spiritual diversity, tolerance, and understanding. Through online and offline media, events, and community activities, *Muslim WakeUp!* champions an interpretation of Islam that celebrates the Oneness of God and the Unity of God's creation through the encouragement of the human creative spirit and the free exchange of ideas, in an atmosphere that is filled with compassion and free of intimidation, authoritarianism, and dogmatism. In all its activities, Muslim WakeUp! attempts to reflect a deep belief in justice and against all forms of oppression, bigotry, sexism, and racism.[2]

The website, which gets more than two hundred thousand visits a month, is not afraid to shake things up. In its early days it ran a feature called "Hug a Jew," consisting of interviews with Jewish figures, complete with photos of, you guessed it, a Muslim embracing the interviewee. One story suggested that readers put down their suicide bombs and pick up guitars in order to spread peace in the world. A popular column on Islam and sexuality, written by Mohja Kahf, is called "Sex & the *Ummah* [community]"; it tackles the still-taboo idea that Muslim women have sex drives and that this is perfectly normal.

In 2004 Nassef joined with three other young American Muslims to form the Progressive Muslim Union (PMU) of North America, which supports the rights of women and gays and lesbians, among other forms of inclusiveness, and calls for a reexamination of Islamic teachings. One of the founders, Omid Safi, a professor of Islamic studies at Colgate University, is the editor of *Progressive Muslims: On Justice, Gender, and Pluralism*, a collection of powerful essays that lay out the activists' arguments. The Progressive Muslim Union has a website (pmuna.org), a necessity in creating a community among like-minded people who otherwise would not have the chance to communicate or even know about each other, and who may be afraid to voice their controversial opinions without the protection of some level of anonymity. "The *Muslim WakeUp!* website gave us a community," Patricia Dunn tells me. "It's put me in touch with amazing women—women I never thought I would meet, women who argue over all the issues but who are really good people. It's nice to be united. I feel so close to some of these women even though I've met some of them [in person] only once or twice."

As the community grew, some of the leaders saw that there was room for another organization. In 2006 two board members of the PMU, Pamela Taylor and Zuriani "Ani" Zonneveld, founded Muslims for Progressive Values (MPV). In its statement of principles, MPV affirms "the equal worth of all human beings, regardless of race, gender, ethnicity, nationality, creed, sexual orientation, or ability"; it supports "women's agency and self-determination in every aspect of their lives," a principle that is "enshrined in the Qur'an"; it endorses the rights of "lesbian, gay, bisexual, and trans-sexual individuals"; and it "condemns all forms of extremism."[3]

Women's religious rights have emerged as a key issue for the new progressives. The way women are treated in mosque, they argue, is demeaning, ethically wrong, and contrary to the Qur'an; moreover, it creates an environment in which women are regarded as less than men in all areas of life. "A lot of the misogyny is not from the tradition, but from a break with tradition," claims Nakia Jackson, a young activist who has been denounced for speaking up about the filthy conditions in the women's section of her former mosque. Her argument is similar to that of equality-minded Christians who say that Jesus sought equality between women and men, but his followers lost sight of his mission. "Originally, Islam was egalitarian. There was flexibility. There was a belief that if woman-led prayer was okay for the community, then it was okay. There was woman-led prayer during the Prophet's time, and there has been woman-led prayer since. But over the last few hundred years, there has been a break with the juristic tradition." This break with tradition has turned off countless women, who don't want to have anything to do with mosques. "I haven't found a mosque yet where I have felt spiritual fulfillment," says Asra Nomani, the author of *Standing Alone: An American Woman's Struggle for the Soul of Islam* and a leading organizer of women-led prayer services, in a sad voice. "I find spiritual fulfillment in Islam, but not in the mosque."

"I'd had no idea how bad it was for women in Islam until after I started studying the history of religion," confesses Laury Silvers, a professor of Islamic studies at Skidmore College in Saratoga Springs, New York, and a leader in the movement for woman-led prayer.

"There are many romantic apologists for Islam and women. They take an imagined golden period from the Middle Ages, the high point of Muslim culture, and they park it right there. Many conservative Muslims, meaning those who have respect for the law and the scholarly tradition, are romantic apologists. And I went through a phase of being a romantic apologist myself. If you have the perfect husband and the perfect world, Islam is paradise. But God forbid you should live in the real world. Ultimately I saw that and struggled with that—without losing my own conservative sense of Muslim identity." After all, she adds, "the intellectual tradition is flexible and rich and worthwhile."

The movement's most radical move has been to organize and support woman-led mixed-gender prayer services. The most publicized woman-led prayer ever held took place on March 18, 2005, in New York City, with the Islamic scholar Amina Wadud serving as imam and more than a hundred men and women in attendance. It was reported in media around the world. Since the service was jum'a, the Friday noon prayer and the most important salat of the week, Wadud not only led the women and men in prayer but also delivered the khutba. Women stood in one section, men in another, with families in the middle: there was no front or back. "People became frightened" about the Wadud service, says Silvers, who participated in the service and collected and made available on the Progressive Muslim Union website the hundreds of *fatwas* (Islamic legal judgments) from around the world. All except four denounced Wadud and the service. "Their sky was falling. Their gendered cosmos was turning upside down. She was making trouble, and it was *fantastic*."

Not all progressives support woman-led mixed-gender prayer, as we will see. Nevertheless, this issue has roused countless American Muslims. Most Catholics do not support the ordination of female priests, but that issue has triggered a movement of Catholic reformers who question blind obedience to the pope and prefer a return to what they see as Catholicism's core values. Similarly, progressive Muslim women and men are discovering that woman-led prayer can pull a peg out from a structure that has illegitimately promoted inequality, leading to a new way of ordering Qur'anic interpretation. Ultimately progressive Muslims want, in addition to the transformation of mosques, female theologians and female community leaders. They want new hermeneutical models to be respected, studied, and taught. They want, in other words, fundamental change—but within the parameters of their tradition.

Islam is based on a body of law, sharia, which is derived from the Qur'an and hadith (collections of traditions of Muhammad) and is considered divine. The Qur'an today is the same Qur'an that Muhammad taught his peers in the seventh century. The hadith are considered valid only if they are authenticated by multiple sources. Sharia regulates public and some private aspects of daily life. Since the Qur'an and hadith do not cover every legal issue affecting daily life, sharia is supplemented with jurisprudence (*fiqh*), a legal system formulated by experts on the Qur'an and hadith. For many centuries, these experts used *ijtihad* (struggle within the mind), a hermeneutical method of critically interpreting the sacred texts. They used reason and took into account historical and cultural circumstances. These scholars, like those in every place and time, were influenced by the prevailing beliefs of their culture; when they formulated legal decisions, they incorporated negative beliefs about women.

By the eleventh century, there were 135 Sunni schools of thought. (Sunni Muslims, who today total 90 percent of the world's Muslims, are distinguished from Shiite Muslims through their choice of successor to Muhammad after the prophet's death.) However, by the end of the century, this number shrank to four. In an effort to consolidate power, the ruling Sunnis discouraged ijtihad. From then on, there was pressure applied to the remaining jurists to rely on seventh-century–based interpretations of the Qur'an and hadith. Thus orthodox Islamic jurisprudence effectively became a fossil, embedded within an era (and looking backward to an even earlier era) that has little or no relevance to today's realities. Outdated, discriminatory ideas about women's roles are included in this fossil and therefore have never been overcome.

Today's progressive Muslim scholars want to "re-open the gates of ijtihad" by applying the principles of the Qur'an to today's world. They decry fundamentalists who cite the Qur'an to justify terrorism and rigid gender roles. In response to "fanatics" who cite the Qur'an and say, "We're going to tell you what God says on every single issue," Sheikh Hamza Yusuf of California says, "That's not Islam. That's psychopathy."[4] Together with Imam Zaid Shakir, Sheikh Yusuf has built the first Islamic seminary in the United States, the Zaytuna Institute, which they created precisely as an antidote to ossified, reactionary interpretations of Islam that have migrated to American mosques courtesy of clerics trained in Saudi Arabia. Through contemporary attempts at ijtihad, progressive scholars intend to show that Islam is, fundamentally, about justice for marginalized members of society— the poor, women, anyone on the fringes. Muhammad himself was orphaned and had a vested interest in protecting the most vulnerable.

Those who call for ijtihad regard the Qur'an not as an embalmed body in a museum, but as something alive with which to engage and communicate. The Arabic language itself is a living thing. In Arabic script, as in Hebrew, there are no written vowels. Vowels are pronounced by the speaker, who infers them. "A set of consonants can have several meanings and only acquires final, specific, fixed meaning when given vocalized or silent utterance," writes Leila Ahmed, the first professor of women's studies in religion at Harvard Divinity School. Arabic words do not have, and do not appear to have, fixed meaning the way European words do. "Until life is literally breathed into them, Arabic and Hebrew words on the page have no particular meaning. Indeed, until then they are not words but only potential words, a chaotic babble and possibility of meanings."[5]

In the medieval period, interestingly, women were permitted to become involved in religious scholarship. There were at least eight thousand female hadith scholars who taught Qur'an and who even served as jurists, according to Mohammad Akram Nadwi, a scholar who has spent eight years collecting their biographical information. He has found that citations of female religious experts dwindle after the sixteenth century. One woman from seventh-century Damascus, Umm al-Darda, was accepted by her male contemporaries as an esteemed jurist. She sat with male scholars in the mosque and even lectured in the men's section. Her students included the caliph (community leader) of Damascus; she prayed shoulder to shoulder with the men and issued a fatwa that allowed women to pray together with men.[6]

Today there are a few isolated pockets of female religious study. Al-Azhar University in Cairo has a women's college, and girls' religious schools and women's study groups do exist. Yet most Muslim women around the world are prevented from participating in religious study, let alone taking on leadership roles.

What would Islamic law look like if women joined men to create jurisprudence? We will find out: the first international all-female Shura (advisory) Council on Islamic law is currently in formation. In November 2006 an organization called the Women's Islamic Initiative in Spirituality and Equity, or WISE, held a series of meetings and lectures at a hotel in New York City's Times Square. Approximately 125 people from twenty-five countries came to lay the groundwork for the council, which is sponsored by the American Society for Muslim Advancement (also known as ASMA), a cultural and educational organization, and the Cordoba Initiative, a multi-faith organization whose objective is to heal the relationship between the Islamic world and America. The Shura Council, comprised of scholars, activists, and specialists, met a second time in New York City in February 2008. Members of the council are developing strategies to articulate Islam as ethical and egalitarian.

"Islam is a religion of law, and it is important to express the principles of social justice within the framework of Islamic law," says Daisy Khan, executive director of ASMA. "This is why we need *muftias* [women officially sanctioned to issue fatwas], in order to do that. Otherwise, it falls on deaf ears."[7] "Women must be included in the decision-making process," Ingrid Mattson, president of the Islamic Society of North America, says to me. "The ideal is to work peacefully with men in leadership and engage in dialogue with them, but you also have to ask, 'Is the law being broken if women are being excluded?' Women often just agree to these rules that marginalize them. But we have a right to stand up and fight for our rights. And if I have some rights, I have to stand up and fight for rights for other women."

"The future lies with these women speaking out," the Qur'an translator Laleh Bakhtiar tells me. "I've been to so many conferences where people come and give their lecture, and then you go home and forget everything that was said." But it's different with the WISE women. "You just feel that change is going to happen because these women are not going to let it go."

In many U.S. mosques, to be sure, women are treated with dignity and respect. In Masjid al-Farah, a tiny, blink-and-you-miss-it Sufi (mystical tradition) mosque tucked in downtown New York City, several blocks from the site of the former World Trade Center, women are greeted with "As-salaam aleikum." The women's section is behind the men's, separated by several low footstools. The mosque is led by a woman, Sheikha Fariha al-Jerrahi, head of the Nur Ashki Jerrahi Sufi Order, which is groundbreaking in itself. One of the imams is Feisal Abdul Rauf, founder of ASMA and often quoted in the press denouncing violence and what he has called "Islamic fascism." At a jum'a when I visited, Imam Feisal—a charismatic man with perhaps the calmest voice I've ever heard—paused before he began his khutba. He instructed that the space be reorganized so as to enlarge the women's section—even though this meant that the two-hundred-plus men were jammed together while the dozen women were given the luxury of a bit of space.

Meanwhile, in San Francisco, the largest downtown mosque was renovated in 2006, and the eight-foot wall that separated the women from the men and cut off the light was demolished. Today there is one large room, well lit for all; men and women do not pray immediately adjacent to each other, so gender separation remains, but there is no physical barrier between them. In the Islamic Center of Greater Toledo in Ohio, a three-foot-high movable partition—tall enough to satisfy many conservatives but short enough to enable the women to see and hear everything the men do—runs down the center of a mosque.

The interior worship layout in most U.S. mosques more closely resembles that of the Islamic Cultural Center of New York, which was financed by the Kuwaiti government.[8] To be sure, the exterior of this mosque is far from ordinary. A grand, ornate building with a greened copper dome and a minaret, it offers architectural splendor in an otherwise bland neighborhood of high-rise apartment buildings on the northern edge of Manhattan's Upper East Side. Inside, this mosque has ample space for four thousand male worshippers in its main sanctuary, with a women's balcony that can squeeze in eighty at best. This majestic sanctuary is reserved for jum'a. There are cubbyholes for the men's shoes, but the women have to stash theirs on the steps of the staircase leading up to the balcony. The imam stands on a raised platform that is suspended slightly above the main floor, but the women's section is so high up (the equivalent of being on the third floor, looking down on the first) that it's impossible to see him unless one manages to snag a space for oneself in the very front of the balcony.

During regular salat on other days, a much smaller room is used, in which the women pray behind a curtain in what looks like a walk-in closet. In fact, if you didn't look closely, you would have no idea that women were participating in salat at all. Before my first visit to this mosque, I had contacted one of the assistant imams and asked for permission to observe salat; he welcomed me and allowed me to sit on a comfortable chair in the back of the men's section. I noticed the curtain only when salat was concluded. I watched as it was pushed aside and several women tumbled out to find their shoes and get back to their daily routine. Instantly I felt humbled: as a non-Muslim woman, I had been given the best seat in the house. I had been allowed to witness the beauty of communal Muslim prayer. Yet these devout women who were actual participants had been segregated in a separate room (if you could call it a room), unable to see the imam and no doubt unable to hear him clearly either.

The physical barrier between the sexes did not originate with the prophet Muhammad. The sexes were segregated during prayer, but the prophet did not require a barrier between them; there is no verse in the Qur'an or hadith establishing the need for a barrier. But after the prophet's death, as prevailing ideas about the dangers of female sexuality and the need to seclude women found their way into Islamic jurisprudence, women's rights were whittled away. Progressive scholars insist that separating the sexes has no legitimate basis in Islam. Ironically, in one of the most repressive countries for women today, Saudi Arabia, women and men may pray side by side, with no barrier at all, in some of Islam's holiest sites.

It is not required to place a division in the mosque between men and women, according to Muzammil H. Siddiqi, chairman of the Fiqh Council of North America, past president of the Islamic Society of North America, and a prominent scholar. "There is no verse in the Qur'an or *hadith* of the Prophet—peace be upon him—that tells us that we must do so." Siddiqi adds that not only is it permitted for men and women to be included in Islamic settings, including prayer, without a curtain, partition, or wall, it is *preferable*.

> In America we are living in a very mixed society. Our brothers and sisters are all going out for work, shopping, study or just for outings. Our mosques should be the places where we should learn and teach our children the etiquette of living in a mixed society with Islamic manners. If we make artificial barriers between men and women inside our places of worship, where are we going to learn Islamic manners of being together as believing men and women?[9]

At most, says Siddiqi, a low barrier should be placed merely to demarcate the separate spaces for men and women. Women should not be placed in a separate room unless there is no space in the mosque and there is no other proper arrangement.[10]

Belief in the necessity of a fixed barrier has a foothold in the United States because mosques here tend to be associated with a specific national-cultural identity—there are Pakistani mosques, Iranian mosques, and so on—which can lead to an atmosphere of cultural insularity. Many of our mosques are financed by fundamentalist Muslim groups that adhere to Wahhabism and Salafism, which promote rigid, ahistorical interpretations of Islamic texts. (Wahhabism, based on tribal customs, is the law of the land in Saudi Arabia.) Many Wahhabi and Salafi Muslims have come to the United States and now serve as imams, mosque presidents, and mosque board members. Their anti-Western attitudes are volatile enough, but they are also combined with a feeling of insecurity in the face of anti-Muslim sentiment, leading to extreme rigidity in their thinking. As Ingrid Mattson observes, many Muslims "mistake rigidity for piety."[11] In religious matters, the path considered most righteous, which tends to be the most rigid, is regarded as the most authoritative and authentic.

A common argument against "mixed-gender prayer"—when women and men are side by side, though not necessarily touching shoulders—is that men are weak and unable to control themselves sexually. Remember, Muslim prayer involves extensive bending, bowing, and prostrating.

Opponents to mixed-gender prayer claim that seeing women's back-sides during prayer will cause *fitna*, conflict or temptation into sin—that it would be too sexually arousing and distracting, and besides, it is inappropriate for women to kneel in front of men, because this is not modest behavior. Progressives retort that when you pray, the last thing you should be doing is checking out the ladies. In any event, it is de rigueur for women to wear baggy, modest clothes when they go to mosque, with many opting to wear an *abaya* (gown) that covers the contours of their bodies completely.

Concern about the effects of female sexuality on men, but not vice versa, is connected with an ancient belief that female sexuality is dangerous and must be controlled. A thirty-eight-year-old Pakistan-born woman now living in Arlington, Texas, tells me that she always speaks up to ensure religious equality. She has two daughters, and she does not want them excluded from anything. She proudly tells me that she is so quick to offer her opinion that she has gotten into public arguments with her imam. For her, the ideal mosque setup would have women on the main floor behind the men, not upstairs in a gallery, but also not side by side with the men. "I agree that women should be behind the men. I don't want someone looking at my backside!" she says with a laugh. This woman is embarrassed and self-conscious about her body because of the argument that women's bodies cause fitna.

No matter how much a female covers up, boys and men who want to sexualize her will. In Egypt, where 80 percent of women cover either their entire body or their neck and head, 98 percent of foreign women visiting the country and 83 percent of native women have been sexually harassed, according to the Egyptian Centre for Women's Rights. Most Egyptian women never report their harassment because either they feel ashamed and responsible or they worry, legitimately, that their reputation could be damaged.[12]

Girls and women internalize the belief that their bodies cause problems for men, leading them to feel ashamed and worried. A thirty-year-old American-born woman told the *San Francisco Chronicle* that now that the wall has been torn down in her mosque, she worries that the men are looking at her and that perhaps she is dressed too provocatively.[13] Many girls and women become embarrassed about their bodies even when they are not engaged in religious practice.

Most young American-born Muslim women recognize this sexual inequality. In the ideal mosque, "the sisters would not be upstairs," says Kimberly Harper, and as she excitedly tells me her vision, her languid southern tempo speeds up as the words spill out. "I would make the sisters' area bigger, with bigger bathrooms, and make it more family-friendly, with changing areas for the babies. But the brothers don't want to give us more room, so we have to build masjids, with women on the planning and design committees. Women need to be active and involved in their communities. There needs to be money for scholarships for women to study Islam within the context of U.S. culture. You know, women often find themselves raising their children alone, no matter what the reason—divorce, abuse, death, whatever. They need to have access to be able to make decisions to benefit their children's lives. Luckily the tide is turning."

As to the question of whether a woman may lead men and women in prayer according to Islamic law, most Muslims believe that women are not permitted to take on this role. But there is no prohibition in the Qur'an and hadith. Furthermore, there is a precedent in the example of a woman named Umm Waraqah who lived during the time of Muhammad. According to several hadith, the prophet commanded Umm Waraqah, who had collected his recitations, to lead prayer. According to Nevin Reda, a student at the University of Toronto who has researched Umm Waraqah, she had her own *mu'adhdhin* (person who calls everyone to prayer). The precedent of Umm Waraqah led several medieval scholars to permit female imams.[14]

But even many progressive Muslims believe that Umm Waraqah is not a strong enough precedent. In an essay that directly responds to Reda, Imam Zaid Shakir objects that the narrators of the Umm Waraqah hadith are considered questionable, and therefore one cannot use this tradition as the basis for establishing law. Shakir, who is actually enormously sympathetic to the issue of women's equality, also argues, not unpersuasively, that it appears that Umm Waraqah led prayer in her home, not in a mosque, and that the service was attended only by the mu'adhdhin and two servants (one male and one female). It is even possible, based on how the narrative is interpreted, that she led only women in prayer. As for the medieval rulings mentioned by Reda, Shakir responds that these are no longer valid, because their schools are extinct and their legal methodologies lost. Thus, jurists have deduced that a woman can lead prayer only for other women. Some modern scholars allow a woman to lead men within her home if there are no men qualified to lead prayer. Shakir concludes that Islamic law does not sanction a woman leading mixed-gender, public, obligatory congregational prayer.[15]

Based on her reading of the sources, Ingrid Mattson agrees. She stresses that women can and do lead prayer for women, but that the matter of a woman leading a mixed-gender congregation is a technical one. "It's a question of Islamic law and how we approach Islamic law," she tells me. "The point of the legal methodology is to be guided by God, not to just do what you want. The struggle is to try to submit ourselves to the law. But it's always an open question as to whether we have a good understanding or not."

One of Shakir's main arguments against female imams is that there is no clear, specific statement of permission for women to lead mixed-gender congregational prayer. Laury Silvers, the Skidmore professor, rebuts that "since there is no clear prohibition in the sources, woman-led mixed prayer is permissible if a particular Muslim community agrees to it."[16] But using different legal reasoning, Mattson tells me that although there is a fundamental principle in Islamic law that if something is not forbidden, it is permissible, this principle does not apply in the area of worship. In worship, the principle is the inverse: if something is not permissible, it is forbidden. This is why Muslims around the world, though astoundingly diverse, pray in a remarkably identical way. Prayer has not changed since the time of the prophet— and most Muslims want to keep it this way.

The challenge, then, is not to debate whether or not Umm Waraqah's prayer is a legitimate or illegitimate precedent, since the debate can be argued either way. Perhaps at some point American Muslims will organize into separate denominations, so that those who want innovations in prayer can find one another and create the worship experience they crave, and those who cherish the status quo can continue as they have been. Those who want an egalitarian prayer service would flock to mosques run by boards with similar values, and traditionalists would be involved with mosques more in line with their own interpretations of the law. Denominations, by definition, emphasize differences, which can fracture a community. However, if more American Muslims felt comfortable in a community of like-minded believers, more would observe Islamic law and Islam would ultimately be strengthened and enriched.

In this post–September 11 world, there are no uncluttered critical discussions about anything having to do with Islam. American Muslims are on the defensive because politicians have felt completely at ease denouncing their religion. When the first Muslim member of Congress, Representative Keith Ellison of Minnesota, chose to be sworn into office in 2006 with a Qur'an instead of the Christian Bible, Representative Virgil Goode of Virginia expressed "fear" of the increasing number of Muslims in the United States. Evangelical Christians have publicly described Islam as "a very evil and wicked religion" (spoken by Franklin Graham, son of Billy Graham) and a "dangerous religion" (Pat Robertson), with Muhammad labeled a "demon-obsessed pedophile" (Jerry Vines, the former president of the Southern Baptist Convention). During the 2008 presidential campaign, Barack Obama was described (falsely) by opponents as Muslim—which was supposed to terrify voters. Given this atmosphere, it's no surprise that many Muslims prefer to converse only among themselves about their internal disagreements.

It is particularly difficult for non-Muslims to talk about the issue of women's rights in Islam. Most non-Muslims are astonishingly ignorant about Islam yet imagine themselves experts—on women's issues and beyond. When the journalist and Progressive Muslim Union board member Mona Eltahawy participated in a panel discussion in New York City intended to showcase the diversity of Muslim voices in the United States, two women from the well-heeled audience later complained about the event. "They're trying to convince us they're the mainstream?" asked one, while the other replied, "They're not the mainstream." During the question-and-answer period, one of the audience members asked, "What does a Muslim home look like?"—the implication being that a Muslim home looks foreign and strange. When she gives lectures on Muslim issues, Eltahawy can guarantee that she will be asked, "How representative are you?" "Implicit in all these questions," she continues, "is the disturbingly prevalent view that there is only one way to be a Muslim." If you're a man, you must be "Angry Bearded Muslim Man," an anti-American terrorist yelling "Allahu Akbar"; if you're a woman, you must be "Covered in Black Muslim Woman," an oppressed being who walks silently and despairingly. Since Eltahawy does not wear hijab and is educated and opinionated, the thinking goes, she can't really be Muslim.[17]

We all know that women in a number of Muslim countries *are* oppressed. Horribly, unimaginably oppressed. Many are forced into arranged marriages, may not travel, and may not work—restrictions that are placed in the name of Islam. Many are victims of horrific human rights violations—again, committed in the name of Islam. In 2002 in Saudi Arabia, fourteen schoolgirls were burned to death in a fire at their Mecca school because the doors were locked from the outside; the girls running out to safety were not covered up, and therefore they were not allowed to exit the building. Also in Saudi Arabia, in 2008 a nineteen-year-old who was abducted and gang-raped by seven men was ordered to be whipped by ninety lashes because she was in a car with an unrelated man before her abduction. When she appealed her sentence and publicized her plight, the court increased her punishment to two hundred lashes and six months in jail.[18]

In rural Turkey, young women are stoned to death, strangled, shot, or buried alive for wearing a short skirt, wanting to go to the movies, stealing a glance at a boy, having consensual sex, or being raped. In Pakistan, the rape of a girl or young woman is a common punishment meted out by tribal councils to avenge crimes committed by other family members. Several years ago in Yemen, a man shot his daughter dead on her wedding night after her new husband claimed she wasn't a virgin. The mother had her daughter's body examined, and it was discovered that she indeed had been a virgin—but her husband was impotent and lied to protect his honor and avoid the shame of displaying their bridal sheet without bloodstains. The list goes on and on.

Every single one of us in the West has a responsibility to speak out against these atrocities; more fundamentally, we must denounce the societal hatred of women that leads to these atrocities. American writers and activists, Muslim and non-Muslim, including Eltahawy, Irshad Manji, Margaret Atwood, and Phyllis Chesler, among many others, have urged Western non-Muslims to stifle the feel-good liberal ethic of "multicultural acceptance," because human rights violations are *never* acceptable, in the United States or abroad.

Yet at the same time, non-Muslims must recognize that these atrocities are based on tribal laws and are not supported by the Qur'an or the example of Muhammad. Similar atrocities are also committed worldwide by non-Muslims. "Many of the most egregious issues have nothing to do with Islam," says Pamela Taylor of Muslims for Progressive Values, "and would in fact be alleviated if people tried to implement Islam."[19] Also, not all Muslim women experience woman hatred. Even in predominantly Muslim countries, many Muslim women do not consider themselves oppressed.[20] When Karen Hughes, a senior Bush administration official, spoke with five hundred elite women at a university in Saudi Arabia in 2005, they openly criticized her for depicting them as mistreated, and they burst into applause when one audience member told Hughes that they're "all pretty happy."[21] In North America, it is true that Wahhabi, Salafist, and tribal beliefs are imported here, and we must be vigilant that these beliefs are not put into practice in a way that harms a single person. But for all their obstacles to religious equality, North American Muslims live in a democratic society with the legal right to speak up and educate people regarding the fact that honor killings and related abuses of women are not only violations of human rights but also violations of the Qur'an and the spirit of Islam. Although they stand in solidarity with their oppressed sisters in other lands, North American Muslim women do not want to be confused with them.

In any event, although Islam obviously is connected with Arab culture, today fewer than 15 percent of the world's Muslims are Arab. Half of the world's Muslims live in South Asia and Southeast Asia. In the United States, there are millions of Muslims who are not immigrants—from any country, let alone an Arab country. Converts to Islam, a group that includes many black Muslims and is a huge segment of the U.S. Muslim population, tend to be overlooked by the media, who consider immigrants more "authentic." To American-born Muslims of whatever race and ethnicity, it is doubly insulting to suggest that they are oppressed, because this not only misrepresents them—it erases them.

In all my conversations with white Christian women rising up for religious equality, not once did anyone express concern that she was betraying her community or that she would be perceived as airing dirty laundry. White Christian women in this country are members of the dominant culture, so even when they are dissident, they still have the protection that comes from being part of the majority. But Muslim women, again and again, expressed concern to me that their desire for reform not be mistaken for rejection of their beloved heritage. You can't blame them for their caution. Westerners have a sordid history of seizing on criticism of Islamic customs involving women—for the purpose of denigrating Islam entirely. Western missionaries in the nineteenth century attacked Muslim countries under the guise of "saving" the women, even though in reality they didn't care at all about women's rights. The most blatant example is that of the British consul general in Egypt, Lord Cromer, who insisted in 1882 that Egyptian women cease veiling their faces, while back at home he opposed giving British women the right to vote.

Western women seeking religious equality have also exacted a double standard from Muslim women. Although it is considered acceptable for Christian and Jewish feminist theologians to criticize their own religious traditions within a framework of acceptance, equality-minded Muslim women have been expected to renounce Islam entirely, which is seen as unredeemable. Leila Ahmed recalls her involvement with panels and conferences on Muslim women, mostly attended by white women, when she first came to the United States in 1980. In her memoir *A Border Passage: From Cairo to America—A Woman's Journey*, Ahmed writes,

> We could not pursue the investigation of our heritage, traditions, religion in the way that white women were investigating and rethinking theirs. Whatever aspect of our history or religion each of us had been trying to reflect on, we would be besieged, at the end of our presentations, with furious questions and declarations openly dismissive of Islam. People quite commonly did not even seem to know that there was some connection between the patriarchal vision to be found in Islam and that in Judaism and Christianity. Regularly we would be asked belligerently, "Well, what about the veil" or "What about clitoridec-

tomy?" when none of us had mentioned either subject for the simple reason that it was completely irrelevant to the topics of our papers . . . In contrast to their situation, our salvation entailed not arguing with and working to change our traditions but giving up our cultures, religions, and traditions and adopting theirs.[22]

In the face of prejudice, cardboard stereotypes, and misinformation, progressive U.S. Muslims have to be careful when they call for reform. After all, internal dissent can be seized upon by non-Muslim Westerners as evidence that even its practitioners find the religion lacking in value. Nevertheless, progressives are willing to stick their necks out. Murmuring quietly does not help the cause. "People need to feel that there is an alternative Islamic space that has some legitimacy that they can turn to," explains one of the founders of the Progressive Muslim Union, Sarah Eltantawi.[23]

In response to her loud, unabashed call for Islamic reform, Irshad Manji has received numerous death threats and has lived under police protection. She was born in Uganda in 1968 to a Pakistani family; they fled the dictatorship of Idi Amin Dada and settled in Canada when Manji was four years old. In 2004 she wrote a book, *The Trouble with Islam*, which became an international bestseller. It is a blunt open letter to Muslims that takes to task those who uncritically accept narrow, medieval interpretations of Islam, tribal ideas about "honor," and knee-jerk anti-semitism. Manji informs her readers of the legacy of independent thinking in Islamic jurisprudence and asks that the "gates of ijtihad" be reopened.

Although purportedly addressed to Muslims, her book is obviously written with non-Muslims in mind; thus, Manji has angered many Muslims who believe she is misrepresenting their faith to a world that is already unsympathetic to Islam. A polarizing figure, she has been accused of falsely presenting herself as the first critic to address the need for contemporary ijtihad.

In person, it's hard not to like Manji. She is cheeky and funny. At an event in New York City in May 2006 at the 92nd Street Y, she addressed the crowd, "Salaam, shalom, and to the atheists out there, how the hell are you?" She went on: "Welcome to an evening that I like to call putting the 'her' into heretic." Wearing jeans, a blood-orange–colored Indian tunic, and a pendant necklace, with her trade-mark spiky hair and glasses she looked like a well-groomed radical. She made it clear that despite her criticisms, she loves her religion and is committed to it. She told the audience of several hundred that grow-ing up with Islam gave her the values of "discipline, empathy, compas-sion, and mercy."

I met up with Manji one week later on campus at Yale University, where she was spending the semester as a fellow. On my way to our meeting place, a diner called the Educated Burgher, I marveled at the gorgeous blue-sky day. It was seventy degrees in New Haven; students and townspeople were flip-flopping down Broadway in sundresses, jeans, and T's, sipping iced teas. It was a day so magnificent it could turn an atheist into a believer. I found the diner and sat down at a booth a few minutes before Manji, wearing a faded orange crewneck T-shirt with a picture of Gandhi, slipped in opposite me. I was sur-prised that she was alone—didn't she have bodyguards?

"I do have them," she replied, "but not on a regular basis. I decided several months after the book came out that if I'm going to have con-tinued legitimacy conveying to young Muslims that it's possible to dis-sent with the clerics and live, I can't have a big, burly guy at my shoulder everywhere I go. It would be a hypocritical message. But when I go to problem areas of the world, I do have personal security with me. I was in Yemen recently, and I had to have three bodyguards. The govern-ment of Yemen provided them."

"The first thing I do every morning is turn on my computer and check my in-box for overnight death threats," she continued. "I'm not concerned about the ones that say, 'I wish you will die' or 'You will die soon.' Those are par for the course. The ones that are trou-bling are the ones that are personal and specific, like, 'You will die, I will be the one to kill you, and here is how I will do it.' At that point I have to take it seriously and contact the police. I've been spat at; I've had things thrown at me. An Arab man at the Montreal airport went up to the friend I was traveling with and put his hand in the shape of a gun in my direction and pulled the trigger. I know what to look for beneath a car and inside a car before I turn on the ignition. I've had good training over the last couple of years. The reality is that if you do this kind of work, you are a marked woman. But my work is absolutely worth the risk. If I go tomorrow, I will die a very happy woman."

In the year 610 in what is today Saudi Arabia, a merchant and member of the Meccan tribe of Quraysh named Muhammad received revelations from God through the angel Gabriel. These revelations, believed to be the literal words of God, came to Muhammad over a period of twenty-three years, bit by bit. Together they form the text of the Qur'an (recitation), which was written down after the prophet's death.

The Qur'an's primary message is that Islam entails creating a just and equitable society. Islam gave women rights within marriage (including the right to sexual satisfaction), the right to divorce, and inheritance law centuries before women in the West were granted these rights. The pre-Islamic custom of female infanticide was prohibited. Muhammad repeatedly declared that women must be treated with respect. Once, the women of Medina complained to him that they were behind the men in their study of the Qur'an; Muhammad helped them catch up.[24] There is a famous hadith in which a man came to the prophet Muhammad and said, "Messenger of God, I desire to go on a military expedition, and I have come to consult you." Muhammad asked if the man had a mother, and when he replied that he did, Muhammad said, "Stay with her, then, for Paradise is at her feet [is found in serving her]."[25] There is a well-told tale that the women asked Muhammad why the Qur'an addressed only men. In response, the prophet received a revelation that addressed the women and the men and emphasized the moral and spiritual equality of the sexes (33:35).[26] Many other Qur'anic passages refer to the equality of women and men—"I waste not the actions of ones who work among you, male or female; each one of you is as the other" (3:195); "One who has acted in accord with morality, whether male or female, and is one who believes, such shall enter the Garden where they shall be provided in it without reckoning" (40:40).

Nevertheless, reading the Qur'an from the perspective of the twenty-first century, one finds passages that describe women as less than men. This is true of the Christian and Jewish sacred texts too. As with all these texts, the meaning is dependent on how the words are interpreted and whether the historical context is taken into account. One Qur'anic verse permits a man to marry up to four wives, although only if he can treat them all equally (4:3). However, later in the same chapter, another verse reads, "You shall never be able to be just between wives, even if you are eager" (4:129). Read together, the two verses can be understood to endorse monogamy without actually prohibiting polygamy. It is important to know that in tribal culture, women needed the protection of a husband, so polygamy protected women in that it insured that every woman could be partnered with a man. Polygamy is also permitted in the Hebrew Bible.

In a verse about inheritance, the Qur'an stipulates that when her parents die, a daughter should receive half of what her brother inherits (4:11, 176). On the face of it, this appears to be blatant prejudice against women. But not so fast—one must also consider that at the time, giving a woman *any* inheritance was unheard of, and therefore the Qur'an actually improved the status of women. Muslim women arguably were given more rights than women from any other culture at this time in history. Moreover, women in Islamic society had no financial obligations, while the men had to support their families, so on balance, the allocation of inheritance was reasonable.

Muhammad helped with household chores and treated his wives as companions rather than helpers, relates the historian Karen Armstrong. His first wife, Khadijah, was a successful businesswoman and widow who offered him a business opportunity leading her caravan into Syria, and then she asked if he would like to marry her. She was forty, and he was twenty-five. They had a monogamous marriage of partnership until she died twenty-five years later. Khadijah was instrumental for Islam because she encouraged Muhammad in his prophecies. One of his other wives, Aisha, is notorious because it is claimed that she was extremely young at the time they were married, possibly only nine years old. But she is also known to have been intelligent and opinionated, and it is reported that most of Muhammad's revelations came to him while he was in her presence. In addition, many of the hadith are attributed to her. In fact, nearly half of the Islamic jurisprudence of the Hanafi school of thought, followed by 70 percent of Muslims, is based on the hadith communicated by Aisha. (Hanafi is one of the four orthodox schools of Sunni law.)

So what *is* Islam? Does it force schoolgirls to die in a blazing fire—rather than spare their lives—because their hair is exposed? Or does it elevate women as the gatekeepers of Paradise?

Every Muslim I spoke with, whether an immigrant or a child of immigrants or a convert, emphasized to me the spiritual dimension of her religion. One Pakistani-born woman told me that she loves Islam because of "the constant contact with God." A daughter of Pakistani immigrants told me that Islam offers "assurance that there is cosmic justice in the world."

Juliet Gentile-Koren is particularly eloquent. Raised Catholic as a child, in her twenties she became a *dervish* (member) of the Nur Ashki Jerrahi Sufi Order (a branch of the Halveti-Jerrahi Tariqat of Istanbul that is led by a woman, Sheikha Fariha al-Jerrahi). Gentile-Koren, now twenty-nine, has a luminous beauty, with large brown eyes and thick brown hair, set off when I met her by a stunning cobalt tunic worn over loose-fitting pants. She spoke to me as she fingered a string of ninety-nine prayer beads, called a *tasbih*, that symbolizes the ninety-nine names of God. Gentile-Koren connects her experience of Islam with the words *"Bismillah al-Rahman al-Raheem"* (In the name of God, most merciful and most compassionate). These words commence each sura (chapter) of the Qur'an. In her Sufi order, the dervishes recite these words "each time we take a sip of water, each time we speak. Ideally we say it as many times as we take in a breath, since each breath out into the world would be Bismillah. And then the day outwardly is punctuated by the five prayers, which is a return to an inner state of connection with God, a time to stand before the presence of God. These punctuations of the day are very important for me, to feel a constant connection with God. Of course, we are always connected, but we try to maintain an awareness of the connection through ritual practices like prayer or the tasbih. Allah is merciful and compassionate, and this is the truth: that everything is God's mercy. That to me as a worldview is profound and very beautiful, to see everything within a tapestry of mercy and compassion."

On the theoretical level, Islam is a religion of mercy and compassion. But on the level of practice, of daily life, it is understood in widely divergent ways by different communities. Even within the same community it can be approached and practiced differently. Riffat Hassan, the author of *Women's Rights and Islam*, was born into an upper-class family in Pakistan and came to the United States in the 1970s. She became aware that there is a "glaring discrepancy between normative Islam and Muslim practice . . . The more I saw that justice and compassion formed the core of the Qur'anic teachings regarding women, the more anguished and angry I felt seeing the injustices and inhumanity to which a large number of Muslim women are subjected in actual life."[27]

Leila Ahmed similarly distinguishes between two ways of approaching her religion. She relates in her memoir that when she was growing up comfortably in Cairo, the men understood Islam narrowly, rigidly, and patriarchally from a textual tradition, while the women learned about Islam from an aural tradition, leading them to extract broader values of equality, justice, and mercy. The women did not attend mosque and did not hear the sermons that the men heard; they were not exposed to the orthodox interpretations presented each Friday at the khutba. Instead, they listened to recitations of the Qur'an and formed their own opinions about what the Qur'an meant. Moreover, the women had little regard for the sheikhs, whom they regarded as bigoted and superstitious. Rather, the women believed that they did not require an interpreter or intermediary between themselves and God: they were perfectly capable of understanding Islam by themselves on their own terms, thank you very much.

The men, claims Ahmed, immersed themselves in a textual heritage that was locked in a medieval mind-set. The women, on the other hand, passed down to their daughters the idea that Islam

> was gentle, generous, pacifist, inclusive, somewhat mystical . . . Religion was above all about inner things. The outward signs of religiousness, such as prayer and fasting, might be signs of a true religiousness but equally well might not. They were certainly not what was important about being Muslim. What was important was how you conducted yourself and how you were in yourself and in your attitude toward others and in your heart . . . a way of holding oneself in the world—in relation to God, to existence, to other human beings . . . Generations of astute, thoughtful women, listening to the Qur'an, understood perfectly well its essential themes and its faith. And looking

around them, they understood perfectly well, too, what a travesty men had made of it.[28]

Amina Wadud, an associate professor of Islamic studies at Virginia Commonwealth University and one of the world's preeminent scholars on women and Islam, affirms that although men have long interpreted Islam from their own point of view and declared that point of view universal for all believers (just as male Christian and Jewish theologians and religious leaders have done throughout history), Islam at its essence regards women and men as coequals before God. In her book *Qur'an and Woman: Rereading the Sacred Text from a Woman's Perspective* she writes that the more research she did into the Qur'an, the more she recognized that "in Islam a female person was intended to be primordially, cosmologically, eschatologically, spiritually, and morally a full human being, equal to all who accepted Allah as Lord, Muhammad as prophet, and Islam as *din* [religious way of life]."[29]

Wadud, an African American who was raised Methodist and converted to Islam, has formulated a hermeneutical method of reading the Qur'an that she calls "the *tawhidic* paradigm." "Tawhid" means unity, referring particularly to the oneness of God. Wadud emphasizes the unity of the Qur'an, meaning that the Qur'an has an overall framework and coherence, with overarching meaning that must be applied to all verses. "Tawhid" also refers to the ultimate unity of all human beings beneath one God. Within the oneness of God, all human beings—female and male—are on the same level of social interaction, with no gender stratification.

Wadud further argues that "seventh-century Arabian particulars in the Qur'an should be restricted to that context unless a broader basis of understanding can be developed from them."[30] That is, the particulars of seventh-century Arabian culture do not apply to today's world, but the overarching values of the Qur'an, which are universal and transcend specific eras and circumstances, do. Further, she maintains that "in order to maintain its relevance, the Qur'an must be continually re-interpreted."[31] This theological concept—that a sacred text can be divine and also alive and fluid—has also been embraced by some Orthodox Jewish feminists, as we will see in the next chapter. In approaching sacred writings from this theological standpoint, a believer can reconcile core divine values with modernity without sacrificing tradition.

Wadud instructs that each Islamic society must apply the eternal principles to its own particulars. To take one example, the principle of modesty, which is discussed in the Qur'an, is always important, but the manner in which women and men must display modesty varies throughout time and culture. This process is never final; it is an ongoing, eternal process. As other scholars have done, Wadud has closely examined the verses on polygamy, inheritance, and other family legal matters, showing that in essence they affirm women's equality, and she has argued that we must extract this essence from the context of seventh-century Arabia in order to apply it to today's situations.

However, there is one verse that—despite trying for years to reconcile with today's norms—she cannot accept. That is the verse understood to permit wife beating, 4:34. It reads that when wives do not obey their husbands, the husbands should "admonish them and send them to beds apart and beat them," according to popular translation.[32] This verse has been used to legitimate violence against women. (When religious authorities have been benevolent, they have reassured that nothing thicker than a twig may be used as a beating instrument.) When she wrote her first book, in 1992, *Qur'an and Woman*, Wadud interpreted this verse to mean that beating is permitted only as an extreme last resort in marital strife, after first, verbal mediation, and second, sleeping in separate beds. Since there was excessive violence toward women in pre-Islamic culture, Wadud read this verse as a severe restriction on the existing practices, which meant it was an *improvement* for women.

Fourteen years later, in her 2006 book, *Inside the Gender Jihad: Women's Reform in Islam*, Wadud revisited this interpretation and changed her position. Now, after rereading the verse extensively and taking into account the fact that Muhammad never once struck a woman or a slave, she cannot allow a reading that permits *any* force against a woman, under *any* circumstances. In a radical move, she writes, "I have finally come to say 'no' outright to the literal implementation of this passage . . . This verse, and the literal implementation of *hudud* [penal code], both imply an ethical standard of human actions that are archaic and barbarian at this time in history. They are unjust in the ways that human beings have come to experience and understand justice, and hence unacceptable to universal notions of human dignity."[33]

This is not a rejection of the Qur'an, but a rejection of the literal application of one verse. Wadud calls this an "intervention" with the text or, using the terminology of Islamic legal scholar Khaled Abou el Fadl of UCLA, a "conscientious pause." This would not be the first "conscientious pause," she reminds her readers. The Qur'anic acceptance of slavery has been abolished, for the simple reason that scholars have followed their conscience rather than the strict letter of the text. Christians and Jews have also rejected their Scripture's acceptance of slavery. And yet no one today says that slavery must be reinstituted in order to be faithful to the text. Wadud continues:

> We finally arrive at a place where *we acknowledge that we intervene* with the text. The next step is to admit that we are continuing the process of intervention between text and meaning, as believers of Allah and in revelation . . . We must now simply acknowledge that it has always been done and accept the responsibility of agency in doing so openly and in consultation with the community. Since we live in the time when at least the conceptualization of women's complete human agency and equality between women and men is conceivable, then we must dance the delicate dance between text and agency to assert a movement of complete gender justice . . . We are the makers of texual meaning.[34]

Like evangelical Christian feminist scholars, Wadud engages with the sacred text by extracting the universal principles. Wife beating just does not mesh with the essence of the Qur'an. To Wadud and like-minded progressive Islamic scholars, this is a signal to us. We must pause and consider whether or not wife beating is part of God's plan for today. The answer, increasingly, is no. God is eternal and transcendent. Therefore, God transcends seventh-century Arabia and the particular practice of wife beating. To allow wife beating, or any other practice that is oppressive to women, is un-Islamic.

Other scholars, sharing the same bafflement that the Qur'an could ever possibly condone violence, have approached the problem differently. The translator Laleh Bakhtiar has persuasively argued that the Arabic term commonly translated as "beat" ("*daraba*") instead means "to go away." Bakhtiar discovered this translation in a 3,064-page nineteenth-century Arabic-English lexicon. The implications are enormous: God did not instruct husbands to beat their wives as a last resort, but to dissolve the marriage. "The word 'daraba' has twenty-five meanings," Iranian-born Bakhtiar, a sixty-eight-year-old grandmother and convert to Islam who lives in Chicago, said to me, "so why do we use the one that's going to harm someone?" She added that her translations make sense logically within the context of the Qur'an: "For instance, it says in the Qur'an that a woman who wants a divorce cannot be harmed. And if a husband accuses his wife of adultery without witnesses, each one has to swear an oath to God five times that they are telling the truth and that the other one is lying. And once the woman does that, the accusation is over and can't move forward. But because 4:34 has been misinterpreted by men to allow husbands to beat their wives, a wife never gets to take advantage of her rights as spelled out in other verses. Let's say a husband and wife are having an argument and the wife says, 'I want a divorce.' According to misinterpretation of 4:34, he can interpret [her behavior] as rebellion and beat her before she even has a chance of getting a divorce. Or he can accuse her of adultery and beat her to a pulp, if that is how you understand 4:34, even though the accusation must end after she swears five times that she is telling the truth. The husband [in this misinterpretation] is both judge and jury. It is totally inconsistent. But the Qur'an is not inconsistent; *we* have made it inconsistent."

The same conclusion was reached by the Saudi scholar Abdul-Hamid A. AbuSulayman:

Considering the context, the purpose of this verse is reconciliation in a dignified manner and without coercion or intimidation as each spouse has the ability and the right to dissolve the relationship. Therefore, the meaning of *daraba* cannot imply the infliction of injury, pain, or disgrace. The most straightforward interpretation is hence that of departure, separation or seclusion.[35]

Because they began with the premise that the Qur'an advocates for the empowerment of women, these two scholars came to recognize that daraba could not possibly be understood to permit husbands to inflict pain on their wives. Thus, different interpretations result from different presuppositions. The new understanding of daraba is perfectly consistent with timeless adherence to the divine message of the Qur'an.

Progressive scholarship by itself will not transform Islam. It must be combined with activism.

Asra Nomani, a former reporter for *The Wall Street Journal* who was born in Bombay in 1965 and moved to West Virginia with her parents when she was four, has gone to great lengths to experience Islam as it should be. Within the rigid framework through which so many Muslims understand Islam, Nomani is an outsider. Not only is she a woman agitating for women's equality, she is also a single mother. While she was living in Pakistan, her Muslim boyfriend left her upon hearing that she was pregnant with his child. Instead of running away from the religion that seemed to endorse the view that she was guilty of a sexual crime and that her child was illegitimate, she has done precisely the opposite: she has returned to Islam. Her journey has been a literal one. In 2003, with her three-month-old son in a baby carrier on her chest, Nomani went on *hajj*, the holy pilgrimage to Mecca, Saudi Arabia—one of the requirements for every Muslim during her lifetime.

In her riveting book *Standing Alone*, Nomani describes her arduous hajj. Along with two million other Muslims, she walked in the footsteps of the prophet Muhammad. Her journey brought her closer to God and also to other Muslims who, like her, had traveled from around the world. Throughout her hajj, strangers were affectionate with her son. She relates that when she first entered Saudi Arabia, she found herself in a restroom where there was an enormous sink for everyone to perform the ritual ablution, wudu, before prayer. The woman next to her was from Iran, and Nomani was excited to perform the same rite beside a woman who spoke a different language but shared the same tradition. Later she was moved when she observed an elderly woman lifting her index finger while making the *sha-hada*, testimony of Islamic faith, during prayer at the exact same moment that she herself suspended her own finger in the air. "It was quite profound that this woman and I were separated by culture, language, and economy, but we were both making a proclamation of faith at precisely the same moment," she writes.[36]

What was most thrilling to Nomani was that while she was performing Islam's most sacred rituals, she did so side by side with men. The women were covered up, of course, in loose, flowing gowns and head scarves, but they prayed together without physical barriers. In the Masjid al-Haram, the Sacred Mosque in Mecca, in one of the most restrictive countries for women, there was no wall, curtain, or balcony. After traveling to Medina, Nomani continued on to Jerusalem and prayed at the al-Aqsa Mosque—again, with no physical barrier. (The al-Aqsa Mosque is believed to be the site to which Muhammad traveled on a "night journey" from Mecca; from there he ascended to heaven, was instructed about the five daily prayers, and returned to Mecca to tell the people.) There, Nomani prayed ten yards behind a row of men, but, she says, she was not made to feel that her spot was subordinate.[37]

Nomani returned to her hometown, Morgantown, spiritually energized. She was bursting with desire to be part of her community. Her parents were overcome with joy; her father had helped found the town's original mosque in 1981 and sat on the board of the Islamic Center. At the time, Morgantown was opening a new mosque, a three-story building near the campus of West Virginia University. Knowing that the new mosque was being financed by a group aligned with Saudi Wahhabis, and concerned that women would not be welcomed there, she created a "Manifesto for Equal Participation by Women"—calling for equal access and facilities within the mosque—and her father brought it before the board the night before Ramadan. The board listened to the manifesto but did not respond, Nomani's father told her. "With hope," she writes,

> I walked with great enthusiasm to the freshly painted green doors of the new mosque. It was the eve of Ramadan, the holiest of months for Muslims and a time when we abstain from

food, drink, and sex from sunup to sundown on the path to liberate us from our attachments to worldly desires. I had enjoyed this month since my childhood days as a sort of spiritual boot camp. I wore the same flowing *hijab* I had worn in Mecca, Medina, and Jerusalem.[38]

When Nomani reached the door, she was not greeted with "Assalaam aleikum." Instead, the board president yelled at her, "Sister, take the back entrance!" Most mosques in the United States do not have separate doors for women, but the attitude toward women she encountered was far from uncommon. Stunned, Nomani relates that she "had never been treated so rudely at the Sacred Mosque in Mecca or in the Holy Sanctuary in Jerusalem," and that even though she "opposed most of Saudi Arabia's policies toward women, the government made the *hajj* experience more equitable than I could ever have imagined . . . And yet it was unacceptable for me to walk through the front doors of my own mosque in Morgantown, West Virginia."[39]

It went downhill from there. Nomani watched as a medical student arrived at the new mosque with a covered dish for *iftar*, the ceremonial dinner breaking the fast at sunset. The student enthusiastically walked up to the front door to offer her homecooked food, only to be met by a man who pointed to the old mosque, where kids were running around wild, and barked, "Women—over there!"[40] Nomani herself, fed up with the way women were being treated, decided to take action. On the eleventh day of Ramadan, together with her mother and her thirteen-year-old niece, she walked through the front door of her mosque and climbed the front staircase for the first time. She walked into the hall for men. Despite the board president and other men booming out threats and insults, Nomani remained where she was, in the back of the men's section. She felt it demeaning to sit upstairs in the women's section, with a wall so high that the women could not see the imam and had to watch the service on closed-circuit television, so she stayed put and prayed behind the men.

At the Friday evening sermon, a visiting imam preached about the permissibility of wife beating. On another Friday, a graduate engineering student delivered the khutba and told the worshippers that "a woman's honor lies in her chastity and modesty. When she loses this, she is worthless."[41] All the while, Nomani complained to the mosque leadership about women's second-class treatment. After being ignored by mosque leaders, she took her complaints public—to the op-ed page of *The New York Times*. Several months later the mosque leadership voted to expel Nomani from the mosque. They said that her behavior was disruptive to prayer and harmful to the community. Her father resigned from his position on the board.

The mosque leadership may have kicked Nomani out, but it did not silence her. She created an Islamic Bill of Rights for Women in Mosques, which she has distributed at mosques across the United States. The ten "principles of equality for women in mosques" include the following: "Women have an Islamic right to enter through the main door"; "Women have an Islamic right to pray . . . without being separated by a barrier"; "Women have an Islamic right to hold leadership positions"; and "Women have an Islamic right to be full participants in all congregational activities." (The full text is available on Nomani's website, www.asranomani.com.) In June 2004 she and her family joined with four prominent Muslim writers—Saleemah Abdul-Ghafur, Mohja Kahf, Samina Ali, and Sarah Eltantawi—and marched through the front doors of the Morgantown mosque. Nomani had alerted the Associated Press, which gave her cause wide news coverage.

Meanwhile, a twenty-five-year-old African American woman named Nakia Jackson was voicing her concerns about women's treatment at her own mosque in Boston. At the Mosque for the Praising of Allah in the Roxbury section of the city, women prayed in a smelly, all-purpose room that was also used as a closet. There was a rat's nest, as well as a urine stain on the carpet, left there uncleaned for many years after a worshipper was incontinent. Religious study classes were held only for men, and all the leadership slots were reserved for men. Jackson, then a student in music education who had worked part-time in the mosque's administrative office for two years, complained about the conditions. "They would say to me things like, 'I don't see it!' or they would blame the rat's nest on the restaurant next door, or they would say they had other priorities," she told me. "The mosque redecorated the office and bought new computers" during the time of her complaints but did not improve the women's section.

I met Jackson for pizza on a mild Sunday evening in Manhattan during Memorial Day weekend. She gave the appearance of being pious and serious but also a little funky, in a loose-fitting fuchsia blouse, long black skirt, dove gray hijab, and horn glasses. She related to me how one day, as Nomani had done, she snapped. She walked into the main prayer space for men and refused to budge. She stood in the back in loose-fitting clothing, to demonstrate that she wasn't trying to grab attention; she just wanted to pray in a dignified space. Like Nomani, she says, she was banned from her mosque. Also like Nomani, she was media savvy: she offered her opinions to *The Boston Globe* and in a PBS program on the way she and her Muslim sisters were being treated.

Jackson and Nomani, who met each other at a convention of the Islamic Society of North America in 2004, were both restless. The media attention was an auspicious start, but they wanted to create real change. Nomani decided to organize a woman-led prayer service. "I called Amina Wadud, and she told me she would be in New York, and I was going to be in New York at the same time to promote my book, which had just come out. So I asked her if she would lead prayer and she said yes. Then I called my friend Saleemah Abdul-Ghafur and asked if she wanted to help organize it, and she said yes. And then I called Ahmed Nassef and asked if he would promote it, and he said yes. It was so exciting because it was the realization of a dream."

Wadud was a brilliant choice for imam. She has the academic credentials. She is learned. She is sincere in her devotion to God. In 1994 she delivered a pre-khutba sermon at jum'a in Cape Town, and she did so with dignity and piety—despite the fact that her participation led to violent protest and denunciation. And as an African American convert, she puts a different face—not the ubiquitous immigrant face—on the progressive movement.

Nomani approached three mosques in Manhattan, requesting them to host the service, and all three turned her down. Luckily, she was able to get a green light from an art gallery in SoHo. But at the last minute, after receiving a bomb threat, the gallery pulled out. The service ended up taking place at the Episcopal Cathedral of St. John the Divine in upper Manhattan, a stunning landmark and tourist attraction notable for its Gothic design.

On March 18, 2005, more than a hundred men and women prayed behind Wadud. (There would have been far more worshippers had the bomb threat not occurred and the location changed.) Wadud stood at the podium. As tradition dictates, her khutba was recited in Arabic; Wadud also translated her words into English.

> Praise be to Allah, Lord of all Worlds (or all alternative universal possibilities). I begin in the name and praise of Allah *ta'ala* [exalted]. I bear witness that there is no god but Allah, One, with no partners; and I bear witness that Muhammad, Ibn-'Abd Allah [Muhammad's full name], is the Prophet (and Messenger) of Allah. May Allah's praise be upon him, and upon his *ahl* [people], and his (immediate) companions, and his wives, and upon all who follow the guidance, (all of them) together until the day of reckoning; Amin . . .
>
> O Existent One, O Thou who art Present in all difficulties, O Thou of Hidden Kindness, of Subtle Making, O Gentle one, Who does not hasten, fulfill my need, with Thy Mercy, O Most Merciful of the Mercifuls. Glory be to Thee on Thy Grace, after Thy Knowledge. Glory be to Thee on Thy Forgiveness, after Thy Power. But if those [who are bent on denying the truth] turn away, say: Allah is enough for me! There is no deity save Her. In Him I placed my trust for It is the Sustainer, in awesome almightiness enthroned. There is none like Him, and He is the Hearer, the Knower.
>
> *Amin.*
>
> Please join me in reciting al-Fatihah, the Opening chapter of the Qur'an.[42]

Saleemah Abdul-Ghafur issued the call to prayer, and Wadud faced the direction for prayer, toward Mecca, made her silent prayer of intention, and raised her head with her hands at the sides of her face to recite "Allahu Akbar" and to begin the units of prayer.

There were swarms of journalists and photographers from news outlets from around the world, and of course the requisite protesters. Guards searched everyone's bags, and flashing cameras were everywhere. But to Nomani, the distractions didn't bother her.

"I felt like I was flying. I felt free for the first time of all of this garbage we have been taught to keep us in our place. For the first time, I felt that I was among Muslims who were kindred spirits [during prayer]. I overcame many fears, like my fear of standing in the front row. I overcame my fear of taking off my scarf during prayer. For the first time, I felt like I was not living in contradiction. For that moment, we had created something very right and very appropriate. We were doing something that was important for each one of us privately, but there was also global importance. I felt that we could really recast the image of women in Islam."

"It was one of the most moving moments of my life to pray behind Amina Wadud," Mona Eltahawy tells me. "It was the first time I had prayed publicly in a congregation with fellow Muslims since I arrived in the United States. It was a very special day for me. I dressed up and wore my best jewelry."

Says Patricia Dunn, one of the founders of *Muslim WakeUp!*, "I don't usually get emotional, but the day I could pray in public with Ahmed and Ali [our son] was incredible."

"I've never seen so many people smiling after a prayer service," reports Nakia Jackson. "There was so much joy. Everyone was rapt during the sermon. We all laughed at her jokes. It was everything a prayer service should be."

Although most of the women wore head scarves, Eltahawy and Nomani decided to pray that day with their hair uncovered. "We debated this amongst ourselves: should we wear it or not?" Eltahawy tells me. "I did wear the head scarf for nine years when I lived in Saudi Arabia and Egypt, but I don't any longer." She relates that Pamela Taylor, then chair of the Progressive Muslim Union (and now chair of Muslims for Progressive Values), wears hijab, "and she saw our e-mails to one another on this. She wrote, 'If you don't pray without a head scarf on this day, then on what day would you do it?' Because I don't believe that a woman should have to wear a head scarf under any circumstances, so why now on this day should I? I wanted to proclaim publicly: this is the kind of Muslim I am."

The international response was fast and furious. Islamic leaders condemned the prayer itself and Wadud personally. However, taking great personal risk, four recognized Islamic leaders—one from Spain, one from Pakistan, and two from Egypt—publicly approved of the prayer. In the United States, the Beverly Hills Islamic Center also issued an approval of woman-led prayer as well as suggestions for how it should be practiced. One of the Egyptian supporters is the grand mufti (highest official of religious law in a Sunni Muslim country), Sheikh Ali Guma. He declared in an interview on Egyptian television that woman-led prayer of mixed-gender congregations is permissible as long as the congregation agrees to it. However, his religious institution issued a fatwa condemning the Wadud service (which the sheikh did not sign). Thus, it's unclear how influential his support will be.[43]

Most religious authorities have charged that when a woman leads men and women in prayer, she causes fitna because they consider her sexuality distracting. People can become very emotional when they denounce female sexuality. One protestor outside the cathedral told the Associated Press that Wadud "is tarnishing the whole Islamic faith. If this was an Islamic state, this woman would be hanged."[44]

Wadud has steadfastly turned away from all media attention. Before the prayer itself she participated in a press conference, as Nomani and the other organizers requested of her. Her comments included, "The only thing different about this for me was that I do not do press conferences before prayer." She followed that by saying, "After this, I would not be giving any more interviews." In the first two weeks immediately following the prayer, she declined fifty media requests a day.[45]

The Wadud service inspired others. One week later, on March 25, Nomani led a small daily prayer outside Boston and Jackson led an intimate jum'a service in Newton, Massachusetts, on the bank of the Charles River. "Figuring out what to say in the khutba was as easy as pie," Jackson tells me with her deadpan humor. "We had the service by a duck pond, and a few swans were in attendance. It's pretty much accepted by the mainstream that a woman can lead prayer for other women, so you need a man for [woman-led prayer] to be considered radical. We stood shoulder to shoulder. I felt sheer panic that I would monumentally screw it up. But I didn't call for anyone's death, I didn't scare anyone, and I didn't put anyone to sleep." She laughs. Since then, other woman-led services have taken place not only in the United States but also in Canada and South Africa, with Laury Silvers and others acting as imams.

"Why does women's religious leadership matter?" asks Ingrid Mattson. The answer: when women are excluded from religious leadership, they are suppressed. Even when those in power are the most compassionate of men, they still overlook some aspects of women's needs. "More compellingly, experience teaches us that when women are not in leadership positions in their communities, they are often assigned inadequate prayer spaces (if any), they are cut off from much vital religious education, and they have few means to access the rights they possess in theory. There are many reasons why women's leadership is important; the most important one for Muslim women is so they will not be prevented—by being blocked from sacred texts or houses of worship and study—from accessing the liberating message of obedience to God alone."[46] And women are curtailed not only in the religious realm. A dominant mind-set is that since women are formally excluded from religious leadership, they are not competent in *any* area of leadership. As the former mufti of Egypt, Nasr Fareed Wassel, has put it, "In order to lead Muslims in their worldly affairs, the ruler must be eligible to lead them in their prayers, and since by consensus of the Muslim community women never lead men in prayers, they cannot rule them."[47]

Mattson, an Islamic studies professor at Hartford Seminary in Connecticut who is fluent in Arabic, was raised Catholic in a Toronto suburb and converted when she was twenty-three. As the first woman (as well as the first convert) elected president of the Islamic Society of North America, the largest umbrella organization for Muslim groups in the United States and Canada, she has a particular interest in the issue of women's leadership. I spoke with her over the phone in between her travels, teaching, academic writings, and leadership of a program that trains Muslim chaplains. "The word 'imam' itself means 'leader,' and it can mean leadership in any capacity," she tells me. Mattson has written that it would be most useful to rethink the role of the imam. The way things are structured today in American Muslim communities, the imam performs multiple functions within the community. He leads daily prayers, gives the Friday sermon, drafts marriage contracts, issues divorce decrees, teaches children and adults, offers social counseling, and represents the community to the public. In some cases the imam also makes policy decisions for the community, such as how the prayer space will be divided between the men and women and how charitable contributions will be spent.

"It is no wonder that so many American Muslims are dissatisfied with their local religious leadership," claims Mattson. "No one person could perform all these functions well. Even if he could, given that the imam for the general congregation has to be male, placing all religious authority with the imam means that women will necessarily be excluded from this field." Thus, the answer is not to give women the authority to lead prayers, but to give them legitimacy in the roles of religious scholars, spiritual leaders, social workers, and youth directors.[48]

Mattson does not agree with the legal interpretation allowing women to lead mixed-gender prayer, and in fact she finds this to be a marginal issue to most women. Yet she has found that the activism around woman-led prayer has helped women. "When I travel around the country," she says, "I meet with women who are concerned on a more basic level about their general participation and about getting access to leadership such as positions on mosque boards, so that they can develop programming and be involved in governance. These things affect their lives and the lives of their community far more [than woman-led prayer]."

But because of the public attention on woman-led prayer, many mosques have been pressured to do *something* for the women in their communities. Thus, even if a particular community does not approve of the Wadud prayer, the very fact that the prayer was conducted and received so much publicity has forced issues of women's participation and leadership to the forefront. Mattson laughs. "It makes my job easier. I've been invited to mosques where I'm the first woman scholar they've ever had come to speak, and they have had to figure out where to put me. There have been instances where I have spoken in the front of the mosque, where the imam stands during prayer. That is something that many communities would not have been comfortable with a number of years ago."

Wadud has called her involvement as a pre-khutba speaker in 1994 in Cape Town "a radical but legitimate Islamic act."[49] There are ardent, persuasive, and devout Muslims on both sides of the debate on whether woman-led prayer of mixed-gender congregations is legitimate (though everyone agrees that it is radical). But from the point of view of equality-minded Muslim women and men, these prayer services are effective. They are forcing communities to look inward and to examine issues of justice, inclusiveness, and the tension between tradition and modernity.

SEVEN

God Gave the Torah
to Jewish Women Too

I must admit being a little envious of my Christian and Muslim sisters. They have the comfort of knowing that their traditions, at least in the beginning, sought to improve the status of women. According to the New Testament and the Qur'an, Jesus and Muhammad explicitly communicated their respect for women and a desire to allot women rights that previously had been denied them. As we have seen, in both religions this goal was thwarted as they expanded and were interpreted by succeeding generations of theologians and jurists.

But when I go back to my sacred texts, I face a complicated, contradictory narrative about women. In the words of the Talmud scholar Judith Hauptman, this narrative is "schizophrenic" and "at war with itself."[1] On the one hand, the Torah clearly values women. (The Torah, in its most limited sense, is the five books believed to have been revealed by God to Moses on Mount Sinai. "Tanakh" is the Hebrew acronym for all the written components of the Hebrew Bible, which includes the five books of Moses. Many people use the word "Torah" to refer to the whole Tanakh, as I will do here.) The Torah includes stories of many powerful, shrewd women: the matriarchs Sarah, Rachel, Rebecca, and Leah, as well as Miriam, Shifra, Puah, Rahav, Deborah, Yael, Esther, the daughters of Zelophehad, and others. The Torah discusses women as fully human as men. Women together with men are created "in the image of God." Mothers together with fathers must be honored according to the fifth commandment. Women together with men are commanded to rest and enjoy the peacefulness of the Sabbath.

Yet at the same time, biblical law reflects a patriarchal social system in which women are treated as commodities. In fact, women are essentially the property of their fathers or husbands. Aside from a few exceptions, men are the ones with power and status.

"Judaism informs my life in every way and every day," says Carol Newman, an elegant woman in her sixties with short blond hair, wearing stylish rimless glasses, tasteful gold jewelry, and a well-cut suit. If your eyes fell on Newman, you would never guess that this refined-looking grandmother is president of the Jewish Orthodox Feminist Alliance (JOFA), an organization considered radical and even dangerous in some Orthodox circles. "Judaism pushes me to be kind and ethical. I love so much about being Jewish. I love our customs. The parts that hurt really hurt me so deeply," she continues. "When I pray to God, I have to believe that God hears my prayers."

Jewish belief is that God brought our people out of the land of Egypt, from slavery to freedom. God gave us the Torah, which among other things spells out the terms of a covenant between God and the Jewish people. The Torah gives my people a framework for daily living that infuses us with a feeling of holiness. Those of us who embrace the Torah consider it a gift, which makes us especially disappointed when it is interpreted in ways that stifle us. Surely when God liberated us from Egypt and gave us the Torah, God did not intend to favor men over women—how could that be?

I happen to like contradictions: they lend texture to otherwise flat narratives. They transform stories into puzzles that need to be solved. I suspect that many other observant Jewish women feel the same way. Those of us who have studied Talmud—texts containing the debates of the great rabbis—are especially apt to view contradictions as opportunities to delve deeper into the material, rather than as obstacles to level and trample over; Talmudic study trains us to think this way. Besides, the Torah's mixed messages about women's place in society may be comforting, in a somewhat perverse way, because they are so familiar. Don't we, living in American culture today, experience similar conflicts in our own modern lives? (Don't we Americans trumpet women's equality even while we limit women's reproductive decision making and their ability to earn a living while mothering young children? Don't we Americans tell women that their beauty comes from the inside even while we praise them for their physical appearance?)

Puzzling over these questions does not mean rejection of the Torah. To the contrary, it is precisely those who love the tradition and can't bear to dismiss it who are involved in Orthodox feminist activism. JOFA proudly wears the term "feminist" on its sleeve but also reassures that feminism does not equal rejection of tradition. Its mission is

> to expand the spiritual, ritual, intellectual and political opportunities for women within the framework of *halakhah* [Jewish law]. We advocate meaningful participation and equality for women in family life, synagogues, houses of learning and Jewish communal organizations to the full extent possible within *halakhah*. Our commitment is rooted in the belief that fulfilling this mission will enrich and uplift individual and communal life for all Jews.[2]

I asked the rabbi of my synagogue, Haskel Lookstein, if feminism and halakhah can ever be reconciled. Rabbi Lookstein, the eminent leader of the synagogue Congregation Kehilath Jeshurun in Manhattan—which was founded in 1872 and has an illustrious history at the center of modern Orthodoxy—and the principal of the Ramaz School, was emphatic in his response. "Feminism and *halakhic* [observant] Judaism *have* to be reconciled," he told me. "Feminism is here to stay. We *have* to find a way for women to express themselves within the confines of halakhah. I believe women should have opportunities to express their religious needs as fully as they possibly can, as long as this is done within the realm of halakhah."

But what if halakhah cannot support women's equality? This is a question that equality-minded observant women grapple with. Like the sacred texts themselves, these Jewish women are torn, at war with themselves. "I want to be treated the same way the men are," says Sara Shapiro-Plevan, a thirty-four-year-old Jewish educator in Manhattan. "But that's impossible in the halakhic world. In the secular world I can insist on equal treatment, because that's the way our secular society operates. But in the Jewish traditional world, I can't. And I hate it."

"I wish the sexism didn't bother me so much," says Carol Newman. "When I sit in the balcony in shul [synagogue], I want to scream. I feel it's a spectator sport that I'm not a part of."

"I can't give up Orthodox Judaism. I don't want to," says JOFA board member Idana Goldberg, "and I can't give up how I feel about women's equality and gender roles. I try to bridge the two, but I end up living with a lot of cognitive dissonance. Yet I don't feel I have a choice. These two things are too important for me, and I can't give up either one."

It would be easier to withdraw from observant Judaism by aligning with a liberal denomination, but these women love their Orthodox tradition too much. They truly believe that God's commandments were a gift given to the Jewish people on Mount Sinai, and they have no interest in joining with a Jewish community that does not view the Torah the same way they do.

Moreover, many observant Jewish women desire to be treated as men's equals, but they do not want to be treated the same as men. Orthodoxy is unique among the Jewish denominations in its insistence that women and men have different roles. Those seeking equality desire a challenging reconciliation: to be given the same religious rights the men have while simultaneously holding on to separate spheres of responsibility. In a struggle that is itself quintessentially Jewish, they argue with their tradition, turning it over and over, always trying to figure out how to put the pieces together.

Goldberg remembers the precise instant that her love of traditional Judaism was transformed into a complicated relationship. In 1988, when she was a junior in a coed Orthodox high school, a group from her school went to Russia for ten days to show support for refuseniks—the Jews who, before the collapse of the Soviet empire, were not allowed to emigrate and were harassed, arrested, and often imprisoned for merely applying for permission to leave the country. The group smuggled in kosher food and ritual objects, and the agenda, as Goldberg understood it, was that the students would teach the refuseniks. But when they arrived, the plan changed: some boys were allowed to participate in teaching, but none of the girls was permitted to participate.

"It was not what I had expected," said Goldberg. "While we were there, we met with a group of young men who had just become observant and had just started studying Talmud for the first time. They were telling us how much they enjoyed it. And I said, 'I also love Talmud. It's my favorite subject in school.' And one of the men said, 'But girls don't learn Talmud, do they?' And I said, 'In our school, the girls also learn it.' And he said, 'But surely they don't learn it as well as the boys do.' I was all of seventeen years old, and I said, 'No, actually the girls learn as well as the boys do. In fact, the girls in our school are known to be the strongest Talmud students in the school.' At that point, one of the teachers who was with us got very angry with me and told me that I had to leave the room. Later I got a very strong lecture about how I had insulted these men in telling them that girls can learn Torah and Talmud as well as the boys. They had been so proud of their accomplishments and I had ruined things for them by telling them that even girls can study Talmud, so it wasn't such a big deal, and I had shattered their egos.

"I was very taken aback because I had never encountered this kind of thinking before. I really didn't understand. The experience changed me. I came back from that trip awakened. Until then, it had never occurred to me that—wait a minute: I didn't count in a *minyan* [quorum of ten men needed for public prayer], and my bat mitzvah didn't involve any ritual. From that point on, I started thinking about Judaism in a feminist way."

The Torah did not invent patriarchy. The male-dominated social system was a product of antiquity, and the Torah was framed within that context, so it is not at all surprising that women in the Torah have low social status. Still, women's subordinate status rankles me and countless other Jewish women. Why didn't the Torah reverse the sexism of the era? Why didn't God decree that women could *own* property rather than *be* property? When giving the Torah to the Jewish people at Mount Sinai, the most central event in all of Judaism, why does it appear that God addressed only the men, even though women were present too? In Exodus 19:15, Moses warns the people, "Be ready for the third day; do not go near a woman." Comments the theologian Judith Plaskow in her 1990 book *Standing Again at Sinai*:

Here, at the very moment that the Jewish people stands at Sinai ready to receive the covenant—not now the covenant with individual patriarchs but with the people as a whole—at the very moment when Israel stands trembling waiting for God's presence to descend upon the mountain, Moses addresses the community only as men. The specific issue at stake is ritual impurity: An emission of semen renders both a man and his female partner temporarily unfit to approach the sacred (Leviticus 15:16–18). But Moses did not say, "Men and women do not go near each other." At the central moment of Jewish history, women are invisible.[3]

We feminist optimists maintain that gender equality is God's ultimate goal, but God took into account the sociological fact of women's subordination during antiquity when addressing the Jewish people. It is up to us to use the tools God has given us to transcend women's subordination. If one believes the Torah is not the literal word of God, but inspired by God and written by men, an alternate explanation is that the male authors were ambivalent about women's equality: they supported it in a general sense, but they were torn because they also wanted to maintain their own power. Regardless of who one believes authored the Torah, one can also argue, as the late biblical scholar Tikva Frymer-Kensky did, that the women of the Torah are not depicted as *inferior* to men, only powerless—that is, women's powerlessness is descriptive, not prescriptive.

Ever since the Torah was given to the Jewish people, great rabbis have pored over it and debated it. The Talmud (study) is a record of rabbinic debates spanning many generations, and it is believed to be part of the Torah itself: Orthodox Jews consider it "oral law" that was revealed on Mount Sinai, passed down by religious leaders from one generation to the next, until it was finally recorded. The first set of documents of the Talmud, the Mishnah (repeating), was codified at around the year 200. The second set of documents, the Gemara (learning), which commented on the Mishnah, was produced over the next 550 years. Overall, the Talmud is a discussion of the underlying values and ethics of the Torah and an extraction of legal principles, leading to the creation of an intricate legal system that continues to guide the daily lives of observant Jews. Thus, the way Talmudic rabbis regarded women centuries ago has real-life consequences for Jewish living today.

Despite God's male-centered language at Mount Sinai, the rabbis "went to great lengths to read women into the text and to argue for their inclusion in both the moment [of divine revelation] and the message [the giving of the Torah]," writes the Israeli Talmud teacher Rachel Furst.[4] They were as disturbed as Plaskow at the thought that God (through Moses) spoke only to the men. They found it inconceivable that women were excluded from the giving of the Torah. And on a few occasions in the Talmud, women are praised. It is said that a man should respect his wife more than himself (Yevamot 62b) and that the people of Israel were saved from slavery in Egypt because of its righteous women (Sotah 11b).

In some cases the great rabbis improved women's status. According to the Torah, a marriage is a purchase by a man of a woman for money, with the man promising the woman food, clothing, and sexual pleasure. The marriage may be valid without the woman's consent (Exodus 21:10). The rabbis of the Talmud (in Kiddushin) added extra protections for the woman, including financial support in the event that she is widowed or divorced, and they transformed the *ketubah* (marriage contract) from a simple purchase to a negotiated contract to which the woman must consent. The rabbis were cognizant of women's lesser social status and, through the legal mechanisms available to them, elevated their societal position, even when this meant modifying the laws of the Torah to synchronize with evolving ethical standards.

But at the same time, the great rabbis of the Talmud undermined women terribly. Women were to be confined to the domestic sphere. Their value came from enabling their husbands and sons to perform *mitzvot* (religious commandments) and study Torah, which gave their husbands and sons social prestige. They were exempted from performing many "time-bound" mitzvot (obligations that must be performed at specific times), and before long this exemption became understood as a prohibition. They were not to learn Torah themselves. Many passages are painful to read. The rabbis described women as sexually licentious (Mishnah Sotah 3:4), too sexually tempting to men (Brakhot

24a), light-minded (Kiddushin 80b, Shabbat 33b), frivolous and dis-honest (Genesis Rabbah 18:2), and sullied by excretions and menstrual blood (Shabbat 152a).

When the rabbis formalized the prayer service, they instructed each man to bless God each morning for not having made him a woman (Tosefta Brakhot 6:23, Yerushalmi Brakhot 63b). The rationale was that women were exempt from certain mitzvot, and men were consid-ered especially blessed because they had the opportunity to perform all of the obligations. Even if this blessing was not intended to deni-grate women, it *reads* like a denigration of women—and when a woman opens up her prayer book each morning and sees it in print and hears the men in synagogue recite it, it *feels* like a denigration.

The fact that men have greater religious obligations than women has enormous implications for the way men and women are regarded within the Jewish legal system. Mitzvot are considered privileges. They are opportunities to be holy, to be close to God. Although indi-vidual men may bemoan the weight of all the obligations and may choose not to fulfill any or all, men have status within this system pre-cisely because they are regarded as chosen by God to fulfill them in the first place. The Mishnah (Kiddushin 1:7) tells us that women are ex-empt from time-bound mitzvot, but no rationale is stated. Later com-mentators offered various explanations connected to women's roles as mothers and homemakers: women needed a flexible schedule in order to do "women's work" and therefore could not be expected to per-form every obligation that had to be performed at a specific time. One medieval commentator said that women were exempt because if they weren't, they wouldn't be able to serve their *husbands* (never mind the children), and the result would be tension in the home.[5]

But there are many exceptions to the exemption—for example, women must light Shabbat candles and recite grace after meals. They must light Hanukkah candles, eat *matzah* (unleavened bread) at the Passover seder (ritual meal), listen to the reading of the scroll of Es-ther on the holiday of Purim, and so on. If women were too busy taking care of their children and husbands, then why weren't they ex-empted from these as well? And why are they exempt from mitzvot that are not time-bound—like studying Torah? Could it be that the rabbis wanted to keep many of the privileges and honors for themselves alone? These are not simply academic questions. Because women are exempt from many mitzvot, their lives are considered to be of less value than men's lives. Thus, the Mishnah rules that in a life-threatening situation, a man's right to life precedes that of a woman's (Mishnah Horayot 3:7).

Equality-seeking traditional Jews regard these rabbis as unsurpassed in intelligence, scholarship, and loyalty to the Torah. They are our role models. But we recognize that they were human beings and therefore were flawed and limited. They reflected the values of their time. But that was a long time ago. And because of the central place the Talmud occupies in Jewish religious thought and practice, this means that very old values about women, values we have come to reject in our secular lives, continue to inform daily observant Jewish life.

Overall, Jewish women in the United States have been fortunate to claim for themselves many mitzvot that previously were the province of men alone. This is because here in the United States, Jews can choose to be affiliated with any of four denominations. The Orthodox movement, comprising less than 10 percent of the American Jewish population, is the strictest in adhering to Jewish law. It is guided by the idea that God is a supernatural, transcendent being who revealed the Torah to Moses and created a covenant with the Jewish people. Orthodox Judaism is split between modern Orthodox Jews, who embrace modern Western culture (such as scientific progress, secular education, the arts, and so on) and ultra-Orthodox or Hasidic Jews, who tend to isolate themselves from modern culture to the extent that they can and who understand the Torah in ways that could be described as fundamentalist. The women in this chapter are modern Orthodox.

The Conservative movement, like modern Orthodoxy, tries to balance observance of Jewish law with a positive attitude toward modern culture, but it tends to have a significantly more lenient interpretation of Jewish law. It also tends to have a much more positive attitude toward women's rights, as well as gay and lesbian rights.

The Reform movement, numerically the largest Jewish movement in the United States, is the most inclusive and liberal denomination. In contrast to the Orthodox and Conservative movements, the Reform movement does not view Jewish law as something that Jews must adhere to. Instead, each individual may determine which laws to follow within a system of Jewish ethical guidelines. Reform synagogues often hold prayer services mostly or entirely in English, and they may incorporate innovative practices, deviating from centuries-old Jewish tradition.

Finally, there is the Reconstructionist movement, which, like Reform Judaism, is open to new forms of Jewish expression, but which emphasizes the role of the religious community more than that of the individual. Reconstructionist synagogues tend to be midway between Conservative and Reform in their adherence to traditional practice.

In an Orthodox synagogue, women sit separately from men, just as in a mosque—either in an upstairs balcony or on the same level as the men but separated by a *mehitzah* (partition). They do not officially count as part of the congregation; they don't count in the mandatory quorum of ten men, called a minyan; and they may not lead any part of the prayer service. Their participation, even when expressed with gusto, is effectively passive. Orthodox prayer books do not include the matriarchs (Sarah, Rebecca, Rachel, and Leah), only the patriarchs (Abraham, Isaac, and Jacob) in the central prayer, and they use male language to describe God and the Jewish people.

In the non-Orthodox synagogue world, women and men have parity. Women and men sit side by side. Women count in the minyan, are called to the Torah, read the Torah, and serve as rabbis and cantors. For those who want the prayers changed to reflect gender equality, there are prayer books that include the matriarchs and use gender-neutral language.

This advancement has spilled over into the Orthodox world, especially the modern Orthodox world, to some extent. In some cases the Orthodox rabbinic establishment is willing to allow some religious practices that reflect at least some value of females.

A number of Orthodox synagogues periodically invite female speakers to deliver sermons in synagogue on Shabbat, though only after prayers are concluded and often in an adjacent hall, not the sanctuary. In a few Orthodox synagogues, when the Torah scroll is passed around the sanctuary, a woman is allowed to bring it into the women's section so that female congregants may kiss it as the men do. Then the

Torah is returned to the men's section, out of range (and sometimes out of sight) of the women. Birth ceremonies for girls are now commonplace, allowing families to publicly rejoice for a daughter just as they do for a son with a *brit milah*, the circumcision ceremony when a boy enters into the covenant with God. But this is optional, completely up to the parents, and there is no mandated date as there is with a boy, who must be circumcised on his eighth day of life. Therefore these affairs tend to be regarded as less important than brit milah ceremonies.

Bat mitzvah ceremonies are also now de rigueur among the modern Orthodox. The first recorded bat mitzvah (daughter of the commandment) ceremony was celebrated in 1922, when twelve-year-old Judith Kaplan, daughter of the Reconstructionist Judaism founder Mordecai Kaplan, was called to the Torah in a public demonstration that she was now ready to fulfill Jewish laws. Orthodox boys at age thirteen had long celebrated their bar mitzvah (son of the commandment) with much pomp. The Kaplan ceremony struck a chord with American Jews, and eventually, after decades of entrenchment in the liberal movements, a watered-down version became accepted by the Orthodox too, following extensive deliberation by such great rabbis of the twentieth century as Moshe Feinstein (1895–1986) and Yechiel Weinberg (1878–1966). In fact, the towering rabbis of the twentieth century did recognize the value of this ceremony in the formation of a girl's attachment to Judaism. Although he argued that a bat mitzvah ceremony should not be held in a synagogue, Yechiel Weinberg also noted that:

> Sound pedagogic principles require that we celebrate a girl's reaching the age of obligation to fulfill commandments. Discrimination against girls in celebrating the attainment of maturity has an adverse effect upon the self-respect of the maturing girl who in other respects enjoys the privileges of the so-called women's liberation.[6]

In a bar mitzvah, the boy reads from the Torah and might also lead part or all of the prayer service. But because in an Orthodox synagogue a girl over the age of twelve is not allowed to go anywhere near the Torah—except for a second or two if she's a member of one of the few Orthodox synagogues that allows it in the women's section during the procession of the Torah—the Orthodox bat mitzvah is purely ceremonial. It is deeply ironic that the day a girl is obligated to take on the commandments is the day she becomes officially excluded from much of traditional ritual.

It is also increasingly common to see women in mourning recite Kaddish (the mourner's prayer) in modern Orthodox synagogues, though not without controversy. All human beings need an outlet for their grief. Eventually everyone faces the death of a family member, and many Jews find the recitation of Kaddish comforting and spiritually fulfilling during a period of bereavement and anguish. When a parent dies, Kaddish is recited by the Orthodox for eleven months, three times a day. It may be recited only in a minyan, and women do not count in an Orthodox minyan. Non-Orthodox synagogues, which *do* count women in their minyans, generally do not hold daily prayer services (only Shabbat services), forcing non-Orthodox Jews to attend an Orthodox synagogue, at least during the week, if they choose to recite the mourner's prayer daily. But technically, according to the Orthodox, women are exempt from this time-bound obligation, and very often when a woman is exempt from an obligation, she is considered forbidden from performing it, even though there is no formal prohibition.

The issue of women wanting to say the Mourner's Kaddish was first raised in the halakhic literature of the seventeenth-century rabbi Yair Chaim Bacharach (1638–1702). He explained that technically it was legally permissible for a daughter to recite Kaddish for her father, but he concluded that it could not be allowed, because it violated the social custom.[7] But other highly influential rabbis—including Israel Meir Kagan, known as the Chofetz Chaim (Desirer of Life, 1838–1933), and Joseph B. Soloveitchik, known as the Rav (the Rabbi, 1903–93)—did permit women to say Kaddish in the presence of a minyan, as long as they remained in the women's section.[8] Today many Orthodox rabbis follow the lead of these authorities and do permit women to recite the Mourner's Kaddish in the synagogue. Nevertheless, many others continue to forbid the practice, particularly when there are no men reciting it at the same time (and therefore the female mourner's voice is not drowned out). Many women have learned to mumble Kaddish as quietly as possible so as not to possibly offend any of the men, but if no one can hear a mourner say Kaddish, no one can affirm her prayer with "Amen."

In 1916 Henrietta Szold, the founder of Hadassah Hospital in Jerusalem and the Hadassah organization of Zionist women in the United States, expressed her frustration with the narrow vision of halakhah held by Orthodox authorities. In a letter to her friend Hayim Peretz, after he offered to say Kaddish on her behalf for her mother, she wrote,

> It is impossible for me to find words in which to tell you how deeply I was touched by your offer to say *Kaddish* for my dear mother. I cannot even thank you—it is something that goes beyond thanks. It is beautiful, what you have offered to do—I shall never forget it.
>
> You will wonder, then, that I cannot accept your offer. Perhaps it would be best for me not to try to explain to you in writing, but to wait until I see you to tell you why it is so. I know well, and appreciate what you say about, the Jewish custom; and Jewish custom is very dear and sacred to me. And yet I cannot ask you to say *Kaddish* after my mother. The *Kaddish* means to me the survivor publicly and markedly manifests his wish and intention to assume the relation to the Jewish community which his parents had, and that so the chain of tradition remains unbroken from generation to generation, each adding his own link. You can do that for the generations of your family, I must do that for the generations of my family.
>
> I believe that the elimination of women from such duties was never intended by our law and custom—women were freed from positive duties when they could not perform them, but not when they could. It was never intended that, if they could perform them, their performance of them should not be considered as valuable and valid as when one of the male sex performed them. And of the *Kaddish* I feel sure that this is particularly true.
>
> My mother had eight daughters, and no son; and yet never did I hear a word of regret pass the lips of either my mother or

my father that one of us was not a son. When my father died, my mother would not permit others to take her daughters' place in saying the *Kaddish*, and so I am sure I am acting in her spirit when I am moved to decline your offer. But beautiful your offer remains nevertheless, and I repeat, I know full well that it is much more in consonance with the generally accepted Jewish tradition than is my or my family's conception. You understand me, don't you?[9]

Szold was a pioneer in her insistence that Jewish custom be enlarged to accommodate women's spiritual needs. She remained committed to Jewish tradition, but many women who were barred from saying the Mourner's Kaddish end up turning away. Supreme Court justice Ruth Bader Ginsburg has said that when her mother died, the day before Ginsburg's high school graduation, the house was filled with women, but religiously, they were invisible. Judaism made her feel secondary, and despite having been very involved in ritual as a teenager, she became alienated from the religious tradition.[10]

Even today the Kaddish problem affects countless women. Nina Mogilnik recounts that when reciting Kaddish after the death of her father, in February 2006, she was forced to stand behind a wall at one Orthodox shul. Finally the rabbi allowed her to pray in the upstairs balcony, but he couldn't understand what she was doing there. He told Mogilnik that her husband could say Kaddish for her father in her place; the wife of the sexton asked, "Your father didn't have any sons?"[11]

An Orthodox prayer book, the *ArtScroll Women's Siddur*, contains commentaries designed to inhibit rather than encourage women to participate actively in synagogue prayer. The Artscroll series of prayer books is popular in modern Orthodox institutions because precise instructions, historical asides, and other tidbits related to the liturgy are interspersed with the prayers. Every single time the Mourner's Kaddish appears in the women's prayer book—and it appears dozens of times, since it is recited frequently throughout the day—the commentary reads:

The prevailing *minhag* [customary practice] is that a woman does not say *Kaddish*, even if she is the only mourner, whether in *shul* or even if the *minyan* is in the house [for example, during the week of mourning] . . . Although reciting *Kaddish* is a comfort for the soul of the departed, even silent recitation by a woman is generally frowned upon.[12]

That women's voiceless recitation of *any* prayer, let alone one intended to offer comfort to the bereaved, could offend someone boggles the mind. This suggestion is far more powerful than it might at first appear. It is true that women's recitation of the Mourner's Kaddish "is generally frowned upon," primarily in ultra-Orthodox communities, not modern Orthodox communities. However, the publisher of this prayer book has aggressively marketed the book to modern Orthodox schools and synagogues, and the retrograde commentary could become a self-fulfilling prophecy. Other notes in this prayer book declare that women are not obligated to recite some of the most important prayers in Jewish liturgy, including the Shema (statement of faith). This prayer book has sold more than 750,000 copies.[13]

To my mind, prohibiting a woman from reciting Kaddish or even questioning her decision to do it in the first place—which sends a message that she shouldn't do it—communicates a blatant disregard for the well-being of women. And remember, we are discussing women at the most vulnerable, needy time of their lives. There is no technical halakhic prohibition for them to recite Kaddish; some of the greatest rabbis of the modern era have confirmed this. This begs the questions: Could it be that some Orthodox rabbis forbid females from some of the mitzvot for reasons that are not halakhic? Is it possible that they want to reserve some mitzvot for themselves only, greedily refusing to share?

In the examples above, there has been progress. Many of the leading modern Orthodox rabbis of our time are empathetic, open-minded people; they have recognized the need to tip the balance of ritual life at least somewhat toward females. But there is one area of Jewish life—divorce law—in which many of today's Orthodox rabbis have interpreted halakhah unnecessarily rigidly, barring women from equality and justice.

We have seen that the traditional Jewish marriage ceremony is essentially a commercial transaction: the husband "acquires" the wife (although she is protected in a number of ways). This has not changed over the centuries. Because of the nature of the ceremony, a wife may not unilaterally divorce her husband. She requires his consent. If a woman wants to divorce her husband for any reason, even that he has abused her, she may not without his willing cooperation. A woman who wants to divorce but cannot because her husband refuses to co-operate is called an *agunah*. (This term means "chained woman" and technically refers to a woman whose husband is missing through aban-donment or death, but it is most commonly used to refer to a woman with a recalcitrant husband.) "The Orthodox Jewish marriage, as it exists, is very dangerous for women," agunah advocate Susan Aranoff tells me. "No lawyer could ethically recommend that their client enter into this agreement with the terms under which a woman enters into [the marriage contract]. You would be violating your responsibility to your client if you advised her to agree."

In the United States, a woman who married in an Orthodox cere-mony with a recalcitrant husband can obtain a civil divorce, but with-out a religious divorce she cannot remarry Jewishly. If she does, any children she would have in her new marriage would be considered illegitimate. There are enormous consequences to illegitimacy: her children, completely innocent, would be consigned to a shameful reli-gious status in which they would not be accepted as Jews by the Or-thodox community. It is the specter of this status that prevents women with recalcitrant husbands from moving on with their lives. Mean-while, with their wives stuck in marital limbo, many husbands can and do remarry other women—believe it or not, a number of Orthodox rabbis issue decrees allowing men to remarry without a divorce, even though polygamy was decreed outlawed in the Middle Ages. Many husbands can and do extort their agunah wives for serious sums of money. Many can and do want to torture them emotionally, claiming that they would grant the divorce only in exchange for custody of the children.

There are several possible solutions to the agunah problem. Rab-binic authorities *could* force a recalcitrant husband to grant the divorce (called a *get*). A Jewish court of law *could* be empowered to dissolve the marriage without the husband's cooperation. Husbands *could* be re-quired to pay heavy financial penalties for refusing to grant the divorce.

These solutions have been proposed by a number of forward-thinking rabbis over the years, but ultimately they have been rejected by the majority of establishment Orthodox rabbis.

One solution that is standard operating procedure in Conservative movement marriage contracts in the United States is a prenuptial agreement written into the contract itself. Called the Lieberman Clause, it stipulates that if the marriage is dissolved under civil law, either partner can involve the Conservative movement's court of law to intervene. However, this so-called solution can actually increase the chance of an inequitable financial settlement (because a husband can declare he will give the *get* only on condition that his wife waive her interest in their assets and in reasonable financial support). It's also shunned by many Orthodox rabbis because they claim the halakhic process through which it was created was problematic. The Orthodox movement has affirmed its own version of the prenuptial agreement, but it is not universally recognized by Orthodox rabbis officiating at weddings. In any event, a prenup maintains the one-sided nature of the marriage contract intact.

The only real remedy to the plight of future *agunot* is to rewrite the marriage vows, transforming them from a one-sided transaction to a partnership of equals. If leading rabbinic authorities wanted to institute this change, they could. But year after year, as more and more women suffer, these authorities claim that they cannot, because halakhically their "hands are tied." To date, none has taken the aggressive step of gathering support for a rewrite of the marriage vows. Thus it is up to women in the grass roots to force the issue themselves.

Solving the agunah issue has become a rallying cry for Orthodox women and their supporters seeking religious equality. In fact, the agunah issue has nearly single-handedly galvanized the Orthodox feminist movement. Year after year, JOFA reminds its members that until this issue is resolved, no Orthodox woman has equality in her marriage, regardless of how enlightened her husband may be. At JOFA's tenth anniversary conference in New York City in 2007, all nine lunchtime sessions addressed different aspects of this problem, forcing every participant to engage in the issue. And there are some modern Orthodox rabbis who work with JOFA and do want to help agunot. Counted among these is Haskel Lookstein, the rabbi of my synagogue, who is on the front lines of advocating for a prenuptial document affirmed by the Orthodox Rabbinical Council of America. (He was among the very first to raise awareness among Orthodox rabbis, in the early 1980s.) In 2007 a group of prominent Orthodox rabbis even castigated a fellow rabbi who issues decrees allowing recalcitrant husbands to remarry.

In the United States alone, there are thousands of agunot, with between two hundred and four hundred new cases each year. (In Israel, where Orthodox law is the law of the land for all Jews even if they do not consider themselves Orthodox, the problem is even more severe.) But it's not the numbers that have made the agunah issue so compelling; it's what this issue represents: rabbis who choose not to find a solution to a problem that hurts women, even though they have the power to solve it once and for all. Jewish women, Orthodox and not, feminist and not, have been moved by the stories of women whose husbands have been unbearably cruel to them—and then must suffer all over again because of the rabbinate's refusal to intervene. Who has "tied" the hands of the rabbis? The rabbis themselves. "There's no payoff for the rabbis to make changes," charges Aranoff. "Men still hold most of the power, and in feminist issues the men feel undermined. So why should the rabbis, as leaders, not only as men, make changes? It's like any political situation. The women don't hold enough cards. They don't have the clout. Why should the rabbis expend political capital on the women when it's the men who hold the cards?"

The religious establishment is not the only barrier to gender parity. Orthodox women themselves have created their own obstacle: fear. They are often afraid to be religiously assertive. Many have relied on male religious leadership their entire lives and have become reflexively dependent on men, even when they themselves, or other women they know, are knowledgeable about Jewish law. This timidity leads them to assume that they are forbidden from performing certain mitzvot even though they are merely exempt from performing them.

Sally Berkovic, a journalist and the wife of an Orthodox rabbi in London, relates that years ago she was traveling, and she spent Shabbat in Williamsburg, New York, with a young ultra-Orthodox widow and her five young children. Berkovic assumed that with the absence of a husband, this young woman would recite the Friday night blessing over the wine (which she is halakhically permitted to do). "But no, we had to wait about an hour until one of her brothers-in-law came to her cramped apartment, crawling with over-tired and over-hungry children, in order to say the blessings so that we could eat our meal."[14]

Even when they know that certain mitzvot are permitted, many women hesitate to take them on, because they have never seen other women do so. And with less practice than the men have, they worry that they will not carry out the rituals properly. Carol Newman remembers trying to persuade a fellow congregant at her synagogue to participate fully in Sukkot, the holiday in which observant Jews eat in a temporary outdoor booth and wave "the four species"—a citron (called an *etrog*) and a palm branch, myrtle, and willow, together called a *lulav*. The congregant said to her, "Oh gosh, I wish I could have a lulav and etrog." Newman looked at her and said, "You *can*. You buy yourself a Cuisinart, why not buy yourself a lulav and etrog?"

Nearly all Orthodox women shy away from mitzvot that are heavily associated with masculinity. Even in the Conservative movement, which on paper espouses equality for women, it is still unusual to see more than a handful of women in synagogue wearing ritual garments. "If a whole bunch of women wore *tefillin* [two boxes, containing biblical verses on parchment, with leather straps, worn on the arm and head during morning prayer] and *tallitot* [shawls with fringes], they would stop being seen as masculine," says Devorah Zlochower, the head of the beit midrash (house of learning) of the Drisha Institute, a progressive institution for Jewish study for women in Manhattan, "and they would lose that forbidden edge." One observant woman who was a pioneer in wearing ritual garments is Haviva Ner-David, who began to wear tefillin in 1991, when she was twenty-two. In a memoir about her religious life, *Life on the Fringes*, she explained that even though as a woman she is exempt from this obligation, "I could not feel religiously authentic if I took advantage of that exemption. Since assuming this obligation, I have found it to be neither a burden nor an action that clashes in any way with my womanhood." But even today Ner-David remains, in many ways, "on the fringes." Nearly all observant women, no matter how committed they are to feminism, are still terrified of being seen in public wearing ritual garments.[15]

Still, many Orthodox women, including feminists, enjoy certain aspects of Orthodoxy's gender roles and don't want to let go of them. For example, a woman may want to wave lulav and etrog but cover her hair with a hat, or wear a *tallit* but not tefillin or a *kippah*. Orthodox feminists are still sorting things out. To my mind, this is not necessarily a bad thing; after all, one of Orthodoxy's big appeals is its differentiation between women and men. One can be different and still equal.

For most of Jewish history, all Jews were essentially Orthodox. Facing discrimination, suspicion, and hatred, if not mass murder, Jews banded together, forming their own self-sustaining, segregated communities. Religious observance was the glue that kept these communities together; the rabbi of the community made all religious decisions, and his word was accepted as the final say. Quite simply, there were no alternative ways of being Jewish aside from the traditional way.

In the age of Enlightenment, beginning in the eighteenth century, Jews began to think about Jewish practice in alternate ways. New ideas about science, philosophy, ethics, and government spread throughout Europe, laying the groundwork for the American and French revolutions and stirring up excitement among many Jewish intellectuals. A number of German Jews, arguing that the Torah was not written by God and that much of Jewish law was not necessary or relevant, formed the Reform movement.

Modern Orthodoxy was a reaction to the Reformers. It was an assertion of the old way, but with a twist. Jews should remain committed to Torah Judaism, but they should also engage with Enlightenment ideas and the larger world. German rabbi Samson Raphael Hirsch (1808–88), the architect of modern Orthodoxy, coined the motto *"Torah im derekh eretz"* (Practice Torah together with the way of the land). Ultra-Orthodoxy, in contrast with modern Orthodoxy, adopted a less tolerant stance toward interaction with the larger world. (Although the comparison is not perfect, the modern Orthodox/ultra-Orthodox split is similar to the evangelical/fundamentalist Christian division of the 1940s discussed in Chapter Four.)

In the United States, the first modern Orthodox organization—the Orthodox Union—was created in 1898, and others followed, such as the National Council of Young Israel in 1912. The seminary of Yeshiva College, later Yeshiva University, was founded in 1915. Meanwhile, the Conservative movement, which like modern Orthodoxy had roots in Germany as a reaction against Reform Judaism, became established in the United States. The Jewish Theological Seminary (JTS), founded in 1886, had originally bridged the modern Orthodox-Conservative worlds, but with the creation of the Orthodox Union the modern Orthodox broke off their affiliation and JTS became identified exclusively with the Conservative movement.

The historian Regina Stein has argued that in the early and mid-twentieth century, the modern Orthodox and Conservative movements were not altogether that different. They were both committed to halakhah, and they both approached the secular world with openness. But over the years they divided, developing distinctive identities. According to Stein, this split occurred primarily because of disputes over such gender issues as mixed seating. The mehitzah, Stein maintains, came to symbolize the denominational barrier between the two movements. "The more the two denominations argued over seating, the more divided they became," she writes. "And the more the denominations moved further and further apart from each other, the more crucial seating became as the paramount issue in the debates which created and then strengthened each movement's sense of identity."[16]

As the modern Orthodox movement solidified its identity as "not Conservative," it gradually began to reject mixed dancing (women and men dancing together) and general social mixing of the sexes—which had been considered acceptable within modern Orthodoxy earlier in the century. Conservative Jews, influenced by the American legal system and its concept of equality, sought more and more to equalize Jewish practice between women and men. Modern Orthodoxy, on the other hand, became increasingly rigid in its adherence to halakhah and the inequality of women and men.

Modern Orthodoxy has taken a "sharply dogmatic turn" since the nineteenth century, agrees Tamar Ross, a professor of Jewish philosophy at Bar Ilan University in Israel. It has taken a "view of halakhah as a rigid and static system, impervious to outside influences and considerations," she writes in *Expanding the Palace of Torah: Orthodoxy and Feminism*.[17] Aside from the desire to strengthen a distinctive denominational identity, this trend has a number of causes. After the Holocaust, when the Nazis obliterated six million Jewish lives, and in the face of renewed anti-Semitism across the globe today, many Jews (not only the Orthodox) feel that their way of life is under attack. To preserve it, they turn to a past way of life that seems stable and safe. Also, Jews today lack a centralized religious authority figure. Individual Orthodox rabbis are reluctant to make halakhic decisions that may be controversial, because they fear they don't have the proper authority. It's easier to offer a strict interpretation rather than a lenient one, because many people, of all religious stripes, believe that stringency is more religiously authentic than leniency. Yet as Ross observes, "stringency, as much as leniency, can be a deviation from mainstream tradition." For example, she points out that for centuries it was considered acceptable to recite Jewish prayer in any language (although Hebrew was always preferable by far), but in the nineteenth century it became mandatory among the Orthodox to pray in public only in Hebrew.[18]

Stringency, in and of itself, is not necessarily a problem. What *is* a problem is that many leading Orthodox rabbis choose when to be strict and when to be lenient—and when it comes to issues involving women's equality, you can guess which way they tend to rule. Moreover, these rabbis pull out all sorts of halakhic rabbits from all kinds of Talmudic hats to stave off women's insistence that they participate fully in religious practice. In the application of halakhic principles to protect the status quo from feminism, Ross demonstrates, there are arbitrary rulings, inconsistency, excessive scrutiny of women's motivation, and bias owing to denominational politics. "Going over these sources [used by rabbis to justify keeping women down] always leaves me with a sense of amazement over how many legal contortions are created in order to withhold religious autonomy from women, so that women may participate only in a manner that leaves them dependent upon men," says the Orthodox feminist Rochelle Millen.[19] Even those who have the best of intentions, adds Ross, cannot escape their own class and gender biases and "have no less natural a stake in perpetuating a status quo that is right and proper in these terms."[20]

Here's the rub: Orthodox women today are the best Judaically educated Jewish women in all of Jewish history. Over the course of the twentieth century and continuing into the twenty-first, there has been an explosion of desire of Orthodox girls and women to study the sacred texts in depth, and the rabbinic injunction that women should not study Torah has effectively been overturned. (Most schools and programs offering advanced study to women, however, admit only women. It is still taboo in most Orthodox communities for women and men to study together.)

The single-sex Bais Ya'akov school began in Poland in 1917 and today boasts an international network of institutions for ultra-Orthodox girls. Although these schools prepare girls for traditional lives as wives and mothers, not Torah scholars, they teach halakhah at a level that previously had been denied them.

Before and after World War II in the United States, modern Orthodox coed yeshiva day schools were created, in which girls learn Torah and Talmud along with geometry, physics, and world history. One of the first of these schools, the Maimonides School in Boston, was created in 1937 by the great Rabbi Joseph B. Soloveitchik (together with his wife, Tonya Soloveitchik), who explained, "Not only is the teaching of [Gemara] to girls permissible but it is nowadays an absolute imperative."[21] Rabbi Joseph H. Lookstein, father of Haskel Lookstein, was also a leader in educating girls in Judaic texts when he founded the Ramaz School in 1937. Today there are eighty-seven modern Orthodox coed day schools dotted across the country.[22] For many modern Orthodox day school graduates, it is a rite of passage to spend a year in Israel in religious seminary before matriculating to college in the United States.

In New York City the Drisha Institute serves adult women (from any Jewish denomination) who want to immerse themselves in advanced Judaic study. Founded in 1979, Drisha offers full-time programs that train women to be scholars, educators, and community leaders. When Drisha started its Scholars Circle program, an intensive, three-year course of study, "it was revolutionary, it was in *The New York Times*," remembers Zlochower, a member of the program's first graduating class (of three) in 1994. "We really felt like pioneers, and we weren't sure what it all meant." Just a decade later, she tells me, "the great success of our revolution no longer seems revolutionary. For me, and certainly for those before me, the right to learn Gemara, for example, and access to all Jewish texts, was a battle. *A battle*. In my [ultra-

Orthodox] day school in Pittsburgh, we girls didn't get any Gemara at all. But for my students, it's a given."

Orthodox women today know the halakhah. They know which mitzvot they are permitted to perform. They can cite the Gemara upside down and sideways. And that is precisely what they are doing. They are speaking up, drawing from their extensive knowledge to collect their religious rights. But overall, there is a profound disconnect between the Judaic knowledge that women have attained and their ability to put that knowledge to practical use.

The feminist Orthodox movement of the United States has its roots in the late 1960s and early 1970s, when American Jews burst with pride over Israel's victory in the Six Day War and Jewish consciousness was at an all-time high. Young Jews formed informal worship and study groups. The women's liberation movement, which included many Jewish women as intellectual leaders and grassroots organizers, was coming into its own. It was a heady time to be Jewish and to be a feminist. But what about being a *feminist Jew*?

Women began to discuss among themselves the contradictions of being committed to women's equality and committed to traditional Judaism, and they slowly began to take action. First came an organization called Ezrat Nashim (the help of women), which winked at the issues they were addressing—*"ezrat nashim"* is also the term for the women's courtyard in the ancient Temple. In 1972 the Reform movement voted to admit women to its rabbinical program. In 1973 a National Jewish Women's Conference drew five hundred women to New York. Meanwhile, "the people of the book" were busy writing. Articles, journal essays, and books about feminism and Judaism were published at an astonishing pace. Cynthia Ozick, Laura Geller, Sara Reguer, Aviva Cantor, and others wrote essays that were collected by Susannah Heschel in her anthology, *On Being a Jewish Feminist*.[23] Rachel Adler, Judith Plaskow, Blu Greenberg, and other women were also busy writing and formulating new theological and halakhic approaches. The glossy feminist Jewish magazine *Lilith* began publication in 1976, and in its inaugural issue it ran a shocking photo of a woman wearing tefillin. As the movement matured, organizations sprang up—the

Jewish Feminist Organization, the New York Jewish Women's Center, B'not Esh—and dissolved. In the early 1980s Blu Greenberg wrote two books, *On Women and Judaism* and *How to Run a Traditional Jewish Household*, that sought to bridge feminism with traditional Jewish practice. In 1988, three hundred women from twenty-four countries (with a large American contingent) gathered in Jerusalem for the first International Jewish Feminist Conference. Throughout the 1970s and 1980s, several Orthodox rabbis, including Avi Weiss, Saul Berman, Emanuel Rackman, Irving Greenberg, and Eliezer Berkowitz, were also writing dense halakhic essays on gender that sought to find ways to improve the status of women.

By the time 1997 rolled around, the idea of being feminist and Orthodox still seemed like a contradiction to most people: the prevailing belief was that a woman had to choose one identity or the other, the two being utterly irreconcilable. Yet there was enough of a groundswell to create an organization specifically for Orthodox women, not just for Jewish women in general. And so it was that Blu Greenberg founded the Jewish Orthodox Feminist Alliance. As with nearly all of the equality-seeking religious women we have met so far, Greenberg's appearance does not square with most people's caricatured idea of what a feminist looks like. She wears the modern Orthodox woman's uniform of knee-length skirt and hose, modernizing it with a turtleneck sweater and a colorful silk scarf around her neck, her hair pulled back neatly at the nape. I can visualize her stirring a pot of chicken soup in the kitchen as easily as my mind's eye sees her hunching over a page of Talmud in a house of study. She is the quintessential unapologetic Orthodox feminist activist—religious, devoted to God and family, yet comfortable at a podium raising the consciousnesses of an audience of a thousand restless women.

The first JOFA conference, held over Presidents' Day weekend at a midtown Manhattan hotel in 1997, was electrifying. I attended, and I was astounded by how many women had shown up. Who knew that there were so many observant women who not only didn't mind being called feminist but actually embraced the label? I certainly had had no idea. There were easily more than a thousand participants—even though only a few hundred had been expected to show up—some modestly dressed in wigs, long-sleeved, high-necked blouses, and ankle-grazing skirts, and others wearing slacks and V-neck tops. Some were college students with freckles and book bags, earnestly taking notes during the presentations; some were mothers taking advantage of the on-site babysitting, maneuvering their young children with the skill and tactics of four-star generals; others were midlife and older women with energy to rival that of the college students. In the hallways of the conference center I kept bumping into friends and colleagues and recognizing writers and rabbis I admired. When all the participants gathered in the hotel ballroom and we listened to Greenberg officially introduce this new organization at her keynote speech, every woman present knew that she was part of something monumental and historic.

JOFA women are not radicals on the fringes of Jewish life. They are mainstream, devout women heavily involved in their religious communities and their children's day schools. They daven (pray); they learn Torah; they cook meals for people in the community in mourning or blessed with a newborn. As Tova Hartman, a professor of education at Hebrew University in Jerusalem, declared to mirthful laughter and applause at the tenth annual conference, in 2007, "We've proven we're good girls. We make *cholent* [stew] every Shabbat."

So here we have a group of fiercely well-educated women who know their way around a complicated legal argument, are committed to both women's equality and the rigid code of Jewish law, refuse to be treated as outsiders within their tradition, and draw strength from being part of a national organization of like-minded and equally committed souls. How do they make the case that their religious tradition, which presumes that women are lesser than men, can be transformed to accommodate women's equality without compromising its core essence as the timeless word of God?

First, one must distinguish between different components of halakhah—that which is immutable and that which is contingent. As Tamar Ross reminds her readers, the great rabbis have always regarded some elements of the law "as emanating directly from God, explicitly conveying some form of absolute truth," while other elements have always been regarded as subject, to some extent, "to the arbitrariness and fallibility of human judgment."[24]

Moreover, halakhah has always recognized the role of the community in establishing customs, which can eventually become law. Historically, grassroots customs have been woven into the fabric of halakhah, and this has been considered a positive aspect of the system. Halakhah is always ultimately a dialectic and negotiation between rabbinic authority and the lived experience of the people.

Most crucially, one can be a believing, practicing, observant Jew and also reject the idea that God's revelation was a onetime event on Mount Sinai. This is hardly a new idea, as Ross points out; it has been embraced by a number of revered traditionalists such as Rabbi Abraham Isaac Kook. Indeed, although in some cases the Talmud suggests that everything the rabbis ruled was predetermined by God when God revealed the Torah to Moses at Mount Sinai, in other cases there is indication that God actually learns Torah from the rabbis. We can understand the word of God as both timeless *and* evolutionary.

Rabbinic authorities have long regarded halakhic development as intimately connected with the unfolding of history. That is to say, God's will is revealed cumulatively throughout history. Ross writes:

> Revelation is a cumulative process: a dynamic unfolding of the original Torah transmitted at Sinai that reveals in time its ultimate significance. This deviation from the common picture of an absolute and one-time affair at Sinai favors a more fluid view of Torah as a series of ongoing "hearings" of the voice at Sinai throughout Jewish history. The idea that this voice is always there waiting to be heard is well anchored in the sources . . . The conception of a written Torah whose full meaning is only revealed incrementally, via the prism of history, exists within mainstream Jewish tradition.[25]

The revelation at Mount Sinai was "the initial core divine message," Ross continues. At the time of that revelation, the patriarchal model made sense for economic, sociological, and other reasons that served the best interests of the Jewish people. However, it does not make sense today, and since divine revelation is "an ongoing, accumulating process," rabbinic authorities may resolve inequities for which there are no valid rationales.[26]

The Muslim theologian Amina Wadud, we have seen in Chapter Six, argues that the overarching values of the Qur'an transcend seventh-century Arabia. That is to say the Qur'an must be constantly reinterpreted in order to reveal God's will in each particular time and culture. Tamar Ross suggests similarly that while God gave the Jewish people the Torah at a specific moment on Mount Sinai, the process of revelation continues; otherwise we will remain forever stuck in a patriarchal social model that God does not intend for us in today's day and age.

To those who oppose it, Ross's theology is radical. But in fact it is the theology of traditional Judaism. Anyone who is honest about the history of halakhah will tell you that the great rabbis have always invented creative legal rulings to address the needs of the people, even if this meant contradicting previous Torah laws. For example, the Torah says that every seven years, lenders must cancel loans to give borrowers a fresh start (Deuteronomy 15:2). The great sage Hillel took a drastic action when he created a legal loophole to stall debt remission for the sabbatical year so that lenders would not be reluctant to lend for fear of not being repaid (Gittin 36a). The rabbis created a legal strategy to sidestep the biblical prohibition of usury (Leviticus 25:37), because otherwise it became impossible for businesses to operate. In the Middle Ages, polygamy was outlawed, even though the Torah permits it—in fact, many of the heroes of the Bible had multiple wives and concubines, including Abraham, Jacob, Moses, and King David. The Torah instructs Jews to eliminate all leavened products during Passover (Leviticus 23:6), but the rabbis created a loophole so that Jews could sell their leavened products to Gentiles and therefore would not need to throw or give away food that they would require post-Passover (Pesahim 13a). And so on. Great rabbis have felt comfortable creating legal innovations to improve the lives of the people. They have done so with the supposition that revelation of the divine will can be expressed through the people on an ongoing basis. But in our era, no one is doing any innovating.

"Halakhah is always slow to change, but it's especially slow with issues pertaining to women. The *halakhot* that pertain to me and my life are left somewhere in the Middle Ages," complains Batya, a twenty-six-year-old modern Orthodox woman who is associate director of a small nonprofit organization in Washington, D.C. "Society changes, and then halakhah changes in accordance with society. Women decide to do things for themselves, and that causes discussion, and then hopefully halakhah catches up."

Blu Greenberg has famously said, "Where there is a rabbinic will, there is a halakhic way," which has become a slogan for the Orthodox feminist movement. This does not mean that anything goes—that halakhah can be bent any which way. Activists in this movement remain committed to the limits that are built into the legal system. But at the same time, they know that within the constraints, halakhah can be as fluid as the leading rabbis and the people themselves want it to be.

It is not the halakhic system that holds women back; it is rabbinic leaders, affiliated with dogmatic Orthodox institutions, who choose to interpret the halakhah overly rigidly in matters that pertain to women's rights. For modern Orthodoxy to succeed in bridging Torah with the "way of the land," it needs an alternative to the towering U.S. Orthodox rabbinical institution, Yeshiva University. Since 1999 there has been a new option for Orthodox men pursuing rabbinical degrees who reject the insularity of the Orthodox establishment. That year, Rabbi Avi Weiss, an independent thinker and leader at the forefront of women's rights in halakhah, founded the Yeshivat Chovevei Torah (YCT) Rabbinical School in Manhattan. YCT openly encourages women to become involved in Jewish ritual, learning, and communal leadership to the full extent of halakhah. YCT is tiny and relatively new, but between its rabbis and the grassroots pressure of Orthodox feminist women, there is a real chance for positive change.

As with devout Muslim women, most Orthodox Jewish women don't mind being separated from the men during worship. But many do mind being seated in an upstairs gallery or behind an extra-tall mehitzah that obscures most or all of their view. Carol Newman observes that when the mehitzah is very high, the men forget that the women are there. During the week, when they pass around the *tzedakah* box (to collect money for charity), they often forget to bring it to the women's section. When she said Kaddish after her mother died, she went to a synagogue with a short mehitzah. "If I davened someplace else one day, the next day the men would ask, 'Where were you yesterday? We missed you.' So even behind the mehitzah, if it's short, you can become part of the congregation. But when the mehitzah is high or if you're upstairs in the balcony and you say Kaddish, you feel very lonely."

I hate tall mehitzahs. I consider a tall mehitzah—one over which I can't see the men, or the podium with the Torah resting upon it, when I'm standing or even sitting—a personal affront. Is my presence so disturbing to the men that I must be completely walled off? In my opinion, a tall mehitzah is even worse than a balcony. In the balcony, at least, if I sit in one of the first few rows, I can see the action. And although I tolerate a short mehitzah, with women to the side of men or behind the men, it makes me feel vaguely ridiculous. I remember the first time I attended a women's *tefillah* (prayer) service at Lincoln Square Synagogue in New York City. The service took place in an annex to the synagogue, not in the main sanctuary, and there was a short mehitzah, with several men sitting behind it. When I gazed around the room and my eyes rested on the men in the back, I nearly gasped with how trivial, how inconsequential, and how distant they appeared. I realized that that is the same way I must appear to the men when I sit behind a mehitzah.

But the actual presence of a mehitzah, in and of itself, is not what ticks off equality-seeking Orthodox women, since they tend to favor separation of the sexes for communal prayer anyway. (If they prefer mixed seating, they usually pray in a Conservative synagogue, where men and women sit together.) What does bother them is what the mehitzah represents: women's lack of meaningful participation in communal worship. Thus feminist-minded Orthodox women in a number of communities across the United States, Israel, and other countries have formed women's tefillah groups in which women lead the entire service, including reading Torah.

The first women's tefillah group began in the 1970s in the Riverdale section of the Bronx under the halakhic guidance of Rabbi Avi Weiss and at Lincoln Square Synagogue with the blessing of Rabbi Shlomo Riskin. Today there are more than forty such groups in the United States alone.[27] In some cases men may attend, but as mentioned, they must sit in the back behind a mehitzah, and they must number nine or fewer. If there are ten men present, the prayer service technically becomes a minyan, and boom, women cannot take on leadership roles. The women are forbidden from reciting Kaddish and several other prayers that require a minyan. In the late 1990s, the sociologist Ailene Cohen Nusbacher interviewed twenty-seven participants in women's tefillah groups in the New York metropolitan area. She found that as a group, the women were exceedingly well educated—70 percent had master's degrees. "As educated women," writes Nusbacher, "this group felt frustrated that their success and achievements could not be replicated in religious spheres."[28]

When she asked why they wanted to participate in a female-only prayer group, the most frequent response was that they wanted a meaningful religious experience and also to participate actively in services. One woman commented that in this type of service, "you felt close to God"; another said that "you get the feeling people are doing this out of true love for their religion . . . it's really inspiring." Three-quarters of the women reported feeling excluded from their synagogues. One woman commented that when the rabbi announced on Simhat Torah (the holiday in which Jews celebrate the completion of reading the entire Torah over the course of the year by dancing with Torah scrolls) that "everyone will get" a chance to dance with the Torah, "he wasn't talking about me." In Orthodox synagogues, only the men get to dance with the Torahs. I know exactly how that respondent feels—and so does every woman who attends Orthodox synagogue on Simhat Torah. Over in the men's section, the men have the time of their lives. They get the Torah scrolls, they get to dance, they get to sing, they get to put their young children on their shoulders and bounce them around. And what do the women get to do? Watch the men have fun. Many women don't bother showing up, and I don't think anyone can blame them.

Given the choice of sitting in the women's section and watching the men—on Shabbat, on Simhat Torah, on any day of the week—or participating in a service for women only, many women have chosen the latter. But since women-only services are not minyans and not all the prayers, including Kaddish, may be recited, they are decidedly separate and unequal. "I'm glad they exist," says Batya, "but it's also the cop-out answer." In segregating themselves, those who participate in women's tefillah groups essentially concede defeat in the quest for women's rights within a minyan. Rather than contest the status quo, they choose women-only services so that at the very least they can derive some religious fulfillment and be part of some religious community.

Given how tame these groups are, you would think they would be tolerated by rabbinic authorities. In fact, it seems to me that the rabbis should *rejoice*: women's tefillah groups are one way to enable women to become more personally involved in prayer and thereby become more connected to Torah Judaism. This is the position of Rabbi Haskel Lookstein, who told me that although he prefers to keep his congregation together and tends not to favor breakaway services, a once-a-month or occasional women's tefillah group "serves the needs of certain women, and it can be a very meaningful religious experience for them. I respect that need, and since it can be done halakhically, the opportunity should be there."

Yet astoundingly, to a number of other Orthodox rabbis, women's tefillah groups go *much too far*. When these prayer groups were first established, in the late 1970s, two prominent rabbis, Meir Twersky and Moshe Meiselman, prohibited them.[29] In 1985 five prominent rabbis affiliated with the rabbinical school of Yeshiva University officially condemned women's tefillah groups. In a single-spaced responsum (halakhic ruling), they denigrated the groups as a "falsification of Torah," a "total and very apparent deviation from tradition," and a product of feminism, which is synonymous with "licentiousness." In a follow-up article, the rabbis offered three rationales for their condemnation: One, the women are imitating a minyan. Two, the prayer groups represent a break with tradition. Three, the women are not genuinely motivated by a desire to fulfill the commandments, but rather by feminism, a non-Jewish fad. Thus, their motives are suspicious.[30]

By and large, American women who want to participate in these groups have ignored this ruling, dismissing it as utterly ridiculous. Remember, these women take consequential steps, such as forgoing Kaddish, precisely so as not to imitate a minyan and not to break with tradition. Besides, no one questions the impetus of men who attend synagogue and seek out honors. Are the men all genuinely motivated by their love of mitzvot, or is it possible that some—many?—are spurred by ego and the desire for congratulations and attention?

In 1997, controversy over women's tefillah groups erupted again, this time specifically concerning a Queens group that was planning a bat mitzvah. The girl was to read from the Torah to mark her religious coming-of-age, a routine occurrence in women's tefillah groups, as Orthodox girls are prohibited from reading the Torah in synagogue. The Va'ad HaRabbonim, an organization of Queens Orthodox rabbis that usually concerns itself with the kosher certification of food, issued a one-page resolution forbidding the ceremony to take place. The Va'ad admitted that there was nothing halakhically forbidden about females reading Torah, but it claimed that nevertheless it was not to occur, because it would be an innovation and therefore a break with tradition. The ceremony was held anyway, in defiance of the rabbis, with an additional hundred women in attendance to lend their support.

The rabbinic attempt to quash women's prayer groups and Torah reading is not limited to the United States. In Jerusalem a women's tefillah group that meets monthly on the Festival of the New Moon has been forbidden by the Israeli government to gather directly near the Western Wall. (This is a retaining wall dating back to the time of the Second Temple, 586 B.C.E.–70 C.E. It is a remnant of the Temple Mount and is considered the holiest location in Jerusalem.) When this group, Women of the Wall, has met at the Western Wall, it has been harassed and abused by ultra-Orthodox men and women who have screamed insults, hurled chairs over the divider, and thrown feces at them. The government claims that women reading Torah at the Western Wall violates the "custom of the place." But surely assaulting Jews who want to pray is a violation of the "custom of the place." One member of Women of the Wall, a friend of mine, has been forced on occasion to cover her slung infant with her arms to protect her from the physical violence.

Modern Orthodox women who know their halakhic rights and are determined to pray meaningfully have not backed down. In fact, some have pushed the envelope even further: They have formed minyans in which women take on ritual leadership roles to the fullest extent possible within the boundaries of Jewish law, including serving as Torah readers.

Women are not forbidden from reading from a Torah scroll. In fact, they are not even forbidden in the presence of men in a minyan. In the Talmud, Megillah 23a, a teaching from the time of the Mishnah reads, "Our Rabbis taught: All may be included among the seven [called to the Torah on Shabbat], even a child who has not reached the age of bar mitzvah and even a woman. But the Sages said that a woman should not read from the Torah because of the dignity of the congregation."[31]

Translation: Women are technically *permitted* to read from the Torah in a minyan. However, they *should* not, because this practice would embarrass the men of the congregation, as this would imply that there are men unable to fulfill this leadership role.

The first principle—that women are permitted to read from the Torah—is an absolute statement of halakhah. The second principle—that they shouldn't read from the Torah—is a relative statement. At the time that the rabbis of the Talmud had this discussion, hearing a woman read Torah would have made the men feel shamed, since women were regarded as subordinate to men. Today, of course, we have different standards. Women hold leadership roles throughout society. Men would not feel embarrassed in the presence of a woman in a leadership role in synagogue. They are accustomed to relating to women as leaders. In addition, other practices that were shunned at the time of the Talmud because they violated the "dignity of the congregation," such as scrolling the Torah in the middle of the service, are now considered acceptable.

In a comprehensive 2001 analysis of the textual sources and halakhic issues raised by women's public Torah reading, the Jerusalem Orthodox rabbi Mendel Shapiro argued that the relative statement about "the dignity of the congregation" no longer applies, and that the absolute halakhic ruling, that women are permitted to read from the Torah, may be invoked. He writes:

> Orthodox women participate in all aspects of professional and communal life, and most Orthodox Jews would select a competent woman professional or representative without giving the matter second thought. Does it make sense to accept as *halakhah* an opinion that is based on anachronistic cultural presumptions? . . . [The dignity of the congregation] is not an absolute, unyielding consideration, but one that can be overcome by other prevailing factors . . . [Customs] should be cherished, faithfully observed, and certainly never mocked, but they may, indeed should, change with the times.[32]

Shapiro also comments that in the Talmud, Hagigah 16b, Rabbi Yosi permitted women bringing sacrifices into the Temple to "lay hands" on their offering prior to its slaughter—even though women were exempt from this requirement—simply because this practice gave them "satisfaction." This is an example of women being permitted to participate in religious ritual purely for the pleasure and satisfaction it brings them.

Shapiro concluded his essay with the recommendation that Torah reading by women in a minyan, a "radical innovation," be introduced in a gradual and respectful way, and only in congregations in which the consensus is that this would not violate community standards. In women-only services, there is no reason to prohibit women from reading Torah.

To date, no Orthodox institution has publicly endorsed Shapiro's view. Yet those who disagree with his conclusions admit that he is halakhically correct. In a response to Shapiro, the esteemed Rabbi Yehuda Henkin wrote that yes, the practice of women being called to the Torah at a minyan is technically permissible. As long as women are called to the Torah only occasionally, "without fanfare," and "not in a synagogue sanctuary or hall," it could "be countenanced or at least overlooked."[33] Commenting on this response, Tamar Ross clarifies that "halakhic authorities might be prepared to condone this practice, or to look the other way, if women keep a very low profile and do not blow up *aliyot* [and Torah reading] into a revolutionary ideological statement."[34] Since the publication of Shapiro's essay, additional halakhic support has come from Orthodox rabbis Daniel Sperber and Joel Wolowelsky.[35]

With this halakhic validation, more than a dozen modern Orthodox communities around the world over the last several years have felt empowered to form their own minyans in which women are called to the Torah and lead parts of the service that are halakhically permissible for women to lead. Different communities have different names for this type of minyan; JOFA calls them "partnership minyans." The first was Jerusalem's Shira Hadasha congregation, founded in 2001, which attracts an overflowing crowd of hundreds of worshippers in a vibrant service every Shabbat. In the United States, there are partnership minyans in Los Angeles, Chicago, New Haven, Cambridge, Queens, the Bronx, Manhattan, and several other communities. They deliberately choose to meet in spaces that are not regularly or permanently used for synagogue worship, and only once or twice a month, so as not to compete with their local Orthodox synagogues.

These minyans are not egalitarian: women do not have equality with men. After all, women are not permitted to lead all parts of the service; and women and men are segregated. There is a mehitzah, often made of fabric, which is moved aside to make room for those called to the podium—which is situated in the middle of the room—to read Torah. Some of these minyans sidestep the issue of women reading Torah by holding their services only on Friday nights, when the Torah is not read, not on Saturday mornings. Nevertheless, the establishment of these minyans is arguably the most exciting thing to come out of the feminist Orthodox movement. They are rooted simultaneously in Jewish law and in the commitment to women's full participation in ritual life.

Judy Abel had long felt a personal desire to be part of a partnership minyan, but as a resident of Manhattan's Upper East Side she was getting tired of schlepping across Central Park to attend Darkhei Noam, the popular partnership minyan on the Upper West Side founded in 2002. So in December 2006 she and her husband, Michael Brill, started one themselves, called Yavneh.[36] It wasn't just for her and her family; "There is a community need for a minyan like this," she tells me.

I have been an enthusiastic participant in Yavneh since its inception. It meets once a month in a rented space, with attendance ranging from forty to more than a hundred men and women. On Yavneh mornings I don't sluggishly get myself and the kids ready for shul as I typically do on other Shabbat mornings. No, on Yavneh mornings I am awake bright and early, dragging everyone out the door the moment I've yanked the boys' arms into the jackets they're always growing out of. When I arrive at the minyan, I am invigorated to be part of a group of worshippers who take the Jewish law seriously yet have found ways for women to lead and be meaningful members of the community. Many women who've never received a Torah honor in their life are called up to the Torah; at just about every service, there has been at least one woman reciting the *Shehiyanu*, the special prayer for accomplishing something important for the first time. To tell you the truth, it almost seems too good to be true. After its half-year anniversary, I asked Abel if she had encountered any hostility or resistance from the larger Orthodox community. "No one in authority has said anything to me about it," she said.

But in smaller communities, there has been negative backlash. One New Jersey woman, Jennifer Kotzker, co-organized a partnership minyan in her community that met two times in the winter of 2005 for Friday night services. The minyan met in the gym of a local school, was intended to meet on an occasional basis, and was by invitation only; participants were asked not to discuss the minyan publicly, out of respect for the several local Orthodox synagogues. Between seventy and eighty people attended both times, and a third service, for Saturday morning, was in the planning stages. At that point the rabbi and the president of one of the Orthodox synagogues together visited the homes of six or seven families who had attended the minyan. In the Orthodox equivalent of saying "You'll never eat lunch in this town again," the rabbi and president told those families, "If you wish to continue your board position and/or to continue to receive [synagogue honors], you must stop participating in [the partnership minyan]." Did anyone stand up to the rabbi and president, I asked Kotzker? "Not a single person stood up to them," she replied. "Not a one. People called us in a panic, and we didn't want them to feel they had to choose between us and the shul. We were not a shul, and where would people go? So we disbanded it."

For the two minyan organizers, their fate was sealed. Kotzker related to me that her stepfather had recently died, and no one in the community, including the rabbi, called her to offer condolences. The other co-organizer, Daniel Geretz, was punished for speaking out in the local Jewish newspaper about the importance of discussion of the merits of such a minyan. Until then he had been a regular Torah reader and occasional cantor, but he is now no longer asked to perform those status-laden functions. In effect, both organizers have been ostracized.

At the tenth annual JOFA conference, two speakers, Elitzur Bar-Ascher and Michal Bar-Ascher Siegal, discussed their role as halakhic advisers to two partnership minyans, in Cambridge, Massachusetts, and New Haven, Connecticut. When Bar-Ascher spends Shabbat with his parents and attends their synagogue, he is denied honors. Bar-Ascher Siegal said, "We have had people stop talking to us; we have had people ban us." She related a time during the winter in New Haven when everyone who was affiliated with an Orthodox synagogue was invited to a dinner, but "those of us from the partnership minyan were left out in the snow."[37]

JOFA board member Idana Goldberg is a fervent supporter of and participant in partnership minyans, and she tells me that knowing they exist gives her hope. But overall, she continues, these minyans "do not have an impact on the wider Jewish world. No mainstream Orthodox rabbi is publicly supporting them. And most people in the wider Jewish world have never heard of them. Most Orthodox people are far removed from these kinds of modern innovations."

Rabbi Haskel Lookstein does not support partnership minyans, but he concedes that they have halakhic justification. So why does he not support them? "Because they absolutely fly in the face of *minhag yisrael* [the custom of the people of Israel]. I think especially in matters of prayer, minhag yisrael is very, very important." But custom can change, and Rabbi Lookstein acknowledges this. "It is of course entirely possible that this type of service could take off, and in twenty or twenty-five years nobody will be able to say, 'It is not minhag yisrael.' But I'm not ready to be part of that process."

Halakhah does change—just slowly. "It will take a long time for modern Orthodox rabbis to accept them," agrees Abigail Tambor, a JOFA activist. "I take the long view. I grew up going to women's tefillah groups when they were just starting and were not accepted at all at the time. They're not mainstream now, but they're more accepted and prevalent than anyone ever thought. I think the more people get exposed to the partnership minyan, the more it will help in getting wider acceptance."

I believe that these minyans will, eventually, have an impact on Orthodox synagogue life. Just as innovations with Muslim prayer cause traditional mosques to reevaluate their treatment of women, these minyans will impel Orthodox synagogues to consider ways to recognize women too. "Sometimes it feels like guerrilla warfare, where you're engaging rabbis, engaging other people one-on-one and pushing them to expand their ideas of what is permissible within the tradition," says Lili Kalish Gersch, a former leader of the D.C. Beit Midrash, the house of study affiliated with the partnership minyan in

Washington, D.C. "There is a chasm between what is permissible [for women] to do and what people allow themselves to do within the context of traditional Judaism. They have allowed themselves to honor modern ideas in other areas of their lives, so we engage with them to honor modern ideas about women also. We ask people to go in a place that's a little uncomfortable."

Rabbi Lookstein adds another concern of his: that eventually women who participate in partnership minyans will feel that they have to take the next step—toward an egalitarian service. "I have wonderful friends who worship in egalitarian services, but these are not Orthodox services," he says to me. I agree that as women gain more of a participatory role within prayer services, some *will* choose to leave Orthodoxy. But some will stay who might have left. In the end, my guess is that most will remain in Orthodoxy, just as they've remained all these years. Even without gender equality, Orthodoxy is still compelling to many observant feminists.

Orthodox Judaism needs female leaders. Yeshivat Chovevei Torah graduates, though crucial for the future of a nondogmatic and forward-looking Orthodoxy, are not enough. The word "rabbi" means "my teacher," and there are countless women as learned as the most eminent male rabbis. If women were ordained as Orthodox rabbis, the Orthodox movement would be strengthened: more women would flock to Torah study and Torah observance, leading to more families involved in traditional observance. Sally Berkovic asks what would change for Orthodox women if there were female rabbis. She eloquently muses,

> At the time of my *bat mitzvah*, she might have given me inspiration to participate more meaningfully. I might have been able to look up to her as a role model. I could have asked her my questions about boys, about suffering and all those other meaning-of-life questions I was obsessed with . . .
>
> When my parents died, an Orthodox woman rabbi might have been able to empathize in a constructive way. She would have given me the option to say the *Kaddish* and would have

taught me the right pronunciation had I decided to say it. She would have held my hand and told me not to be embarrassed that the words were foreign to me . . .

When I got married, she would have been more sympathetic to a request that the name of my mother be included in my *ketubah*, and she would have calmed my nerves before going to the *mikvah* [ritual bath] on the night before my wedding. She might even have come with me . . .

When I had daughters, she would have helped me to develop an appropriate service to herald their births. She might have popped in to see how I was managing, and offered insights from her own experience . . .

She would be particularly concerned about the problems of *agunot* . . . There are other legal issues where her "touch" would have a great influence—for example, in the use of the *mikvah* [since each month a wife must immerse herself in the ritual bath after her menstrual period before she may have sexual relations with her husband] and the area of sexual relations . . . [T]he female rabbi could encourage the use of the *mikvah* for symbolic healing after a rape, abortion or miscarriage . . .

She would be a teacher, like the male rabbi, but she would include the wisdom and literature of women in her teaching. She would highlight the practices of women in the past which could inform our practices of today. She would inspire other educators to think about the role of women in the development of Jewish thought and lifestyle.[38]

Men also need female teachers and role models; this would enhance their own appreciation and understanding of the Torah. Yosef Kanefsky, the rabbi of an Orthodox synagogue in Los Angeles, has said, "The stupidest thing the Orthodox community does now is not having women rabbis. It wastes intellectual and spiritual talent."[39]

The Reform movement ordained its first woman rabbi, Sally Priesand, in 1972. The Reconstructionist movement ordained its first woman rabbi, Sandy Eisenberg Sasso, in 1974. It took the Conservative movement a while to follow suit because the faculty of its seminary was split over the issue. But in 1985 it, too, ordained its first woman, Amy Eilberg. In 2006 there were 829 female rabbis in the United States alone.[40] As for the Orthodox movement, the title of rabbi continues to be withheld from its women.

Well, to be precise, there is no Orthodox institution that trains women to be ordained as rabbis. But in Israel there are women who have been granted a certain measure of religious authority. Women who have studied Jewish divorce law are permitted to act in the rabbinical courts as legal advocates for women. In addition, Nishmat, a Jerusalem center for advanced Jewish study for women, offers a twenty-four-hour hotline with trained women, experts in the halakhah of family purity law, to answer questions from women who are unsure if they are following the legal regulations correctly. It is worth noting that Nishmat emphasizes that it does not train women to become rabbis, and in fact, those who complete the program of study in family purity law are granted no title. The dean of Nishmat, Chana Henkin, uses the title *rabbanit* (in Hebrew) or *rebbetzin* (in Yiddish), which means "wife of a rabbi." In Jerusalem, a new nondenominational program at the Shalom Hartman Institute will ordain women and men alike as "rabbi-educators." However, these leaders will be trained to teach in North American Jewish day schools, not to take on pulpit positions or be authorities in Jewish law.

Also in Israel, there are three women who have been privately ordained by respected Orthodox rabbis. The first, Mimi Feigelson, a dual citizen of Israel and the United States, was ordained by a panel of three rabbis in 1994 after having studied with the late Rabbi Shlomo Carlebach. The second, Eveline Goodman-Thau, was ordained by Rabbi Yonatan Chipman in 2000. Chipman explained, "I was convinced of her knowledge and mastery of practical halakhah. I researched it, and as strange as it seems, there is not really a halakhic obstacle. Strictly speaking, in our day, the title of rabbi is a person proven to have mastery of Jewish sources, Jewish law and method of ruling."[41] The third woman, Haviva Ner-David, who immigrated to Israel in 1997, was ordained in 2006 by Rabbi Dr. Aryeh Strikovski after studying with him in Jerusalem for eight years.

Ner-David's ordination was covered in *The Jerusalem Post*, and the Orthodox world both in Israel and the United States, where Ner-David grew up, experienced shock waves. The Orthodox blogosphere lit up with hostile comments that belittled women's abilities. Even the rabbi who ordained Ner-David shies away from the word "ordination." He told *The Jerusalem Post*,

> It is more of an official recognition of her achievements in her studies, that covered exactly the tractates and the issues men have to master in order to get an ordination . . . Practically, it is the same, since there is no objection to Ner-David providing answers and religious rulings to women who would come to ask her halakhic questions, but in the Orthodox world and society it is not acceptable yet to ordain a woman . . . [I would be] more than happy to see more and more women entering the world of Torah and Talmud. The only difference between Ner-David and any Orthodox rabbi is that it is not acceptable. But in all issues related to her learning and abilities, I see no difference.[42]

Ner-David studied the same texts as male rabbis and jumped through the same hoops they do, but at the end of the day she may not be called a rabbi, for one reason alone: she is a woman.

Feigelson kept her own ordination a secret for many years, explaining, "I live within the Orthodox world; that is my spiritual community. I did not want to be marginalized for something that is halakhically permissible."[43] She does not use the title rabbi, because she does not want to antagonize the Orthodox establishment. Likewise, Goodman-Thau also downplays her ordination. But Ner-David refuses to keep her ordination a secret, though she calls herself a "Jewish rabbi" and not an "Orthodox rabbi."

Rabbi Ner-David, a writer and teacher with a doctorate in Jewish studies, is a friend of mine since childhood. We attended the same modern Orthodox day schools from kindergarten through twelfth grade. I was with her the night her baby sister was born. I was one of the four people who held up her wedding canopy. When a mutual friend e-mailed me the news about her ordination, I cried with happiness for her, just as I had on the day of her wedding. Immediately I called her, and we scheduled a time to speak. The only opportunity she had was at the end of the day, on her way back home to Jerusalem, to her husband and five children (she now has six), after attending an academic conference on religion and gender near Tel Aviv. On her cell phone, she said, "People are questioning, 'Is it *smikhah* [ordination]? Is it not smikhah?' Rabbi Strikovski is having second thoughts and is saying it's not really smikhah exactly because I'm a woman. He told me that if one day there are female rabbis who are recognized in the Orthodox world, then it will automatically be considered Orthodox smikhah. He's worried about repercussions from the Orthodox world. So I see my smikhah as one small step forward, until the day comes when there is an absolutely, positively, everyone-can-agree-on-it smikhah for Orthodox women."

I asked her if she thought that day will come. "I do think it will," she replied, "but it might not be called smikhah."

Some of Ner-David's supporters assert that the terms "smikhah" and "rabbi" are not the main issue—proficiency in Jewish law is. "The nuances—whether it is a usual smikhah or not—are of no importance," says Hanna Kehat, founder and leader of Kolech, an Israeli organization similar to JOFA. "What really matters is that women should turn to her and ask for her religious rulings, acknowledge her achievements and support her. Nobody will give us our rights, we will have to struggle for each step. So be it. The important thing is to remember that it can be done. This is very happy news, for all of us."[44]

But names do matter, and the title rabbi—as with priest for Catholics—brings with it a high level of respect and awe that "teacher" or an equivalent does not replicate. When I met with Devorah Zlochower of the Drisha Institute at her office, the title problem came into full relief. I announced my presence by telling an administrative assistant that I was there "for my appointment with Devorah." The instant the words came out of my mouth, I realized that something was wrong. Surely Zlochower must have a title, and I worried that I had been disrespectful. Here I was, on my way into the office of an individual fearsomely learned in Jewish texts and law, and I was calling her by her first name. It seemed so mixed up. (In fact, her job title at Drisha is *rosh beit midrash*, head of the house of learning.) At the end of our meeting I told Zlochower my concern, and she reassured me: "I'm pretty casual, so that's not a problem! But it *is* all mixed up. To some extent, I wear the non-title [not being called rabbi] as a sign of protest. It says something. You have to look at me and acknowledge the fact that I am not called rabbi, even though if you went down the list of criteria for smikhah, I fit many of those. I've named babies. I've led tefillah. I teach Torah. People call me up and ask me questions about halakhah. I speak publicly on lots of panels with female rabbis [from the liberal denominations], and that's always very ironic, where it's me and two female rabbis, and yet I'm the one who is asked the halakhic questions—and I'm Devorah."

In the United States, no Orthodox rabbi to date has ordained a woman, but several modern Orthodox institutions currently have women on staff as religious leaders. A Manhattan synagogue, Kehilat Orach Eliezer, appointed Dina Najman as "spiritual leader" in 2006. The news made it to *The New York Times*, and Najman—another learned woman who would be "rabbi" if she were a man—was photographed in her study, rows upon rows of sacred books lined up on the bookshelves behind her, with a beret on her head and a modest skirt suit demonstrating her adherence to modest dress (and thus her piety). "We think that the larger community benefits when women have more opportunities," said the copresident of the congregation, Robert Sacks, in the *Times* article. "But that doesn't mean we're not trying to be very careful to adhere to Jewish law. For us, the law comes first."[45]

Another institution, the Hebrew Institute synagogue in the Riverdale section of the Bronx, has hired women to whom female congregants can turn with halakhic and pastoral issues. The job title is "religious mentor," and the women who have occupied this position have performed many of the functions that an assistant (male) rabbi does, such as teaching, helping others make halakhic decisions, counseling, and delivering occasional sermons. Currently Sara Hurwitz occupies this position. In Manhattan's Lincoln Square Synagogue, Elana Stein Hain likewise serves as "community scholar." In Manhattan's Spanish and Portuguese Synagogue, Lynn Kaye is "director of Jewish life and learning." And at Anshe Sholom B'nai Israel in Chicago, Rachel Kohl Finegold is the "programming and ritual director."

In some cases, the women who have held these positions have considered their work a success. Hurwitz is not a rabbi, but she points out that she is "a *de facto* rabbinic figure . . . I have undoubtedly acclimated people to seeing women stand up on the pulpit and assume roles of leadership."[46] The hiring of these women represents an enormous change in modern Orthodoxy. Finally, learned and capable Jewish women are being recognized and are serving their communities. This is a tremendous achievement. But to put a twist on the song we sing every Passover at the Seder, *lo dayyenu*—it is not enough.

"As a group," writes Kohl Finegold, "we lack a name. In a world of labels, we have no label with which to define ourselves to the outside world and to identify ourselves with each other. Because we have no collective name, we tend to be defined by what we are not. We are not rabbis, although we may fill rabbinic roles. We do not have *smikhah*, although we have received much of the same training."[47]

These women will always be second-class within the system of religious authority. Assistant rabbis can become senior rabbis; these women have nowhere to advance when their position expires. They can't lead their congregation in prayer. They may possess identical skills, charisma, and Judaic literacy, but they will never be given the salary, credentials, and professionalism that men will. "I don't think we've arrived," Finegold has said. "The reality of my situation is that in X number of years, when I want to move on to whatever the next logical step would be in my career, there is no logical step. It's what some of us call the 'glass *mehitzah*.'" Indeed, the academic head of an advanced Talmud program for women at Yeshiva University, at which two of these five women studied, declares that the new trend "is something whose time has just come." But when asked if Orthodox women could become ordained as rabbis, he responded, "That's not on our radar screen."[48]

For all Orthodox women seeking expanded religious rights, the law comes first. And according to Jewish law, there are no obstacles to women becoming rabbis—or participating in partnership minyans, or doing a number of other things that are being withheld from women. The obstacles are purely attitudinal, and surely they can be overcome.

EIGHT

The Sexual Lives of Religious Women

"Sex is a bad thing that hurts women." This is what Christine remembers being told over and over by her conservative born-again-Christian parents when she was growing up. A thirty-eight-year-old stay-at-home mother in North Carolina, Christine recalls her parents quickly changing the channel when anything remotely sexual flickered on the television screen. If they rented a movie, they fast-forwarded through the scenes that even hinted at sexual behavior.

"I grew up thinking that I would never be able to get pregnant, because it would be too embarrassing for everyone, especially my parents, to know that I'd had sex," Christine says, not altogether unembarrassed even now. "I was embarrassed to date; I was embarrassed to talk with my parents about liking boys. There was never any, 'Hey, this is a normal part of life.' It was just 'Sex is bad until you're married.'"

As a parent myself, I believe that parents *should* tell their children to wait until they are in a committed, secure, long-term relationship before having sex. But this message must be served up with a few significant facts: that the ideal may not work for everyone, that sexual desires are a perfectly normal part of human development, and that females as well as males are entitled to sexual expression. In many religious households this message is conveyed in such rigid terms that anyone who does engage in sexual behavior—even well into adulthood—without being married is made to feel ashamed and like a failure. Many religious people therefore get married too young (Christine married at twenty-two) and to the wrong person, setting themselves up for many years of dejection, anger, and possibly abuse. If they are gay, they are made to feel deviant; they, too, may enter into marriages for all the wrong reasons.

This message also leads to a deliberate withholding of sexual information, especially for girls. "When I married, there was a lot I didn't know," says Christine. "I did not know that women could have orgasms. I did not have a clue that women masturbated. I knew that guys did it, but not that women did too." We will see that religious ideas about sexuality have far-reaching consequences, for when girls and women are denied information about sexuality and reproduction, they lose the ability to control their very lives.

Christian Attitudes

"You can say that 'marriage is the only place where sexual activity is allowed,' but what does that actually mean?" asks Gusti Newquist, a Presbyterian studying for ordination at Harvard Divinity School. "How do you talk about cultivating healthy relationships when you can't even talk about premarital sex?" Newquist, a former staff person for the National Network of Presbyterian College Women, clarifies that she doesn't advocate making a blanket statement about sex before marriage being good or bad. "I just want to create a space where we can discuss people's real lives instead of saying 'Don't do it.' It's not fair to college students, and it's not fair to the average churchgoer either. The Presbyterian Church does not deal with adult sexuality and with people's real lives."

The prohibition of sexual relationships between unmarried people goes hand in hand with the belief that all nonheterosexual and nonprocreative sex is against God's will and therefore fundamentally wrong. The essayist and Tucson resident Nancy Mairs, who converted to Catholicism as an adult, recalls meeting with a Dominican brother to discuss a matter that had nothing whatsoever to do with sexuality. Brother Tim asked her about her relationship with her husband and began querying about their sex life. Mairs was confused about the direction of the conversation but was too polite to quash it. Brother Tim asked if she and her husband had ever had oral intercourse. "Well, of course we'd had oral intercourse," she writes in her book *Ordinary Time: Cycles in Marriage, Faith, and Renewal.* "Aha, there lay the trouble," he told her with "obvious satisfaction," for "the devil uses sodomy to gain access to the world," and Mairs and her husband had "repeatedly flung wide the gates."[1]

Mairs, a woman in her sixties, is hardy enough to handle being told that she is the source of evil in the world. But Brother Tim was stationed at a ministry at the University of Arizona, and Mairs worries about the undergraduates, their sexual identities still in formation, who might go to him for guidance and walk out convinced that their bodies are disgusting and shameful.

Many Christians, both Catholic and Protestant, get the impression from their churches that human bodies are tainted—no, make that filthy and corrupted. Leading theologians have concluded that since God decided to have the divine son born from a virgin, an asexual body is superior and more godlike than the regular bodies mortals have, complete with urges and appetites. One should devote him- or herself to a life of the mind (as if the body and mind were not connected). Anyone who engages in sexuality in any way can never approximate the holiness of the divine. If one cannot refrain from sexual behavior, the next best thing is to limit all sexual activity to the procreative—and only within heterosexual marriage.

This view of Christianity as being antisex has been corrected in the last fifty years by such scholars as Letha Dawson Scanzoni and M. O. Vincent, but popular misconceptions remain.[2] The idea of sexuality as something to be avoided or limited hurts everyone, male and female alike, but women bear the worst brunt of it. The theological framework that denigrates bodily needs and privileges the mind is a breeding ground for misogyny because women have been historically likened to the body and men to the mind. There is also a critical piece of early Christian history that explains the development of Christian misogyny. The hierarchy of the priesthood was solidified in reaction to the growing power of women in early churches. It was precisely the creation of a male hierarchical elite, writes the theologian Beverly Wildung Harrison, that "engendered the rise within Christian theology of myths of feminine evil and images of woman either as temptress or perpetual Eve, as virgin or harlot. What this means is that a concrete power struggle over the definition of and the control of Christianity took place in the church and that the 'male dominance' party won."[3]

This theology also cultivates homophobia, as we will see. Harrison points out that misogyny and homophobia are entwined and that gay men are perceived as "failed men, no better than females."[4] Since anything having to do with females became disvalued in Christianity, homosexuality likewise became—and remains—denigrated.

One consequence of Christian misogyny is the policing of women's sexuality. The virgin mother Mary is said to be the only virtuous woman in all of history; it goes without saying that it is humanly impossible to emulate her. No woman can be both virgin and mother, but she can choose to be either virgin or mother. Very few commit to lifelong celibacy; for nearly all, being a "good" Christian woman is translated as being mother extraordinaire. She bears many children, even if she does not have the economic support and psychological strength for a large family. To ensure that women actually do bear baby after baby, Pope Paul VI issued the encyclical "Humanae Vitae" ("Human Life") in 1968, asserting that all birth control is prohibited. Only the so-called rhythm method—known as "Vatican roulette" because of its high failure rate—is morally acceptable. The overwhelming majority of American Catholics reject "Humanae Vitae," but the underlying belief that a "good" Catholic female is either a virgin or a mother of as many children as possible frames the way millions of Catholics regard females.

Moreover, a sexual double standard has always been prevalent in Christian societies, classifying girls as "good" and marriageable or "bad" and unmarriageable. Boys who can't wait until they're married to engage in sexual behavior turn to a "bad" girl, whom they discard once it's time to get serious and marry a virginal "good" girl. The theologian Rosemary Radford Ruether points out that this system causes the sexual repression of one group—the "good" girls—and the sexual exploitation of another—the "bad" girls.[5]

But even good girls are never good enough. They are still, after all, girls. Laura Eppinger, a Catholic and student at the Jesuit Marquette University, wonders aloud to me why priests can't be married. "It's bad enough that women can't be priests, but they can't even get near a priest by being his wife. Is it that a woman would contaminate the soul and the body of the priest?" The Catholic attitude about women is that when they're not involved in mothering, they are pollutants.

Evangelical Protestants do not overvalue celibacy, but their valorization of the nuclear family can be just as oppressive. James Dobson, the leader of the powerful evangelical organization Focus on the Family, which includes a network of internationally syndicated radio programs listened to by more than two hundred million people daily, demonizes "intentionally childless" couples who marry but choose not to have children. (He does not criticize those who wish to bear children but cannot for reasons beyond their control.) Dobson's colleague Rev. R. Albert Mohler, Jr., the president of the Southern Baptist Theological Seminary, calls this attitude "a willful rejection of God's procreative purpose for marriage." He continues: "Marriage, children and sex are part of one package. To deny any part of this wholeness is to reject God's intention in creation—and His mandate revealed in the Bible."[6] But not everyone is suited to parenthood; isn't it better to choose childlessness rather than inept or possibly abusive parenthood? And since women are the ones who give birth, lactate, and do most of the hands-on work of parenting, why don't they have a say in this system?

Islamic Attitudes

Islam historically has celebrated nonprocreative sexuality. Al-Ghazali, the famous medieval Persian Muslim scholar, thanked God for having created sexual pleasure. In his *Book on the Etiquette of Marriage*, he wrote,

> In the name of God, the Merciful and Compassionate, Praise be to God, the marvels of whose creation are not subject to the arrows of accident. Minds do not reflect on the beginning of such wonders except in awe and bewilderment. Praise be to God, the favor of whose graces continue to be bestowed upon all creatures . . . One of God's marvelous favors is creating human beings out of water, causing them to be related by procreation and

marriage, and subjecting creatures to desire through which God impelled them toward sexual intercourse and thereby preserved their descendants.[7]

This belief that sexual pleasure is in and of itself a positive thing was also expressed by the sixteenth-century hadith scholar Ali Muttaqi, who wrote,

> A man's sexual play with his partner, when accompanied by sincere intent, causes him to be rewarded by Allah. As the Prophet is reported to have said, "Allah is pleased with a man's playing with his wife, and records a reward for him and makes a worthy provision in the world for him because of it."[8]

Scott Siraj al-Haqq Kugle, religion professor at Swarthmore College, notes that historically, Islam did not limit sexual relationships to marriage. An informal contract, *mut'a*, could be drawn between two individuals (such as a man and a concubine) to formalize a sexual relationship outside of marriage.[9]

Nevertheless, there is a powerful Islamic taboo against nonmarital sexuality, particularly for women. Originally a tribal morality, veneration of female virginity has come to be considered an essential element of Islamic morality. Today many Muslims around the world consider an unmarried woman's virginity priceless, leading to tragedy if it is believed that her hymen has been prematurely broken.[10] In a number of countries a Muslim woman suspected of having sex outside of marriage is considered "dishonored." Her punishment ranges from social ostracism to murder, sometimes exacted by a member of her own family. Thousands of Muslim girls are murdered each year in Islamic and Western countries because they have "dishonored" their families. Muslim families go to great lengths to protect girls' virginity, often refusing to let them interact in the larger world, and girls grow up learning that they pose a danger to their family. They know that on their wedding night—after having married, in many cases, a virtual stranger—they must have intercourse whether they want to or not and then display a bloodstained sheet for the guests waiting outside for proof that the bride's hymen was intact.

This mind-set continues to prevail among Muslim communities in the United States. Mohja Kahf, a novelist and sex columnist for *Muslim WakeUp!*, has written about the pressure on unmarried Muslim women to remain virginal until their wedding night. In her 2004 short story "The Rites of Diane," about a group of Arab American young women preparing for a friend's wedding, she refers to "the hymen hang-up." "Don't tell me they still do that bedsheet ritual," says one female character. "Hanging the bloodstained wedding night sheets out for everyone to see. Didn't that go out at least a generation ago?" Responds her friend, "It did. And it didn't. It's still in people's heads even if they don't hang the sheets up anymore."[11]

There is no directive in the Islamic sacred texts for brides to prove their hymenal intactness with blood. Both men and women are expected to be chaste before their wedding, and for men it's sufficient that they give their word that they have been. "So why should a woman have to offer physical proof of her virginity?" asks Laila Al-Marayati, a physician and prominent speaker on Muslim women's issues. "Why isn't her word good enough? In a religion that argues for egalitarianism, it doesn't make sense that a woman has to prove she's a virgin but a man does not."[12] Yet many Muslim women, virgins and nonvirgins alike, undergo "vaginal reconstruction" surgery to "demonstrate" their purity. Such are the stakes of sexual shame that women are willing to begin their lifelong marital bond with dishonesty and painful surgery. In 2008 a French court annulled the marriage of two Muslims because the groom said his bride was not a virgin, as she had claimed to be. Consequently, young French Muslim women are increasingly turning to this surgery. One twenty-three-year-old patient awaiting the surgery told *The New York Times*, "In my culture, not to be a virgin is to be dirt. Right now, virginity is more important to me than life."[13]

In the 2005 anthology *Living Islam Out Loud: American Muslim Women Speak*, which is meant to provide snapshots of a range of American Muslim women's lives, the topic of virginity recurs throughout. The book is not about sexuality, but so many of the contributors discuss the social pressure for a "good" Muslim woman to remain "pure" until she marries that it becomes transparently obvious that the "hymen hang-up" is very much in force. "When we were married,

I was a virgin," comments the editor, Saleemah Abdul-Ghafur, a tid-bit that most non-Muslims would sooner keep private. Samina Ali writes that she grew up believing she was a "priceless vase" that "could easily shatter," which would in turn shatter her family's reputation.

Another contributor relates that although she was a virgin when she married, she bled only a little bit when she and her husband had sexual intercourse the first time. Behind her back, her husband queried a gynecologist, Dr. Stephanie, via e-mail to determine if the lack of blood indicated a lack of virginity. The gynecologist advised him to simply ask his bride. "In addition to the distrust that it demon-strated," the e-mail "also made me feel as if my identity as a Muslim and Arab woman had been called into question," writes Manal Omar. Khalida Saed laments that "sexuality of any kind is not discussed . . . A woman's virginity is the most valuable bargaining chip she can bring to marriage. And she *will* get married one day, or else it reflects badly on her entire family and ruins the chances of marriage for her younger siblings."[14]

Progressive Muslims want to do away with the "hymen hang-up." Activist Asra Nomani has written a list of ten sexual rights for women, an "Islamic Bill of Rights for Women in the Bedroom." Tellingly, she focuses on the excessive attention paid to women's private lives. "Women have an Islamic right to sexual privacy," reads Number 7. "Women have an Islamic right to exemption from criminalization or punishment for consensual adult sex," reads Number 8.[15] These rights can be exercised only when Muslim women cease to become symbolic of "honor" and are allowed to exist simply as worthy human beings.

Hijab

"Islam is oppressive to women—just look at how the women have to cover up!" The issue of hijab (the word refers to modest dress, but in this country it is used mostly to refer to the scarf that covers women's hair and neck) is a sore one for American Muslim women. Hijab has become a symbol of individual women's conformity to a simplistic no-tion of Islamic piety. Whether a woman must wear hijab or chooses to wear it—or not—she is scrutinized and judged, her allegiance to Islam praised or questioned. Many non-Muslims believe that the hijab is a symbol of Muslim women's oppression. They feel entirely comfortable criticizing the hijab, which is by extension a criticism of the women themselves, who are said to be complicit with their own subordination. Yet we have seen that the theologies of conservative Christianity and Orthodox Judaism deny women a number of freedoms, leading in many instances to cramped lives. Still, Muslim women are singled out in a way that their Christian and Orthodox Jewish sisters are not.

Hijab is a loaded topic because white Westerners, including feminists, have associated it with Muslim ignorance and primitiveness and used it as a symbol to demonstrate Western superiority. In fact, the head scarf was long considered a sign of status and prestige. The head scarf per se is not mentioned in the Qur'an; instead, several verses discuss the need for women to dress modestly. In one verse (24:31) God tells women to cover their bosoms and jewelry. In another verse God instructs the wives and daughters of Muhammad and the wives of believers to wrap a garment tightly around them, for the stated reason that they would be recognized and not harassed (33:59). In another verse, believers are told to speak with Muhammad's wives, but not all wives, from behind a curtain (33:53).

The head scarf became widespread among the Muslim elite in the fourteenth century, but it was understood as a cultural practice, not one mandated by Islam. It was five hundred years later, when British colonialists in the Ottoman Empire "discovered" the practice of hijab, that it became associated with Islam. Colonialists claimed to be appalled that Muslim women were "oppressed" by hijab, but it appears that they were not as interested in improving women's lives as they were in denigrating Islam.

How Muslim women dress continues to have political ramifications, although today the lines of debate tend not to be about Islam being "backward." Instead, a woman's attire is read by other Muslims as a symbol of how pious she is—and by extension, how pious are her family, her community, and even her country. To non-Muslims, her dress indicates whether or not she (and her family, community, and country) is "fundamentalist." The content of the debate has shifted, but women and their sexuality are still caught in the center.

Muslim women's attire around the globe is politicized. In Saudi Arabia and Iran, it is mandatory for women to cover practically their entire bodies. In several democratic countries with large Muslim populations, such as France and Turkey, hijab is banned in educational institutions. Meanwhile, British schools are permitted to bar female students from wearing the *jilbab*, a loose ankle-length gown, and the *niqab*, a face veil that leaves only the eyes exposed. In the United States, many American Muslims choose to wear the head scarf. Some regard it as a sign of piety and say it makes them feel close to God. Others want to demonstrate solidarity with fellow Muslims, especially because there is blatant discrimination against Muslims after September 11, 2001.

Does hijab oppress women? It depends. For those who do not choose it but are required to wear it by their government or family, the head scarf marks them as subservient and powerless, their sexuality policed—although they may not regard themselves as restricted. Those who willingly wear it often claim that it is liberating—that it frees them from preoccupation with feminine appearance and the pressure to conform to fashion, that it allows them escape from sexual objectification, that wearing it causes others to respect and validate them, affording them more freedom than they otherwise would hold. However, as theologian Amina Wadud has pointed out, whether a woman is required to wear the head scarf or chooses to, her appearance looks the same to anyone whose eyes rest on her. Wadud, who herself chooses to wear hijab, writes that

> the *hijab* of coercion and the *hijab* of choice look *the same*. The *hijab* of oppression and the *hijab* of liberation look the same. The *hijab* of deception and the *hijab* of integrity look the same. You can no more tell the extent of a Muslim woman's sense of personal bodily integrity or piety from 45 inches of cloth than you can spot a fly on the wall at two thousand feet.[16]

The Muslim woman is prejudged on the basis of her wearing or not wearing hijab, regardless of the context for her wearing it, by non-Muslims and Muslims alike. And she never can tell which direction the judgment will fly. "Hijab is a war ground between women," one woman fumed to me. The Muslim Women's League, an American organization that promotes equality for women, has lamented that hijab has become a "litmus test" for piety. One woman, whom I met only on the phone, described herself to me as "observant, even though I don't wear the head scarf." Another woman I spoke with, who had converted to Islam, enjoys wearing hijab—although she complained that it's difficult in the hot summer months. "Spiritually it's good," she said, "because it keeps you in tune with Allah. And people treat you with respect. Men treat me totally differently when I'm wearing it. Women do too, in a good way. I think it's a blessing, but it has to be a woman's choice. A woman has to be ready for it." Yet Wadud, who has led congregational prayer of women and men, has been dismissed as a "devil in hijab." Still, if she did not wear hijab, she would surely be criticized for that too. A Muslim woman can't win—no matter what she does.

Even within her own mind, a Muslim woman sometimes just can't win. There can be a great deal of anxiety and ambivalence behind the decision to wear or not wear the hijab. The Muslim journalist Mona Eltahawy wore hijab herself from the ages of sixteen through twenty-five while living in Egypt and Saudi Arabia. During those years, she tells me, "people had a whole set of assumptions about me, and I wasn't even given the chance to tell them who I am. This was true of Muslims and non-Muslims. It was not for me. I felt suffocated by it. I was treated like I was the walking embodiment of the Qur'an. The last straw for me was one day when my mom, a physician with a Ph.D.—who still wears the hijab—told me that she had run into another doctor, a colleague of my dad's, who asked if I was married yet. My mom said no, and he asked if I wore the head scarf. My mom said yes, and he said, 'Well, then she'll be married soon.' And I thought, Is that all I am—a girl who wears a head scarf? But on the positive side, I chose to wear the hijab. My mother never pressured me to do it. I felt that it was a way for me to say, Pay attention to my intellect, not just my body. I was not oppressed, stupid, or brainwashed. Some feminists have a mentality of 'I believe in women's choices as long as they choose what I would choose for them.'"

It saddens me to imagine Eltahawy's gorgeous, thick, shiny hair covered up, but she tells me that during her hijab years she wore her hair very short. She began to let it grow only several years after she took off the head scarf. The implications for her sense of bodily self were enormous.

"The day I took off my hijab, I went to a hairdresser I knew was terrible. I didn't want a good haircut, because I didn't want anyone to think I had taken off my hijab to look good to attract men. I used to wear shirts with the neck all the way up, the long sleeves, the long skirt. I didn't want people to think, Oh, Mona is just trying to attract guys. I went out of my way to not look good. It took me a long time to feel comfortable with my body, to accept that I am physical and I am intellectual."

Competition over who is most pious gets played out especially with niqab, the face veil. Few American Muslims choose to cover their faces; those who do, stand out. I asked Eltahawy what she thought about niqab, and her serious, intelligent face became flushed with fury at even the thought of it.

"Niqab is different from hijab. Niqab scares the hell out of me because it completely negates who you are. If you wear niqab, I don't know who you are. It gets me on a really visceral level, niqab does. I once got into an argument with a niqabi woman on the Cairo subway back when I wore hijab. She got into the car I was riding in and sat opposite me and tried to convince me to wear niqab. I said, 'Isn't what I'm wearing enough?' And she said, 'If you wanted to eat a piece of candy, and you had one piece that was in a wrapper and one piece that was not in a wrapper, which would you choose?' I said to her, 'I'm not candy. I'm a human being!'"

Adds Laury Silvers, a professor of Islamic studies at Skidmore College and a convert to Islam, regarding niqab in the United States, "You know how you feel when you have your big movie-star sunglasses on? You feel protected. You can hide behind your glasses. Some women feel that way. Others want to act like they're more pious than other women and can act superior. Others are really pious, and it's genuine."

Both Muslims and non-Muslims must stop using hijab as a vehicle to judge others. For many Muslim women, their sexual identities are stunted because they are treated like candy that must be wrapped at all times—and if the wrapper comes off, they are told, they are dirty and disgusting. The author Irshad Manji tells me that "if you go back to the Qur'an, you can see that all you need is a turtleneck and a baseball cap to meet the theological requirements of dressing modestly. A few years ago I interviewed the political leader of Islamic Jihad, and I didn't have hijab with me, because I didn't think I was going to get the interview. So I wore a baseball cap and joked with him about it, and he accepted it."

Meanwhile, when non-Muslims criticize hijab as a vehicle of women's oppression, they rarely apply the same critical lens to their own lives. Does not Western fashion imprison most of us, who feel endless pressure to conform to a narrow, if not impossible, beauty ideal? An anecdote about Lady Mary Montague, the eighteenth-century wife of the British ambassador to Constantinople, says it all. While visiting a Turkish bath, she showed the women the corset beneath her blouse. The Muslim women believed she was "imprisoned in a machine which could only be opened by her husband." Both groups of women could see each other as prisoners and of course they were right.[17] We don't have the corset any longer, but we are hobbled and shackled just the same by high heels, pencil skirts, slinky fabrics, thong underwear, and Botox. Are non-Muslims entitled to judge?

Jewish Attitudes

As with Islam, Judaism traditionally cherished the concept of sexual pleasure for its own sake, although only within marriage. It is said that when a husband and wife engage in sexual relations, God is present. According to the Torah, the husband *must* give his wife sexual pleasure in order to fulfill his marital obligations (Exodus 21:10). The lush love poem Song of Songs, included in the canon of the Jewish Bible, includes verses like this:

> I have come to my garden,
> My own, my bride;
> I have plucked my myrrh and spice,
> Eaten my honey and honeycomb,
> Drunk my wine and my milk . . . (5:1)
>   My beloved is clear-skinned and ruddy, . . .

His belly a tablet of ivory,
Adorned with sapphires.
His legs are like marble pillars
Set in sockets of fine gold . . .
His mouth is delicious
And all of him is delightful. (5:10, 14–16)

The rabbis of the Talmud were far from prudish. Sexual topics—oral sex, masturbation, multiple orgasms—came up occasionally in the crosshatches of their legal debates. They were clearly interested in sexuality and recognized its importance in a healthy (marital) relationship. They set down strict guidelines of how often a husband was to pleasure his wife: if he was unemployed, every day; if he was a laborer, twice a week; mule driver, once a week; camel driver, once a month; sailor, once every six months (Mishnah Ketubot 5:6).

The medieval scholar Nachmanides (1194–1270) was quite explicit in his *Holy Letter*, which has been likened to a Jewish *Kama Sutra*. The great medieval rabbi reminded men that sexual play is a holy, sacred act. He also instructed them to pleasure their wives first before pleasuring themselves:

Know that the sexual intercourse of man with his wife is holy and pure when done properly, in the proper time and with the proper intention. No one should think that sexual intercourse is ugly and loathsome, God forbid! . . . [Aristotle was incorrect] for stating that the sense of touch is shameful for us. Heaven forbid! The matter is not like the Greek said . . . Everything created with divine wisdom is complete, exalted, good, and pleasant.

. . . When engaging in the sex act, you must begin by speaking to her in a manner that will draw her heart to you, calm her spirits, and make her happy. Thus your minds will be bound upon one another as one, and your intention will unite with hers. Speak to her so that your words will provoke desire, love, will, and passion, as well as words leading to reverence for God, piety, and modesty.

. . . A man should never force himself upon his wife and

255

never overpower her, for the Divine Spirit never rests upon one whose conjugal relations occur in the absence of desire, love, and free will . . . A man should not have intercourse with his wife while she is asleep, for then they cannot both agree to the act. It is far better, as we have said, to arouse her with words that will placate her and inspire desire in her.

To conclude, when you are ready for sexual union, see that your wife's intentions combine with yours. Do not hurry to arouse her until she is receptive. Be calm, and as you enter the path of love and will, let her insemination come first, so that her seed be the substance and your seed like the design.[18]

Yet for all the gorgeous sexually positive imagery in the Jewish tradition, members of many Orthodox communities today tend not to discuss sexual matters at all, leading to profound discomfort and awkwardness among young singles, especially women. In the modern Orthodox world, there is sex segregation in many schools and social events, although not as much as in the ultra-Orthodox world. Even still, there is a lot of anxiety and fear about sexuality, compounded by an elaborate and rigid set of rules regarding sexual abstinence during and after menstruation, euphemistically called the "laws of family purity."

Because there is so much sexual ignorance, Orthodox couples engaged to be married typically enroll in a premarital class to get up to speed. The men and women are segregated, with the men taught by a rabbi and the women taught by a rabbi's wife or another woman considered modest, pious, and knowledgeable. The women's classes are called *kallah* (bridal) classes. Although not all officiating rabbis require brides to enroll, most brides do anyway because the classes teach the regulations of family purity, which they are required to master.

Many kallah classes present sex as something secretive and dirty, causing excited young brides fantasizing about their wedding to become confused, even ashamed, of the sexual life awaiting them. One twenty-six-year-old modern Orthodox woman told me about the class that both she and her sister had attended in New Jersey.

"My sister had gotten a horrible sex education from this rebbetzin [wife of the rabbi], to the point where my sister was already pregnant and I had seven months to go before my wedding, but I was educating my sister! And she was saying things to me like, 'You're kidding!'

I knew more because even though I took the same class, my fiancé and I had in addition attended a second premarital class that was not negative about sex. But my sister's whole sex education was from this one rebbetzin. The rebbetzin had said that you have to wait until dark to have sex, and she said things like, 'It's all really overwhelming' and that having sex the first time 'will probably hurt you.' The eighteen-year-old girls she speaks to are terrified. It's all negative, nothing positive.

"The other class I took was a great class. The woman who led it taught us how to have good sex, because most of the engaged couples had not had sex and some of them had never even held hands. She said, 'I know there are some people who say that going down on your husband is not allowed, but it's really okay and it's nice once in a while.' She was sitting there with a beret, this frum [pious and modest] lady!

"I feel bad for my sister that she didn't get to take a class like that. There's this air of secrecy. Nobody talks about sex; nobody compares notes with each other. A friend of ours who took that same class with the rebbetzin once burst out crying and said that she hates sex, that it hurts so much, and that she doesn't know what to do or who to talk to. She had no outlet. There's an air of dirtiness around this. The rabbis approach this from the point of view of purity and impurity, which makes women look at themselves negatively and at sex negatively."

Another modern Orthodox woman in her mid-twenties, from Washington, D.C., expressed alarm about the damage done by teachers of kallah classes. "I've heard stories of teachers saying, 'Don't worry, it won't hurt for too long,' or 'Don't worry, you won't have to do it that often,'" she told me. "You're taking a population of young women who don't know much about sexuality. It's scary and sad. These women don't expect to have a pleasurable experience and so they don't know that it's even possible for it to be pleasurable."

Sexuality education is too important to assign to uninformed, unprepared, unhelpful kallah teachers. In March 2008, the Jewish Orthodox Feminist Alliance decided enough was enough: it convened a ground-breaking conference, "Demystifying Sex and Teaching Halakhah: A Kallah Teacher's Workshop." (The conference, held in New York City, was also cosponsored by the Drisha Institute and Yeshivat Chovevei Torah.) Fifteen women ages twenty-five to fifty-two spent four days exploring the halakhic and biological issues of sexual response. The chair of the conference, Bat Sheva Marcus, is herself observant and is also the clinical director of the Medical Center for Female Sexuality in New York. Many of her Orthodox Jewish patients are completely ignorant about human sexuality. One young Hasidic woman came to see her after having been married for two years and not being able to become pregnant. Marcus discovered that not only had the patient not had sexual intercourse, the patient and her husband did not even realize that they had not had sexual intercourse.[19]

Kallah teachers typically describe sex as a holy act, but where are women—and men—supposed to go with technical questions and their need to discuss the emotional side of sexuality? An online discussion board at Calm Kallahs (www.calmkallahs.com), founded by Marla Lemonik, is one of the best places around for Orthodox women and men to anonymously ask and respond to questions. "Once in a while sex is a holy coming together," Marcus told *The Jewish Week*. "Sometimes it's OK. Sometimes it can just be fun. You don't want to have a Shabbat dinner every time you sit down to a meal. Sometimes you eat a sandwich because you're just hungry."[20]

Laws of "Family Purity"

According to the Torah (Leviticus 15:19–29), a woman must not have sexual relations with her husband while she experiences normal menstrual bleeding, for a minimum of seven days, during which time she is considered ritually impure or unclean. She becomes ritually purified, rabbis later decreed, after she immerses herself in a special pool of water called a mikvah. However, if the bleeding is abnormal and unexpected—caused perhaps by hormonal fluctuations—she is ritually impure until her bleeding stops, as well as for an additional seven "clean" days.

The rabbis of the Talmud conflated the two categories of bleeding into one, so that whether a woman experienced regular monthly bleeding or irregular bleeding, she was to follow the same course of action. In other words, all bleeding was from then on to be treated as irregular, abnormal bleeding. The period of ritual impurity was decreed to last a minimum of five days (even if a particular woman bleeds only for three or four), with an additional seven "clean" days before a woman may immerse herself.[21]

Although the Torah warns that anyone who touches a ritually impure woman becomes impure, the rabbis strengthened the prohibition. All touching—including kissing and holding hands—was prohibited. Spouses may not share the same bed during a woman's ritually impure days. (Typically, an observant couple has two beds that are pushed together or spread apart, depending on the time of the wife's menstrual cycle.) Thus, there is a *minimum* of twelve days each month when a couple may not have sexual relations or even touch each other.

How does a woman know if bleeding has truly stopped? Through a self-performed internal exam with the vaginal insertion of a white cloth. She is supposed to perform this exam each day of her period or, minimally, at the beginning and the end of her period. The seven "clean" days do not kick in until bleeding has ceased, and if a woman finds a spot on her cloth and is unsure whether it is blood, she must show it to her rabbi to check. Yes, you read that correctly: a Jewish woman who observes the laws of family purity—a modest woman who chooses to live a devout life—is expected to bring a cloth that had been inside her vagina to her rabbi so that he may inspect her secretions. You might be wondering why she would bother to do something so embarrassing. Why not just wait another day or two if necessary? Because when a woman is trying to conceive a child, waiting extra days beyond what is required can be disastrous. It is critical that it be determined how long she must wait before resuming relations with her husband, lest they miss her fertile days. There is also the fact that she and her husband have waited long enough and just don't want to wait any longer to touch each other.

I believe that the laws of family purity evolved because of male feelings of disgust, revulsion, and fear over menstruation. (The Qur'an, in verse 2:222, also prohibits sexual relations with a menstruating woman, but Islam does not share Judaism's extensive set of regulations surrounding the prohibition.) Although today Orthodox Jews use the inclusive language of "family purity," the language of the Torah and Talmud is that of women's defilement, and women and men today continue to regard a woman in *niddah* (state of ritual impurity) as unclean at some spiritual level. Even if she is not actively bleeding, the fact that she is capable of bleeding renders her, in the minds of many Orthodox Jews, as one with the potential to defile others.

Recognizing that no self-respecting woman in today's era can follow the laws of family purity without feeling diminished or ashamed, modern Orthodoxy to its credit has tried very hard to put a positive spin on these laws. And to some extent, the effort has been successful. A number of Orthodox communities and a few Conservative ones have poured money into creating mikvahs with beautiful tiles, plush towels and robes, scented candles, and Jacuzzi bathtubs. One mikvah near my home on Manhattan's Upper East Side is so luxurious that I am tempted to immerse even when I don't need to. A sound system pipes in instrumental Jewish music; a female attendant provides a pair of slippers. With a mikvah like this, who needs a spa?

Many modern Orthodox women today, especially those who do not suffer from fertility problems, enjoy adhering to these laws, saying that being sexually off-limits for nearly half the month makes the rest of the month seem like a honeymoon. Some find spiritual meaning in the water itself, or they find the experience sensuous. Some have reclaimed mikvah immersion to assert they are not a sex object, since for twelve days a husband must communicate with his wife without any sexual overtones. They claim that although they must follow these laws because they are divinely authored—and you can never argue with divine authority—there's an added bonus in the fact that when all is said and done, it's nice to have a period of time in which one can be inwardly focused. Still others appreciate time to reflect on the loss of potential life signaled by their menstrual period. "I actually kind of like it," one young woman sheepishly told me. "I didn't expect to like it, but somehow I separate the intellectual side of it—that deals with women's impurities—and the actual experience of it."

On the other hand, this woman does not observe the laws every month: occasionally she manipulates her menstrual cycle by taking the contraceptive pill without a break, leaving her with no period (and in fact, when a woman is on the pill, she doesn't truly menstruate in the first place). "I feel very committed to the twelve-day issue and not to the once-a-month issue," she tells me. In other words, she is committed to adhering to the laws of ritual purity for twelve days after bleeding begins, but if she does not bleed, because she has manipulated her cycle, she doesn't mind skipping observance of the laws during that time frame. Plus, although she and her husband have separate beds at home for when she is in niddah, when they travel, they share a bed. "I make it more convenient for me. If I can mess with things a little without losing the [fulfillment of the commandment] entirely, then I will do it." Some women wait only the seven days proscribed in the Torah and dismiss the extra days added by the rabbis.

The fact that it is the woman alone who is considered "impure" before immersion is more than some women are willing to take. It's not just the act of going to the mikvah, but the sexual messages behind it. "I feel guilty when I have my period," another woman tells me. "I can't give my husband pleasure, and it's *my fault*. If my body bleeds for an extra day, it's *my fault*." Another woman, a Judaic educator, tells me that when she first married, she "was really into it. I thought it was spiritual. But then I began to feel dirty and angry. And the rabbis checking the cloth? It is so perverted, so sick."

Increasingly, observant women are refusing to turn to rabbis with these intimate matters. In Israel, an organization called Nishmat trains and certifies women to serve as experts on the laws of family purity. Nishmat runs a toll-free hotline and online support. "This improvement notwithstanding, the very notion that women must submit themselves to . . . outside surveillance is questionable," writes the theologian Tamar Ross, who supports Nishmat but questions the need for anyone other than the woman herself to weigh in on her niddah status. "The mystique surrounding the degree of expertise such questions [about bleeding] require raises the suspicion that here is merely another device for keeping women in their place."[22]

Reproductive Rights

Muslim and Jewish beliefs about sexuality lead to the policing of women's sexuality within Muslim and Jewish communities, but conservative Christian beliefs about sexuality affect every one of us in the United States. Many of our lawmakers are themselves conservative Christians who want to impose their beliefs on the private lives of all Americans. This is most stark in the area of reproductive rights. The political reproductive rights battle used to center completely on abortion, but now the field of attack is much wider. The goal is not only to restrict a woman's ability to terminate a pregnancy at any gestational stage but also to withhold critical information about sexuality from young people and to restrict access to contraceptives from women of all ages, especially if they are not married.

Conservative Catholics and conservative evangelical Protestants are increasingly in sync in this cause. The two groups have different theological approaches. To conservative Catholics, abortion and some forms of pharmaceutical contraception violate divine nature. To conservative evangelical Protestants, there must be moral accountability for sexual activity: women who engage in nonmarital, nonprocreative sex are promiscuous sluts who deserve to suffer the "consequences"—disease and/or pregnancy leading to childbirth. Most conservative Catholics and conservative evangelical Protestants who oppose reproductive rights are united in the belief that God created men and women as essentially different, with different roles, and that motherhood is the primary role God has given women.

The battle begins with sex education in schools. George W. Bush, himself born-again, maintained that teenagers must not be given any information about contraceptives except with regard to their failure. His support of "abstinence-only" education was based on religion, not science or concern for the health of young people. Over and over, researchers have found that abstinence-only programs—which dictate that unmarried people should not have sex, full stop—have no effect whatsoever on children's sexual behavior. They do not curb teen pregnancies or halt the spread of HIV and other sexually transmitted diseases.[23] According to a 2007 congressionally mandated report based on four communities, elementary and middle school students who received abstinence education were just as likely to have sex in the following years as students who did not get such instruction. Approximately half became sexually active in each group—and at the same age (14.9 years on average), with the same number of sexual partners.[24]

Moreover, according to a 2004 report released by Representative Henry Waxman, D-California, many abstinence-only curricula teach false, misleading, or distorted information: abortion can lead to sterility or suicide; half the gay male teenagers in the United States have tested positive for HIV (in fact, no one knows how many are HIV-positive); touching a person's genitals "can result in pregnancy"; a forty-three-day-old fetus is a "thinking person"; HIV can be spread through sweat and tears; and condoms fail to prevent HIV transmission 31 percent of the time in heterosexual intercourse (the correct percent is less than 3). Since 1999 millions of children ages nine through eighteen have participated in more than a hundred federally funded abstinence programs in at least twenty-five states. In 2005 alone, Bush proposed to spend $270 million on the funding, with Congress reducing the amount for that year to a still-sizable $168 million, bringing total funding to nearly $900 million over five years.[25]

The abstinence educator Leslee Unruh, founder of the Abstinence Clearinghouse, claims outrageously that couples who wait until marriage to have sex routinely have simultaneous orgasms. "The hormonal symphony between the two, you can have it right away," she told the journalist Michelle Goldberg, author of *Kingdom Coming: The Rise of Christian Nationalism*. "It's reaching it together. It's the fireworks. It's a bonding. It's intimacy." Intimacy is not possible for those who have sex with more than one person, Unruh continued. "The secretions from one person are different from the next person." People with more than one sex partner "mess up their body processes." However, those who give up sex with multiple partners and pledge abstinence or "secondary virginity" can rest assured: their physical equilibrium will be restored in time. Unruh's organization received a $2.7 million contract in 2002 from the Department of Health and Human Services.[26]

Leading pediatricians are unequivocal in their opinions that teenagers need information about and access to birth control and emergency contraception. Unruh's fantasyland scenarios about "hormonal symphonies" do not count as information. Abstinence-only education, experts say, makes it more likely that once teenagers initiate sexual activity, they will fail to use contraceptives, having unsafe sex that can lead to pregnancy and/or disease.[27] Even those teenagers who *themselves* espouse belief in abstinence until marriage—and prove it by taking a "virginity pledge" stating that they will remain virgins until they marry—become sexually active before marriage and engage in unsafe sex. According to the March 2005 *Journal of Adolescent Health*, male virginity-pledged teens are four times more likely than their non-pledged peers to have engaged in anal sex (did someone forget to tell them that anal sex counts as sex?), and overall rates of sexually transmitted diseases among both groups are the same.[28] Parents agree with pediatricians. Although nearly all parents (95 percent) believe that schools should encourage teenagers to wait until they are older to have sex, they also (94 percent) believe that schools should teach about birth control.[29]

Access to birth control is also being severely restricted—and not only to teenagers. "The mind-set that invites a couple to use contraception is an anti-child mindset," says Judie Brown, president of the Catholic American Life League. "So when a baby is conceived accidentally, the couple already have this negative attitude toward the child. Therefore seeking an abortion is a natural outcome. We oppose all forms of contraception."[30] Sex is for making babies, echoes Rev. R. Albert Mohler, Jr.:

The effective separation of sex from procreation may be one of the most important defining marks of our age—and one of the most ominous. This awareness is spreading among American evangelicals, and it threatens to set loose a firestorm . . . Prior to [the pill], every time a couple had sex, there was a good chance of pregnancy. Once that is removed, the entire horizon of the sexual act changes. I think there could be no question that the pill gave incredible license to everything from adultery and affairs to premarital sex and within marriage to a separation of the sex act and procreation.[31]

In 2006 Missouri state representative Cynthia Davis wrote in an e-mail to a fellow Republican legislator that she disapproves of pharmaceutical contraceptives because they "tamper with mother nature" and that "even if you solve a physical problem" by halting insemination, "you still have not solved the moral, emotional and spiritual problems that come with a promiscuous lifestyle." She wondered "what kind of man would want to enjoy free sex and then expect [his partner] to provide for her own contraceptives? These are the kind of men who want free whores . . . I have concluded that the chemicals and drugs [i.e., pharmaceutical contraceptives] are their way to have all the goodies and not pay the price."[32] This lawmaker believes that if you have nonmarital, nonprocreative sex, you deserve to "pay the price"—pregnancy or disease. If you are an unmarried woman using contraception, you are a "whore."

In her eye-opening book *Full Frontal Feminism*, Jessica Valenti points out that more and more states are introducing "conscience clause laws" allowing pharmacists, nurses, and other health-care professionals to refuse to distribute any medication that goes against their moral, ethical, or religious beliefs. According to the National Women's Law Center, four states currently permit pharmacists to refuse to fill prescriptions that contradict their personal beliefs: South Dakota, Arkansas, Mississippi, and Georgia. More than ten others have introduced "conscience clause" legislation. In the states in which this law is in force, a pharmacist who believes that it is wrong for an unmarried woman to have sex is legally allowed to refuse to fill her contraceptive prescription. So far, Valenti observes, pharmacists have taken matters into their own hands, even without a conscience clause law in their state, and have refused to fill contraceptive prescriptions. Pharmacists have focused on women alone. They are not refusing condoms for unmarried men.

This is not mere inconvenience. What if every pharmacist in a woman's neighborhood refuses to do his or her job? What if her pharmacist refuses not only to fill her prescription but also to return the prescription to her? (On its website, the organization Pharmacists for Life International does not offer a clear response to the question about whether the prescription should, from a moral standpoint, be returned to the customer.) What if the customer is picking up not her monthly Ortho-Cyclen but emergency contraception (also called Plan B or the morning-after pill)? This contraception prevents pregnancy in the uterus and must be taken within seventy-two hours after unprotected sexual intercourse, but it is more likely to be effective if taken within twenty-four hours. A woman may become pregnant against her wishes and lose the ability to control the direction of her own life.

In 2005 a Kmart pharmacist in Scottsdale, Arizona, recommended to other pharmacists who, like himself, oppose emergency contraception, to lie to their customers: "The pharmacist should just tell the patient that he is out of the medication and can order it, but it will take a week to get here. The patient will be forced to go to another pharmacy because she has to take these medicines within 72 hours for them to be effective. Problem solved."[33]

In 2006, after being stalled for years in the Food and Drug Administration pipeline, emergency contraception finally became available without a prescription. As it is, emergency contraception may be called "over-the-counter," but in truth it is "behind-the-counter"—a woman must present ID to prove she's at least eighteen years old. In more than thirty-eight countries it is available over the counter. The reason it took so long to get even behind-the-counter status in the United States can be summed up in one word: religion.

In 2005 the Government Accountability Office, a nonpartisan investigative arm of Congress, concluded in a report that the FDA's initial rejection of emergency contraception was "unusual," "novel," and based on politics rather than science. Indeed, both an independent advisory committee as well as the FDA's own scientific review staff had recommended availability of the contraceptive. Dr. Janet Woodcock, the FDA's acting deputy commissioner of operations, and Dr. Steven Galson, acting director of its drug center, had planned to reject the contraceptive even before the agency's scientific review of the application process had been completed.[34] Woodcock said she was concerned that over-the-counter status could lead to "extreme promiscuous behaviors such as the medication taking on an 'urban legend' status that would lead adolescents to form sex-based cults centered around the use of Plan B."[35]

Dr. W. David Hager, a Christian conservative obstetrician-gynecologist appointed by George W. Bush to lead the FDA's committee on reproductive health drugs in 2002, said he worried that if emergency contraception were easily available, it would increase sexual promiscuity among teenagers—even though medical research made available to Hager and the other committee members proved no connection between sexual activity and access to emergency contraception. Hager's medical credentials include authorship of *As Jesus Cared for Women: Restoring Women Then and Now*, which recommends biblical readings and prayers to cure headaches and premenstrual cramps. In his private practice, he refuses to prescribe contraceptives to unmarried women.

As an obstetrician-gynecologist, Hager's job is to protect women's health. But in addition to his adherence to religion above medicine and science, there is another problem to consider. His wife of thirty-two years, Linda Davis, has publicly stated that he repeatedly raped her with forced, painful anal sex. She spoke to a *Nation* reporter in 2005 in a very credible interview; the facts were corroborated by several friends and her attorney.[36] Davis divorced Hager. His patients can find another doctor. But we American citizens are stuck with the supposed custodians of women's health our right-wing Christian lawmakers appoint for us.

Make no mistake about it: attempts to revoke women's reproductive rights are based on religious ideas about women's God-given role as virgin or mother. This set of beliefs frames debates about the legal availability of abortion. Changes on the Supreme Court bench may lead to a reversal of *Roe v. Wade*, which would make abortion law fall to the states.

Eleven states are trying to ban abortion completely. In 2006 South Dakota passed the most sweeping ban on abortion in the country, prohibiting abortion even for raped women and victims of incest. Later that year, South Dakota citizens voted down the ban, but it was close. The South Dakota state senator Bill Napoli said on a PBS *News-Hour with Jim Lehrer* that there was only one instance in which he could ever imagine a female being entitled to an abortion: She "would be a rape victim, brutally raped, savaged. The girl was a virgin. She was religious. She planned on saving her virginity until she was married. She was brutalized and raped, sodomized as bad as you can possibly make it, and is impregnated."[37]

The late commentator Molly Ivins observed that with Napoli's restrictions, another South Dakota woman interviewed on the same program would not be eligible for an abortion. "Michelle," a woman in her twenties with a low-paying job and two children, said that she just could not afford a third. She had driven five hours to the state's only abortion clinic, and she said, "It was difficult when I found out I was pregnant. I was saddened because I knew that I'd probably have to make this decision. Like I said, I have two children, so I look into their eyes and I love them. It's been difficult, you know, it's not easy. And I don't think it's, you know, ever easy on a woman, but we need that choice."[38]

Salivating over the punishment of nonvirginal, nonreligious, nonsodomized rape victims, lawmakers in Alabama introduced a similar ban, with no exception for rape and incest. Valenti, whose book is filled with lawmakers' statements so frightening I didn't believe they were accurate until I verified them myself, dug up this comment by the state senator Hank Erwin: "I thought if South Dakota can do it, Alabama ought to do it, because we are a family-friendly state."[39]

Currently, thirty-four states require an underage teenage girl to obtain the consent of a parent in order to have an abortion. Most of these states at least offer the possibility of judicial bypass, for the intrepid teenage girl actually willing to go in front of a judge to explain why she can't tell her parents about the pregnancy—for instance, because her parents would kick her out of her home, or because her father/stepfather is the one who impregnated her. But in Utah, the state senator Chris Buttars argued that *no* girl should be allowed the judicial bypass option, not even an incest victim. He explained, "Abortion isn't about women's rights. The rights they had were when they made the decision to have sex." Throwing logic out the window, he continued, "This is the consequence. The consequence is they should have to talk to their parents."[40]

There are more Christian antichoice centers, called "crisis pregnancy centers," than health clinics offering abortion. These centers pressure or trick pregnant women into remaining pregnant until it's too late to get an abortion. There are four thousand crisis pregnancy centers in the country, with names such as Women's Resource Center or Pregnancy Help Center. Women walk in assuming that they will be given full and accurate information or assistance with terminating their pregnancy. These centers use deceptive practices to avoid helping women who want to abort. The manual of a foundation that ran dozens of these centers nationwide instructed, "Never counsel for contraception or refer to agencies making contraceptives available" because such counseling "is not only inaccurate but unacceptable and against the general pro-life philosophy, and Christian principles."[41]

The ultimate goal of Christian antiabortion activists is a nationwide ban on abortions at every gestational stage. Although this possibility seemed remote in the years following *Roe v. Wade*, it appears quite feasible today. A 2007 ban, upheld by the Supreme Court, on late-term "intact dilation and extraction"—called partial-birth abortion by

Christian abortion opponents—is a very real threat to all abortion rights. This procedure involves aborting a fetus after partially extracting it from the woman's uterus rather than while it is inside the uterus. I admit: it is gruesome to contemplate this procedure. But it is used only late in the pregnancy, when no other method is appropriate. According to the Guttmacher Institute, 88 percent of all abortions take place during the first twelve weeks of pregnancy, with an additional 10.8 percent being performed before week twenty. Only 1.2 percent take place after the twentieth week.[42] The women who require abortions late in their pregnancies are in dire circumstances. (Ironically, one reason a woman may require a late-term abortion is that religious antiabortion activists have denied her information and resources earlier in her pregnancy.) But the Supreme Court did not make any exception for women who might require this procedure for health reasons.

In this decision, the Court shone a spotlight on the fetus as a being with value *greater* than that of the woman carrying it. Thus, the Court opened the way for *all* abortions to be challenged, at any stage and under any circumstance. In 2005, fifty-two state laws were passed restricting abortion. In 2006 more than a hundred new state measures were considered to limit abortion, either by making it more difficult to obtain or by pressuring pregnant women to reconsider.[43] The 2007 Supreme Court ruling, said Dobson on his Focus on the Family radio program, "reminds us that elections matter. Bush's appointment of Samuel Alito [as justice of the Supreme Court] provided the swing vote to protect this law. If John Kerry were president, partial-birth abortion would still be legal in the land . . . I applaud the president for nominating two pro-life justices to the Court and for having the courage and conviction to stand firm for human life."[44]

Women of financial means will always figure out a way to terminate their pregnancies. It is women with few financial resources who do not and increasingly will not have the ability to do so. Low-income women are more likely than women of means to have an unplanned pregnancy in the first place—their rate has increased by 29 percent since 1994, according to the Guttmacher Institute, compared with a 20 percent decrease in unplanned pregnancies among higher-income women. These women are the ones most affected by religion-driven bans on federal funding for abortion. On average, they must undergo the procedure three weeks later than higher-income women.[45]

Whether or not abortion is legal, a woman seeking an abortion will make sure to get an abortion. According to a global study, abortion rates are similar in countries where it is legal and those where it is not, which suggests that making abortion illegal does not deter women who are desperate for the procedure. However, it is crucial to keep abortion legal because only in countries that allow the procedure is it safe. In countries where abortion is outlawed, women are forced to have it performed on them clandestinely in dangerous, dirty conditions. Around the world, abortion accounts for 13 percent of women's deaths during pregnancy and childbirth.[46]

It is a lie that those who are "pro-choice"—who believe that women must have the legal right to an abortion—celebrate abortion. No one with a heart and a soul believes that abortion is a good thing. Every abortion causes sadness and loss. The ideal is to reduce the number of abortions to the smallest number possible (and preferably in the beginning of gestation). Pro-choice advocates maintain that this can be accomplished with better, cheaper, more widely available contraception, including emergency contraception, and with comprehensive sex education—not abstinence education. Because abstinence is hard to come by even among the virginity-pledged, and contraceptive failure and coerced sex are inevitable, abortion must be available as a last-resort backup.

When women choose abortion, they offer multiple reasons. Three-quarters cite concern for or responsibility to other individuals; three-quarters say they cannot afford a child; three-quarters say that having a baby would interfere with work, school, or the ability to care for dependents; and half say they do not want to be a single parent or are having problems with their husband or partner.[47]

Millions of religious Americans are pro-choice. Frances Kissling, who served as president of Catholics for a Free Choice (CFFC) for twenty-five years, works to expose the myth that all Catholics are opposed to abortion. Many disagree with the Vatican's position on abortion and other reproductive issues. In fact, 56 percent of American

Catholics believe that abortion should be legal.[48] In 1984 the CFFC ran a full-page advertisement in *The New York Times* stating that American Catholics held a diversity of opinions on the question of abortion. In response, the Vatican punished those who signed the ad, with some losing their jobs and two nuns being forced to leave their religious communities. In 2004 the organization conducted a poll and found that the vast majority of American Catholics rejected the Vatican's actions to get voters to oppose pro-choice presidential candidates.[49]

In 2007 the Catholic theologian Daniel C. Maguire published two pamphlets in which he argued that abortion, contraception, and same-sex marriage are morally permissible under Catholic doctrine. The U.S. Catholic bishops' Committee on Doctrine denounced the pamphlets. Maguire, who teaches at Marquette University in Milwaukee, a Jesuit institution, responded that the bishops are "simply uninformed. There is no one Catholic view on contraception, abortion or same-sex marriage. There's a diversity of views. And it's not just Dan Maguire versus the bishops. There's a large school of thought that agrees with everything I've said in these pamphlets."[50]

Most American Jews are pro-choice, holding that under certain circumstances—such as a woman's physical or mental health being in peril—abortion is not only permitted but required. According to the Talmud, the fetus is part of the pregnant woman's body—it is "like its mother's thigh"—and is not considered a living person; therefore if the woman's health is in danger, an abortion is permitted (Hulin 58a). What it means for a woman's life to be endangered is open to different interpretations, with some rabbinic authorities, especially among the ultra-Orthodox, upholding many restrictions, but the underlying ethic is one of concern for the woman.

American Muslims tend to hold a wide spectrum of views. One traditional Islamic belief is that until the fetus is 120 days old (17 weeks of pregnancy), it may be aborted. After 120 days, however, the fetus is believed to have a soul, and it may not be terminated unless the mother's life is in real danger. Nevertheless, according to the Council on American-Islamic Relations, 55 percent of American Muslims believe that even prior to 120 days of gestation, abortion should be against the law (except to save the life of the mother).[51]

Religious Jews and Muslims who interpret religious law in the strictest terms would like to have abortions restricted to all but the most dire cases. But in general, religious Jews and Muslims in the United States do not try to impose their own religious beliefs on other Americans. Antichoice Catholics and evangelical Protestants, on the other hand, want their religious viewpoint to be the law of the land.

There is no biblical (or Qur'anic) position on abortion. Christian opposition to abortion is based on inference from several biblical passages. Exodus 21:22–25 discusses a situation in which two men are engaged in a fight and one pushes into a pregnant woman, causing a miscarriage. The offender must pay a fine of whatever amount the woman's husband demands and the court allows. But if there is other serious injury, then "eye for eye, tooth for tooth, hand for hand, foot for foot, burn for burn, wound for wound, bruise for bruise" must be taken as retribution. This can be understood to mean that the woman's life has serious value, but the life of the fetus does not. But some people interpret the verse differently and argue that the case does not describe a miscarriage but a premature live birth. The "eye for eye" retribution would then be applied to either the baby or the woman, in which case they are of equal value.

Psalm 139:13–16 reads:

It was You who created my conscience,
You fashioned me in my mother's womb.
I praise You,
for I am awesomely, wondrously made;
Your work is wonderful;
I know it very well.
My frame was not concealed from You
when I was shaped in a hidden place,
knit together in the recesses of the earth.

This can be interpreted as a poetic celebration of God's creation of humankind, without scientific meaning. Or it can be understood to refer to the developing human life before birth.

Luke 1:41–42 reads: "When Elizabeth heard Mary's greeting, the child leaped in the womb. And Elizabeth was filled with the Holy

Spirit." This could mean that a fetus in the sixth month (stated in Luke 1:26) has some awareness, which would mean that late-term abortions are problematic. Or it could mean that the fetus at every stage of development requires protection.

These passages are ambiguous and are understood differently by different people, all equally thoughtful and committed to their sacred texts. There are, to be sure, millions of Americans who genuinely believe that fetuses have the same rights as humans after birth, and that abortion at any stage under any circumstances is murder. But this belief is entwined with other religious ideas about woman's role as childbearer. As we have seen, anxiety over the separation of sex from procreation, and the belief that nonprocreative sex should have repercussions, drives much of the antichoice rhetoric.

A thorough analysis of the biblical interpretations and the theological foundations behind both Christian antichoice and pro-choice positions is beyond the scope of this book. But I would like to offer the perspective of Beverly Wildung Harrison, who observes that "the equation of abortion with murder is dubious." After all, she reminds us, "we live in a world where men extend other men wide moral range in relation to justifiable homicide."[52]

Religious pro-choice people generally hold a nuanced approach to abortion. "I don't know whether to call myself pro-choice or pro-life," Katie Markey says to me. A feminist evangelical grad student in Pennsylvania, she worries that if she calls herself pro-choice, it would imply "that I'm pro-abortion, and I'm not pro-abortion. I don't want it to happen, but I also sympathize with women who are in a situation where an abortion is the best solution." Concern for women who need to abort is also cited by Christine, another evangelical. "I just don't understand how compassionate people can think that it's okay for women to be in back alleys or using coat hangers," she tells me. "The antiabortion people are so unforgiving. Christianity is supposed to be about forgiveness and compassion. [Antiabortion Christians] have compassion only for an unborn baby and not for women and girls going through a pregnancy under dire circumstances."

Frances Kissling best expresses the complex thought process of a thoroughly devout woman. She disagrees with religious antichoice people that women should have few reproductive rights, but she does agree with them that fetal life has value. In a much-discussed 2004 es-say, "Is There Life After Roe?," Kissling upbraided the pro-choice movement for failing to acknowledge, out of fear that they might weaken their cause, the sad elements of abortion.

> In theology, the question has traditionally focused on when is it most likely that God gives the developing fetus a soul, a dis-course pretty much abandoned by both traditional and innova-tive theologians; in sociology, most often the capacity for relationships is central—when can one say a meaningful rela-tionship exists between the fetus and society; in medicine, the weight is on viability and on the physical and mental capacity of the fetus—when could it survive outside the womb, when is there higher brain development. Fascinating speculation, but similar to arguments over the number of angels that could dance on a pinhead. The precise moment when the fetus be-comes a person is less important than a simple acknowledgment that whatever category of human life the fetus is, it nonetheless has value, it is not nothing . . .
>
> We would do well as prochoice people to present abortion as a complex issue that involves loss—and to be saddened by that loss at the same time as we affirm and support women's deci-sions to end pregnancies. Is there not a way to simply say, "Yes, it is sad, unfortunate, tragic (or whatever word you are comfort-able with) that this life could not come to fruition. It is sad that we live in a world where there is so little social and economic support for families that many women have no choice but to end pregnancies. It is sad that so many women do not have access to contraception. It is sad that this fetus was not healthy enough to survive and it was good that this woman had the right to make this choice for herself and her family, to avoid suffering, and to act on her values and her sense of what her life should be."[53]

Kissling is adamant that abortion is not something ever to be taken lightly. "If some twenty-two-year-old woman suddenly decided at twenty-four weeks of pregnancy that she'd made a mistake and just doesn't want to be pregnant and she were denied an abortion, I wouldn't spend five minutes working to get her an abortion," she told the journalist Angela Bonavoglia. "No. I wouldn't care if the law said she couldn't have an abortion. Nobody is fighting for the untrammeled right to have an abortion up to nine months of pregnancy, for any reasons whatsoever. This is just bullshit."[54]

This message is welcomed by religious Christian women who support the legal right to an abortion. Their voices often get lost in the shouting matches that, on the surface, appear to be between the religious and the secular. But there are many religious women who are pro-choice. One devout Catholic woman I spoke with told me, "I'm pro-life, but in the broadest sense. I oppose the death penalty. I support reproductive rights, but I have a problem with the phrase 'pro-choice.' It makes it seem that life is expendable. I want abortion to stay legal, but I also think that life is considered too expendable. There is too much disrespect of life."

Religious Christians, including those who oppose abortion, have abortions. Of those who identify their religion, 20 percent of women who have had abortions are evangelical, and 27 percent are Catholic.[55] In her powerful book *Abortion: My Choice, God's Grace*, the evangelical writer Anne Eggebroten collected the heartbreaking stories of devout Christian women who have had abortions. "Count up half of the women in any Catholic church on Sunday morning and one out of three in the Protestant churches, and you're counting the women who have had abortions," writes Bunnie Riedel in the foreword. (She is the founding director of the organization now known as the Religious Coalition for Reproductive Choice.)[56] The women in Eggebroten's book, from the most right-wing religious communities in the country, have prayerfully chosen legal abortion.

One of the women relates that she and her boyfriend were students at a Christian university, on a mission to help people in the inner city in 1974. They made love, and she became pregnant; he insisted she have an abortion, but she refused. Instead, she turned to a home for unwed mothers. "I spent hours praying and talking over my concerns with God. I spent a lot of effort asking God to help find the right family for the baby. I also told God how wonderful it was to have a precious life inside of me." Her Christian friends treated her coldly and told her it was her fault she had gotten pregnant.

After the nurse came and took my daughter from my arms, I stood for a long time with my arms out in the same position as when I had been holding her. I couldn't put them down. I was out of breath as if I had been punched in the stomach. When the nurse came back, I was still holding my arms out and staring at them. Straining to speak, I could only gasp out one word: "Empty."

She became pregnant again soon afterward and this time made a different decision.

I had an abortion, and God was with me as much on that table as earlier on the delivery table. If you love me, you won't call me a murderer. You'll try to understand the horror of being pregnant when you don't have the resources or emotional strength to have a child.

For me, carrying a baby nine months and then giving it up is too horrible to recommend to another person. I might as well suggest that she burn her eyes out with branding irons, drink ammonia and sleep on razor blades—because that pain could not hurt as much.

Choosing an abortion, for me, was choosing life. It was, in fact, the first time I had ever acted as if my life mattered.[57]

A pastor's wife shares her abortion story and the "lonely secrecy" of the experience. Her husband was the one who suggested the abortion: they already had one child, she was coping with the fallout from major surgery and taking heavy-duty medication, and he was completing seminary. "Although I never expected to be in a position to consider abortion," she writes, "I learned that abortion does not happen in isolation. It is a personal decision that is made in the context of the circumstances of a woman's life at the time. And through it all, there is God."[58]

Many devout people of faith understand their Scripture to support abortion when it is necessary. The doctrine of loving one's neighbor as oneself affirms the value of existing life, as does the doctrine of free will, with its emphasis on human responsibility. Eggebroten also points to the compassion and grace of Jesus, who protected the adulterous woman.

There simply is no biblical prohibition of abortion, a fact that even conservative antichoice Christians concede. The few Scripture passages pertaining to miscarriage or gestation can be interpreted in multiple ways by equally religious, serious people. One person's interpretation is not the only way of understanding a passage in its context. Thus that interpretation, especially when it concerns contested public policy, should not be imposed on everyone.

Gay Rights

"Every once in a while the pastor would preach on homosexuality, and the reason given that homosexuality is wrong is that it's not the way God designed the family to be," remembers Emily Wurgler, an undergraduate at the University of California, San Diego, who grew up attending an evangelical church. "Pretty much everyone believed it was wrong, so there was never any debate about it. When I would ask questions in Sunday school, the answer was always, 'This is the way it is in the Bible, and the Bible is true, therefore this is right.'" Wurgler was not satisfied with this theological argument, and she would press for some other explanation. "Then they would say things like, 'We need to protect the morality of the country' and 'The family is the best environment for children.'"

The religious fight against gay rights, like that against women's reproductive rights, unites conservative Catholics and evangelical Protestants. Both groups believe that homosexuality is a violation of "natural law" and God-given roles for men and women. (Evangelicals additionally hold that God's prohibition of homosexuality is a moral code and that there must be moral accountability for those who do not uphold the code.) Both groups worry that gays and lesbians threaten the nuclear family, the foundation of church life. From a societal standpoint, they are concerned about children raised outside the traditional mom-and-pop family unit. Who will stay home with the kids? Who will take care of them financially?

But in today's economy, nearly *all* families scramble to meet their children's basic needs. Could the real fear be that—as with reproductive rights—women might recognize that the world doesn't explode if they choose not to follow the conventional religious script? If gay and lesbian rights were legitimated, the "women must do this, men must do that" blueprint would be meaningless. Women would have more choices. So would men, for that matter, but they would lose the ability to control and contain women, leading to a diminution of male power.

Many people forfeit their own freedom in exchange for order, security, and the opportunity to practice their religion as they believe it should be done. That is their own choice, and I believe they should be allowed to make that choice for themselves. For instance, in observing Jewish law, I choose to restrict a number of personal freedoms. I am content with this lifestyle; it fits me and my family well. But it's unthinkable to me to force others to follow the same religious regulations. Yet a population of conservative Christians is intent on snatching away the personal freedoms of other Americans who do not share the conservative Christian perspective.

Roughly half of Americans today believe that gay men and lesbians should have the right to same-sex marriage, which provides the economic and legal benefits available to heterosexual married people.[59] In addition, many other Americans support civil unions for same-sex couples. Though civil unions do not provide the legal benefits of marriage, support for the unions indicates at least lukewarm tolerance of same-sex couples. This widespread acceptance of same-sex unions alarms conservative evangelical Protestants, who have become ever more vociferous in their attacks on gay people. In his 2004 book *Marriage Under Fire*, James Dobson charged that heterosexuality is under siege. He warned that legal recognition of gay unions would topple the institution of marriage, which would lead to the suffering of children and rampant pedophilia. "But now let me give you some very good news," he continued.

> Just as the attack on Pearl Harbor in 1941 by the empire of Japan served to energize and mobilize the armed forces of the United States, it would appear that the vicious assault on marriage and the church in recent months has begun to reinvigorate people of faith. I see indications that the church is marshaling its forces and preparing to meet the challenge. Evil has a way of overreaching, and that appears to have happened regarding the

blatant and lawless assault on marriage and biblical morality. In a strange way, the threats we are facing today could be the vehicle for a revitalized church. It is an exciting thing to watch.[60]

This is a revealing passage. Denunciation of gay rights, Dobson says, is as much about asserting the superiority of evangelical Christianity as it is about protecting children and families. Conservative evangelicals are quite deliberately using gay rights as a "vehicle"— Dobson's own word—for the expansion and growth of their churches and to accrue political power.

Conservative Christians as well as Orthodox Jews have largely adopted the position of "loving the sinner but hating the sin" in an effort to show compassion for gay men and lesbians and allowing them to be part of their religious community while refusing to condone gay sexual behavior. What this means in practice is a demand that gay men and lesbians remain celibate their entire lives. But sexuality is an integral part of the human experience, and to deny someone the right to be sexual seems cruel and even a denial of his or her full humanity.

Conservative Muslims likewise condemn homosexuality, which is widely understood as strictly forbidden. Same-sex intercourse is a crime punished by execution in several Muslim countries and punished with jail time, fines, or corporal punishment in several others. In the United States, many Muslims abhor homosexuality. Muzammil H. Siddiqi, a prominent scholar and theologian who is past president of the Islamic Society of North America and currently serves as president of the Fiqh (Jurisprudence) Council of North America, has said that "homosexuality is a moral disorder. It is a moral disease, a sin and corruption . . . No person is born homosexual, just like no one is born a thief, a liar or murderer." Siddiqi does not condone violence against gay men and lesbians, but he does support laws in countries where homosexuality is punished by death.[61] (I don't understand the logic either.) To help gay and lesbian Muslims (along with "bisexual, transsexual, intersex, and questioning Muslims") who are made to feel ashamed of their identities, an advocacy group called Al Fatiha provides support.[62]

What does the denial of rights to gay men and lesbians have to do with the denial of rights to women (whatever their affectional orientation)? Everything. The enforcement of heterosexuality shuts out both groups with the rationale that this is how God wants it to be: only heterosexual men may have religious power. Men are in charge of "masculine" responsibilities, and women take control of the "feminine" tasks. Families must look a certain way. Families that do not conform to the mom-dad-kids structure are illegitimate.

The enforcement of heterosexuality is connected with a mind-set in which women are lesser than men. Putting aside considerations of compassion and justice, heterosexual women seeking religious equality have a vested interest in contesting discrimination and denunciation of gay men and lesbians. Those of us who are heterosexual need to remember that their struggle is our struggle too.

In Judaism, Christianity, and Islam, women as well as gay men are required to sacrifice some of their sexual expression in the service of God. The privileging of heterosexual masculinity, validated by the argument that God wills it this way, is peculiar: after all, God is not a heterosexual male. It's the religious authorities who are heterosexual males.

NINE

Lost in Translation:
Women's Language in Worship

In Michelangelo's famous rendering of God's creation of humanity, God and the first human look astonishingly alike. God leans forward from the heavens, his finger outstretched to touch that of the human, who reclines with insouciance. They are both represented as muscular, sinewy, broad-shouldered white men—although God appears to be sixty-five years old and has a white beard and flowing white hair, while the human, Adam, has the face of a sixteen-year-old and short-cropped light brown hair. The five-hundred-year-old fresco on the ceiling of the Sistine Chapel symbolizes the predominant belief, still held today, that if God had a gender, God would be male, and that God created man, not woman, in his image.

This understanding of a male God, reflected in the language of Christian, Jewish, and Muslim liturgy, is severely limited. Those who believe in God as a transcendent yet imminent being do not think that God is a man, nor that God is a woman. (They also do not believe God is Caucasian.) God is thought to be beyond sexuality. Yet in choosing to represent God in worship in literal male terms exclusively and to shun the use of any feminine imagery, Christianity, Judaism, and Islam have cut off numerous alternative ways of imagining God that would enrich believers' faith and understanding of divinity. No one can understand God, this is true; so why further limit human understanding of the divine through incomplete language?

For me, the way God is described in English (or Greek or Latin) is primarily an academic issue. I pray to God and even think about God in Hebrew. And the Hebrew I use is not the modern Hebrew language spoken by Israelis, but the Hebrew of traditional Jewish prayer, which dates from late antiquity, with some medieval poetry and a sprinkling of Aramaic added to the mix. This language is formal, elegant, and, to my mind, holy. It is true that God is mostly represented as a father figure and king; undeniably the language is masculine. But all objects and pronouns in Hebrew are assigned a gender—there is no gender-neutral "it"—and Hebrew speakers do not think of most objects in gendered terms. (The word for butter is in the feminine form, for instance, and the word for milk is in the masculine form, but no one considers butter feminine and milk masculine.) And since the Hebrew of the traditional Jewish prayer book is not a vernacular tongue, the language has a sacred, timeless quality that (to me) smoothes over the masculinist edges. I tend not to focus on the literal meanings of the Hebrew words themselves; rather, the very act of reciting words in Hebrew has deep meaning for me in a way that speaking in English does not. I don't pay mind to the gendered God language, and it doesn't seep into my consciousness.

Prayers in the vernacular are a different story. When prayers are recited in English in synagogue, or when I have occasion to visit or observe Christian worship, the masculine God language is glaring. There it is, completely transparent, with no emperor's clothing, no sacred language to cover it up: God is likened to a man, a father, a lord, a king. Therefore I support enriching the language used to describe God—when transferring sacred texts to the vernacular and when composing new texts in any language—to clarify that God is not really masculine. The original sacred texts should be left intact and untouched, however.

Sister Elizabeth A. Johnson, a prominent Catholic theologian and author of *She Who Is: The Mystery of God in Feminist Theological Discourse*, reminds us that God "is mystery beyond all imagining." No concept or image can truly capture the divine reality. We "can never wrap our minds completely around this mystery."[1] All language about God is metaphorical, not literal. To pay proper respect to God, believers should use many names for God, since one (or two or three) is supremely insufficient. There are many names and metaphors for God in the Scriptures, including feminine ones, so it makes sense to use a multiplicity of names and metaphors today. "I believe that attempting to understand God with the human mind is like attempting to clothe yourself with a postage stamp," says the progressive Muslim activist Nakia Jackson. "There is so much left uncovered."

Though I believe that God language in the vernacular should be enriched, it's not just for the sake of being sensitive to the feelings of a feminist minority of believers. No. God language should be enriched for two different reasons. One: if we don't, we reduce the awesome and wondrous divinity to just a handful of overused, formulaic metaphors. Does this not reduce God to a cliché or to an idol, as graven as if in stone? Two: how people understand God has consequences for how they understand the world. A male God translates into an undermining of women and the creation of male-centered religious institutions. If God were supposed to be thought of as male, then our hands would be theologically tied. But since that is not the case, we must reimagine God while we rethink the status of women.

The feminist theologian Mary Daly said in 1973 that "if God is male, then the male is God."[2] Other Christian feminist theologians since then, including Letty Russell, Rosemary Radford Ruether, and Virginia Ramey Mollenkott, along with such Jewish feminist theologians as Judith Plaskow and the Jewish poet Marcia Falk, have also explored the implications of male-centered language on theology. They have shown that when we imagine God as literally and exclusively male and when we ban feminine images from the menu of metaphors, we are led to believe that men are closer to God than women are—even though the Bible states unequivocally that both man and woman were created in the image of God. Thus, men are given priority over women within religious life and beyond. If men are "closer" to God, they are superior to women and more deserving of power, status—and salvation. In this framework, women are always Other. They understand themselves as lesser and they are understood by other people, including other women, as lesser.

In Christianity these assumptions are reinforced by the fact that Jesus was male. His maleness is upheld as evidence that maleness is close to godliness. The Catholic Church has used this logic to ban women from the priesthood—on the grounds that only men can represent

Christ. But the maleness of Jesus was not essential to his role and identity. Jesus was male because, had he been female, he would not have been able to serve as an authority figure. He needed the social privileges associated with maleness in order to preach; it's not that being male is superior to being female.

Elizabeth Johnson has invoked Gloria Steinem's response, on turning forty, to a reporter who said, "But you don't look forty." Steinem replied, "This is what forty looks like." Similarly, says Johnson, women "must simply declare of themselves, 'This is what Christ looks like,' affirming in this way their deepest baptismal identity and resisting its denial until the heart of officialdom be converted."[3]

So what is the solution—to replace male imagery with female language? No, to do that would be equally restrictive and idolatrous. Exclusive feminine imagery would also not be faithful to the sacred texts. Nor should we just use the word "God" exclusively without gendered pronouns, since the term is so impersonal. Besides, male metaphors are not the problem; it is their exclusive, literal use that has been the problem. Johnson proposes using a multiplicity of names and metaphors, masculine and feminine—what is known as inclusive language. She notes that "insofar as God creates both male and female in the divine image and is the source of the perfections of both, either can equally well be used as metaphor to point to divine mystery. Both in fact are needed for less inadequate speech about God, in whose image the human race is created."[4]

Conservative Catholics and conservative evangelical Protestants tend to oppose the use of feminine metaphors for God, even when mixed with masculine ones. They argue that calling God "Mother" or "Sophia" is akin to paganism or goddess worship. But if God is not male, because God transcends gender, then what difference does it make if God is called she as well as he? Feminine God imagery would be indicative of paganism or goddess worship only if God were truly male, in which case avoiding male language would be honoring a different god. There are feminists who have abandoned Christianity in favor of paganism or goddess worship; this is true. However, the use of occasional feminine metaphors does not lead to paganism or goddess worship if it's done within a Christian context. It just expands believers' understanding of the one true God.

Another argument is that the attempt to desexualize or de-gender God has caused the opposite to occur—it has represented God as sexualized. This, too, makes sense only if one is trying to protect a male understanding of God. Mary Kassian, the evangelical author and a professor at Southern Baptist Seminary in Louisville, Kentucky, betrays her own understanding of God as sexualized. She has attacked those who question the exclusive use of Father, Master, and King to describe God, because in so doing, they have "castrated His character, for the words are not merely figurative, but reflect true aspects of God's character."[5] If Kassian does not believe that God is a sexualized male, why does she imagine God's character as something that can be castrated (metaphorically speaking, I presume)?

Kassian also denounces the premise that people may decide which words to use to describe God. "It is not our right to name ourselves, the world, and the Creator," she claims. "Rather it is God's right to name Himself, the world, and the people He has created . . . Feminism's attempt to rename God is a blasphemy that comes out of the very depths of hell."[6]

But in fact, equality-seeking believers are not renaming God or fabricating modern imagery. The Bible itself contains many feminine metaphors for God. God is repeatedly described as a mother figure within both the Hebrew Bible and the New Testament. In Exodus 34:6, God is *rahum* (compassionate), from the Hebrew word for womb, "*rehem.*" When you think about it, it makes sense for the Creator of the universe to be described as having a womb, as a mother who gives birth.

In Deuteronomy 32:18, Moses admonishes the people of Israel, "You neglected the Rock that birthed you, forgot the God who brought you forth."[7] In Isaiah 42:14, God says, "I will scream like a woman in labor, I will pant and I will gasp." Isaiah likens God to a mother who relieves the distress of her child: "As a mother comforts her son, so I will comfort you; you shall find comfort in Jerusalem" (66:13). In Hosea 13:8, God is a mother bear violently protective of her children: "Like a bear robbed of her young I attack them [the enemies of Israel] and rip open the casing of their hearts." God is also likened to a midwife or baby nurse who helps the mother give birth: "You drew me from the womb, made me secure at my mother's breast" (Psalm 22:10).

The most powerful figure in the Bible after God is represented in feminine language. This is "*hokhmah*," the Hebrew word for wisdom ("*sophia*" in Greek). Wisdom, known as Sophia among Eastern Orthodox churches, appears to the people of Israel as a prophet. But she is not a human being. She is depicted in the eighth chapter of Proverbs as God's first creation, who was beside God during the creation of the world. Throughout Proverbs, the figure of Wisdom/Sophia is described as a divine figure who is God's companion. She is transcendent and seemingly a cocreator of the universe.

Further references to Wisdom/Sophia appear in the book of Sirach (Ecclesiasticus), a second-century B.C.E. Hebrew work not included in the Hebrew Bible, but considered biblical by the Catholic and Eastern Orthodox traditions and apocryphal by the Protestant traditions. In chapter 24 she sings a song of self-praise, describing herself as God's intimate partner who dwells among the people of Israel. Wisdom/Sophia also appears in the Wisdom of Solomon, a Greek text thought to be written by a Jew living in Egypt in the first or second century B.C.E. In chapters 7 and 10 she is represented as part of the mystery of God and is described in decidedly godlike terms, with the power to arrange the universe and redeem the people of Israel. Wisdom/Sophia also appears in other prophetic apocryphal books of the Greek Bible, such as the book of Baruch and the book of Enoch.

Jewish and Christian theologians alike have understood Wisdom/Sophia as God in female imagery. Judaism was in formation during a time when people in the Near East worshipped many gods, including goddesses such as Isis, the giver of life, whose cult began in Egypt during the third millennium B.C.E. Many biblical scholars have concluded that the figure of Wisdom/Sophia was created to revitalize the Jewish tradition for those who would have preferred to worship such goddesses as Isis. Goddess worship was too popular to ignore, so Wisdom/Sophia was a strategic theological construction. Without resorting to goddess worship, Jews were given a way to think about their monotheistic God as having feminine (as well as masculine) attributes.[8]

In some strands of Jewish thought, it has been perfectly acceptable to describe God in both feminine and masculine terms. In the Talmud, God is occasionally called *Shekhinah*, a grammatically feminine

Hebrew name that refers to God's close presence among the people. In the mystical tradition of Kabbalah, Shekhinah, or the "divine feminine," is given great theological significance.

Early Christians were also drawn to feminine God imagery, and the authors of the Gospels described Jesus as embodying elements of Wisdom/Sophia. Many New Testament scholars believe that the characteristics attributed to Wisdom/Sophia were transferred onto Jesus.[9] Jesus is the "firstborn of all creation" (Colossians 1:15), "through whom are all things and through whom we exist" (1 Corinthians 8:6), and like Wisdom/Sophia, Jesus was present with God "before the world existed" (John 17:5). Jesus called out in a loud voice in public places, speaking both blessings and threats, in a manner very similar to that of Wisdom/Sophia (John 7:28, 37).[10] Jesus referred to himself in feminine terms, "as a hen gathers her brood under her wings" (Matthew 23:37; Luke 13:34), and also referred to God in feminine terms. In the parable of the yeast (Matthew 13:33), Jesus likened God to a baker woman who mixes and leavens the yeast to create the kingdom of heaven.

But femininity became devalued, and concern arose that Jesus should not be described in feminine terms. Therefore, the Gospel according to John, written at the end of the first century, substitutes "*logos*" (word) for "*sophia*" (wisdom): "In the beginning was the Word, and the Word was with God, and the Word was God. He was in the beginning with God. All things came into being through him" (John 1:1–3).

When the association between Jesus and Wisdom/Sophia was broken, theological beliefs not only about the Creator but also about Jesus became limited. Before, it had been entirely legitimate and biblical to consider God, together with Jesus, as both feminine and masculine. Now God and the son Jesus were more associated with the masculine; it would take careful reading and research to recover their links to feminine images and experience.

Within centuries, all feminine imagery was transferred onto the Virgin Mary, mother of Jesus, who became venerated as the supreme but human mother. Thus, feminine metaphors for God became contained and diluted, and God's full dimensionality was sliced off. Moreover, early Christianity allowed space for the veneration of real women, but now that space was closed off. These observations are not meant to diminish the power of the symbolism of Mary, but merely to point out that as much as Catholics may revere Mary and consider her connected to God, no one believes that she *is* God.

In the late Middle Ages, European Christian mystics, male and female, developed female God language and symbols in an effort to conceptualize God as possessing both male and female characteristics. Jesus Christ was likened to a mother who nourishes and saves her young, and the Eucharist was said to feed the soul as a mother nurses her baby. Breast-feeding images abounded. According to the medieval historian Caroline Bynum, this imagery was especially popular among male mystics, who wanted to understand God as more loving and less authoritarian.[11] The historian Gerda Lerner notes that the twelfth-century nun Hildegard of Bingen, whose mystical visions were acknowledged as authentic by Pope Eugenius III, repeatedly invoked Sophia and described the church as a maternal, life-giving body. The fourteenth-century mystic Julian of Norwich described God as androgynous. She wrote, "And thus in our Creation God almighty is our kindly Father, and God Who is all wisdom is our kindly Mother, with the love and the goodness of the Holy Ghost—all of Whom are one God and one Lord."[12]

Today, opponents of inclusive God language insist that God must be represented only as male. "We have no right to assume, as evangelical feminists do, that because God 'gives birth' to creation (Deuteronomy 32:18; Job 38:29), 'comforts us as a mother comforts her child' (Isaiah 66:13), and is as protective as a 'bear robbed of her cubs' (Hosea 13:8) that we have the right to call him 'Mother,'" says Kassian. "The only right we have, as created beings, is to address God in the manner He has revealed as appropriate. It is not we who name God; it is God who names Himself."[13]

But it seems evident, according to the sacred texts, that God *likes* to be imagined as feminine, at least in some aspects. Could the real fear be not about God, but about humans? For if God is not male, then the male is not God. If God is truly beyond gender, then maleness should not be privileged in churches and society, and if that were the case, we would understand Scripture from a different point of view. No longer would there be a divinely sanctioned hierarchy of males over females. No longer would gay men be a threat to the power structure of males over females. No longer would the Catholic priesthood be reserved for men alone. No longer would wives have to submit to their husbands. No longer would women's sexuality be regarded as dangerous and licentious. No longer would women's procreative role overshadow their entire lives. There is a lot invested, you see, in imagining God as exclusively male.

What does inclusive God language ("vertical language," in the jargon of scholars) look like? To start with, it goes hand in hand with inclusive language about people (horizontal language). To destroy the "God is male, male is God" mind-set, we can refer to humanity as including female as well as male. We can speak not of "brothers" but "brothers and sisters" or "humanity." We can change "mankind" to "humankind." And so on. If we are quoting Scripture, however, and the original text refers only to males, opinion is divided on whether or not the language should be changed. In some mainline Protestant and liberal Jewish congregations, all such references are made gender-neutral, so that even if the word used in Scripture refers to males alone, the congregation will hear a reference that includes both males and females. Other congregations remain faithful to the original Hebrew or Greek of Scripture when citing it directly, making changes only when it's clear that the new language is clarification, not translation.

In some cases the original language of the New Testament was gender-neutral but had been translated as masculine (the Greek term "*adelphoi*," meaning "siblings," became "brothers" in English). The New Revised Standard Version (NRSV) of the Bible, released in 1989, uses gender-inclusive language when possible (changing "brothers" back to "siblings.") It is used in Episcopal, Presbyterian, United Methodist, United Church of Christ, and other mainline churches.

The traditional language of the Trinity—Father, Son, and Holy Spirit (or Holy Ghost)—has also come under fire for its blinding masculinity. A popular hymn, known in many Protestant traditions as the Doxology, reads,

Praise God from whom all blessings flow;
Praise Him, all creatures here below;

Praise Him above, ye heavenly host:
Praise Father, Son, and Holy Ghost.

Observes the New Testament scholar Reta Finger, "We're hit in the stomach by the 'Hims.' The last line, a grand finale meant to call forth praise from human, bird, or blade of grass, ends up sounding like an all-male team that women can only cheer on from the sidelines."[14] The problem is not just that the masculine language of the Trinity sounds like a nail on a chalkboard to modern ears, but that this masculine language has implications for women in the church.

Although most mainline churches continue to refer to God as He or Him, increasingly they are substituting language such as Creator, Redeemer, and Sustainer, or Speaker, Word, and Breath to replace Father, Son, and Holy Spirit. In 2006 the Presbyterian Church (USA) endorsed other phrases to describe a "triune" God. Admittedly, some of these phrases are wacky. "Compassionate Mother, Beloved Child, Life-Giving Womb," "Overflowing Font, Living Water, Flowing River," "Rainbow of Promise, Ark of Salvation, Dove of Peace" are more than a little bit forced and will certainly not sway traditionalist holdouts. "You might as well put in Huey, Dewey, and Louie," commented Rev. Mark Brewer of Los Angeles.[15]

But the attempt to try alternative ways of referring to God should not be dismissed. For instance, it is not terribly difficult to avoid the English words "Father," "Lord," and "King," which have meanings specific to men in positions of power. "As a Christian woman, I feel it's a sign of respect when a church is aware of these issues and doesn't just do it the same way it's been done for centuries, with the assumption that the way we've always done it is the right way," Rev. Emily Goldthwaite Fries, a United Church of Christ pastor in Urbandale, Iowa, tells me. "I think just my presence, my being a woman at the pulpit, is another sign that we're not doing things exactly the same way they've always been done." Pastor Emily does not refer to God as She, because, "to me, that's as specific as He, and it doesn't sound right to me, but the senior pastor does. We say God instead of He most of the time. When we read Scripture, I want to stay as close to the authentic text as much as we can, but we do experiment with taking out the masculine language as we read it, although that becomes very difficult."

Mary Louise ("Mel") Bringle is a skillful writer of hymns, used in Protestant congregations, that convey a full spectrum of divine images. She achieves a balance between preservation of the traditional masculine language and incorporation of creative imagery—which is itself traditional because it is rooted in the Bible. Bringle is the president of the Hymn Society of the United States and Canada, an organization that promotes congregational song. A tall and charismatic woman, with a beautiful shock of short gray-white hair, she is the author of two hymn collections, *Joy and Wonder, Love and Longing* and *In Wind and Wonder*,[16] and is a professor of philosophy and religion at Brevard College in North Carolina. I asked her how she chooses God language.

"The church does not need more masculine language, so I try to find ways around it. What's tricky is the word 'Lord,' which is a darned good rhyming word! Adored, soared—there are lots of choices. But what do you rhyme with God—trod? Plod? [laughter] I do use Lord, particularly when I'm translating Spanish-language hymns into English for bilingual people, because it's a key part of Spanish-language hymns.

"But there are a lot of gender-neutral terms and images for God: Rock, Fountain, Mountain, Power, Breath, Spirit. All of those get away from the masculine language altogether. I never use masculine language—I think my computer would crash! The thing is, you can use gender-neutral language without people even noticing. If you do it well, you can have people focus just on the content without noticing gender at all."

Among Bringle's hymns is "As Tender as a Mother Hen":

As tender as a mother hen
who spreads her wings to shield her brood,
Christ Jesus stretches out His arms
and sheds His life as holy food.
    We seek His pattern in our hearts,
    amazed by such unselfish grace,
    and tend the children of the world
    in whom we see God's face.

Courageous as a mother bear
who guards her young from danger's path,

Christ Jesus wields His zealous love
and shows the gift of rightful wrath.
    We heed His call, opposing powers
    that thwart the cause of life and health,
    and strive to reach the prophets' dreams
    to build God's Commonwealth.

A phoenix rising from the flames,
a mother eagle, soaring high,
Christ Jesus lifts the weary world
and conquers death for all who die.
    In Him, we find our strength renewed
    and, mounting up on fledgling wings,
    we rise to share the gospel hope
    that resurrection brings![17]

Bringle uses biblical metaphors (Matthew 23:37 and Luke 13:34, Hosea 13:8, Exodus 19:4) to imagine God as a mother hen, a mother bear, and a mother eagle, but she alternates these images with references to Christ Jesus that use masculine pronouns. She skillfully draws in maternal references without being pushy about it. In doing so, she has created a hymn that allows worshippers to pray to God as a being who is both imminent and transcendent and can be imagined in multiple ways.

This kind of creativity is verboten by the Vatican. Inclusive language is not permitted in Catholic liturgy, even in horizontal language, an area where even many traditionalists have come to support inclusiveness. In 1991 U.S. bishops, in order to replace an outdated translation, overwhelmingly approved use of a revision of the New American Bible that contains some inclusive horizontal language. But in 1992 Cardinal Joseph Ratzinger, prefect of the Vatican's Congregation for the Doctrine of the Faith (CDF), now Pope Benedict XVI, forbade the new translation on the grounds that it would erode doctrinally important language and lend legitimacy to heretical feminists.

    Thus in Catholic worship, Genesis 1:26 is translated as "Let us make man in our image" instead of the NRSV's "Let us make humankind in our image," even though the original Hebrew word "*ha'adam*" is correctly translated as "the human," not "the man." Likewise, 1 Corinthians 1:10 is read as "I appeal to you, brethren" (in this case following the Greek) instead of "I appeal to you, brothers and sisters." The lectionary (book containing biblical readings for use in the Mass) also preserves male-centered language, despite the protests of most U.S. bishops. "Men" may not be replaced with "people," even when the original Hebrew or Greek clearly refers to men and women. Likewise, a 1993 translation of the Psalms (collectively known as the Psalter) that had been created by the International Commission on English in the Liturgy, a body organized after the Second Vatican Council (1962–65), was also rejected by Ratzinger.

In 2001, with the approval of Pope John Paul II, Ratzinger, as head of the CDF, issued a comprehensive prohibition of modern translation of the Hebrew and Greek Bibles. The document was titled "Liturgiam Authenticam" ("The Authentic Liturgy"). The CDF claimed that the most authoritative version of both the Hebrew and Greek Bibles, the one from which all translations must spring, is the 1979 edition of the Latin translation made by Saint Jerome in the early fifth century, known as the Vulgate. Yet biblical scholars say that the new version of the translation, known as the Neo-Vulgate, should absolutely not be the norm, because it is not the original Hebrew and Greek biblical text and contains many errors.

According to "Liturgiam Authenticam," a faithful translation of a Latin word in the Vulgate that includes both genders must be masculine only. For example, the Latin word "*homo*" is widely understood to mean "human being" but must be translated as "man." The most accurate, faithful translation of "homo" is thus forbidden. The CDF has argued that the word "man" in English includes women, but today most Americans, especially those under the age of fifty, do not understand man to include women. To them, man refers only to males. The Vatican's edict is that *even when inaccurate*, male-exclusive language in translation is necessary.

This rejection of inclusive language amounts to a rejection of the legacy of the Second Vatican Council, with its call for spiritual and liturgical renewal. Vatican II had called on the Catholic Church to engage in the modern world, to open itself up to greater involvement of laypeople, and to use vernacular language instead of Latin in the Mass. Pope Benedict XVI reinforced this rejection in 2007 when he signed a document allowing more churches to use the old Latin Mass, known as the Tridentine Mass, that had largely faded from use since Vatican II. "The long and short of it is that we have had a regression in Catholicism," the theologian Mary Hunt tells me. "It is now decreed that the language used in the Eucharist, in the Mass, is from before the Second Vatican Council. It's backpedaling. The Catholic Church is very far from ever allowing inclusive God language."

Nevertheless, there are Catholics who assert their desire to pray using the language that provides the best bridges between them and their God. Sister Joan Chittister, a member of the Benedictine Sisters of Erie and a leading voice heard internationally for church reform, has written prayers that are decidedly not Vatican approved. Among them is a litany (a traditional way of calling upon the saints for help) titled "Litany of Women for the Church":

> Dear God, creator of women in your own image,
> Born of a woman in the midst of a world half women,
> carried by women to mission fields around the globe,
> made known by women to all the children of the earth,
> give to the women of our time
>> the strength to persevere,
>> the courage to speak out,
>> the faith to believe in you beyond
>> all systems and institutions
> so that your face on earth may be seen in all its beauty,
> so that men and women become whole,
> so that the church may be converted to your will
>> in everything and in all ways.
>
> We call on the holy women
> who went before us,
> channels of Your Word
> in testaments old and new,
> to intercede for us

so that we might be given the grace
to become what they have been
for the honor and glory of God.

The litany continues with an appeal to sixteen female saints and concludes with a call to Mary, mother of Jesus,

who turned the Spirit of God
into the body and blood of Christ, pray for us. Amen.[18]

This litany, a favorite among progressive-minded Catholic women,
puts women front and center in the history of Catholicism. It affirms
a God who created holy women who have been devoted believers—
yet were also leaders and visionaries. Some of these women were unafraid to approach God without the authority of the patriarchal
church; others spoke out for justice. While it conforms to a traditional
liturgical style, the litany gives Catholic women a new way to express
their love of God. It offers a petition for a renewed church in which
women's contributions are recognized and honored, a church in
which women have power and influence.

The Arabic words that name and describe God are understood to
include feminine as well as masculine aspects of divinity. Each recitation of the Qur'an begins, "In the name of Allah, the Compassionate
[*al-Rahman*] and the Merciful [*al-Rahim*]." Note that just as the
Hebrew word "rahum" (compassionate) is from the grammatical root
that becomes the word for womb, so too are the divine names al-
Rahman and al-Rahim linked with womb imagery. It is said that
there are ninety-nine names of Allah within the Qur'an. (Actually, there
are more than ninety-nine, but the poetry of the number is the point.)
In addition to al-Rahman and al-Rahim, other names are *al-Malik*
(the King), *al-Quddus* (the Most Holy), and *as-Salaam* (the Peace
and Blessing). The hundredth name, believed to be most expressive
of divinity, is hidden and therefore never uttered. This name is believed to represent God's transcendence and ultimate mysteriousness.

The Arabic language has fourteen "declensions," or grammatical cases, Laleh Bakhtiar tells me, while English has only six. Bakhtiar is an Iranian-American Muslim author and translator of the Qur'an. "There is a lot of variation" with verb forms, which "makes the language extremely rich." When translating the Qur'an, it is enormously challenging to capture the fullness of the original Arabic; this is why Muslims value recitation of the Qur'an in the original. Even the most beautiful, elegant, and faithful translation cannot mirror the feeling of transcendent divinity of the original.

I asked Bakhtiar why the standard in translations is that God is always He. She responded, "I'm a believer in my faith, and I believe that the Qur'an is the word of God, that the Qur'an is the way that God revealed Himself. I believe one must be faithful to the original. The word for the essence of God is '*dhat*,' which is a feminine word. So God in His essence is feminine, but becomes masculine in the descriptions of the creation of the heavens and the earth [and in other contexts]. I don't feel that the Qur'an negates me or doesn't include me when it says 'He.'

"I feel that we have so many deep issues as women of faith caused by misinterpretation of the Qur'an, like the misinterpretation of 4:34 about wife beating. Women's lives are at stake because of misuse of the sacred text. So I don't worry about the pronouns. Whether God is called He or She is not as important."

The activist Nakia Jackson agrees that in the original Arabic it's clear that God transcends gender. However, when referring to God in English, she prefers to reveal both the feminine and masculine elements of the divinity. Jackson has considered skipping pronouns entirely when she refers to God, "but that would sound very stilted. So I've decided to switch pronouns. But when I do that, some people react in shock: 'How can you refer to God as *She*?' But God is not male. God is beyond gender. And they say, 'Well, of course God is beyond gender, but we must refer to God as *He*.'"

On January 10, 2006, in Cambridge, Massachusetts, Jackson led a mixed-gender congregation in prayer for the Eid-ul-Adha, the festival at the end of hajj. This was her khutba:

Asalaamu alaikum wa rahmatullah wa barakatuhu. Bismillah Ar-Rahman Ar-Rahim . . . Peace, mercy and the blessings of

Allah be upon you. In the name of Allah, the most gracious, the most merciful. Peace and blessings be on Muhammad, his family and companions. I bear witness that there is no god but Allah; He has no partner, and I bear witness that Muhammad is Her servant and messenger . . .

One of the deeply resonant rituals of hajj is the *sa'i*. We run between the hills of Safa and Marwa to commemorate Hagar's search for water for her infant son, Isma'il, whose story comes to us through the *hadith* of the Prophet Muhammad, peace and blessings be upon him. Ibrahim had left Hagar and Isma'il alone in the Arabian desert, and as their food supply diminished, Hagar's desperation to provide for her son grew. She ran from Safa to Marwa and back again, seven times, searching for any sign of water in the desolate valley. At last, upon discovering water bubbling from the earth near her son, Hagar dug into the spring later called Zamzam. Millennia later, this spring still gives life-sustaining water to millions of pilgrims and residents of Mecca . . .

Mothers the world over perform the *sa'i* of Hagar daily, racing between low-paying jobs, meager welfare payments, inadequate health and child care, and other formidable challenges in a no less desperate search to help their children survive. These women race not through the desert, miles from human habitation, but in our cities and towns today. Yet where is their Zamzam? . . . God has established a Zamzam for the Hagars that struggle before us daily to provide for their children, but it is one that has become clogged with apathy, fear, and despair.

We often become overwhelmed when we are confronted with the vast desert of need, sure that our meager contributions couldn't possibly make a difference . . . I call upon you not to give all that you have, but to give what you can, so that you may have more than you could ever imagine . . . We must remove those obstacles in our lives that keep our compassion and love from bubbling to the surface. Once we have done so, that drop of the divine that we have all been imbued with can flow through us, offering divine love and bounty to those modern day Hagars . . .

Glory to God, praise to God, God is Greater. There is no God but Allah, He is one and has no partner, Hers is dominion and Theirs is praise, and He is capable of all things . . . Oh Allah, bring light into my heart. Oh Allah, grant me light, and make light in my mind, and light in my body and light in my blood. Oh Allah, make for me a light in my grave, and a light in my bones. Increase me in light, increase me in light, increase me in light. Grant me light upon light.[19]

This khutba connects contemporary Muslims with Hagar, enabling women to take ownership of their rightful place in Islamic tradition. It calls upon them to take responsibility for the Hagars of the world today. Jackson's words are especially powerful because of the way she refers to God. In this khutba God is male, female, and plural—a hidden treasure that desires to be known.

In liberal Jewish denominations, inclusive horizontal language is used in many synagogues. Inclusive vertical language is also common in many Reform and Reconstructionist (but not Conservative) synagogues. Orthodox women generally believe that the words of the siddur (prayer book) are sacred and should not be changed. If they are uncomfortable with exclusive male language, horizontal or vertical, they have the option of turning to private vernacular prayers, not found in a conventional prayer book, that supplement traditional communal prayers. Sephardi women (whose ancestors are from Spain) historically wrote songs in Ladino, a Judeo-Spanish dialect, while Ashkenazi women (whose ancestors are from eastern Europe) have a legacy of private Yiddish prayers called *tehines* (supplications).

After Sephardi Jews were expelled from Spain in 1492 and from Portugal in 1496, Ladino became their native tongue as they migrated to North Africa and the Mediterranean. Hebrew remained the language of synagogue and ritual, but Ladino was the vernacular. A number of Sephardi women wrote and sang Ladino songs about life-cycle events, such as a son's circumcision ceremony, and about liturgical themes, such as Rosh Hashanah and Havdalah, the ceremony marking the end of Shabbat. These songs were sung aloud, often by a woman, at public events. They tended to be intimate in tone and they mentioned the matriarchs along with the patriarchs.

In medieval and early modern Europe, most Ashkenazi Jewish women could not read the Hebrew of the prayer book and were unfamiliar with the liturgy. But they did attend synagogue, so they routinely appointed an educated woman, such as the rabbi's wife or daughter, to lead them in prayer in the separate women's section. Eventually some women's prayer leaders began to write and publish their own Yiddish-language prayers, as has been documented by the historian Chava Weissler. The first tehine to appear in print was published in Kraków in 1577. By the eighteenth century, printed editions of Yiddish tehines were widespread, often as pocket-size books. Men also wrote tehines intended for women.[20]

Some tehines were meant to be recited in synagogue, but most were for private recitation during observance of what's known as the three special women's commandments—baking hallah and separating a small portion of dough when preparing the bread; separating from one's husband during the days of ritual impurity and immersing in a ritual bath; and lighting candles for Shabbat and holidays. Some were connected with women's life-cycle events—pregnancy, giving birth, nursing—and with other issues of concern to women such as a child's recovery from illness or a husband leaving home for a business trip.

Unlike the prayers recited in synagogue, tehines were written in the vernacular, Yiddish, rather than Hebrew. They were voluntary, flexible, and usually written in the first person singular, lending an intimate and emotional tone. They often called up the legacies of the matriarchs, whose names are absent from almost all the prayers recited in synagogue. Women continued to write tehines throughout the eighteenth, nineteenth, and twentieth centuries; in ultra-Orthodox bookstores (such as in Borough Park, Brooklyn) you can purchase tehine collections, sometimes with English translations.

Renée Septimus, the social worker and lecturer who spoke eloquently about her struggle as an observant Jewish woman in Chapter 2, writes her own modern tehines in English. This is an outlet for her desire to communicate directly with God. In 1999 she stood before the guests at her son's bar mitzvah ceremony and read "The Voice of a Mother":

Ribono shel olam [master of the world], I stand humbly before you, a mother like Sarah, Rivkah, Rachel, Leah and Hannah, watching her son take steps towards adulthood and towards assuming his role and responsibility for the Jewish people. Always I've felt intimately our partnership in the creation and maintenance of the children you have blessed me with. But as they leave my womb and the womb of our household, I feel and need your presence ever more as I confront the limitations of my own ability to protect them.

From the moment I knew he lived inside me, this son has inspired joy in my life and the lives of those around him. *Ribono shel olam*, help him maintain his love of life and laughter, his integrity and honesty, his sensitivity and compassion. Guide him to think for himself with an open mind, seeking truth and goodness. And keep him always safe from harm, ready to do your sacred work, his desire and motivation always towards Torah and *mitzvot* [Jewish commandments] . . . Help my son grow to be a good man with fine qualities, aware always of your presence, wise and dedicated to good works, charity, and acts of loving kindness.

Dear God, I believe and trust in you and I come before you, my soul in my hands and I beg you, my Creator, the force which sustains all life, to accept my prayer with mercy, this prayer which comes from the depths of my heart.

Amen.[21]

In this prayer, Septimus is proud of her role as a mother who nurtures her children and guides them to independence and a life of good deeds and actions. She uses womb imagery to express the way God nurtures human beings. In this way she suggests that as a mother, she is carrying out God's desires and is reflecting the image of God. You don't have to be a mother or a woman yourself to be moved by this direct, unmediated appeal to God, using language that is profound to her.

I have reprinted these alternative prayers—in the Protestant, Catholic, Islamic, and Orthodox Jewish traditions—to demonstrate that prayer has the potential to empower believers in their faith. God does not have to be She or Sophia, although for some, that specific terminology is important and meaningful. There are other options, as we have seen, to bring in references to women's lives—references that are conspicuously absent from traditional liturgies. Women and men should be encouraged to use prayers of this variety if doing so allows them to draw closer to their tradition.

Fear of innovation is a hallmark of traditional religious communities. This makes perfect sense: our traditions—Christian, Jewish, and Islamic—have endured precisely because they have remained relatively unchanged at their core for so many centuries. Their stability gives them power and meaning, and through them we acquire power and meaning.

But feminine God imagery is as old as the Bible and Qur'an themselves. "People like to cling to ancient tradition, but the further you go back, the more diversity there may have been," observes Rev. Goldthwaite Fries. "There are so many different words to describe God in the Bible, and we use a very tiny few of them with any frequency." When we describe God in both feminine and masculine metaphors, we are in fact returning to tradition, not departing from it.

Conclusion

For the sake of remaining rooted to traditional Judaism, I'm willing to make some compromises. For example, although it goes against the grain of much I hold dear, I tolerate sitting in a separate women's section in my Orthodox synagogue, provided that the physical barrier is not high or otherwise obscures my view. I send my sons to Orthodox day school, where only boys wear Jewish ritual garments, even though religious authorities admit that girls are permitted to wear them too. In my household, I alone set aside my professional obligations every Friday to undertake "women's work"—the myriad domestic tasks that enable my family to enjoy a restful Shabbat, complete with delicacies we don't eat during the rest of the week.

But I'm not willing to compromise on everything, and there is one area where I feel passionately that women must be given the same opportunities as men: religious leadership. When women are excluded from religious leadership positions solely because they are female, it's a very short step to making the argument that women may be excluded from secular leadership positions and that women are not as capable as men. This I cannot tolerate. Besides, when a woman is removed from leadership roles, it is all too easy for her to consequently become distanced from the tradition. This doesn't mean that she doesn't love her religion, but she isn't given the chance to form as close a bond as her male peers and family do.

Several years ago I began leading the weekday morning service on occasion at a Conservative synagogue where my children attended nursery school. In the beginning I took on this role because the synagogue had trouble finding capable laypeople who were up to the task, and even though I had never led a service, I knew I could do it. My only obstacles were stage fright, which to this day I still suffer from, and an intense self-consciousness about my singing voice, which I also continue to experience. But knowing that the community needed someone gave me the impetus to stand at the podium with my annotated prayer book and wobbly voice. And when that first service was over, after I had closed and kissed my prayer book, I realized that I was just as capable as my husband, who had led services many, many times. I could serve the community just as he and so many other men routinely do without giving it any more thought than they do to breathing.

As a parent, it's my job to show my children that women can be religious role models. I began bringing my sons with me whenever I led this service, planting them in the back with books and small magnet toys, so that it would appear natural to them that Ima, like Abba, has Judaic skills. But it began to gnaw at me that they were not being exposed to women chanting from the Torah or other sacred writings. I resolved that I would learn how to layn (chant) the special musical cantillation (or *trope* in Yiddish) for the scroll of Esther. I chose this text as my first because the story—about how Queen Esther, at great personal risk, saved the Jewish people—features a positive female role model and therefore seemed appropriate for my "coming out" as a woman who layns. Again at the Conservative synagogue—because women are forbidden from doing this at Orthodox synagogues—I chanted the third chapter of this scroll. When my children ran up to me when I was done to show their pride by hugging my legs, I knew I was doing something right.

I also began attending a traditional monthly Shabbat service, called Yavneh, that had just been established in my neighborhood on Manhattan's Upper East Side. Strictly speaking, Yavneh probably occupies no denominational niche. I consider it Orthodox yet cutting-edge. Women and men sit separately with a curtain between them; the prayer book is Orthodox; and the prayers themselves are recited according to Orthodox regulations. But at Yavneh, women may lead some parts of the service and also may layn. I have layned Torah at this service too. My husband has made sure that the boys are in the sanctuary, not the playroom, when Ima is chanting.

Learning how to layn, still very much an ongoing process for me, is an incredible experience. Having been denied the education of how to layn from an early age (only boys took classes in trope at my elementary school), I had never thought much about what it really entails. I had always figured it was a skill that either you were taught and you mastered, or you weren't and you didn't. But I discovered that layning is much more than a skill. It is a sensory way of experiencing the Torah. In order to layn, one must crack a code of squiggly lines and markings, as well as vowels and punctuation, none of which actually appears in the Torah scroll itself. Therefore, when preparing to layn, one learns by heart not only the words of the Torah but also its rhythms, as well as something intangible—its soul. When I am learning and practicing my layning, I feel as though the Torah is inside my head, heart, and body. It is an organic part of me.

Why would anyone want to deny this experience to girls and women?

I have come to believe that the primary reason male religious authorities exclude women (and gay men) from full participation is that this act defines their faith in opposition to the contemporary world and to competing denominations. The exclusion of women (and gay men) is an identity marker that demonstrates authenticity. Catholicism stands in opposition to Christian reformation. Evangelical Protestantism resists the liberalism of mainline Protestantism. Orthodox Judaism staves off the individualism of the Conservative and Reform movements. Traditional Islam distances itself from contemporary culture and from other religious worldviews. Curbing women is a symbol, a shorthand of resistance to change. When you hear that a specific religious community does not allow women's ordination or men and women to sit together in worship, you know that it sees itself as the last distinctive holdout against a chaotic culture lacking in boundaries.

I understand and respect the need for a community to take a stand in favor of a particular worldview and to reject alternative worldviews. As I've made clear, I support firm boundaries in many contexts, religious and otherwise. But it seems wrongheaded to put women in the cross fire. Women do not need to be sacrificed for the sake of tradition. It doesn't even make sense to deny full religious experience to women, since they are usually the ones with power within the home and can determine the extent to which their family will adhere to religious tradition in the first place.

The movement for girls and women learning Torah at an advanced level was not motivated by rebellion against the contemporary world or established Orthodoxy. Those who want to rebel tend to leave Orthodoxy for another denomination or ditch the tradition altogether. Rather, says the theologian Tamar Ross, the movement stems from "a genuinely conceived need both to intensify women's attachment to the Jewish tradition and upgrade women's Jewish literacy to the level of their general knowledge. Nonetheless, irrespective of the original catalyst or purposes, there is no denying that the phenomenon of women's learning has become a time bomb, in providing women potential access to positions of leadership and authority that were traditionally held only by men."[1] Now that women have access to the inner sanctum of tradition, it's not possible, or desirable, to tell them they can go only so far but no further.

This phenomenon is hardly limited to modern Orthodox Jewish women. We have seen that religious women from different communities similarly embrace Bible and Qur'an study, which empowers them to become more actively involved in their faith. They are taking back their faith intellectually. The more they learn, the more they discover that they love their tradition and want to honor it as faithfully as they can—which means being full, active participants, if not leaders. The historian Gerda Lerner has pointed out that women have been involved in creating alternative biblical criticism since the third century, and that the first woman's reinterpretation of the story of creation was done by the twelfth-century mystic Hildegard of Bingen.[2] Women today are not engaging in something new and radical by any means. They are in fact continuing a long-standing tradition.

There is always more than one way to interpret sacred texts (as with any text). It is impossible "to strip away all interpretations to get at the transparent truth of the Bible," says the Southern Oregon University communication professor Alena Amato Ruggerio, a member of the Evangelical and Ecumenical Women's Caucus. "Every reading of the Bible inherently implies interpretation. Reading and interpreting are the *same thing*. So if every reading of the Bible is always already an interpretation, it then becomes a question of whose interpretation, and *what set of assumptions* they used to arrive at that interpretation."[3]

This does not mean that "anything goes"—that any interpretation is as valid as any other. It does however remind us that different pre-suppositions yield different understandings of God's intentions. No one knows exactly what God intends. It is up to us to figure things out. We will always have multiple answers to our questions. And this is a good thing: wrestling with interpretation can yield only a richer understanding of our religion. Cutting off this process of study by claiming "This, not that, is what God wants" yields a poorer understanding of our religion. As the progressive Muslim activist Nakia Jackson tells me, "The Qur'an is full of meaning. But if you rely on an old translation, it's like using an old computer. As language progressively changes and people progress and change, it's always important to have alternate perspectives."

If you have any doubt that these people are truly committed to their faith, listen to these voices from women, ages ranging from their twenties through their seventies:

"The best thing about Catholicism is the Eucharist. The ability to receive the body and blood of God, of Jesus, it's so intimate. It's almost too good to be true! It's more intimate than sex! It becomes part of my body. That is what always keeps me in the Catholic Church—the Eucharist."

"You can go almost anywhere in the world and find a church, and I like that idea, especially since a sense of community is falling away as we get more technologically advanced."

"The best thing about Islam is the constant contact with God. God is always there to help you and love you."

"With Islam there is assurance that there is cosmic justice in the world. Although we have yet to realize it, it's there—waiting to be found, to be realized. I think that is the most comforting part of Islam for me. To realize it, you have to struggle and you have to be patient."

"Judaism should inform your life in every way. It's not just for Shabbat, it's every day. It's my Judaism that tells me to make a condolence call, even early on a Sunday morning, and to stay late because the mourner needs someone to talk to. My Judaism affects my moral life. It pushes me to be kind and ethical. And it has to be a part of your daily life so that it can inform your ethical life."

"To me there is such security in the feeling of being a child of God. I get the feeling that God can wrap his arms around me. I have a feeling of security, a safety net. It's nice to know that in spite of my shortcomings, there is still somebody who loves me."

These are not women who want to rebel for the sake of rebelling. These are women who simply want to experience their faith to the fullest.

To the religious woman reading this book, I suggest:

- If you want equality in your faith, educate yourself about your religion. Self-assurance, independence, and empowerment flow from literacy. Join or start a Bible or Qur'an study group or other type of religious reading group. If you can, lead a group to educate others. Or read and learn by yourself. Don't feel ashamed or embarrassed if you know too little: no one, no matter how learned, fully understands divine truth.
- Press your religious leaders to be as innovative as possible. Schedule an appointment with them; e-mail them; come up to them after worship. Although we need grassroots pressure from laywomen and -men, we also need knowledgeable leaders who are unafraid to push against boundaries that limit us all. Leaders and laypeople must work together.
- Put your money where your faith is. When you tithe, give *zakat*, or give tzedakah, choose the beneficiary of your money wisely. Many people unreflectively give their charitable dollars to traditional religious organizations that promote ideas about women they themselves do not hold. But we have seen that there are alternatives such as Call to Action; the Women's Ordination Conference; FutureChurch; Catholics for a Free

Choice; the Evangelical and Ecumenical Women's Caucus; Call to Renewal; *Sojourners*; Women's Alliance for Theology, Ethics and Ritual; Muslims for Progressive Values; Progressive Muslim Union; *Muslim WakeUp!*; the Women's Islamic Initiative in Spirituality and Equity; the Jewish Orthodox Feminist Alliance; Agunah International; *Lilith*; the Foundation for the Advancement of Women in Religion; and many others. Support the organizations, institutions, and publications that reflect your values about women and religion.

- Learn about other faiths; reach out to members of other faiths. The more we know about each other, the more connected we become and the more we can learn from one another.

Sister Joan Chittister has said, "Today's heresy is tomorrow's social dogma."[4] We are entitled to—no, we must—question our tradition even while we honor it. The value of religion comes not from a stamp of divine approval, but through the process of interpreting, questioning, and wrestling. Absolute certainty is never just around the corner, and if someone says it is, I say find another corner.

NOTES

1: Women on the Verge of an Uprising

1. Miriam Therese Winter, Adair Lummis, and Allison Stokes, eds., *Defecting in Place: Women Claiming Responsibility for Their Own Spiritual Lives* (New York: Crossroad, 1995), 1.

2. Vivian Gornick, *The Solitude of Self: Thinking About Elizabeth Cady Stanton* (New York: Farrar, Straus and Giroux, 2005), 45.

3. According to the Jewish Publication Society translation of Genesis, the verse reads "And God created man in His image," but the Hebrew "ha'adam" is more accurately translated as "the human."

4. Elisabeth Schüssler Fiorenza, "Women in the Early Christian Movement," in *Womanspirit Rising: A Feminist Reader in Religion*, ed. Carol P. Christ and Judith Plaskow (HarperSanFrancisco, 1992), 84.

5. Mary Daly, "After the Death of God the Father: Women's Liberation and the Transformation of Christian Consciousness," in Christ and Plaskow, 54.

6. Judith Plaskow, "Male Theology and Women's Experience," in *The Coming of Lilith*, 53–54 (Boston: Beacon, 2005).

7. Presentation by David Gibson, "Pope Benedict XVI and the Future of Reform," given at the 2006 Call to Action conference, held in the Midwest Airlines Conference Center, Milwaukee, Wisconsin, November 4, 2006.

8. Christel Manning, *God Gave Us the Right: Conservative Catholic, Evangelical Protestant, and Orthodox Jewish Women Grapple with Feminism* (New Brunswick, NJ: Rutgers University Press, 1999), 6.

9. In 2005 *Newsweek* commissioned a national poll together with the website Beliefnet and found that 88 percent of Americans describe themselves as either spiritual or religious. *Newsweek*, August 29/September 5, 2005, 54. In a separate poll in 2006, 92 percent said they believed in God, and only 37 percent said they would even consider voting for an atheist for president. *Newsweek*, September 11, 2006, 47.

10. The 10 percent statistic is from a 2006 survey conducted by the Baylor Institute

for Studies of Religion; the 14 percent figure is from a study conducted in 2001 by the Graduate Center of the City University of New York.

11. City University of New York Graduate Center News press release, October 2001, "Graduate Center Survey of Religion in America Complements U.S. Census"; the figure for Muslims is from a 2007 Pew Research Center survey, "Muslim Americans: Middle Class and Mostly Mainstream," May 22, 2007, available on-line at http://pewresearch.org/pubs/483/muslim-americans.

12. Researchers at the Baylor Institute for Studies of Religion isolated evangelical Protestants from mainline Protestants and found that a third of Americans are evangelical. AP, "Survey: Americans More Religious Than Believed," on MSNBC.com and other news sources, September 11, 2006.

13. Intelligent design is the belief that an intelligent entity created the natural world. Creationism is a narrower belief that God created the world. Some creationists adhere to a biblical understanding of the natural world and argue that the earth is only a few thousand years old. Others embrace some aspects of evolutionary theory. For an explanation of the distinction between intelligent design and creationism, see Daniel Engber, "Creationism vs. Intelligent Design: Is There a Difference?" *Slate*, May 10, 2005, available online at www.slate.com/id/2118388/.

14. "People are interested to know why I picked Harriet Miers," George W. Bush said in the Oval Office following a radio program with James Dobson of Focus on the Family. "They want to know Harriet Miers' background. They want to know as much as they possibly can before they form opinions. And part of Harriet Miers' life is her religion." John Riley, "Bush: Harriet Miers' Faith Had Role in Nomination," *Newsday*, October 13, 2005, available online at www.newsday.com.

15. Gornick, 18.

16. Catherine A. Brekus, "Restoring the Divine Order to the World: Religion and Family in the Antebellum Woman's Rights Movement," in *Religion, Feminism, & the Family*, ed. Anne Carr and Mary Stewart van Leeuwen (Louisville, KY: Westminster John Knox Press, 1996), 169.

17. Cited in Gornick, 29–30.

18. Gornick, 117–18.

19. Brekus, 169.

20. Gornick, 118.

21. Helen LaKelly Hunt, *Faith and Feminism: A Holy Alliance* (New York: Atria, 2004), 8.

22. Gornick, 120.

23. Gornick, 124.

24. Sojourner Truth, the black slave turned abolitionist and women's rights activist, ripped the concept of women's purity to shreds in 1851 when she delivered her famous impromptu speech, "Ain't I a Woman?" She said, "That man over there says that women need to be helped into carriages, and lifted over ditches, and to be in the best place everywhere. Nobody ever helps me into carriages, or over mud-puddles, or gives me any best place! And ain't I a woman? . . . I have borne five children and seen them all sold off to slavery, and when I cried out with my mother's grief, none but Jesus heard me! And ain't I a woman?" In Nell Irvin Painter, "Sojourner Truth," in *Facts on File Encyclopedia of Black Women in America: The Early Years, 1619–1899* (New York: Facts on File, 1997), 174–75. Cited in Hunt, 62.

25. Keynote speech at the 2006 conference of Call to Action, held in the Midwest Airlines Conference Center, Milwaukee, Wisconsin, November 3, 2006.
26. Frances D. Gage, "Reminiscences: Sojourner Truth," in Elizabeth Cady Stanton, Susan B. Anthony, and Matilda Joslyn Gage, *History of Woman Suffrage*, 6 vols. (New York: Fowler & Wells, 1881–1922), 1:116. Cited in Gerda Lerner, *The Creation of Feminist Consciousness: From the Middle Ages to Eighteen-Seventy* (New York: Oxford, 1993), 106.
27. Mary Daly, *Beyond God the Father: Toward a Philosophy of Women's Liberation* (Boston: Beacon, 1973).

2: A Love-Hate Relationship with Tradition
1. Nancy Mairs, *Ordinary Time: Cycles in Marriage, Faith, and Renewal* (Boston: Beacon, 1993), 99.
2. Julie Ingersoll, *Evangelical Christian Women: War Stories in the Gender Battles* (New York University Press, 2003), 137–38.
3. Karen Armstrong, *A History of God: The 4,000-Year Quest of Judaism, Christianity, and Islam* (New York: Ballantine, 1993), 394.
4. Carol P. Christ and Judith Plaskow, eds., *Womanspirit Rising: A Feminist Reader in Religion* (HarperSanFrancisco, 1979, 1992), 131–32.
5. Christ and Plaskow, 10.
6. Winter et al, 197.

3: Catholic Women vs. the Vatican
1. Both quotations are from presentations made during the 2006 annual conference of Call to Action in Milwaukee, Wisconsin, November 3–5.
2. These survey results are according to Women's Ordination Conference (www .womensordination.org). I have found other surveys with even higher levels of support for women's ordination, such as a 2000 survey by Georgetown University's Center for Applied Research on the Apostolate, which put the figure at 71 percent supporting women's ordination.
3. Personal interview with Bonavoglia, September 26, 2006, New York City.
4. Deborah Halter, *The Papal "No": A Comprehensive Guide to the Vatican's Rejection of Women's Ordination* (New York: Crossroad, 2004), xiv.
5. Michelle Boorstein, "Reclaiming the Feminine Spirit in the Catholic Priesthood," *The Washington Post*, July 30, 2006, C3.
6. Angela Bonavoglia, *Good Catholic Girls: How Women Are Leading the Fight to Change the Church* (New York: ReganBooks, 2005), 217.
7. The full letter is available online at catholicpittsburgh.org.
8. Quoted in Elizabeth Fernandez, "Going Against Catholic Law, 12 Women Seek Ordination," *San Francisco Chronicle*, July 30, 2006.
9. Patricia Fresen, "Prophetic Obedience: The Experience and Vision of Roman Catholic Womenpriests," keynote speech delivered at the Southeast Pennsylvania Women's Ordination Conference event on March 12, 2005, 9. Available online at www.womensordination.org.
10. Quoted in Halter, 43.
11. Quoted in Catholic League for Religious and Civil Rights News Release, "ABC News Reports Women 'Priests,' " June 20, 2006.

12. Two thorough and very readable books about Catholic women's challenge to the Vatican and the Vatican's responses are Bonavoglia, *Good Catholic Girls*, and Halter, *The Papal "No."* I have relied on the histories related in these two books for this section. I thank Bonavoglia and Halter for organizing the material in a clear and accessible way and for offering sharp, insightful commentary.
13. Halter, 21.
14. Cited in Halter, 22.
15. Bonavoglia, 34–35.
16. See Bonavoglia, 1–18.
17. Cited in Bonavoglia, 9.
18. Both quotations in Bonavoglia, 141.
19. Cited in Bonavoglia, 29.
20. See Halter, 10–11.
21. Halter, 153.
22. Halter, 37.
23. For a feminist analysis of "Inter Insigniores," see Halter, 45–58.
24. Halter, 70–71.
25. For a feminist analysis of "Mulieris Dignitatem," see Halter, 76–77.
26. Bonavoglia, 31–32.
27. For a feminist analysis of "Ordinatio Sacerdotalis," see Halter, 96–105.
28. Halter, 112–14.
29. Quoted in Peter Steinfels, "Vatican Says the Ban on Women as Priests is 'Infallible' Doctrine," *The New York Times*, November 19, 1995, from www.nyt.com.
30. Information about the 2004 "Letter to Bishops" is from a WOC press release dated August 3, 2004. Information about the Vatican documents and responses to them are from Halter, *The Papal "No."*
31. Joan Breton Connelly, *Portrait of a Priestess: Women and Ritual in Ancient Greece* (Princeton, NJ: Princeton University Press, 2007).
32. Elisabeth Schüssler Fiorenza, "In Search of Women's Heritage," in *Weaving the Visions: New Patterns in Feminist Spirituality*, ed. Plaskow and Christ (New York: HarperCollins, 1989), 29.
33. Bonavoglia, 203. Also see Eldon Jay Epp, "Text-critical, Exegetical, and Sociocultural Factors Affecting the Junia/Junius Variation in Rom. 16:7," in A. Denaux, *New Testament Textual Criticism and Exegesis* (Leuven, Belgium: University Press, 2002), 227–92, cited in Bart D. Ehrman, *Misquoting Jesus: The Story Behind Who Changed the Bible and Why* (New York: Harper, 2005), 228.
34. See www.futurechurch.org for information about the omission of women from the lectionary. Ruth Fox, "Women in the Bible and the Lectionary," originally published in *Liturgy 90*, May/June 1996, is reprinted here. Also see Bonavoglia, 206.
35. Gerda Lerner, *The Creation of Feminist Consciousness: From the Middle Ages to Eighteen-Seventy* (New York: Oxford, 1993), chapter 4, "The Way of the Mystics-1," and chapter 5, "The Way of the Mystics-2."
36. Bonavoglia, 225–26.
37. Mary Hunt, "Different Voices/Different Choices: Feminist Perspectives on Ministry," delivered on July 23, 2005, at the Women's Ordination Worldwide conference in Ontario, Canada. Available online at www.wow2005.org.
38. Fresen spoke at the Call to Action annual conference in Milwaukee on November 3, 2006.

4: Evangelical Women Spread the Good News About Women and the Bible

1. This figure comes from a CNN/USA Today/Gallup poll of 1,009 adults nationwide conducted in December 2002. The full figures are available online at www.pollingreport.com, and the 46 percent figure is cited in Nicholas D. Kristof, "God, Satan and the Media," *The New York Times*, March 4, 2003.
2. John Stratton Hawley, ed., *Fundamentalism and Gender* (New York and Oxford: Oxford University Press, 1994), 16.
3. Sally K. Gallagher, *Evangelical Identity and Gendered Family Life* (New Brunswick, NJ: Rutgers University Press, 2003), 8.
4. Virginia Ramey Mollenkott, "Feminism and Evangelicalism," *EEWC Update* 29, no. 1 (Spring 2005), available online at www.eewc.com.
5. Evangelical Manifesto Steering Committee, *A Study Guide for an Evangelical Manifesto*, 2. Available online at www.evangelicalmanifesto.com.
6. Evangelical Manifesto Steering Committee, *An Evangelical Manifesto: A Declaration of Evangelical Identity and Public Commitment*, 9. Available online at www.evangelicalmanifesto.com.
7. Neela Banerjee, "Taking Their Faith, but Not Their Politics, to the People," *The New York Times*, June 1, 2008, A20.
8. Cited in Gallagher, 27.
9. Margaret Lamberts Bendroth, *Fundamentalism and Gender, 1875 to the Present* (New Haven, CT: Yale University Press, 1993), 90–93.
10. Nancy Tatom Ammerman, *Baptist Battles: Social Change and Religious Conflict in the Southern Baptist Convention* (New Brunswick, NJ: Rutgers University Press, 1995 edition; originally published 1990), 83.
11. Gallagher, 78, 84.
12. Cited in Gallagher, 98–99.
13. James Dobson, *Straight Talk to Men and Their Wives* (Waco, TX: Word, 1980), 64. Cited in Gallagher, 54.
14. Stormie Omartian, "How a Husband Should Handle His Wife's Submission," *www.family.org/married/comm/a0019372.cfm*. Excerpted from *The Power of a Praying Husband* (Harvest House Publishing, 2001).
15. Nancy Kennedy, "Eight Points That Show, Christian or Not, He's Still a Guy," www.family.org/married/comm/a0019604.cfm. Excerpted from *When He Doesn't Believe: Help and Encouragement for Women Who Feel Alone in Their Faith* (Colorado Springs: WaterBrook Press, 2001).
16. James Dobson, "Gender Gap?," www.family.org/married/comm/a0009661.cfm. This article was excerpted from *Love for a Lifetime* (Questar Publishers, 1987, 1993).
17. Stephanie Simon, "They Love to Do Their Homework," *Los Angeles Times*, October 11, 2007, available online at www.latimes.com/news/nationworld/nation/la-na-homemaking11oct11,0,900610.story.
18. Billy Graham, "Jesus and the Liberated Woman," *Ladies' Home Journal*, December 1970, 42. Cited in Nancy Hardesty, "Blessed the Waters That Rise and Fall to Rise Again," *EEWC Update* 28, no. 2 (Summer 2004).
19. Information about the formation of the Evangelical Women's Caucus is from Hardesty, "Blessed the Waters," available online at www.eewc.com; and from an interview I conducted with Hardesty on the telephone on July 11, 2006.
20. Letha Dawson Scanzoni and Nancy A. Hardesty, *All We're Meant to Be: Biblical*

Feminism for Today, third revised edition (Grand Rapids, Michigan: William B. Eerdmans, 1992), 5.

21. Scanzoni and Hardesty, 15.
22. Cited in Pamela D. H. Cochran, *Evangelical Feminism: A History* (New York and London: New York University Press, 2005), 47.
23. Cochran, 65.
24. "Letters—Women in the Church," *Eternity* 17 (April 1966), 3. Cited in Bendroth, 121.
25. Cited in Cochran, 70.
26. The full CBE Statement of Faith is available online at www.cbeinternational.org.
27. Julie Ingersoll, *Evangelical Christian Women: War Stories in the Gender Battles* (New York University Press, 2003), 22.
28. Gallagher, 69.
29. Ibid., 77.
30. Tony Evans, "Spiritual Purity," in Bill Bright et al, eds., *Seven Promises of a Promise Keeper* (Colorado Springs: Focus on the Family, 1994), 79–80, cited in Ingersoll, 111.
31. Raymond C. Ortlund, Jr., "Male-Female Equality and Male Headship," in John Piper and Wayne Grudem, eds., *Recovering Biblical Manhood and Womanhood: A Response to Evangelical Feminism* (Wheaton, IL: Crossway Books, 1991), 95.
32. Piper and Grudem, 35–36.
33. Ibid., 40–41.
34. Ibid., 50.
35. Ingersoll, 22–23.
36. Information about Andrea Yates is from Timothy Roche, "Andrea Yates: More to the Story," *Time*, March 18, 2002, and Timothy Roche, "The Yates Odyssey," *Time*, July 26, 2006, both available online at www.time.com; and from Anne Eggebroten, "A Biblical Feminist Looks at the Andrea Yates Tragedy," *EEWC Update* 25, no. 4 (Winter 2001) and Anne Eggebroten, "O Texas, Texas," in the same issue, both available online at www.eewc.com.
37. The $10 billion figure is from 1988, cited in Peter Waldman, "Holy War: Fundamentalists Fight to Capture the Soul of Southern Baptists," *The Wall Street Journal*, March 7, 1988, available online through www.wsj.com.
38. Audra Trull and Joe Trull, eds., *Putting Women in Their Place: Moving Beyond Gender Stereotypes in Church and Home* (Macon, GA: Smyth & Helwys, 2003), xiii.
39. Cited in Trull and Trull, xiv.
40. "Patterson's Election Seals Conservative Control," *Christianity Today*, July 13, 1998, 21, cited in Trull and Trull, xv.
41. Ingersoll, 66.
42. Bart D. Ehrman, *Misquoting Jesus: The Story Behind Who Changed the Bible and Why* (HarperSanFrancisco, 2007), 181–84. Ehrman cites a number of scholars who advance the idea that Paul did not write these passages, including Gordon D. Fee, *The First Epistle to the Corinthians* (Grand Rapids, MI: Eerdmans, 1987).
43. Ehrman, 184.
44. Information about Sehested is from author's interview with her on August 1, 2006; Marjorie Hyer, "Baptist Group Ousts Church with Female Pastor," *The Washington Post*, October 20, 1987; Marjorie Hyer, "Expelled for Hiring Female

Pastor, Baptist Church Celebrates Her Arrival," *The Washington Post,* November 2, 1987 (both articles available online through www.washingtonpost.com); and Vicki Kemper, "Faithful to the Call," *Sojourners,* February 1988, 22–25.

45. The full text of Sehested's extemporaneous speech is in *Sojourners,* February 1988, 24.
46. Associated Press, "Professor Says Seminary Dismissed Her Over Gender," *The New York Times,* January 27, 2007, A14.
47. Associated Press, "Church Says Women Shouldn't Teach Sunday School Classes to Men, Cites Bible," August 21, 2006. Cited in Eggebroten, "Of Buttons, Baptists, and Don Quixotes," *Christian Feminism Today* 30, no. 3 (Fall 2006), available online at www.eewc.com.
48. In conducting the research for this chapter, I made numerous, repeated attempts to reach out to Focus on the Family, the Council on Biblical Manhood and Womanhood, and the Southern Baptist Convention to request interviews with their spokespeople. All of my requests have gone unanswered.

5: Are Mainline Churches Making Men Less Manly and Women Too Prominent?

1. Laurie Goodstein, "A Divide, and Maybe a Divorce," *The New York Times,* February 25, 2007.
2. Quoted in Goodstein, "New Episcopal Leader Braces for Gay-Rights Test," *The New York Times,* February 11, 2007, A24.
3. Adopted by the church in 1992, amended and readopted in 1996 and in 2004. For the full text of the resolution, go to http://archives.umc.org/interior_print .asp?ptid=4&mid=1079.
4. For the full text of "Well-Chosen Words," go to www.pcusa.org/women/ history-theology/well-chosen.htm.
5. See Ruthie Blum, "Feminine Mystique," *The Jerusalem Post,* January 2, 2008, available online at www.jpost.com; and Stewart Ain, "From Boils to Baldness," *The Jewish Week* (New York), April 18, 2008, 1.
6. According to Leon J. Podles in *The Church Impotent: The Feminization of Christianity* (Dallas: Spence, 1999), ix.
7. According to Bret E. Carroll, professor of history at California State University, Stanislaus, quoted in Kristen Campbell and Adelle M. Banks, "Empty Pews: Where Did All the Men Go?" Religion News Service and *The Washington Post,* June 10, 2006, B9.
8. Frederica Mathewes-Green, "Men Need Church Too," *Christianity Today,* May 24, 1999, available online at www.frederica.com.
9. According to Empty Tomb, a mission research and advocacy organization in Champaign, Illinois. Cited in Steve Levin, "Mainline Denominations Losing Impact on Nation," *Pittsburgh Post-Gazette,* July 17, 2006, available online at www.post-gazette.com.
10. Gary Stern, "Mainline Protestants Being Left Behind," *The Journal News,* May 4, 2003, available online at www.thejournalnews.com.
11. Walter Russell Mead, "God's Country?" *Foreign Affairs,* September/October 2006, available online at www.foreignaffairs.com.
12. Podles, xvi, 196.
13. Ibid., 197.

14. Charlotte Allen, "Liberal Christianity Is Paying for Its Sins," *Los Angeles Times*, July 9, 2006, available online at www.latimes.com/news/opinion/commentary/la-op-allen9jul09,1,6911633,print.story.
15. Quoted in F. W. Dupee, *Henry James: His Life and Writings* (New York: Criterion Books, 1956), 11. Cited in Ann Douglas, *The Feminization of American Culture* (New York: Noonday/Farrar, Straus and Giroux, 1977, 1998), 17.
16. Quoted in Campbell and Banks, "Empty Pews."
17. Robin Russell, "Are Churches Too Feminized for Men?" United Methodist News Service, July 19, 2006, available online at www.umc.org.
18. Available online at www.confessingumc.org on March 23, 2003, cited in Leon Howell, *United Methodist @ Risk:* A Wake-Up Call (Kingston, NY: Information Project for United Methodists, 2003), 28.
19. Howell, 121–22.
20. Hilda A. Kuester, "Creating the Sophia Ritual," in Nancy J. Berneking and Pamela Carter Joern, eds., *Re-Membering and Re-Imagining* (Cleveland, OH: Pilgrim, 1995), 18.
21. Said during a question-and-answer session of the conference, tape 3–2, side B, cited in multiple sources including *The New York Times* (Peter Steinfels, "Cries of Heresy After Feminists Meet," May 14, 1994) and in Pamela D. H. Cochran, *Evangelical Feminism: A History* (New York and London: New York University Press, 2005), 111.
22. Berneking and Joern, *Re-Membering*, 69.
23. A Christian Women's Declaration, the Institute on Religion and Democracy, available online at www.ird-renew.org.
24. Peter Steinfels, "Cries of Heresy After Feminists Meet," *The New York Times*, May 14, 1994.
25. Berneking and Joern, 130.
26. Howell, 72–74.
27. Sources of information about the accusations made against the NNPCW from the point of view of the NNPCW: Barbara Dua, "Voices of Sophia: A Community of Theological Conscience and Resistance Viewed from Reformation Insights about the Origins of Sinfulness," unpublished dissertation, San Francisco Theological Seminary, May 1, 2003; Institute for Democracy Studies, *A Moment to Decide: The Crisis in Mainstream Presbyterianism* (New York, 2000), 27–28; author interview with Kate Holbrook, June 9, 2006; author interview with Rev. Dr. Rebecca Todd Peters, June 26, 2006; author interview with Rev. Dr. Barbara Dua, July 31, 2006; and author interview with Rev. Gusti Newquist, August 31, 2006.
28. "A Sampling of Resources Written and Recommended by the National Network of Presbyterian College Women," *The Presbyterian Layman*, January 15, 1999, available online at www.layman.org/layman/news/national-network-college-women/nnpcw-resources-samples.
29. At the time, General Assemblies were held every year. Today they are held every other year.
30. Parker T. Williamson, "College Women's Network Provided Links to Pornographic Material," *The Presbyterian Layman*, July 8, 1998, available online at www.layman.org/layman/news/national-network-college-women/press-release.htm. Williamson's italics.

31. Grace E. Huck, *God's Amazing Grace: Stories from My Life* (Spearfish, SD: Sand Creek Printing, 2005), 79.
32. Statistics cited in "Goals and Recommendations for Full Participation of All Women," adopted 2000 by the United Methodist Church, from *The Book of Resolutions of The United Methodist Church—2004*, available online at http://archives.umc.org.
33. Neela Banerjee, "Clergywomen Find Hard Path to Bigger Pulpit," *The New York Times*, August 26, 2006, A1, A12.
34. According to findings by Barbara Brown Zikmund, Adair T. Lummis, and Patricia M. Y. Chang in their book *Clergy Women: An Uphill Calling* (Louisville, KY: Westminster John Knox Press, 1998), 73.
35. Banerjee, A12.
36. Zikmund et al, 29.
37. Banerjee, A12.

6: The Alarm Has Rung and Muslim Women Are Wide-Awake

1. Laurie Goodstein, "Muslim Women Seeking a Place in the Mosque," *The New York Times*, July 22, 2004.
2. The mission statement of *Muslim WakeUp!* is found on its website, www.muslimwakeup.com.
3. The full principles of Muslims for Progressive Values are available on the organization's website, www.mpvusa.org.
4. Goodstein, "U.S. Muslim Clerics Seek a Modern Middle Ground," *The New York Times*, June 18, 2006, A1.
5. Leila Ahmed, *A Border Passage: From Cairo to America—A Woman's Journey* (New York: Penguin, 1999), 127.
6. Carla Power, "The Way We Live Now: Reconsideration: A Secret History," *The New York Times Magazine*, February 25, 2007, available online at www.nyt.com.
7. Ben Arnoldy, "Bid to Bring Female Voice to Islamic Law," *Christian Science Monitor*, November 21, 2006, available online at www.asmasociety.org/wise/news.html.
8. Kuwait contributed two-thirds of the $17 million to build the center, which was completed in 1991. Katherine Potts, "Leader of New York's Largest Mosque Goes to Cairo," Associated Press, October 24, 1991, available online at www.beliefnet.com.
9. Cited in Asra Nomani, *Standing Alone in Mecca: An American Woman's Struggle for the Soul of Islam* (New York: Harper, 2005), 201. The paperback edition is titled *Standing Alone*. Muzammil H. Siddiqi's statements about the separation of the sexes, among other issues, are available online at www.islamonline.net.
10. Cited in "U.S. Muslims Split on Mosque Separation," IslamOnline.net, June 25, 2006.
11. Cited in PBS program, "Women in Mosques," November 12, 2004, episode no. 811, transcript available online at www.pbs.org/wnet/religionandethics/week811.
12. Mona Eltahawy, "Shame and Sexual Harassment in Egypt," Agence Global, July 29, 2008, available online at www.monaeltahawy.com.

13. Matthai Chakko Kuruvila, *San Francisco Chronicle*, June 6, 2006, available online at www.sfgate.com.
14. Nevin Reda, "What Would the Prophet Do? The Islamic Basis for Female-Led Prayer," March 10, 2005, available online at www.muslimwakeup.com/main/archives/2005/03/women_imamat.php.
15. Imam Zaid Shakir, "An Examination of the Issue of Female Prayer Leadership," March 23, 2005, available in the online archives at www.pmuna.org and on www.zaidshakir.com.
16. "Laury Silvers' Reflections on Woman-Led Prayer," April 18, 2005, available online at www.pmuna.org/archives/2005/04/laury_silvers_r_1.php.
17. Mona Eltahawy, "Firebrands Win the Cliché War as Islam's Moderates Struggle to Prove They're 'Real,'" SaudiDebate.com, February 11, 2007.
18. Mona Eltahawy, "Gender Apartheid," *Middle East Online*, November 26, 2007, available online at www.middle-east-online-cdom/english/?id=23243.
19. Cited in Dave Belden, "Ayaan Hirsi Ali: An Islamic Feminist Leaves Islam," *Tikkun*, July/August 2007, 31.
20. In 2006 the Gallup organization conducted a huge international face-to-face survey of 8,000 Muslim women from Egypt, Iran, Jordan, Lebanon, Morocco, Pakistan, Saudi Arabia, and Turkey and found that they did not see themselves as oppressed. Helena Andrews, "Muslim Women Don't See Themselves as Oppressed, Survey Finds," *The New York Times*, June 8, 2006, A9.
21. Steven R. Weisman, "Saudi Women Have Message for U.S. Convoy," *The New York Times*, September 28, 2005.
22. Ahmed, 292.
23. Rachel Zoll, "For U.S. Muslims, A Push From the Progressive Wing," Associated Press, reprinted in *The Washington Post*, October 16, 2004, B9.
24. Karen Armstrong, *A History of God: The 4,000-Year-Quest of Judaism, Christianity, and Islam* (New York: Gramercy, 2004), 157. Originally published in 1993.
25. Al-Tirmidhi (824–92), collector of hadith.
26. Armstrong, 157.
27. "Riffat Hassan," in Ann Braude, ed., *Transforming the Faiths of Our Fathers: Women Who Changed American Religion* (New York: Palgrave Macmillan, 2004), 182.
28. Ahmed, 121, 127.
29. Amina Wadud, *Qur'an and Woman: Rereading the Sacred Text from a Woman's Perspective* (New York and Oxford, England: Oxford University Press, 1999, first published in 1992), x.
30. Wadud, xii.
31. Ibid., xxi.
32. This interpretation of 4:34 is found in many English translations of the Qur'an, for example in the Penguin Books edition translated by N. J. Dawood, *The Koran* (New York and London, 1974, first published 1916).
33. Amina Wadud, *Inside the Gender Jihad: Women's Reform in Islam* (Oxford: Oneworld, 2006), 200.
34. Wadud, *Inside the Gender Jihad*, 204–205. Wadud's italics.
35. AbdulHamid A. AbuSulayman, *Marital Discord: Recapturing the Full Islamic Spirit of Human Dignity*, Occasional Paper Series 11 (London and Washington: The International Institute of Islamic Thought, 2003), 20.

36. Nomani, 74.
37. Ibid., 164.
38. Ibid., 197.
39. Ibid., 197–98.
40. Ibid., 198.
41. Ibid., 233.
42. From Wadud, *Inside the Gender Jihad*. The English translation is hers except for Qur'an 62:9, which is taken from A. Nooruddeen Durkee, translator and transliterator, *Tajwidi Qur'an*, English edited by Hajjah Noura Durkee (Charlottesville, VA: un-Noor Foundation), 887.
43. Extensive information about international responses to the Wadud prayer is available on the Progressive Muslim Union of North America website, www.pmuna.org. Click on "The Women-Led Prayer Initiative."
44. "Woman Leads U.S. Muslims to Prayer," BBC News, March 18, 2005, available online at http://news.bbc.co.uk/2/hi/Americas/4361931.stm.
45. Wadud, *Inside the Gender Jihad*, 248.
46. Ingrid Mattson, "Can a Woman Be an Imam? Debating Form and Function in Muslim Women's Leadership," available online at http://macdonald.hartsem.edu/muslimwomensleadership.pdf, pp. 4–5.
47. Cited in "Sarah Eltantawi's Reflections on the Wadud Prayer," April 18, 2005, www.pmuna.org/archives/2005/04/sarah_eltantawi_1.php.
48. Mattson, 17–18.
49. Wadud, *Inside the Gender Jihad*, 186.

7: God Gave the Torah to Jewish Women Too

1. Judith Hauptman, *Re-Reading the Rabbis: A Woman's Voice* (Boulder, CO: Westview, 1997).
2. www.jofa.org.
3. Judith Plaskow, *Standing Again at Sinai: Judaism from a Feminist Perspective* (HarperSanFrancisco, 1990), 25.
4. Rachel Furst, "For Men Only? Gendered Language in the *Aseret Ha-Dibrot*," *JOFA Journal* 6:4 (Summer 2007), 16.
5. Rabbi David ben Joseph Abudraham, *Birkat HaMitzvot uMishpateihem*.
6. Yechiel Weinberg, *Seridei Eish* 3:93, cited in Erica S. Brown, "The Bat Mitzvah in Jewish Law and Contemporary Practice," in Micah Halpern and Chana Safrai, eds., *Jewish Legal Writings by Women* (Jerusalem, Israel: Urim Publications, 1998), 250.
7. Yair Chaim Bacharach, Responsa *Havvot Ya'ir* No. 222. Cited in Joel B. Wolowelsky, "Women and Kaddish," *Judaism* 44:3 (1995), 282–90.
8. Cited in Wolowelsky, 282–90.
9. Marvin Lowenthal, ed., *Henrietta Szold: Her Life and Letters* (Westport, CT: Greenwood, 1975), 92–93. Cited in Sally Berkovic, *Straight Talk: My Dilemma as an Orthodox Jewish Woman* (Hoboken, NJ: Ktav, 1999), 39–40.
10. Abigail Pogrebin, ed., *Stars of David: Prominent Jews Talk About Being Jewish* (New York: Broadway, 2005), 19.
11. Nina Mogilnik, "No Direction Home for Kaddish," *The (New York) Jewish Week*, November 17, 2006, 70.

12. *Ohel Sarah Women's Siddur*, based on the *ArtScroll Siddur*, compiled and annotated by Dovid Weinberger with Avrohom Biderman (Brooklyn, NY: ArtScroll/ Mesorah, 2005), 32 and throughout.

13. Debra Nussbaum Cohen, "Feminists Object, But ArtScroll Rolls On," *The Jewish Week* (New York), October 5, 2007, 12.

14. Berkovic, 72.

15. Haviva Ner-David, *Life on the Fringes: A Feminist Journey Toward Traditional Rabbinic Ordination* (Needham, MA: JFL Books, 2000), 4.

16. Regina Stein, "The Boundaries of Gender: The Role of Gender Issues in Forming American Jewish Denominational Identity, 1913–1963," unpublished doctoral dissertation, the Graduate School of the Jewish Theological Seminary, 1998, 361–62. University of Michigan Dissertation Services, microform number 9929541.

17. Tamar Ross, *Expanding the Palace of Torah: Orthodoxy and Feminism* (Waltham, MA: Brandeis University Press, 2004), 58.

18. Ross, 60.

19. Rochelle Millen, "Social Attitudes Disguised as *Halakhah*," *Nashim* No. 4 (Fall 2001), 185, cited in Ross, 96.

20. Ross, 98.

21. Cited in Ross, 272, note 5.

22. This figure comes from a 2003–2004 census of U.S. day schools taken by the Avi Chai Foundation. For more information, go to www.avi-chai.org. There are also ultra-Orthodox institutions, Conservative Solomon Schechter schools, and Reform and nondenominational Jewish schools, bringing the total number of Jewish day schools to 759.

23. Susannah Heschel, ed., *On Being a Jewish Feminist* (New York: Schocken, 1983).

24. Ross, 47.

25. Ibid., 197, 198.

26. Ibid., 211, 216.

27. For an up-to-date listing, see www.edah.org/tefilla.cfm.

28. Ailene Cohen Nusbacher, "Orthodox Jewish Women's Prayer Groups: Seeking a More Meaningful Religious Experience," *Le'ela* No. 49 (2000), 41–46. Available online at www.jofa.org.

29. Tova Hartman, *Feminism Encounters Traditional Judaism* (Lebanon, NH: Brandeis University Press/University Press of New England), 106.

30. The responsum was followed by a fuller explication in Rabbi Hershel (Zvi) Schacter, *Tzei Lakh be'Ikvei haTzon*, in Yeshiva University's halakhic journal *Beit Yitzchak* 17 (March 1985). Information about the responsum and Rabbi Schacter's article may be found in the May 17, 1985, issue of *Sh'ma*, a Journal of Jewish Responsibility.

31. Translation is mine.

32. Mendel Shapiro, "*Qeri'at ha-Torah* by Women: A Halakhic Analysis," 36–37, 47. *Edah Journal* 1:2 (2001). Available online at www.edah.org. The *Edah Journal*, now known as *Meorot*, is an influential modern Orthodox publication.

33. Yehuda Herzl Henkin, "*Qeri'at Ha-Torah* by Women: Where We Stand Today." *Edah Journal* 1:2 (2001), available online at www.edah.org.

34. Ross, 180.

35. Daniel Sperber, "Congregational Dignity and Human Dignity: Women and Pub-

lic Torah Reading, *Edah Journal* 3:2 (2002), available online at www.edah.org; and Joel B. Wolowelsky, "On *Kohanim* and Uncommon *Aliyyot*," *Tradition* 39:2 (2005), available online at www.traditiononline.org.

36. Yavneh is the name of an ancient city in Israel that housed the Jewish court and a house of study after the destruction of the second Temple in 70 C.E.

37. "Beyond Women's Issues: Partnership Minyanim Engage Orthodoxy," with Elitzur Bar-Ascher, Alanna Cooper, and Michal Bar-Ascher Siegal, February 11, 2007, Jewish Orthodox Feminist Alliance tenth annual conference, held at Columbia University.

38. Berkovic, 235–37.

39. Peggy Cidor, "For the Sake of Righteous Women," *The Jerusalem Post*, May 4, 2006. Available online at www.jpost.com.

40. Louise Bernikow, "Female Rabbis Brought Women's Advocacy into Faith," *Women's eNews*, May 31, 2007, available online at www.womensenews.org.

41. Lauren Gelfond, "The Next Feminist Revolution," *The Jerusalem Post*, March 18, 2005, 27. Available online at www.jpost.com.

42. Cidor.

43. Gelfond.

44. Cidor.

45. Michael Luo, "An Orthodox Jewish Woman, and Soon, a Spiritual Leader," *The New York Times*, August 21, 2006, B1.

46. Sara Hurwitz, "Rabbanit Reclaimed," *JOFA Journal*, Winter 2006, 10–11, available online at www.jofa.org.

47. Rachel Kohl Finegold, "What's in a Title? The Roles of Female Religious Professionals," *JOFA Journal*, Spring 2008, p. 24.

48. Ben Harris, "From Liberal Periphery to Conservative Center," Jewish Telegraphic Agency, reprinted in *The Jewish Week* (New York), January 4, 2008, 10–11.

8: The Sexual Lives of Religious Women

1. Nancy Mairs, *Ordinary Time: Cycles in Marriage, Faith, and Renewal* (Boston: Beacon, 1993), 202.

2. See Letha Dawson Scanzoni, *Why Wait? A Christian View of Premarital Sex* (Grand Rapids, MI: Baker, 1982) and M. O. Vincent, *God, Sex, and You* (Urichsville, OH: Barbour, 1985).

3. Beverly Wildung Harrison, *Making the Connections: Essays in Feminist Social Ethics*, ed. Carol S. Robb (Boston: Beacon, 1985), 141.

4. Harrison, 140.

5. Rosemary Radford Ruether, "Sexual Illiteracy," *Conscience*, Summer 2003, available online at www.catholicsforchoice.org.

6. James Dobson, Focus on the Family Action letter, April 2007, e-mailed to subscribers of Focus on the Family.

7. Madelain Farah, *Marriage and Sexuality in Islam: A Translation of al-Ghazali's Book on the Etiquette of Marriage from the Revival of the Religious Sciences* (Salt Lake City: University of Utah Press, 1984), 45, cited in Scott Siraj al-Haqq Kugle, "Sexuality, Diversity, and Ethics in the Agenda of Progressive Muslims," in *Progressive Muslims: On Justice, Gender and Pluralism*, ed. Omid Safi (Oxford, England: Oneworld, 2003), 190.

8. Ali ibn Husam al-Din al-Hindi Muttaqi, *Jarr al-Thaqilfi Suluk al-Ma'il* (Bearing the Heavy Burden on Soul Training of Men Considering Marriage), cited in Kugle, 193.

9. Kugle, 193.

10. Ayaan Hirsi Ali, *The Caged Virgin: An Emancipation Proclamation for Women and Islam* (New York: Free Press, 2006), 19–20.

11. Mohja Kahf, "The Rites of Diane," *Muslim WakeUp!*, May 21, 2004, available online at www.muslimwakeup.com.

12. Laila Al-Marayati, "Medically Speaking: Hymens, Tampons, and Virginity," *Muslim WakeUp!*, August 23, 2004, available online at www.muslimwakeup.com/sex/archives/2004/08/002417print.php.

13. Elaine Sciolino and Souad Mekhennet, "Muslim Women and Virginity: 2 Worlds Collide," *The New York Times*, June 11, 2008, A1.

14. Saleemah Abdul-Ghafur, *Living Islam Out Loud: American Muslim Women Speak* (Boston: Beacon, 2005), 9, 25, 60, 87.

15. Asra Nomani, *Standing Alone in Mecca* (New York: HarperCollins, 2005), 295.

16. Amina Wadud, *Inside the Gender Jihad: Women's Reform in Islam* (Oxford, England: Oneworld, 2006), 219–20.

17. Judy Mabro, *Veiled Half-Truths: Western Travellers' Perceptions of Middle Eastern Women* (London: I. B. Tauris, 1991), 23, cited in Homa Hoodfar, "The Veil in Their Minds and on Our Heads: Veiling Practices and Muslim Women," in *Women, Gender, Religion: A Reader*, eds. Elizabeth Castelli and Rosamond C. Rodman (New York: Palgrave Macmillan, 2001), 427–28.

18. *Iggeret Hakodesh, The Holy Letter: A Study in Medieval Jewish Sexual Morality*, ascribed to Nachmanides. Translated with an introduction by Seymour J. Cohen. (New York: Ktav, 1976), 40–42, 48 (chapter 2); 140–44 (chapter 6).

19. Debra Nussbaum Cohen, "Among Orthodox Jews, More Openness on Sexuality," *The New York Times*, May 3, 2008, B5.

20. Elicia Brown, "Sex Ed for the Jewly Wed," *The Jewish Week* (New York), February 15, 2008, 70.

21. Ashkenazi women (whose ancestors are from eastern Europe) count a minimum of five days, while Sephardi women (whose ancestors are originally from Spain) count a minimum of four days.

22. Tamar Ross, *Expanding the Palace of Torah: Orthodoxy and Feminism* (Lebanon, NH: Brandeis University Press, 2004), 240.

23. Nicholas Bakalar, "Adolescence: Abstinence-Only Programs Not Found to Prevent H.I.V.," *The New York Times*, August 14, 2007, F6.

24. "The Abstinence-Only Delusion," editorial, *The New York Times*, April 28, 2007, A16. The report was issued by the Mathematica Policy Research firm.

25. Ceci Connolly, "Some Abstinence Programs Mislead Teens, Report Says," *The Washington Post*, December 2, 2004, A1, available online at www.washingtonpost.com.

26. Michelle Goldberg, *Kingdom Coming: The Rise of Christian Nationalism* (New York: Norton, 2006), 144.

27. Associated Press, "Doctors Slam Abstinence-only Sex Ed," July 5, 2005, available online at www.msnbc.com.

28. As reported in the National Women's Health Network newsletter, the *Women's Health Activist*, July/August 2005, 7.

29. These statistics are from a 2004 poll by National Public Radio, the Kaiser Family Foundation, and Harvard's Kennedy School of Government. Cited in Russell Shorto, "Contra-Contraception," *The New York Times Magazine*, May 7, 2006, 68.
30. Cited in Shorto, 50.
31. Cited in Shorto, 50, 55.
32. The full text of the e-mail is available online at www.firedupmissouri.com. It is referenced in Jessica Valenti, *Full Frontal Feminism: A Young Woman's Guide to Why Feminism Matters* (Emeryville, CA: Seal/Avalon, 2007), 83.
33. Dan Grasinger, "Absolving Pharmacist's Conscience," letter to the editor, *The Arizona Republic*, April 15, 2005. Cited in Valenti, 87.
34. Gardiner Harris, "Report Details FDA Rejection of Next-Day Pill," *The New York Times*, November 15, 2005, A1.
35. Cited in Shorto, 53.
36. Ayelish McGarvey, "Dr. Hager's Family Values," *The Nation*, May 30, 2005. Posted online May 11, 2005, and available online at www.thenation.com/doc/20050530/mcgarvey.
37. Cited in Valenti, 95.
38. Molly Ivins, "South Dakota's Stand," March 7, 2006, www.cnn.com.
39. Bob Johnson, "Proposals Would Ban Abortion," Associated Press, October 21, 2006, cited in Valenti, 96.
40. Rebecca Walsh, "Senate: Incestuous Dad Knows Best," *Salt Lake Tribune*, February 28, 2006, cited in Valenti, 102.
41. Goldberg, 140.
42. Guttmacher Institute, "Facts on Induced Abortions in the United States," May 2006, available online at www.guttmacher.org/pubs/fb_induced_abortion.html.
43. Shorto, 55.
44. From the transcript of Dobson's statement on April 18, 2007, on his Focus on the Family radio program. The transcript is included in Dobson's monthly e-mail newsletter, June 2007.
45. Guttmacher Institute, "A Tale of Two Americas for Women," news release, May 4, 2006, available online at www.guttmacher.org/media/nr/2006/05/05/index.html.
46. Elisabeth Rosenthal, "Legal or Not, Abortion Rates Compare," *The New York Times*, October 12, 2007, A8.
47. Guttmacher Institute, "Facts on Induced Abortions in the United States."
48. Statistic cited in sidebar to Ian Fisher and Laurie Goodstein, "Hard-Liner with Soft Touch Reaches Out to U.S. Flock," *The New York Times*, April 13, 2008, A1.
49. Angela Bonavoglia, *Good Catholic Girls: How Women Are Leading the Fight to Change the Church* (New York: ReganBooks, 2005), 120.
50. Laurie Goodstein, "Bishops Denounce Writings of a Catholic Theologian," *The New York Times*, May 23, 2007, A15.
51. "Survey of American Muslim Political Attitudes" conducted by the Council on American-Islamic Relations, news release, December 22, 1999, available online at http://islam.about.com.
52. Harrison, 127.
53. Frances Kissling, "Is There Life After Roe? How to Think About the Fetus," *Conscience*, Winter 2004–2005, available online at www.catholicsforchoice.org.

54. Cited in Bonavoglia, 121.
55. "Focus on the Family Challenges Christians on Abortion in the Church," Focus on the Family press release, December 27, 2005, available online at www.family .org; and Bonavoglia, 120.
56. Anne Eggebroten, *Abortion: My Choice, God's Grace: Christian Women Tell Their Stories* (Pasadena, CA: New Paradigm Books, 1994), xiii.
57. Eggebroten, 29, 30, 33.
58. Ibid., 73.
59. According to a Pew Research poll in March 2006, 49 percent of the public support legalizing same-sex marriage. Cited in David D. Kirkpatrick, "A Religious Push Against Gay Unions," *The New York Times*, April 24, 2006, A12.
60. James Dobson, *Marriage Under Fire: Why We Must Win This Battle* (Sisters, OR: Multnomah Publishers, 2004), 23.
61. Ayesha Akram, "Marriage for Gay Muslims?" *The Washington Post*, June 24, 2006, B9. Available online at www.beliefnet.com/story/193/story_19350.html.
62. For more information, visit the organization's website at www.al-fatiha.org.

9: Lost in Translation: Women's Language in Worship

1. Elizabeth A. Johnson, *She Who Is: The Mystery of God in Feminist Theological Discourse* (New York: Crossroad, 1992), 7.
2. Mary Daly, *Beyond God the Father: Toward a Philosophy of Women's Liberation* (Boston: Beacon, 1973).
3. Johnson said this at a keynote address to the annual Call to Action convention, November 3, 2000, in Milwaukee. Cited in Tom Roberts, "Theologian Calls for Recognition of Holiness in Women," *National Catholic Reporter*, November 17, 2000.
4. Johnson, 55.
5. Mary Kassian, *The Feminist Mistake: The Radical Impact of Feminism on Church and Culture* (Wheaton, IL: Crossway, 2005), 170.
6. Kassian, 292, 294.
7. The Jewish Publication Society translation reads "the Rock that begot you," but the Hebrew *y'ladkha* should be translated as "birthed."
8. See Johnson, 92–100. In her notes, p. 289, Johnson cites Hans Conzelmann, "The Mother of Wisdom," in *The Future of Our Religious Past*, ed. James Robinson, trans. Charles Carlson and Robert Scharlemann (New York: Harper & Row, 1971), 230–43; John Kloppenborg, "Isis and Sophia in the Book of Wisdom," *Harvard Theological Review* 75 (1982), 57–84; Elisabeth Schüssler Fiorenza, *In Memory of Her* (Herder & Herder, 1983), 133; Martin Hengel, *Judaism and Hellenism* (London: SCM Press, 1973), 1:157–62; James D. G. Dunn, *Christology in the Making* (Eerdmans, 2003), 195; M. Jack Suggs, *Christology and Law in Matthew's Gospel* (Cambridge: Harvard University Press, 1970), 58; Elizabeth A. Johnson, "Jesus, the Wisdom of God: A Biblical Basis for Non-Androcentric Christology," *Ephemerides Theologicae Lovaniensis* 61 (1985), 261–94. Also see an overview by Harold G. Wells, "Trinitarian Feminism: Elizabeth Johnson's Wisdom Christology," *Theology Today*, October 1995.
9. See M. Jack Suggs, chapter 2; James M. Robinson, "Jesus as Sophos and Sophia,"

in *Aspects of Wisdom in Judaism and Early Christianity,* ed. Robert L. Wilken (Notre Dame, IN: University of Notre Dame Press, 1975), 1–16; and Elisabeth Schüssler Fiorenza, "Wisdom Mythology and the Christological Hymns of the New Testament," in Wilken; all cited in Wells, "Trinitarian Feminism."

10. For more on the Lady Wisdom–Jesus parallel, see Johnson, 95–100.
11. Caroline Bynum, ". . . 'And Woman Her Humanity': Female Imagery in the Religious Writings of the Later Middle Ages," in *Gender and Religion: On the Complexity of Symbols,* ed. Caroline Bynum, Stevan Harrell, and Paula Richman. (Boston: Beacon, 1986), 250–79. Cited in Gerda Lerner, *The Creation of Feminist Consciousness: From the Middle Ages to Eighteen-Seventy* (New York: Oxford, 1993), 88.
12. Lerner, 62–63; 90.
13. Kassian, 295.
14. Reta Halteman Finger, "Feminist Reflections on the Trinity," *EEWC Update* (now *Christian Feminism Today*) 12, no. 1 (Spring 1988), 3, cited in Pamela Cochran, *Evangelical Feminism: A History* (New York University Press, 2005), 112.
15. Cited in K. Connie Kang, "Presbyterians and the Holy Trinity: Let Us Phrase," *Los Angeles Times,* May 30, 2006.
16. Chicago: GIA Publications, 2002; and GIA, 2007. www.giamusic.com.
17. Mary Louise Bringle copyright © GIA Publications, 2007. Used with permission of the author and of GIA Publications.
18. Copyright © Sister Joan Chittister, Order of Saint Benedict. Used with permission. This prayer can be ordered on prayer cards in the catalog section of www.benetvision.org.
19. Used with permission of Nakia Jackson. Translation of Qur'an is Ahmed Ali, trans., *Al Qur'an: A Contemporary Translation,* 9th ed. (Princeton, NJ: Princeton University Press, 2001).
20. Chava Weissler, *Voices of the Matriarchs: Listening to the Prayers of Early Modern Jewish Women* (Boston: Beacon, 1998).
21. Renée Septimus copyright © 1999. Used with permission. This prayer, along with several others, is found on www.ritualwell.org.

Conclusion

1. Tamar Ross, *Expanding the Palace of Torah: Orthodoxy and Feminism* (Lebanon, NH: Brandeis University Press, 2004), 231.
2. Gerda Lerner, *The Creation of Feminist Consciousness: From the Middle Ages to Eighteen-Seventy* (New York: Oxford, 1993).
3. Cited in Nancy Hardesty, ed., "Special Theology Section, Part 2," in *Christian Feminism Today,* Winter 2007, 4. Ruggerio's italics.
4. Chittister made this declaration during her closing address at the National Catholic Education Association meeting in Milwaukee on April 20, 2001.

AUTHOR'S NOTE

If you would like to share your experience of being denied, or achieving, the expansion of women's role in your own religious community, please write to me at leora@takingbackgod.com. After I have collected a good number of readers' experiences I will publicize them either on the website for this book (www.takingbackgod.com) or in a future book. This will enable women from different religious communities to learn from each other and to contact one another for follow-up conversation. Please note that by submitting a written account of your experience to me, you are granting me permission to publish your account, in whole or in part, on my website and in any future book I may write. Please include your name, mailing address, e-mail address, phone number, and an account of your experience, as detailed as you wish. If you want to remain anonymous, that's fine, but please tell me your real name so that I can communicate with you. Also please indicate if you grant permission for others to contact you.

ACKNOWLEDGMENTS

Thank you to those who read the manuscript and incised it with commentaries and corrections: Cyra Choudhury, Patricia Dunn, Dr. Anne Eggebroten, David Feuerstein, Rev. Joan Houk, Rabbi Dr. Haviva Ner-David, and Letha Dawson Scanzoni. Thank you to those who went out of their way to introduce me to interviewees: Rev. Amy De-Long, Sharon Loferski Engler, Rev. Kate Holbrook, Asra Nomani, Helen Markey, Ariele Mortkowitz, and Rabbi Danya Ruttenberg. Finally, thank you to everyone who carved time out of their busy lives to speak with me and share the intimate details of their religious struggles. I am privileged that you trusted me.

I am exceptionally grateful to Jennifer Lyons, my literary agent, for her outstanding professional smarts, and to Denise Oswald, my editor at Farrar, Straus and Giroux, for her wisdom. I am thankful to Jessica Ferri, editorial assistant at FSG, for her excellent guidance, and to Chris Peterson, production editor, for his superb attention.

Thank you to my family—Jonathan, Sasson, and Zev—for supporting me in the writing of this book. You have encouraged my personal efforts to become involved in religious leadership, and for that I am blessed and enriched.

INDEX

124, 132, 162, 197; feminized
depictions of, 130–31, 134, 288;
Gospel of, 63; hymns about, 291–92;
inerrancy and beliefs about, 102;
Judaism of, 12; maleness of, 11, 13,
283–84; ministry of, 81; "muscular"
Christian view of, 136; personal
connection of evangelicals with, 92,
95, 96, 111, 120; and priesthood,
65, 72, 73; as savior, belief in, 17,
27, 28; on sinners versus sins, 138;
symbols of obedience to, 62; wafers
and wine as body and blood of,
34, 66 (*see also* Eucharist); water
symbolism and, 61; women as
disciples of, 76–80, 122
Jewett, Paul, 110, 111, 113
Jewish Feminist Organization, 221
Jewish Orthodox Feminist Alliance
(JOFA), 8, 198, 200, 213, 221–22,
231, 233–34, 239, 257, 309
Jewish Week, The (newspaper), 50
Jews, xi, 3, 23, 24, 29, 38, 51, 108,
159, 185; ancient, xi–xii, 28–29;
ideas of God of, 40; Conservative,
see Conservative Jews; Muslims and,
161, 176; observant, dissatisfaction
of, 43, 46–51, 53; Orthodox, *see*
Orthodox Jews; ultra-Orthodox
Jews; as percentage of U.S.
population, 16; pro-choice, 271–72;
proselytizing by Christians of, 18;
Reconstructionist, xi, 33, 34, 152,
206, 207, 236, 298; Reform, *see*
Reform Jews; *see also* Judaism
Joanna, 78
John XXIII, Pope, 66–67
John Paul I, Pope, 68
John Paul II, Pope, 68–71, 73, 74,
293
Johnson, Sister Elizabeth, 282, 284
Jordan, 320*n20*
Journal of Adolescent Health, 263
Joy and Wonder, Love and Long
(Bringle), 291
Judaism, ix–xiii, 7, 10, 13, 65, 179,
301, 308; dietary restrictions of, 81;

historical changes in, 25–26, 33–35;
imagery of God in, 286–87;
language of, 281–83, 289,
298–300; laws of, xi–xiii, 14, 15,
204–206, 214, 258–61, 278 (*see
also* halakha); liberal, feminization
of, 132; liturgy of, 211, 281; of
Jesus, 12; ordination of women in,
236–39; patriarchy of, 41, 183,
201–205; sacred texts of, *see*
Hebrew Bible, Talmud, Torah;
sexual attitudes in, 254–61, 280;
traditional male practices in, 137; *see
also* Jews
Judas, 73, 79
Julian of Norwich, 81, 288
jum'a (Friday noon prayer service in
Islam), 33, 163, 167, 191, 194
Junia, 74, 78, 79, 80

Kabbalah, 16, 287
Kaddish, 208–211, 225, 226–29,
235–36
Kagan, Rabbi Israel Meir, 208
Kahf, Mohja, 160, 190, 248
Kairos CoMotion, 27
kallah (Jewish bridal) classes, 256–57
Kane, Theresa, 70–71
Kanefsky, Yosef, 236
Kaplan, Judith and Mordecai, 207
kashrut (Jewish dietary laws), *see*
kosher food
Kassian, Mary, 285, 288
Kater, John L., 130
Kaye, Lynn, 240
Kehat, Hanna, 239
Kehilat Orach Eliezer (New York),
240
Kempe, Margery, 81
Kennedy, Nancy, 104
Kerry, John, 98, 269
Khadijah, 14, 36, 180
Khan, Daisy, 166
khutbas (Muslim sermons), 7, 159,
167, 182, 189; delivered by women,
7, 163, 192, 194, 296–98

258, 263, 264; violence in, 184,
186–87; women's rights in, 14, 179
marriage contracts: Jewish, 203,
211–13; Muslim, 195
Marriage Under Fire (Dobson),
278–79
Marx, Karl, 108
Mary of Bethany, 79, 80
Mary Magdalene, 43, 74, 77–80
Mary the virgin, 43, 245, 287–88
Masculinity 101 (Kennedy), 104
Masjid al-Farah (New York), 167
Masjida al-Haram (Sacred Mosque,
Mecca), 188, 189
Mather, Cotton, 132, 138
Mathewes-Green, Frederica, 133
Mattson, Ingrid, 166, 169, 172,
194–96
May, Ann, 42
Mayr-Lumetzberger, Christine, 60
McCartney, Bill, 114
Mead, Walter Russell, 133–34
Medical Center for Female Sexuality
(New York), 258
Meiselman, Rabbi Moshe, 228
Mennonites, 7
menstruation, ritual purification after,
50, 236, 258–61
Messiah College, 90
Methodists, 8, 22, 26–28, 101,
131–34, 143; conservative targeting
of, 138–40, 145; conversion to
Islam of, 183; gender-neutral
language of, 289; men's
organization of, 136; ordination
of women by, 152–54
Michelangelo, 281
Miers, Harriet, 18, 312*n14*
mikvah (Jewish ritual bath), 50, 236,
258, 260–61
Millen, Rochelle, 218
Milton, John, 110
minyan (quorum of ten Jewish men
for Jewish public prayer), 201, 206,
211, 226; for Kaddish, 208, 211,
226; partnership, 231–34; Torah
reading by women in, 229–31

Miriam, 197
Mishnah, 202, 204–205, 229, 255
misogyny: Christian, 138, 244–45;
Jewish, 48; Muslim, 162
Misquoting Jesus (Ehrman), 122
mitzvot (Jewish religious
commandments), 204–205, 211,
214, 215, 220, 228, 300
Mogilnik, Nina, 210
Mohler, Rev. R. Albert, Jr., 246, 264
Mollenkott, Virginia Ramey, 99, 110,
283
Montague, Mary, 254
Moody Bible Institute, 111
Moral Majority, 17, 98
Morgantown (Pennsylvania) Islamic
Center, 188–90
Mormons, 7
Morocco, 320*n20*
Mortkowitz, Ariele, 5
Moses, 197, 201–203, 205, 224
Mosque for the Praising of Allah
(Boston), 190
Mott, Lucretia, 20, 21
Mount Saint Benedict Monastery
(Erie, Pennsylvania), 69, 70
Muhammad, 25, 34, 165, 168, 175,
183, 184, 187, 250, 297; birthplace
of, 158; collection of traditions of,
see hadith; denounced by evangelical
Christians, 173; gender roles and,
36, 180; "night journey" from
Mecca of, 188; revelation of Qur'an
to, 14, 279; rights allotted to
women by, 197; sexual pleasure
encouraged by, 247; successors to,
164; women led prayer during
lifetime of, 162, 171
Muslims, 3–5, 7, 29, 38, 39, 108,
158–97, 225, 320*n20*; African
American, 30, 35, 159, 175, 183,
190, 191; attitudes of non-Muslims
toward, 173–77; clothing
restrictions on, 34, 170, 249–54;
devout, dissatisfaction of, 43,
51–53; fundamentalist, 95, 169; gay
rights opposed by, 279; ideas of

Index